RELIGIOUS LIFE AND PRIESTHOOD

Perfectae Caritatis, Optatam Totius, Presbyterorum Ordinis

REDISCOVERING VATICAN II

Series Editor: Christopher M. Bellitto, PhD

Rediscovering Vatican II is an eight-book series in commemoration of the fortieth anniversary of Vatican II. These books place the council in dialogue with today's church and are not just historical expositions. They answer the question: What do today's Catholics need to know?

This series will appeal to readers who have heard much about Vatican II, but who have never sat down to understand certain aspects of the council. Its main objectives are to educate people as to the origins and developments of Vatican II's key documents as well as to introduce them to the documents' major points; to review how the church (at large and in its many parts) since the council's conclusion has accepted and/or rejected and/or revised the documents' points in practical terms; and to take stock of the council's reforms and paradigm shifts, as well as of the directions that the church appears to be heading.

The completed series will comprise these titles:

Ecumenism and Interreligious Dialogue: Unitatis Redintegratio, Nostra Aetate by Cardinal Edward Cassidy

The Church and the World: Gaudium et Spes, Inter Mirifica by Norman Tanner, SJ

The Laity and Christian Education: Apostolicam Actuositatem, Gravissimum Educationis by Dolores Leckey

Liturgy: Sacrosanctum Concilium by Rita Ferrone

Scripture: Dei Verbum by Ronald Witherup, SS

The Church in the Making: Lumen Gentium, Christus Dominus, Orientalium Ecclesiarum by Richard Gaillardetz

Evangelization and Religious Freedom: Ad Gentes, Dignitatis Humanae by Jeffrey Gros and Stephen Bevans

Religious Life and Priesthood: Perfectae Caritatis, Optatam Totius, Presbyterorum Ordinis by Maryanne Confoy, RSC

RELIGIOUS LIFE AND PRIESTHOOD

Perfectae Caritatis, Optatam Totius, Presbyterorum Ordinis

Maryanne Confoy

Paulist Press
New York/Mahwah, NJ

Cover design by Amy King
Book design by Celine M. Allen

Library of Congress Cataloging-in-Publication Data

Confoy, Maryanne.
    Religious life and priesthood : Perfectae caritatis, Optatam totius, Presbyterorum ordinis / Maryanne Confoy.
        p. cm.
    Includes bibliographical references and index.
    ISBN 978-0-8091-4454-9 (alk. paper)
    1. Priesthood. 2. Pastoral theology—Catholic Church. 3. Catholic Church—Clergy—Religious life. 4. Monastic and religious life. 5. Catholic Church—Clergy—Training of. 6. Vatican Council (2nd : 1962–1965) Decretum de presbyterorum ministerio et vita. 7. Vatican Council (2nd : 1962–1965) Decretum de institutione sacerdotali. 8. Vatican Council (2nd : 1962–1965) Decretum de accomodata renovatione vitae religiosae. I. Title.
    BX1912.C668 2008
    262'.142—dc22

                                                                2007049374

Published by Paulist Press
997 Macarthur Boulevard
Mahwah, New Jersey 07430

www.paulistpress.com

Printed and bound in the
United States of America

CONTENTS

SECTION I
ON THE MINISTRY AND LIFE OF PRIESTS
Presbyterorum Ordinis

SECTION II
ON THE TRAINING OF PRIESTS
Optatam Totius

v

CONTENTS

SECTION III
ON THE ADAPTATION AND RENEWAL OF RELIGIOUS LIFE
Perfectae Caritatis

ACKNOWLEDGMENTS

There are many people to whom I owe a great deal in the completing of this book: friends present and afar; my sister Tricia, whose unfailing support sees me through so many tasks; and my congregation of the Sisters of Charity of Australia. My special gratitude is to Christopher Bellitto, the editor who has been both patient and encouraging. His steadfast attention to detail, his scholarly support, and his advice have kept me moving along.

I am indebted to my Jesuit colleagues, especially Antony F. Campbell, for their support all the way. For the initial impetus, my thanks to Bernard Cooke and Pauline Turner.

For help with research I am grateful especially to Paul Chandler O.Carm and the Carmelite library, to the Boston College Library, and to the librarians, especially Carol Pikos, of Dalton McCaughey Library, Melbourne.

There are several communities that have informed my understanding and enriched my experience of church: the Columban sisters who have given me a home and always a challenging companionship; the community of Kilbride Centre; the Christian Brothers and the Edmund Rice movement for its prophetic engagement with the C21 church; and all at The Way who keep me earthed!

The English translations of both Vatican II and post-conciliar documents are from the Vatican website.

ABBREVIATIONS

Documents of Vatican II

AA	*Apostolicam Actuositatem* (Apostolate of the Laity)
AG	*Ad Gentes* (Missionary Activity)
CD	*Christus Dominus* (Bishops)
DH	*Dignitatis Humanae* (Religious Freedom)
DV	*Dei Verbum* (Revelation)
GE	*Gravissimum Educationis* (Christian Education)
GS	*Gaudium et Spes* (The Church in the World of Today)
IM	*Inter Mirifica* (Means of Social Communication/Mass Media)
LG	*Lumen Gentium* (The Church)
NA	*Nostra Aetate* (Non-Christian Religions)
OE	*Orientalium Ecclesiarum* (Eastern Catholic Churches)
OT	*Optatam Totius* (Priestly Formation)
PC	*Perfectae Caritatis* (Religious Life)
PO	*Presbyterorum Ordinis* (Ministry and Life of Priests)
SC	*Sacrosanctum Concilium* (Liturgy)
UR	*Unitatis Redintegratio* (Ecumenism)

Other Abbreviations

AAS	*Acta Apostolicae Sedis*
CDF	Congregation for the Doctrine of the Faith
CLAR	Latin American Conference of Religious
CPC	Central Preparatory Commission
CSS	Conciliar Commission on Seminaries, Studies, and Catholic Education

ES	*Ecclesiae Sanctae*
FABC	Federation of Asian Bishops' Conferences
FORUS	Religious Life Futures Project, or Future of Religious Orders in the United States
LCWR	Leadership Conference of Women Religious
MP	On the Ministerial Priesthood
PDV	*Pastores Dabo Vobis*
PPF	*Program of Priestly Formation*
VC	*Vita Consecrata*

PREFACE

So much has been written about Vatican II and ministry in the forty years since the conclusion of the council and by so many people with varied levels of expertise and interest in the academy and in the pews that it is impossible to do justice to the range and depth of the ideas that have been presented. This volume deals with the three conciliar documents that were addressed primarily to those who worked professionally in ministry before, during, and after Vatican II: ordained and vowed men and women. These three documents, *Presbyterorum Ordinis* (*PO*), On the Ministry and Life of Priests, *Optatam Totius* (*OT*), On Priestly Training, and *Perfectae Caritatis* (*PC*), On the Adaptation and Renewal of Religious Life, are not numbered among the most notable of the Vatican Council documents in terms of total impact or influence.

It can be argued that the greatest impact on the lives of priests and religious came not from the particular documents addressing their state but rather from the documents on the church, *Lumen Gentium* (*LG*) and *Gaudium et Spes* (*GS*), on liturgy, *Sacrosanctum Concilium* (*SC*), and on the apostolate of the laity, *Apostolicam Actuositatem* (*AA*). The universal call to holiness that was a hallmark of the council had extraordinary and unexpected consequences for all Catholics, whatever their calling or commitment, and it affected the subsequent shape and understanding of ministry for ordained and vowed religious women and men profoundly.

For those of us who lived through the prescriptive and canonically regulated era before the council and who heard the freshness of *aggiornamento* (updating), the new winds blowing through the musty corridors of church structures were both promise and sign of new hopes, new possibilities, and some fears. What were we gaining and what might be lost in this renewal or perhaps revolution? For those who are the equivalents of contemporary "baby-boomers" and later generations in the Catholic Church, Vatican II is simply another experience from the past that seems to barely touch on their lives. The contrast of experiences is real.

Those Catholics who had been brought up on an un-nuanced teaching that the Catholic Church was the one true church, and that all other belief systems were at worst heretical and at best deeply flawed, felt that their hierarchical and ordered world of certainties was breaking down from within. Before Vatican II the dangers were from outside the church; suddenly the world of the religiously certain and secure was collapsing all around them. This was how many Catholics experienced the new directions of Vatican II.

At the same time there was an eruption of ecumenical and interfaith initiatives and connectedness that characterized church relationships in the 1970s and 1980s. These were the stimulating years of interdenominational dialogue and interfaith outreach. This was particularly true when it came to the subject of involvement in church life and responsibilities. The elitism and exclusiveness of pre–Vatican II ministry by the ordained and by religious became, in the post-Vatican decades, a sometimes confusing plethora of diverse ecclesial ministries.[1]

In retrospect we might sum up the years of Vatican II as a time of extraordinary contrasts.

It was the best of times, it was the worst of times . . . it was the epoch of belief, it was the epoch of incredulity, it was the season of Light, it was the season of Darkness, it was the spring of hope, it was the winter of despair . . . We were all going direct to heaven, we were all going direct the other way—in short, the period was so far like the present period, that some of its noisiest authorities insisted on its being received, for good or for evil, in the superlative degree of comparison only.[2]

Surely this quote from Charles Dickens's *A Tale of Two Cities* might well describe the state of the Roman Catholic Church in those years of recovery from the destructive and debilitating effects of two world wars with the consequent changing political relationships between a fragmented Europe and an increasingly powerful United States and United Soviet Socialist Republic. The losses had been real, but new initiatives and new life were springing up in unexpected ways and from unfamiliar places in church and society. New voices from Latin America, Africa, and Asia were beginning to ask questions about their place not only in the global world of politics and economics but also in the ecclesial structures that affected their experiences of identity and community.[3]

Christianity in Europe in the 1950s was still struggling to recover from division and a sense of religious inertia and disillusionment, primarily as a consequence of the failures of the institutional Christian churches to find a voice for those on the margins in time of war and recession.[4] The Catholic Church in the United States, in contrast, had come of age and was flourishing ecclesially and financially. Catholicism had moved from the immigrant faith of the poor and the marginalized to a position of political influence and expansion. Catholic church leaders, episcopal and lay, were finding their voice and expressing their concerns for their nation and its people.[5] The breadth of vision and human warmth of John XXIII had opened doors for communication between unexpected partners and participants in the council.

In contrast to all previous councils, Vatican II was the most genuinely ecumenical and representative of the whole church. The earliest councils, such as Ephesus (431) and Chalcedon (451), numbered 153 and 600 council members[6] respectively, while Vatican II was the largest in the history of the church, with 2,860 bishops and heads of religious orders from all over the world.[7] Laymen and non-Catholics were invited as observers, with women being invited to the third session in 1964.

The interest of the Western world in the happenings at this truly international and ecumenical council was sustained by the consistent and lively media interest in the previously closed and apparently clandestine world of the Vatican that had suddenly opened its doors, making visible a truly global church in a new way.[8] As the council developed during the four sessions over the thirty-eight months of its duration, the diverse media relationships improved and the reporting became more informative, breaking through the "rubric of secrecy" that characterized the official reporting of the early stages.

From its inauguration, the council had proven to be a startling event, providing print journalists and TV and radio commentators with hard news: Pope John was reported as commenting that some of his counselors were "prophets of doom," and there was division regarding the first documents for discussion, as well as concern about the members of the preparatory commissions. A number of cardinals and bishops were looking for opportunities to address the complexities of the situations in which they found themselves in their leadership roles rather than to simply affirm past approaches to church and world, especially in relation to mission and ministry.[9] The preparatory work for the council was carried out by preparatory commissions composed primarily of curial officials. The fear of instability for a church that prided itself on its unchanging identity in a changing world was the basis of the initial working documents prepared by these commissions.

Many bishops in the council saw the activities of the Roman curia as obstructionist from the beginning of the council through to its conclusion.[10] There was an initial negative reaction to the prepared conciliar documents as bishops from countries other than Italy wanted to be involved in the work of the preparatory commissions and in the preparation of council documents. Right from these early stages there were obvious divisions among the council members.

Various commentators on the early period of the council discuss the factional groupings among the bishops. French journalist for *Le Monde* Henri Fesquet named the group of influential bishops in the redevelopment of the preparatory work of the pre-conciliar commissions as "Julius Cardinal Döpfner, Archbishop of Munich; Franziskus Cardinal Koenig, Archbishop of Vienna; Cardinal Alfrink of Utrecht; Archbishop Alfred Bengsch of Berlin; Archbishop Lorenze Jaeger of Paderborn; Cardinal Ottaviani of Rome; Achille Cardinal Liénart, Bishop of Lille; Paul Cardinal Richaud...Giacomo Cardinal Lercaro, an Italian pioneer of liturgical reform, and particularly Giovanni Battista Cardinal Montini whose exceptional worth everyone praises."[11] Within this group there was significant difference of opinion about the way the council should move. Cardinals Liénart and Frings caused an upset at the first council meeting by demanding a free election of the commissions that would produce the council's discussion documents.[12] Frequent skirmishes between curial prelates and their opponents were also recorded.

It was a lively period of hopes and fears, disagreement and affirmation. Correspondents such as "Xavier Rynne" (Francis Murphy CSsR) wrote colorful accounts of formal and informal occasions of both conciliar debates and of the many disagreements among the prelates. Yves Congar criticized the newspaper *France Soir* for what he described as "frivolity, discourtesy and even downright dishonesty" in its headline, "French bishops in revolt at the council."[13] Ecclesial movements toward greater unity within Christianity and interfaith dialogue at the time meant that new networks of communication and relationships were being established: "...developments at the council and especially the approval of the decree on ecumenism aroused among the faithful the widespread hopes that they could set aside at least those doctrinal divisions that had become incomprehensible to many people and initiate common ways of bearing witness to the faith."[14] It was a time of hope that was being ushered in, but doubts were also strong.

While all this ferment was occurring in the global church during the period from the time of the council convocation, December 25, 1961, to its conclusion on December 8, 1965, it was at the level of grassroots parish living that the upheaval was being felt most. The varied levels of reporting were coming through diverse sources. The task of communicating what was happening in their church fell primarily on priests and religious. Their public profession of ministry as preachers or teachers meant that they were called to mediate the messages coming from the council to the people in the pews and classrooms. That the priests and religious were, on the whole, receiving and processing information at the same time as the laity they served meant that they were under pressure to preach and teach with minimal resources.

Theirs was a church in which obedience to hierarchy, church regulations, and religious practice were a primary source of Catholic identity. But these priests and religious had themselves been inducted into their ecclesial and congregational identity and ministry through the same structures and ordinances as the laity, along with their own additional formation for a vowed or priestly life. While they continued to exercise their leadership roles in their communities, they had to deal with the impact that both press releases and rumors were having on their own personal and communal identities and religious worldview and their sense of mission and ministry in a newly changing church.

The years of Vatican II were years of turmoil and strain, particularly for priests and religious. The statement made by a French country priest in 1965, "We are sure of God, but we have no clear notion of what we are ourselves, or of where we are," a statement quoted subsequently in a series of lectures on priesthood in 1966 at the Aquinas Institute, Illinois, indicates something of the experience: "This country

parish priest expresses clearly enough what today's priests feel confus-
edly both at the sociological level and at the pastoral level. They are not
clear on 'what they are.'"[15] An enormous number of books on the
priesthood were published in the years following the council. "In
France alone there was a new book every month on the priesthood in
1965, and the number has been added to steadily ever since."[16]

Now, forty years after Vatican II, both a backlash and a resurgence
are taking place in relation to church ministries, ordained and lay.[17]
Books about priesthood are still proliferating, both in terms of theological and pastoral explications and sociological and statistical analyses.[18]
But the polarization that characterized the council itself and the church
in the post-conciliar years is still evident. "The Church in England
shows an enormous gap between the avant-garde clergy and laity and
the rest of the church. What is more alarming than the extent of the
gap, however, is the incomprehension, and at times, hostility, that exist
on both sides of it."[19] This is still the case forty years later, when polarization at many levels occurs within the priesthood between older and
younger priests and between priests and laity. "The polarization today
mainly concerns ecclesiology, the theology of the priesthood, and the
liturgy."[20]

The division that existed within the pre-conciliar church, particularly at the level of leadership, both institutional and academic, is still
operative in the present ecclesial context. The power struggles that
took place during the decades that followed the council are still obvious
in Vatican documents, in academic and pastoral publications, and at
both hierarchical and grassroots levels of church life.

The impact of the Vatican documents on priests, religious, and laity
during the past forty years is visible in terms of what is described on one
hand as a time of vocational crisis and on the other an unprecedented
expansion of ministries among the laity. The prophetic words of Pope
John XXIII in his convocation of the council on December 25, 1961,
are as pertinent today as they were in the 1960s.

> Today the Church is witnessing a crisis underway within soci-
> ety. While humanity is on the edge of a new era, tasks of im-
> mense gravity and amplitude await the Church, as in the most
> tragic periods of its history. It is a question in fact of bringing
> the modern world into contact with the vivifying and perennial

energies of the gospel, a world which exults itself with its con-
quests in the technical and scientific fields, but which brings
also the consequences of a temporal order which some have
wished to reorganize excluding God. This is why modern society is earmarked by a great material progress to which there is
not a corresponding advance in the moral field.[21]

This was the context of the 1960s, and the same crisis and tasks are
pressing on the Catholic Church at the present time.

The three decrees of Vatican II, *Presbyterorum Ordinis, Optatam
Totius,* and *Perfectae Caritatis,* can be adequately understood only if seen
in the context of the changing ecclesiology that developed during and
after the years of the council. Over the past four decades the ecclesiological context has been affected by sociocultural and political changes
that have generated both fervor and ferment in local communities and
in the global institutional identity of the Catholic Church.

The second session of the council was opened by Pope Paul VI with
the statement that the council had come to free "the noble and destiny-
filled name of church from forms full of holes and from being close to
collapse."[22] To explore what has been happening in priesthood and religious life during the past forty years is to come to realize that in our
"noble and destiny-filled" church the Holy Spirit is alive and well in the
Christian community, even though times of light and darkness, incredulity and belief, the spring of hope and the winter of despair have
tested our faith, hope, and love.

Background to the Three Documents[1]

From the perspective of ministerial leadership in dioceses, parishes, and schools, the image and understanding of church that was communicated by bishops, priests, and religious women and men was of an institution of certainties and security in a world of rapid change, political instability, and uncertainties. Institutionally the church claimed a sure identity and a theological confirmation of its future survival; its belief system and its values were strongly professed and proudly acknowledged by faithful and loyal Catholics who had a clear sense of their own identity.[2] Enemies were clearly defined and those who belonged to the church knew both the blessings and burdens of Catholic identity and communal belonging.

Yet the preaching and teaching about the stable institution did not always connect with the experience of Catholics in the decades preceding the council. While the institutional church, through its political and diplomatic representatives in the various regions, worked to maintain the established network of church and state relationships, local parish communities were confronted with new issues and questions.

Among those priests and religious whose task it was to preach, teach, nurse, and care for people at the grass-roots level, a new approach to complex ministerial situations needed to be addressed and responded to. Affirmations of the changelessness of the church echoed paradoxically for parishioners who had experienced change and uncertainty in most areas of their lives. Both urban and rural parish communities throughout Europe had been radically affected by the impact of world and regional wars. Periods of economic depression had taken their toll, especially among those who found themselves in the ranks of the new poor as a result of neo-industrial activities that drew people from farming areas and small towns to cities to find employment.

Polarization increasingly characterized communities globally and locally, and xenophobia was rife—East versus West, Christians versus Jews, Catholics versus Protestants, rich versus poor—and any stranger was always a possible enemy. This was the context in which priests and religious preached, taught, nursed, and cared for people.

As the opening period of the council drew near "there was a ripple of enthusiasm; but caution, pessimism and indifference were both appropriate and widespread."[3] These were times when ghettoism and triumphalism rather than dialogue or humility were seen to characterize Catholic communities throughout the northern hemisphere.[4] The atmosphere was one of "a real human beehive from which emerges an uninterrupted buzz of confused voices in search of harmony... in which [people] easily become mixed and lost."[5] A key approach used by Pope John XXIII in describing the mandate of the council was that of an attending to the "signs of the times" in the present world in which the church is called to preach, teach, and serve.

> The substance of the ancient doctrine of the Deposit of Faith is one thing, and the way it is presented is another. And it is the latter which must be taken into great consideration with patience if necessary, everything being measured in the forms and proportions of a magisterium which is predominantly pastoral in character. (John XXIII, Opening General Congregation, October 11, 1962)

A major problem for those who were given the task of writing the initial Vatican documents was the mandate from Pope John XXIII that the council was to be pastoral in its approach and documentation. However, the understanding of and approach to the idea of a "pastoral" council was understood in diverse ways, and many council members were diametrically opposed to each other in their responses to what a pastoral council might actually mean. Commentators on the proceedings during the council years noted that the earliest ethos and communications from the essentially Roman preparatory commissions were dominantly juridical, legalistic, and negative. This was the context out of which the initial documents on the priesthood, seminary training, and religious life emanated.

SECTION I
ON THE MINISTRY AND LIFE OF PRIESTS

Presbyterorum Ordinis

PART I
THE DOCUMENT

In the European world, particularly in the late nineteenth century and the first half of the twentieth century, the shape of parish life and that of its priests could perhaps be summed up in Bernanos's fictional depiction of the experience of a parish priest in France.

> Mine is a parish like all the rest. They're all alike. Those of today I mean...My parish is bored stiff; no other word for it. Like so many others! We can see them being eaten up by boredom and we can't do anything about it. Some day perhaps we shall catch it ourselves—become aware of the cancerous growth within us. You can keep going a long time with that in you.[1]

Conciliar historian Hubert Jedin's analysis of the developments in the life and ministry of clergy from 1914 to the 1980s describes a movement from stability and inertia to ferment and upheaval in parish life along with the consequent impact of these changes on priestly identity and ministry.[2]

The postwar experiences of demographic change and of societal reconfiguring had an impact at virtually every level of human interaction, and the hierarchical structure of Christendom began to display its own signs of fracturing. In particular, within the European church some significant changes were taking place. Priestly ministry to French seminarians and members of Catholic Action who had been conscripted to work in German factories during World War II became the seed-bed of the worker-priest movement—a movement that was initiated within the French church and then began to spread.

The consciousness-raising process that this movement initiated among the priests and seminarians who were originally involved in this pastoral ministry meant that in the postwar period the clerical class system gradually became an issue parochially. Priests began to exercise their ministry with workers as their fellow workers. Their commitment to justice and to the rights of the poor unsettled the status quo of those established French parishes where the pastor was a man of influence and position. What had begun as a means of outreach to those on the margins became a source of conflict between the small groups of worker-priests and their communities and the affluent parishes with the middle-class status of their parish priests. Misunderstandings, alienation, and mutual critique of and by worker priests and their more class-conscious peers of the changes in ministerial commitment became disturbing features of French diocesan life.

The tensions between the two groups of priests eventually resulted in the closing down of the worker priest movement, but not before its impetus for social action in the church had spread to other nations. Before long the movement became a force to be reckoned with in and beyond the Catholic community; "[the movement's] failure occupied French and European public opinion until the eve of the council."[3]

Perhaps the summary of the spirit behind this movement, itself a response to the "signs of the times," may still have significance forty years after the council that endorsed similar hopes and planned means for bringing them into reality:

> We need the passion and courage of the worker-priests...We also need a special training centre and a new kind of theological education for priests who will initiate new engagements with the "principalities and powers" of society...Our ablest theological minds should be occupied with the problems of "communication" for we too, to use Poulat's words, need "a new religious language to replace one which (is) now no more than a dead language" and we also need to discover "a new Christian way of life."[4]

The need for priestly solidarity that was expressed at that time through the number of associations of priests that mushroomed has been a consistent feature of the priesthood. There has been a long history of formal and informal confraternities and associations of diocesan priests. Augustine is usually acknowledged as having established the tradition.[5]

Records of meetings in Europe "to improve the feeling of solidarity among the priests as well as their social position and material solidarity" were recorded as early as 1901.[6] The division that was operative among the bishops at the opening of the council was not a new phenomenon. An atmosphere of suspicion and mistrust prevailed throughout the Catholic community, affecting both priests and laity. It stultified theological speculation and research among theologians and in parish liturgical life.

A secret society "was formed for ferreting out and delating to the Holy Office the writings and teachings of Catholics in every field."[7] The circumstances that had brought the condemnation of modernism to a head in Pius X's encyclical, *Pascendi*, of September 8, 1907, had consequences that extended far beyond the pope's original intention of denouncing a heresy that undermined faith and questioned dogmatic beliefs.

Charges of "new theology" were made particularly against those theologians whose originality and non-conventional ideas and approaches to biblical studies and dogmatic theology marginalized them from mainstream thinking. Some fear-filled parishioners reported to the bishop and even to Rome on what they thought might be aberrant behavior liturgically. It was an uneasy world in which to exercise leadership, to exercise scholarship, and to minister in the Catholic Church, and divisions and suspicion abounded between bishops, priests, and their communities. It was a clerical church in which the laity were generally institutionally objectified or rendered invisible in their expected unquestioning conformity to established order.[8]

The decades prior to the council have been described as a time of "two opposing currents of traditionalism and innovation"; the secular and religious intellectual environments were wide-ranging in the ideas and movements they generated.[9] The firm foundation of the Rock of Peter was being battered in unexpected ways both from inside and outside the ministerial community. Defensiveness abounded within the Roman Church as new ideas, worldviews, and lifestyles surfaced ecclesially and societally. But this was as much an issue of a few scrupulous parishioners as it was of the priests themselves. Conformity was the criterion for orthodoxy, theological and liturgical. Parish life was suffering from the failure to connect preaching and ministry with the changing family and working-life circumstances of parishioners.

Episcopal conferences in the period prior to the call for a council expressed hopes for "wide-ranging liturgical reform," the use of the vernacular in the liturgy, and "full participation of the faithful" in the Eucharist.[10] Other problems that were important to bishops and priests in their ministry to their people had to do with mixed marriages, the laws of fast and abstinence, clergy formation, and the ever-present issue of birth control.

In commenting on the issues raised by bishops' conferences during this pre-conciliar period, church historian Giacomo Martina outlines the approach to the Christian devotional and ascetical life that was dominant among the clergy in Rome:

> The basic aim of the religious life was to promote and transmit intact the basic underlying values, such as total consecration to the Lord, a striking austerity, an intense and personal prayer life, authentic and sincere fidelity to the Church, a spirit of service devoid of any career-minded ambition, burning pastoral zeal, and a strong cultural grounding, which tended to be predominantly if not exclusively philosophical and theological, although it was also open to other aspects.[11]

This was the substance of preaching and ministry at diocesan and parochial levels. The prevailing spirituality was personal and private rather than communal, and the devotional and ascetical practices in which priests and people were encouraged to engage reinforced a passive and subordinate form of loyalty to bishops and to church.

In contrast to this static style of faithfulness were the new and continuing Catholic Action initiatives such as the Young Christian Workers movement that had continued as a consequence of the worker-priest consciousness-raising activities.[12] In European cities and rural areas these movements encouraged greater responsibility and societal awareness among their adherents. "See, judge, and act" was the catchword of these Catholic activists on behalf of social justice and peace. The pastoral theology that informed their activities was becoming increasingly important in the period, and one that numbers of priests were using in their own pastoral ministries.[13] Some priests, influenced by the renewal of historical and biblical scholarship of the period, began to argue that there was a one-sidedness to Trent's formulations about priesthood.[14]

They experienced an ambiguity in the traditional emphasis given to the dominant sacerdotal priestly category[15] as that of a man set apart from the people in face of the growing need for a style of servant leadership[16] within and for the community.

Historians who have written about the council have acknowledged the divisions and the factions that existed within church leadership before, during, and after the council. Various nomenclatures have been used to describe the main factions, for example, progressive and conservative, intransigent and forward-thinking. But it is obvious that there were some members of the hierarchy who could not see outside the form of the tradition as they had integrated it into their own lives, while there were others for whom the values of the tradition needed to be expressed in new ways according to historical changes that had taken place in the life of the church. That the Decree on the Ministry and Life of Priests, *Presbyterorum Ordinis* (*PO*), exists at all is because the bishops found the discussion of the priesthood contained in the document on the church, *Lumen Gentium* (*LG*) to be an inadequate treatment of the topic.[17] The decree is a fruit of the bishops' deliberations, particularly during the latter period of the council.[18]

There was much discussion about the ways in which some conciliar documents dealt with contemporary problems according to the time-honored processes of the past without any real understanding of the new issues that were confronting bishops and priests in their dioceses. The history of the Decree on the Ministry and Life of Priests is an example of this problematic approach. It was noted that priests had been largely forgotten at this council.[19] Cardinal Suenens commented in 1965, "In today's church with its attention to bishops and laity, priests feel neglected by the church."[20]

The first schema regarding priests that was submitted to the council by the Preparatory Commission was so inadequate that the council members considered it not even worth debating. The revised text also was only moderately good, and was adopted—by a great majority of votes—more because it was impossible not to say anything at all about priests than because of any real enthusiasm for the actual contents of the document.[21] During the council, Archbishop Hurley of South Africa is recorded as commenting that the "original sin of the council lay in the defective work of the Preparatory Commissions."[22] This certainly applies to the document on the priesthood.

Records of both the proceedings of the council and of comments in relation to priests and the priestly life indicate a dualism in the underlying approach that was prevalent in the 1960s. Priests were greatly appreciated for their services; concern was expressed for them, but many of the comments reveal an idealized understanding of the priesthood and the priestly life. When it came to addressing particular issues of concern in relation to priests, the bishops moved from the abstract ideal of the perfection of the priestly life to negative or juridical remonstrations about priests, their lives, and their ministry.

Nor was there an apparent interest within the commission responsible for priests in the development of a theology of the priesthood. The Decree on the Ministry and Life of Priests was described as "one of the council's stepchildren...the idea was always to deal with the discipline of the clergy and the Christian people without getting into the question of an appropriate theological description of the ministry of priests."[23] This can be seen in the various topics that surfaced as the decree on priesthood changed from the early canonical and pious schema concerned with the spiritual life of priests, their duties, and their discipline to the final version which took their ministry and life into account.[24]

DEVELOPMENT OF THE DOCUMENT

The history of the decree on the ministry and life of priests has its origins in a questionnaire sent all over the world by Pope John XXIII immediately after he had convoked the council. Rather than send out documents for discussion, Pope John proposed that the Antepreparatory Commission invite all bishops to offer their own suggestions for key questions to be considered at the council. More than two thousand responses were returned for the ten preparatory commissions to coordinate and prioritize into discussion documents. These commissions were presided over by curial members for whom the idea and practice of a pastoral council was, to some extent, limited by their own administrative and juridical background and perspective. In its overseeing and presentation of preparatory documents for the respective commissions, the Antepreparatory Commission itself seemed unconvinced about the need to change from the more canonical approach of previous church councils to the requested pastoral approach.[25]

On June 18, 1959 Cardinal Tardini distributed the questionnaire worldwide to 2,594 bishops and 156 superiors of men's religious orders and also to rectors and to deans of Catholic universities and theological faculties. The replies filled around fifteen volumes and amounted to nearly ten thousand pages. These responses were juridical rather than pastoral in tone. The concern expressed by bishops in relation to the priesthood was in terms of clerical duties and devotional practices that were monastic in origin and flavor rather than directly related to the actual life of the diocesan priesthood.[26]

The Preparatory Commission for the Discipline of Clergy and Christian People, with thirty-two members and thirty-four consultants, was appointed on June 5, 1960, to review and coordinate the responses and to present a draft document for discussion at the council. Cardinal Ciriaci, prefect of the Congregation of the Council, was appointed chair. From November 1960 to April 1962, Preparatory Commission members worked on the material sent to them. They constructed a schema that they forwarded to the Central Preparatory Commission (CPC) for distribution. The initial schema, simply titled "On Priests," was composed primarily of summary statements of papal proclamations and of prevailing Roman theology and pastoral practice at that time.[27] The Tridentine model of sacerdotal priesthood held firm.

The first session of the council began before this schema had been dealt with by the Preparatory Commission and the issue of priesthood was virtually off the agenda at this initial stage of the council. On October 16, 1962, new members of the Commission for the Discipline of Clergy and Christian People were both appointed by the pope and elected by council members. Cardinal Ciriaci remained the chair, but a new secretary, Rev. Alvaro del Portillo of Opus Dei, was appointed and remained in office until the end of the council.

When the first meeting of the new Commission for the Discipline of Clergy and Christian People took place on December 3, 1962, the commission members set up processes for revising the material they had received from the initial commission. For the task of composing an appropriate decree on priestly life they had been given seven topics to consider in light of contemporary needs: the distribution of the clergy, the irremovability of pastors, clerical dress, ecclesiastical precepts, catechetical instruction, ecclesiastical benefices, and confraternities. To these the commission members themselves added ten other topics. They set up sub-commissions and went to work on topics and submissions from the bishops.

In all, they wrote seventeen documents on the priesthood for presentation to the Central Preparatory Commission, all of them practical in orientation. In particular, three of these, entitled "The Holiness of Clerics," "Clerical Offices and Benefices," and "The Distribution of Priests," and another on "The Care of Souls" were selected by the CPC, which decided that these documents should be restructured into a single document and used as a basis for discussion in the council. Because the first schema had not been discussed at the first session, the bishops were asked to send in their responses to the revised schema by February 8, 1963, to enable the implementation of responses in time for the second session. The response from the bishops was basically that the schema was too juridical in nature. The texts were both practical and pastoral in approach, but there was little evidence of the commission's awareness of the ecclesiological and sociological discussions of the pastoral involvement of the church in the modern world that had taken place over the previous three decades.[28]

In reviewing the preparatory period of the council as session one came to closure, conciliar historian Giuseppe Alberigo commented that, from a sociological point of view,

> the preparation appears to have been concentrated in the hands of a proportionately restricted group, composed exclusively of males who were celibate, of rather high median age and of European culture... One has the impression during the years between 1959 and 1962 that the major world events did not find much echo within the group.[29]

This was evidence of the inward-looking approach that characterized the early documents that had been distributed for discussion among the council members. Many of the bishops brought the concerns of their dioceses to the council sessions and they found themselves frustrated by the style and substance of these documents. Even John XXIII's most important statements, such as his encyclical on Christianity and social progress, *Mater et Magistra* (1961), had not been taken into account in the council preparation.

Nearly three hundred suggestions for revision of the document on priesthood were sent to the commission, which was ordered to produce a new decree for the second session.[30] It was to have three chapters: chapter 1 on the perfection of priestly life, chapter 2 on the study of pastoral practice, and chapter 3 on the proper use of ecclesiastical possessions. The first chapter was to present the key principles intrinsic to the priestly life, while the second was to look at contemporary approaches to pastoral care. The third chapter was to endorse the need for adequate material support for priests so that they would not be tempted to engage in money-raising activities for their personal or familial gain.

To facilitate this process effectively in terms of time and personnel, it was decided to divide the commission into four sub-commissions, with leaders who would be able to see that the task was completed in time. The expert leadership of Archbishop Marty of Rheims in these tasks was acknowledged by his co-workers. They received the benefit of his scholarship and collaborative competence, along with his ecclesio-political acumen, all of which were exhibited in the presentation of the new schema of twenty-eight pages with its new title "On Clerics" (*De Clericis*) in February. It was circulated among council members in May 1963.

The responses that came back to the commission ran to ninety-nine pages and were used by the commission as the basis for a revised schema which, in order to achieve some sort of representation of the diverse and often contradictory viewpoints in the amendments, was a text of both compromise and adaptation.

That this was a council that represented episcopal conferences from every continent meant that the priestly and ministerial issues addressed had to be related to the larger arenas of church life in the contemporary world. The division of opinion in the responses ranged from those from bishops who were looking for a theological statement on the priesthood and the priestly office to those from others who were looking for a more pastoral and practical approach. Although there was a request by a number of bishops for a theological exposition of the priesthood, the commission's interest remained focused on priestly discipline rather than on doctrine, which they saw as under the purview of the commission on doctrine.

Responses from among the bishops themselves also reminded both commission and council members that it was no longer appropriate to refer to priests as "the lower clergy" or to treat them with condescension.

> Priests share in the priesthood of Christ and not only in the priesthood of bishops. It does not seem just to call them "an order of the second degree." The priest is not only the bishop's delegate. It is because of him that the church takes on democratic meaning. There is also a collegiality of priests.[31]

The statement that the priesthood is a state of perfection, an idea strongly proposed by some bishops, was equally opposed by others. Love as the source of all perfection was however affirmed generally, as was the statement that "the priestly office performed under the beneficent direction of the bishops, is a true exercise of the love of God and of one's neighbor, and this is a sure method of striving for perfection."[32]

The new title of the revised schema, "On Priests," was due to a change in the Latin term from *De Clericis* to *De Sacerdotibus*. However, this change, significant in Latin, is lost in the simple English word "priest." The term "cleric" had offered problems because it encompassed all those ordained—from those in minor orders to bishops and the pope.[33] The title change was made primarily as a result of the discussion that arose from the request of fifteen East African bishops who argued that the decree was meant to address priests specifically rather than clerics in general.

The inclusion of the section on the threefold office of Christ as teacher, priest, and king was requested by a number of bishops and was thus included in the preface. Omission of judgmental or negative comments in regard to those who had left the priesthood was required because such comments were considered not in keeping with the style of the schema, which was to be more pastoral. With regard to priestly spirituality, many bishops wanted to see their own personal devotional practices listed. However, it was decided that only those obligations that were common to the priesthood in both the Eastern and Western churches would be mentioned. While some bishops wanted an end to honorific titles and a simplification of vestments and other such matters, it was realized that the appropriate place for such issues to be addressed was either canon law or local episcopal conferences.

No sooner had this new text been presented for acceptance at the two sessions of December 28, 1963, and January 15, 1964, than the Coordinating Commission made the unilateral decision to reduce the schema, "On Priests," to its basics in terms of a number of guiding principles or propositions on which the council fathers would vote. When this decision was announced on January 23, the Commission for the Discipline of Clergy and Christian People went back once again to rework the document. A special sub-commission, which included the secretaries of the previous four sub-commissions, was appointed and after three days of meetings at the end of January it reduced the text to ten guiding principles, which were approved on April 17. Archbishop Marty, with the approval of his commission, sent with these principles a text concerning the preparatory work that had been done and an account of the evolution of the schema "On Clerics," along with the complete text of the schema "On Priests." Again the material met with more requests for alterations before the third session.

While it is apparent that priests and their ministry were on the back burner rather than in a prominent position during the two first sessions of the council, it is important to realize that in the protracted and sometimes polarized discussions on the Dogmatic Constitution on the Church, issues were being addressed about the common priesthood of the faithful, the role of bishops, and the relation of the ordained and the laity. A new ecclesiology was being shaped, an ecclesiology that took account of the common priesthood and that would have ramifications for bishops, priests, and deacons as well as for all the baptized. However, the relegation of this schema on the priesthood to the last batch of schemas that were taken up at the council, along with the fact that it was being reduced from a text to simple proportions, was a disappointment to some. "The bishops did not realize that in a time of *aggiornamento* the priestly ministry required a doctrinal approach that transcended the level of more disciplinary matters."[34]

The controversies about the restoration of the permanent diaconate as a means of dealing with the shortage of priests (*LG*, 29), the relation of priests with their bishops, and the renewed understanding of the episcopacy (*Christus Dominus* [*CD*], 28) were also feeding into the rising awareness of the need to have a document that would speak to priests in terms of their present situation with a new recognition of the changing demands and complexities of priestly life and ministry. There was a concern expressed by some that the significance of the priesthood was being lost at the expense of the new ecclesiology: "Vatican II must not overlook the priesthood of priests by stressing the value of the episcopacy and the laity as Vatican I rather overlooked the episcopacy by stressing the papacy."[35]

Commentators have pointed out that the council experience was itself an educative process for the majority of the participants. By the end of the second session of the council a better working relationship had been established between the council members and their consultants. The key issues had been under discussion for at least two years and the connections had been made between episcopal conferences and individuals of like mind. The period from November 14 to December 8 was described as:

> a turning point that was decisive for the future of the council and therefore for the future of the Catholic Church itself . . . not because the council fathers already knew all the decisions they would make later, but because in it the council took possession of itself, its nature and its purpose and attuned itself to the intentions of John XXIII, an attunement that had largely been impeded by the work of the preparatory commissions, especially the Theological Commission.[36]

The new awareness had been generated both by the polarization and by the regrouping of episcopal conferences so that they could find their own voices and also hear what the voices of other cultures were expressing. Opportunities were being shared among the bishops to listen to their own consultants and to those of other bishops, and to develop their own understanding of the ideas that were being exchanged in the council hall.[37]

This was the background to the revision of schemas as well as to the debates. Bishops were meeting outside the council hall and working on the documents together. The German-speaking and Scandinavian bishops had held a conference at Innsbruck before the third session to discuss the propositions on the priesthood and they had consequently sent in a large number of amendments that ultimately formed about ninety percent of the changes made on the schema at the third session. They were concerned to include recognition of the importance of the apostolic life of priests, who also needed to develop those human qualities that enabled a priest to be a "brother among brothers."

Some bishops had argued from the beginning of the council against any revisions at all and complained about the rejection of the foundational work of the preparatory commissions. These bishops, predominantly those described by some writers as "intransigents," believed that once a schema had been approved by the pope and the Coordinating Commission for presentation in the council it should be accepted.[38] This opinion was rejected by the majority of the bishops, and by the preparatory commissions themselves, because papal approval was simply for the draft documents to be submitted to the council members. It was not an explicit approval of the content of the documents. Dialogue, debate, and discussion won the day and characterized the subsequent style of interaction of the third and fourth sessions and the developing style and approach of documents such as the revised schema on priests.

The mode of operation that had been decided upon by the CPC for the third session was that schemas presented would simply be voted upon as they stood, and there were to be no amendments. The principles reworked as propositions contained in "On Priests," which ran to twenty-four pages, were presented to the bishops in two parallel columns, with the propositions of March 1964 alongside a revised text that included suggestions that had been received in the interim. The title, at the request of the French bishops, had now been changed to "On the Life and Ministry of Priests," as the document on the church dealt with issues related to priesthood.

On October 13, 1964, toward the close of the plenary session, Archbishop Marty gave his report on the schema on priests that the bishops would be discussing the next day. He pointed out some key features of the document. The pastoral role of the priest and the relation of all priests to the *presbyterium* of their bishops were key issues. The two ways in which priesthood had been under debate and discussion at the council were explained in the document. The emphasis of some bishops on the liturgical leadership of priests was countered by the emphasis of others on the priestly role of evangelization. Both were confirmed as integral to priestly identity and ministry.

Marty pointed out that priests function in relation to their bishops and to the laity; they are not individual ministers on their own. He also affirmed the holiness of the priesthood, with its source in the exercise of ministry in and through Christ and the church.[39] Among the bishops there was still dissatisfaction. A conversation between Cardinal Suenens and Yves Congar on the priesthood text reports Congar supporting Suenens's concern and saying: "I myself am of this opinion and tell everyone that the text ought to be rejected since it is feeble, moralizing, paternalistic, without vision, inspiration or prophetic spirit! It contains no deep questioning, no biblical sources; it does not take up the real and burning questions of priests themselves." [40]

In his report on the third session, Rynne commented on the "October Crisis" that had been generated both by the concern and urgency of many bishops that the council be concluded at this session, and by the tense debates that had taken place over procedures and schemas under discussion, such as those on the church, religious liberty, and the apostolate of the laity. The schema on priestly life and ministry had once again been pushed to the background by these issues. The bishops who gathered to discuss it had just spent four days previously in heated discussion on the schema on the apostolate of the laity.

This was the climate that greeted Marty's opening address, in which he explained the schema as treating the pastoral needs of the church as well as priestly life and ministry in the contemporary world in a positive way.[41] The session opened with Archbishop Marty's report on the troubled history of the text and his statement that the purpose of the revised text was "to relate the life and ministry of the priest to the conditions and needs of today's world."[42] Marty also discussed the expanded contents and number of the propositions, now twelve.

When the discussion began the next day, it was obvious that many bishops wanted to be heard, and perhaps to be on record, on this important schema. There was a diverse and lively reaction from council members to the proposed text. The residue of the earlier debates was obvious in the negative reaction of many bishops to the propositions. Forty-one bishops spoke, along with three groups of bishops, while ninety-two sent in written amendments. Where so much emphasis had been paid to the bishops and laity in fully developed schemas, the priesthood seemed to have fallen between the cracks of the council's concerns. The impression was inevitable that priests were being downgraded in comparison with bishops and the laity. For whatever reason, the members of this commission as well as those of the other commissions whose texts had been reduced to propositions had not had the backbone or "nerve" of the Commission on the Apostolate of the Laity, which earlier in the year had refused outright to adopt the requested reduction of its schema to propositions.[43]

Unease prevailed among the council members as well as within the commission itself in regard to the document on priesthood and the decision was unanimous that "a message from the fathers of the council to all priests of the world—debated the previous year—be taken up again."[44] Cardinal Meyer of Chicago opened the discussion with a critique of the text, commenting on the inadequacy of its organization and its content. He was unable to find a relationship between the revised text and Marty's earlier stated aims that the pastoral needs of the contemporary church would be addressed.[45]

Bishop Latusek of Poland spoke on the importance of stressing the spirituality proper to the diocesan priest. Some bishops urged that the title be changed to: "On the Ministry and Life of Priests, Especially Diocesan Priests." Cardinal Léger of Montreal was critical of the failure in the document to recognize that priestly spirituality could not be separated from priestly ministry. He argued that the reference to the evangelical counsels spoke more to the ordained religious than to the diocesan priest. Others were in support of this criticism, including Cardinal Döpfner, who on the following day spoke on behalf of the German bishops who wanted the second part of the document to address the contemporary situation and spirituality of priests, less in terms of counsels and more in terms of the daily struggles of the diocesan priest in relation to his own ministry and spiritual life.

There was a concern that only priestly obligations to their bishops seemed to be expressed. Bishop Théas from Lourdes and Tarbes noted that "bishops could do nothing without priests . . . To read the propositions, one would think that nothing had changed in the life and ministry of priests since the Middle Ages."[46] He expressed his concern about the increasing number of bishops in contrast with the diminishing number of priests in the context of a steadily growing Catholic population.

Archbishop Gomes dos Santos of Goiânia, Brazil, on behalf of 112 bishops from Brazil and other countries, confirmed the rejections already voiced and in turn criticized the document's failure to deal adequately with either diocesan or religious clergy, and also its failure to critique paternalistic and self-serving aberrations in the church. He described the document as "a great disappointment and an insult to priests."[47] It was seen to be limited in its approach to contemporary priestly life, and it seemed to have been constructed in a rather ghettoist context. Cardinal Alfrink spoke of the lack of any missionary spirit or of global awareness and proposed "the establishment in every diocese of a pastoral council composed of priests and laymen."[48]

Several wanted the document to present an image of the priest which was in greater conformity with the gospel, and more Christocentric in approach. There was little sense that the identity of the priest might need to be addressed in any other way than this, and no sense of the issues that the priest of the future would face in terms of identity.

In contrast to the rejection of the schema by other groups of bishops, Cardinals Ruffini of Sicily and Quiroga y Palacios of Santiago de Compostela, along with Archbishops Rosales of the Philippines and Evangelisti of Meerut, India, supported the text as it stood, without any changes. They believed it served the priesthood well, even though it had been described by some bishops as an institutionally self-serving document. Ruffini praised the "wisdom and prudence" of the commission in the presentation of the schema as it stood.[49]

The idea of priestly associations and of a "common life" for diocesan priests was favored by many speakers as a means of resolving the problems of the loneliness that could be experienced by diocesan priests. The suggestion was made that bishops should promote associations of priests to "live according to the gospel of Christ, in poverty, chastity and obedience."[50] There was an evident tension between those who were proposing an authentic spirituality for the diocesan priesthood and those promoting the monastic or religious spirituality that had dominated priestly training until the council, and which still influenced many bishops.

The equitable distribution of priests, their support, and the procedures and preparation for transfer were also important issues for non-European episcopacies. The postwar consequences for priestly life came to the surface in the issue raised for the appropriate care of those priests who had suffered psychological damage during the war.

A short section on celibacy, originally omitted because the document was for both Eastern and Western churches and their different disciplinary requirements and because of sensitivity to the Eastern Churches,[51] had been added at the request of seventy bishops, one of whom was Cardinal Lercaro, who also asked that "the special obedience which a priest owes his bishop should be shown to derive from his share in the same priesthood and mission as his bishop."[52] This revised draft had a greater insistence on celibacy to reaffirm the present discipline. The ten lines on celibacy and chastity that had been added had now increased to eighty lines exhorting those who had promised to observe sacred celibacy to trust in God's grace and to persevere faithfully in their commitment.

During this period, rumors had been circulating about a possible relaxation of the law of celibacy. There was also a strong call for a more positive view of clerical celibacy, with the comment made that it should not be seen as a "sort of admission ticket to Holy Orders."[53] The three evangelical counsels of poverty, chastity, and obedience were stressed in the revised text.

From Roman, Spanish, and Eastern European bishops there had been requests for the inclusion of practices directed toward priestly holiness, including pastoral courses and annual retreats. Other more personal devotional practices, such as visits to the Blessed Sacrament and the recitation of the Rosary, were requested for inclusion. It was decided to simply recommend mental prayer, asceticism, and contemplation along with a common form of life where possible. Recommendations as to the importance of the discipline of study in the priestly life were made, as was the effort to develop pastoral skills.

The debate that took place from October 13 to 15, 1964, came to closure with Cardinal Lefèbvre of Bourges, speaking on behalf of seventy bishops, who objected to the text because of its failure to deal with the efficacy of the priesthood, especially in terms of the relationship of ordained priesthood to the common priesthood of the faithful. The majority verdict on the document was negative, especially on the grounds of its brevity.

Archbishop Marty summed up the debate and skillfully turned the fate of the decree in favor of the original intentions of his commission. He proposed to council members that a fully developed schema on the life and ministry of priests be developed and that the idea of propositions be dropped. The moderators accepted this on October 12 and put it to the vote at the next meeting on October 19 by a margin of 1,199 for and 930 against. This was in accord with the hopes of the commission. The propositions were to be dropped and a new schema developed. This would allow major revisions to be made without the appearance of a total rejection of the document. Once again, all the written comments were submitted and collated by the commission and they resulted in two volumes that amounted to 250 pages. The new draft needed to be presented to the council members before their departure on November 21.

While the debates had been taking place, the members of the sub-commissions had been beavering away at the task of developing a new schema on the priesthood in light of submissions and discussions, and in the hope that Marty's proposal of a text that addressed the concerns expressed in council by the bishops would be the outcome. Of the various changes to be made, Lécuyer suggests that the inclusion of a definition or description of the presbyterate was of greatest importance.[54] This was at the request of a number of bishops from Indonesia and West Africa who had called for a greater correlation with the Dogmatic Constitution on the Church in terms of the relation between bishops and priests.

The new text was presented in time for a meeting of the Coordinating Commission of the council in early November. The forty-four page text was ratified by this commission on November 9 but, for whatever reason, it was not distributed to the bishops until November 20, the day before their departure. It was requested that any comments on the document be returned by the end of January 1965. The comments sent in accordingly were again collected and arranged in a 165-page booklet containing 446 proposals. This was worked on in plenary commission so that yet another new text was ready by April 1, 1965.[55]

The new title, "On the Life and Ministry of Priests," indicated a new development in the level of understanding of the key issues in relation to contemporary priesthood. The story of the title is the story of the changing approach to the schema. The movement from a schema on clerics (*clericis*), to priests (*sacerdos*), to life and ministry of priests (*sacerdotium*), to the eventual ministry and life of priests (*presbyterorum*) illustrates the change and the new prominence given to priestly ministry and a movement toward a spirituality of diocesan clergy that is related to their apostolic ministry rather than to the previous monastic model.

The completely revised document for discussion at the fourth session was composed of Archbishop Marty's report, the new schema with the original propositions notated nearby, and the report of the secretariat of the Commission on Priesthood on three individual sections of the schema, focusing in the first section on ministry, the second on priestly life, and the third on an exhortation to priests. Commentators point out that the style, tone, and content of this document were quite different from those in all the schemas presented earlier. The renewed emphasis on the threefold function of the priest as preacher, teacher, and pastor was the consequence of the request of more than one hundred bishops and this was clearly stated in the new preface.

In this schema, priestly ministry is contextualized in the common priesthood, while the ordained priesthood is elucidated in relation to the episcopate and laity. A group of bishops had tried to reintroduce the idea that "the essence of presbyteral priesthood is derived from its relation to the Eucharist" (Modification no. 13),[56] but this was rejected by the commission. The council direction was in terms of the priestly office being derived from the episcopal offices and this was the thrust of the document that prevailed in the council. Eucharistic centrality and the importance of the sacramental life are stressed, as is the more comprehensive approach to priesthood as participation in the threefold mission of Christ. The spirituality of the priesthood in terms of engaging in ministry as a means of holiness was developed in some detail.

Once again, celibacy was the major subject that had elicited the most comments from the bishops. While more than one hundred bishops wanted a statement on the traditional foundations for celibacy, reference to canon law in relation to it, and a reaffirmation of celibacy's primary importance in the priestly life, another group, equally large, wanted the clarification that there was no incompatibility between priesthood and marriage.

To find a formula that would satisfy the range of views, including diametrically opposed amendments and quite conflicting positions and ideas being proposed, was not possible. Consequently, a compromise position of dealing with the concerns of the majority became the focus of the commission's efforts. They omitted reference to the decision of the apostles to leave all and follow Christ because of the implications this had for married clergy. They included affirmations of voluntary celibacy as an expression of total commitment to Christ and the ministry. The eschatological value of celibacy and poverty and the implication of greater freedom were reaffirmed. This revised schema, slightly smaller than the draft that had preceded it and with attention paid to criticisms of repetition and overuse of quotations was sent to the council members in May 1965.

The fourth session opened on September 14, 1965, and the re-named decree "On the Ministry and Life of Priests" was due for presentation and debate on October 14. The change of title represented the change in emphasis from the priestly *life* to priestly *ministry*. This was a result of the debates and discussion that had taken place on the title and its importance in determining the direction of the decree. The requirements of priestly ministry determine priestly life and spirituality rather than the opposite. This was a new direction for the commission to take.

When this new text was discussed in October, the bishops were still dissatisfied with it, even though it had changed in structure and content as requested. Although this schema received less time in discussion in the council hall than many of the others, it had received far more interventions and amendments than any other schema.[57]

Individual bishops and episcopal conferences were not all in agreement with the debates on the issue of celibacy that had taken place at the earlier sessions. Their own experience of the shortage of priests and the problems with celibacy among the clergy led many of them to look for a schema that addressed the situations they were facing in their own dioceses.

The problem for Latin American churches had apparently been under discussion since the time of Pope Pius X. Responses were varied, and often at opposition with each other. Bishop Pedro Koop of Lins, Brazil, had earlier distributed his intended intervention in regard to the support for a married clergy among council members and it had found its way into the public press. Two other Brazilian bishops publicly supported Koop in this proposal.[58]

Bishop Larraín Errázuris of Chile, also president of the Conference of Bishops of Latin America, "sent a cable to the Pope denying unofficial rumors that the bishops of Latin America were in disagreement on the present law on priestly celibacy."[59] He affirmed the support of the episcopal conference he represented for the pope's wishes. Koop's statement, while acknowledging the value of priestly celibacy, had reminded its readers of the dire problem of the shortage of priests in Latin America; thus his request that episcopal conferences have the authority to ordain married men of recognized virtue and commitment. Koop had argued that, in dependence upon their bishops,

> married priests could exercise their conjugal, familiar, and socioeconomic experience in service of the ministry. This would undoubtedly make it more effective...Let the bishops be under no illusion: the fate of the Church in Latin America is in great danger. The choice is urgent: either we multiply the number of priests, or we can expect the fall of the Church in Latin America.[60]

His argument had also been used earlier, during the debate on permanent diaconate by another Latin American prelate, Bishop Kémérer of Argentina, who had proposed that married men who had been faithful to their commitment for at least five years and whose leadership was recognized in the community might be ordained. Those bishops who were in support of this proposal believed that the precedent had been set by the ordination of married Lutheran priests who had converted to Catholicism during the reign of Pope Pius XII.[61]

However, on October 11 an unprecedented event occurred. Cardinal Tisserant, secretary general of the council, interrupted the council proceedings for the reading of a letter from Paul VI in which the pope required that any further discussion on the topic of celibacy was to stop. "Public debate is not opportune on this subject which is so important and demands such profound prudence."[62] The letter reinforced the pope's intention not simply to maintain the law of celibacy, but to reinforce its observance for priests of the Latin rite. Any bishop who wished to express a concern on this matter was advised to submit it directly to the pope in writing.

This letter was generally thought to be the consequence of the great deal of discussion in the public arena through the media, with much conjecture about the various perspectives on priestly celibacy and a concern for the possible decisions that might be made in council.

Among the bishops themselves, the decision had been made to bring the issue of married clergy to debate in the council during the decree dealing with the priesthood. That there was a great deal of emotion felt in relation to the intervention of Paul VI's letter might be understood when commentators point out that the reading of the letter was punctuated with (forbidden) bouts of applause in the council.

Earlier discussion and voting on the schema dealing with seminary training had been supportive of the law of celibacy in the Latin church. The vote (1,971 for and 16 against) had been so strong then that it had been generally assumed that the bishops were ready to maintain the status quo in regard to priestly celibacy. With the papal suppression of public debate there were some negative reactions, but approval was voiced by the majority because at this final stage of the council the bishops were clearly divided on the issue, and they realized that the need to do justice to the topic rendered further discussion impractical and would defeat the need to give appropriate time to the other documents that needed to be ratified before the close of the council.

The particular character of the priestly ministry as both worship of God and a service to humanity was endorsed as a safeguard against priestly "activism." Cardinal Richaud of Bordeaux affirmed the principle that priestly ministry is "consecrated to the exterior and interior worship of God," which then renders it a service to humanity through the power of Christ.[63] This was reinforced by the intervention of Cardinal Shehan of Baltimore, who affirmed that it was through the priest's participation in the ministry of Christ, and through the commissioning of his bishop, that the priest was authorized to minister on behalf of the people of God.

The need to articulate a priestly spirituality that suited an apostolically active life rather than the religious or monastic model that was implicit in the original draft of the document was the concern of a number of speakers, including Cardinals Léger, Döpfner, Suenens, and Roy. By midday October 16, the council members decided that the discussion on this text could now be closed. The vote was put on whether this text could be the basis of a final revision in light of the amendments, verbal and written, that had been made. The voting was 1,507 in agreement with this and 12 against it. Yet another revision was to be made in preparation for the final discussion and approval.

The schema was revised and restructured, the latter according to a suggestion of Cardinal Suenens, with a movement away from the structure of brief propositions to a document with a preface, three chapters, and a conclusion. Two diverse perspectives had been evident in the discussions relating to the presbyterate. The majority group wanted to relate the idea of priestly ministry to the threefold ministry of episcopal priesthood with its foundation in Christ as priest, prophet, and king. This connected with the understanding of priesthood established in the Constitution on the Church, with teaching, preaching, and pastoral ministry as focal points. The minority position was related to the maintenance of the sacerdotal or cultic notion of priesthood, with the eucharistic emphasis recognized as a priority.

The commission was able to address the concerns of both groups in the final document, though not without compromise. When the section on celibacy was presented, it addressed celibacy as gift appropriate to but not required by priesthood, the theological character of celibacy in terms of pastoral mission and ministry, and the freedom that celibacy brings to the priest. It affirmed that, although the topic of celibacy required more discussion, the primary concern in the schema was in relation to the formulation of the law of celibacy. In this way, the sensibilities of the Eastern Church, an important issue during all the debates on the topic, could be taken into consideration.[64] There was also a concern to ensure that the words used would not force closure on future decision-making in regard to celibacy.[65]

The final seventy-two-page text presented for debate included Archbishop Marty's report, parallel copies of the original and revised texts for comparison, the report of the commission in regard to changes made and the reasons for them, and the summary of the text for voting purposes.[66] There was some concern about the status of the schema—as decree rather than constitution—the order of the title, and an addition to article 6 in relation to priestly leadership and care in religious orders. Basically the major area of concern for this draft was article 16 on celibacy once again. More than one hundred bishops wanted passages from 1 Timothy 3:2–5 and Titus 1:6, which mention married bishops, cited as references. The clarification between East and West in relation to married clergy caused a number of interventions, with two bishops wanting married and unmarried clergy to be given some attention.

Although a number of bishops wanted to make the superiority of the celibate over the married priesthood made explicit, this was rejected.

More than four hundred bishops had wanted more emphasis given to Marian devotion, and this had been taken into account in the final schema. Eventually the revisions were dealt with and the reworked schema was voted on and approved, with the votes being 2,390 for and 4 against. Paul VI promulgated the decree on December 7, 1965. Alberigo offers a caution in his comment that this final vote "should not blind us to the problems in this text," which sets up "a traditional sacerdotal image of the priest over against a theologically up-to-date understanding of ministry."[67]

PART II
MAJOR POINTS

The structure, headings, and major points of the final version of the Decree on the Ministry and Life of Priests, *Presbyterorum Ordinis* (*PO*), are as follows:

> Preface
>
> Chapter 1: The Priesthood in the Ministry of the Church
>
> Chapter 2: The Ministry of Priests
> > Section 1: Priests' Functions
> > Section 2: Priests' Relationship with Others
> > Section 3: The Distribution of Priests, and Vocations to the Priesthood
>
> Chapter 3: The Life of Priests
> > Section 1: The Vocation of Priests to the Life of Perfection
> > Section 2: Special Spiritual Requirements in the Life of the Priest
> > Section 3: Aids to the Life of Priests
>
> Conclusion and Exhortation

As was pointed out earlier, a major focal aspect of this document can be seen in the changing emphasis in the title from the original document directed toward the functional (and inclusive of bishops and deacons) identity of priests as clerics, *De Clericis*, with the subsequent movement in revised texts to the cultic and sacerdotal emphasis, *De Sacerdotibus*, followed by the larger horizon of priestly identity in "On the *Life* and Ministry of Priests," to the final reworking of the ministerial focus of "On the *Ministry* and Life of Priests." The transition from the earliest concern of the commission to remind priests of their duty to lead a model life eventually moved to the final emphasis on the participatory nature of priestly ministry. [68] The movement of primary emphasis from "Life" to "Ministry" shows the concern of council members to emphasize the function of priesthood rather than its status. The significance of the ordained ministry is in its ecclesial service for the glory of God.[69]

The title change is a consequence of the developing conciliar affirmation that the ministry that priests exercise nourishes their spiritual life. That this is directed primarily to the identity of the diocesan priest is a characteristic of the direction of the total document, which deals much more with the ministry and life of diocesan priests rather than with that of religious priests. It is important to note that, although a number of council members wanted the decree to include a discussion on the theology of the priesthood, there is no attempt in the document to do so.[70]

A clarifying comment on the key elements of the decree was written by (then council expert and now Pope Benedict XVI) Joseph Ratzinger a few years after the council, when its impact on their understanding of their own priestly identity was being felt by priests:

> The emphasis of the entire document is clearly on the second chapter, on the question of the true nature of priestly office. The prime concern of the first chapter is to situate the question within the total pattern of Christology and theology. The fundamental proposition here states that the origin of priestly office is to be found in the mystery of Easter, that the meaning of the priesthood can be grasped only in unity with all the Christian realities in the light of this central mystery.[71]

Ratzinger affirmed the "formal authority" of the decree and commented that it directs readers to its biblical and traditional foundations and enables the recognition of "the contemporary relevance of both."[72]

The influence of *Lumen Gentium* (*LG*) is apparent in the twofold emphasis on priesthood, that of the ordained and that of the common priesthood of the whole Mystical Body. The references to the conciliar documents on the liturgy, *Sacrosanctum Concilium* (*SC*); the church, *Lumen Gentium*; the pastoral duties of bishops, *Christus Dominus* (*CD*); and priestly training, *Optatam Totius* (*OT*) locate priestly identity in the ministerial function of the church. There is a new movement away from the Tridentine and nineteenth and early twentieth century manual theology emphasis on the cultic or sacerdotal identity of priesthood as expressed in "the power of consecrating the True Body and Blood of Christ and of remitting or retaining sins" to a "discussion of the priesthood of the faithful and...ministry in the church as a means of enabling the church to be the one body of Christ."[73] The theological foundation for priestly ministry implicit in the decree rests in the theology of *Lumen Gentium* and *Christus Dominus*. This represents a significant move.

The three chapter headings locate the threefold office of priesthood in the service of "Christ the Teacher, Priest and King." The theology of the priesthood implicit in the decree has its foundation in this threefold office of Christ and his church: "It is a genuine priesthood because it is a sharing in the priesthood of the sole mediator Christ. It includes therefore a sharing in all that the council has accepted as included in the priesthood—namely, the task of ruling, sanctifying, and shepherding the Christian community, the People of God" (*LG*, 21).

PREFACE

The opening line of the preface locates priesthood in the context of the priestly identity of baptized ministers who, participating in the ministry of the bishop, have been ordained to serve the community of believers. "The excellence of the order of priests in the Church has already been recalled to the minds of all by this sacred synod" takes for granted the background of communion ecclesiology that is at the heart of *Lumen Gentium* and links priesthood from the outset with the missionary role of the church.[74] The language change from "priceless—*inaestimabilis*—dignity" of an earlier draft to "the excellence of the order" shows the movement away from the aura of an elevated separation of the priestly caste that characterized the pre–Vatican II sacerdotal model.[75]

The essentially relational character of the ministerial priesthood is affirmed in the opening reference to the documents on the church, bishops, and priestly training. The priest is called to gather God's family together in unity, "to lead them in the Spirit through Christ, to God the Father" (*LG*, 28). Priests are called to be in relation to God's people and to their bishops, and this ordained relationship has its foundations in Jesus Christ, the source and inspiration of the special ministry of priests. The vision of priestly ministry that is integral to this document is more expansively described in terms of the affirmation of Christ's "teaching, sanctifying and shepherding" role (*LG*, 21). This threefold ministry, handed on to the apostles, is now being carried out in priestly ministry to the people of God to build up the body of Christ which is the church.

The emphasis on "order" in the document is an official term that carries over from the original Roman notion of leadership to ecclesiastical usage in terms of grades of hierarchical leadership. It shows the council moving away from the Tridentine emphasis on the cultic notion of priesthood with the emphasis essentially on the consecration of the Eucharist and the office of power over the Mystical Body of Christ, the church.[76] It is a movement toward "a broader vision of priestly ministry as a whole: preaching and pastoral activities are now the primary tasks. These are connected directly with the people of God and not with the eucharist. Only in this pastoral context is the sanctifying task of the priest determined."[77] The three functions are to be understood in light of the ecclesiology for which the "service of the community is not just *a* function; it is *the* function of those who receive the priestly ministry through the sacrament of holy orders."[78]

This new vision of ministerial priesthood is not a playing down of the significance of the eucharistic ministry but it is a relocation of priestly ministry in the context of servant leadership of the community. Commentators point out that participation in the threefold office, "the teaching office (prophetic office), the priestly office (office of sanctification), and the royal office (pastoral office)" is a means of expressing Christ's salvific work as teacher, priest, and king.[79] These are traditional titles found in patristic and medieval writings, titles that were systematized by Calvin into a way of interpreting the ministry of Jesus and that he then applied to all the baptized and subsequently developed in his own approach to salvation in Christ.[80]

The new emphasis on this more comprehensive understanding of priestly ministry is a modification of the traditional approach.[81] The further implications of the threefold ministry in terms of the fullness of orders, as in the grades of, and relationships between, bishop, priest, and deacon are implied rather than explicated in the preface, and are dealt with in greater detail in the Decree on the Pastoral Office of Bishops in the Church and in the Dogmatic Constitution on the Church (*LG*, chapter 3).

The emphasis in the preface is not only on "the care of souls" but on the "increasing difficulty" that priestly ministry involves. The priest is placed in the context of the routine struggles and situations along with the community of the faithful. The communal aspect of the human struggle of priest and people is recognized in the article. The varied references to the setting and circumstances of priestly ministry give this document a contemporary and concrete feel. Both priest and people function "in pastoral and human circumstances which very often change so profoundly" and in ways for which there are no established precedents. This addresses the ministry of both diocesan and religious priests and acknowledges that it is a dynamic rather than a static understanding that is needed for an authentic priestly ministry.

The preface also recognizes a prophetic dimension in and through the preaching, teaching, and liturgical leadership roles of the priest in the contemporary ecclesial context. The priestly "sacred ordination and mission" is received from the bishops so that the building up of the body of Christ may "be carried on more effectively and their lives be better provided for, in pastoral and human circumstances."

In his commentary on the decree, Friedrich Wulf points out that while the last sentence of the preface discusses the increased difficulties of priestly ministry in the contemporary era, it would surely have been more helpful to at least give some extra attention to the crisis of priesthood "for theological, anthropological, sociological and pastoral reasons" that was fermenting even during the conciliar years.[82] The preface offers a "model" of priesthood, simply an intimation of the reality against an idealized background. The decree then moves on to the explication of "The Priesthood in the Ministry of the Church" in chapter 1.

CHAPTER 1
THE PRIESTHOOD IN THE MINISTRY OF THE CHURCH

The context and purpose of priestly ministry are expressed in terms of service of the church in and through the threefold ministry of Christ for the glory of the Father. The order of priesthood, the part that the priestly sharing in the threefold office of Christ plays in the renewal of the church that receives emphasis in this chapter is not so much the consecration and sanctity of the priest but his ministry and function as well as his sacramental activities within the church.

This chapter, perhaps surprisingly, opens with an affirmation of the common priesthood of the faithful. "In Him all the faithful are made a holy and royal priesthood" (*PO*, 2). The two kinds of priesthood are clearly presented as differing in essence, not merely in degree, and yet they are closely related to each other in the "whole Mystical Body" of Christ. By baptism and confirmation Christians give witness to Christ in and through the witness of their own authentic living and worship. The transformation of the world is thus the mission of all the faithful.[83] "There is no member who does not have a part in the mission of the whole Body" (*PO*, 2), but there are different functions in the church. The document states that it is the official ministers who "are able by the sacred power of orders to offer sacrifice and to forgive sins," and theirs is a public office for all people exercised in Christ's name (*PO*, 2).

In this decree, identification with Christ as head of the church comes only through ordination.[84] Various commentators point out that this section has an ambiguity similar to that in *Lumen Gentium* 28, a "certain vagueness and ambiguity which leads us to conclude that the theological concept of priesthood presented by the decree is not quite homogeneous."[85] Priests "are able to act in the person of Christ the Head" (*PO*, 2), but are they representatives of the church? A great deal of theological debate has gone into the question of the way in which the priest is acting *in persona Christi* or *in persona Ecclesiae*.[86] The decree leaves the implications of the question open for further development theologically and pastorally.

Yet Christ's unique role as "high priest" in his salvific activity of life, death, and resurrection is integral to this section. It is through the ministry of the ordained that the "spiritual sacrifice of the faithful is made perfect in union with the sacrifice of Christ." The ministry of the word and the "good news" it offers alongside that of sacrifice and sacrament in the bringing about of God's reign permeates this section. God's loving invitation to all is responded to in and through the Eucharist. The priest is the representative of the church in this missionary role to all people, which has its basis in the New Testament apostolic ministry.[87]

There seems to be some question as to whether the spiritual sacrifice
that the faithful offer is the same as, or separate from, the sacrifice of
Christ.

> But the sacrifice of Jesus Christ is offered by priests in a sacra-
> mental manner and is thus the place where the spiritual sacri-
> fice of the faithful acquires its full effectiveness and meaning. If,
> however, the sentence is thus interpreted, then one asks again
> what it means to say that priests celebrate the Eucharist "in the
> name of the whole Church."[88]

Presbyterorum Ordinis 2 represents a compromise position in response to the conciliar debates on whether the document should focus
on the episcopacy and its threefold office in which presbyters participate or whether it should focus on the traditional category of priesthood. However, in attempting to satisfy both positions that were
represented in the debate, the council had to sacrifice consistency in the
final text. Having said that the presbyterate participates in the same
threefold ministry of Christ as the episcopacy, the text goes on to focus
on Christ's priesthood. It is noticeable that there is no explicit reference
to the "mystery" dimension of the priestly church. This section resonates with tones of the salvific activity of Christ's priesthood in and
through the sacerdotal (the sacred power of orders) and apostolic ministerial emphases which are present. It brings in a new understanding of
the presbyterate as participation in the episcopal ministry, which is the
fullness of ordination. "The fundamental priesthood is that of the
church, the community of those who believe in Christ,...the special
priesthood essentially grows out of the mystery of the priestly church
without simply being under the control of the church." Because of the
divergent opinions expressed in the debate, this point is not made sufficiently clear in this decree.[89]

Implicit in *Presbyterorum Ordinis* 3 is the collegiality and communal
identity of the priesthood. The plural "priests" is consistently used in the
document. The tone of the opening sentence is one of separation; priests
are "taken from" the people. Yet they share the human condition and
circumstances. The cultic separateness of priesthood comes to the fore
once again in the reference to an often quoted "high priestly" passage

from the letter to the Hebrews (5:1). That it is contextualized in a Pauline priestly ministry of being set apart so that in becoming all things to all people, all might be saved (1 Cor 9:19–23) enables a reconnection to be made between priests and their people. But there is still the connotation of apartness from the community in this article.

The key differences between the Vatican II concept of priestly ministry and that of Trent is described by Wulf in terms of the uniqueness of Christ taken seriously in the Vatican II understanding. "Christ alone is the priest and his priesthood is an eschatological one." Sacrament and leadership are key elements in Christ's saving action. In *Presbyterorum Ordinis* the bishop, the *episkopus*, is seen as the fullness of ordained priesthood, while the traditional emphasis saw the priest, the *presbyter*, as the fullness. The cultic character of Trent which was "one-sided, static and personal," in Vatican II is "multiple, dynamic and ecclesial."[90] Wulf notes that the connection between common priesthood and ordained priesthood has not been totally successful in *Presbyterorum Ordinis*, but he argues that the new approach it brings does make a significant contribution toward the understanding of the relationship between the two.[91]

CHAPTER 2

THE MINISTRY OF PRIESTS

The threefold ministry of Christ is the panorama against which the ideas are developed in this chapter. The ecclesiological foundations for priesthood are present in the sections on the functions of priesthood, priestly relationships, and the issues of placement and vocations.

Section 1: Priests' Functions

At the outset the decree states (*PO*, 4) that it is the priestly ministry of the word that is the first task of priests. The source of the identity of priests as "co-workers with their bishops" in the preaching ministry relationship has its foundations in *Lumen Gentium* 21. The emphasis on the preaching role of bishops and priests also connects with thematic developments in the document on liturgy and that on the missions.

This represents a movement away from the approach to ministry of the Middle Ages, which was primarily an emphasis on the sanctifying role and was more sacerdotal in approach.

The difficulty of preaching "in the circumstances of the modern world" is acknowledged; the preacher needs to be able to relate the "lasting truth of the Gospel" to the changing situations in which people find themselves. "Contemporary problems" are to be addressed. The distinction is made between the tasks of evangelizing the unchurched and catechesis of the community of believers. It is noteworthy that the focus here is exclusively on the priest himself, with no allusion to any form of mutuality between him and the community.

Wulf points out the inadequacy of the ecclesial foundations for priestly ministry in this section, a lacuna in the decree as a whole.[92] *Presbyterorum Ordinis* 4 summarizes the responsibility for and confirms the significance of the preaching ministry. "In this context the words 'proclamation,' 'proclaiming' become the key words of this decree. The idea of proclamation (preaching of the Gospel) is the construction center on which the conciliar decree projects and understands the office of the priest."[93]

Presbyterorum Ordinis 5 needs to be read alongside the Constitution on the Sacred Liturgy if it is to be fully appreciated. The priestly ministry is a sacramental ministry through which the bishop is made "present in every congregation" in and through priests' sharing of a "special title in the priesthood of Christ... by the action of his Spirit." It is the responsibility of the priests to catechize the faithful about the meaning and value of the Eucharist, to lead them in worship in the Eucharist, and to make sure that the place of worship is cared for. Priests are responsible to pray the Divine Office and develop their own "knowledge of and facility on the liturgy." These liturgical tasks are to be carried out in such a way that, while being faithful to the tradition, they are also in touch with the present needs and circumstances of the ordinary churchgoer.

The role of unifying the people of God is the main thrust of *Presbyterorum Ordinis* 6. The priest exercises the office of "Christ the Shepherd and Head." Commentators point out that the leadership here is identified with pastoral role of the priest. "Spiritual power is conferred upon them for the building up of the Church. The priest is subordinate to the bishop, but he has a genuine authority, a spiritual one, in his own exercise of his priestly office."[94]

This picks up on the twofold aspect of priestly leadership: the ordained act in the name of the community of believers and in the name and power of Christ conferred on them. It is the risen Christ who "is both immanent to the church and over against it."[95] It is a eucharistic community that nourishes both those present in the celebration and those for whom the community itself is accountable in the witness of their daily lives and in missionary outreach. While the exercise of priestly authority in this section is in continuity with the past, the new emphasis on the Christian community as "effective instrument" opens up new horizons of mutual collaboration between bishop, priest, and the people of God.

Presbyterorum Ordinis 4, 5, and 6 together present a definition of priestly ministry, following the three offices of Christ as teacher, priest, and shepherd. Ratzinger comments that the choice of a Christological framework emphasizes, if indirectly, the Christological character of the New Testament priestly office. The unity of priestly ministry is primary in the decree.[96] Yet here, as in the earlier articles, it would have been helpful if the decree had made the connection with the priesthood of the church, with priests and laity serving together with the same sense of mission that gives a unity to all, particularly in the whole Christ.

Section 2: Priests' Relationship with Others

This section opens up a more hierarchical structure of priestly ministry. Yet *Presbyterorum Ordinis* 7 states that, alongside the "hierarchical communion with their bishops," priests are "the necessary helpers and counselors" to the bishops in their own roles of "teaching, sanctifying and nourishing the People of God." There is an explicit mutuality in the relationship which adds a level of complexity to its pastoral implementation. This may be evidenced in the movement from the relationship described between bishops and priests as "sons and friends" in *Lumen Gentium* 28 to "brothers and friends" in this section in *Presbyterorum Ordinis*. The bishop is responsible for the formation of priests, both initial and lifelong, and for consulting the priests in his diocese through a "senate representing all priests." A dialogical relationship that requires listening and response from both parties involved is integral to this relational network, which has its foundation in the common sharing in the priesthood of Christ. The spiritual and temporal well-being of the priest is the responsibility of the bishop.

The opening-up of consultative processes and responsibility is a new development. Consultative processes, greater opportunities for mutual exchange and for freedom of expression between authorities, and the mutual respect on which all this is built has brought a deeper and richer understanding of the meaning of ecclesial obedience. The importance of unity in the accomplishment of "apostolic undertakings" is seen as a contemporary necessity rather than an option.

Just as unity is a necessity in the bishop-priest relationship, so it is in the fraternal relationships of the "intimate sacramental brotherhood" of priests (*PO*, 8). This can be brought about by the various clergy associations that have been initiated since the council. This section in the decree brings another element to the approach to diocesan priestly life when it discusses the necessity of encouraging "some kind of common life or some sharing of common life." The idea of a *presbyterium* or presbytery community that unites the bishops and priests of a diocese "in a bond of charity, prayer and total cooperation" is intended to be a reclaiming of a previously outdated community model, but one which it was hoped might have something to offer priests in the contemporary context.

The original idea of the "presbytery community" arose in early-church times but died out in the fourth century. What is presented here appears to have monastic roots, but according to Wulf, who was present at the discussions on the document, it refers to "the group of priests in a particular diocese who, under the authority of their bishop, serve the Church in this locality." [97] The mission and ministry of priests is to connect the laity in the diocese with the bishop who cannot minister to them in person, thus the collaboration of all is essential. Christ's salvific mission is brought to the people of God in and through the bishop and the *presbyterium*, the collegiality of priests.

Collaborative ministry requires cooperation and mutual support. At the outset intergenerational divisions are named in *Presbyterorum Ordinis* 8 as problematic issues that affect the well-being of all, ordained and laity. The relationship between younger and older priests has always been problematic for a variety of reasons; some tensions are simply age-related, some are societally based, and others are ideological. Some priests are simply described as "laboring under certain difficulties" or having "failed in some matters," and these also need "fraternal charity and magnanimity."

In the past, priestly failure was usually ascribed to a man not faithful to his vocation, but more recently it has been associated with the prominent sexual abuse of priests and bishops, particularly in North America and Europe. It is not simply a contemporary issue but one that has always been part of the story of priestly ministry.[98] The article tries to address failure while offering encouragement as well as practical recommendations for shared hospitality, "frequent and periodic meetings," and other communal activities. The section concludes by encouraging priests to show fraternal support to all priests who may not have lived up to their vocation.

The initial affirmation of the common priesthood in the preface has been left to *Presbyterorum Ordinis* 9 to develop. The relationship between laity and priesthood is one of the major issues generated in and by the council, in subsequent Vatican communications, and in theological and pastoral discussions. The Tridentine reaction to the broad and general inclusivity of the Reformation understanding of priesthood meant that its emphasis on ordained priesthood came at the expense of the identity of the laity who were usually rendered passive receivers of sacraments, or objects, in any documents related to them.

Vatican II ecclesiology brought a new emphasis to the place of the laity in the exercising of Christ's office of the shared ministry of teaching, sanctifying, and leading, across the orders. The apostolic role of the laity in the church was an important conciliar topic. The relationship between priests and laity is confirmed in the common commitment to Christ and of baptism shared. The leadership mentioned in this article is focused on the priest, who is to "work together with the lay faithful" in following the example of Christ. Priests are encouraged to listen to the laity, to be attentive to their needs, and to "recognize their experience and competence in the different areas of human activity, so that together with them they will be able to recognize the signs of the times."

The fact that among laity there are those who "are attracted to a higher spiritual life" is recognized, as is the importance of giving them "freedom and room for action." The laity should be "invited to undertake works on their own initiative." The context for this leadership is that of "the unity of charity." However, the document does not seem to recognize or acknowledge any real sense of lay ecclesial leadership, of the mutuality and new ways of being in ministerial relationship on behalf of the mission of Christ in the world that could be developed if bishops and priests did take *Presbyterorum Ordinis* 9 to heart and acted on it.

Section 3: The Distribution of Priests, and Vocations to the Priesthood

While the ecclesiological foundation of the decree addresses the internal relational and functional structures, it also addresses the missiological outreach that is integral to the building up of the body of Christ in the world in the present that there may be a future. In his commentary on this section, Wulf points out the contrast between *Presbyterorum Ordinis* 10 and 11 and *Presbyterorum Ordinis* 2 where the co-responsibility of all the baptized is a given. "In this passage the mission seems only to apply to priests."[99] Yet it is the biblical concept of mission to bring about the reign of God that is being addressed here, "a salvation even to the ends of the earth." The line that is confusing reads: "The priesthood of Christ, in which all priests really share, is necessarily intended for all peoples and all times." The inclusion of the word *vere* ("really") reinforces the emphasis on the priority of the ordained priestly responsibility in the preceding article and minimizes the appreciation of the priesthood of the baptized.

The need for "a better distribution of priests" was real then and it is even more real in the present when the disproportionate location of priests in certain areas at the expense of others is still evident and when there are significant increases in the number of Catholics worldwide. The Latin American bishops lamented the absence of priests to serve their people, and this was echoed by bishops in other areas who faced the same problem of priest shortages. But what the bishops also noted in their discussions was that there was not a shortage of lay ministers and, in many cases, of religious and lay women, who were willing to serve the people.

The decision "to set up international seminaries, special personal dioceses and other initiatives" to train priests "for the good of the whole church" does not seem to have had the desired effect of meeting the need to disperse priests to needy areas demographically and geographically.

The complexity of priestly response to the needs of dioceses other than their own has been documented and shown to be more problematic than the ideas described in the decree might sound.[100]

The document also reminds those in leadership of the importance of giving initial preparation and ongoing spiritual, mental, and bodily care to those who are sent "to a new field of labor." The faith affirmation in *Presbyterorum Ordinis* 11 that God would provide priests and that "Christians would never be like sheep without a shepherd" is an important one. But it is followed by the reminder that priests themselves have an important responsibility in the promotion of vocations. The subject of vocations was debated at length in the discussions of this text, but the decision was made to leave it to the treatment of vocations already covered in *Lumen Gentium* and *Perfectae Caritatis* (Decree on the Adaptation and Renewal of Religious Life). The concern of the commission was to alert priests in particular and the faithful in general to the importance of fostering priestly vocations.

CHAPTER 3
THE LIFE OF PRIESTS

This chapter addresses the priestly life in terms of the tension between the inner life of the priests and the demands of service. Joseph Ratzinger summed up the document's response to this tension:

> Holiness through ministry; ministry not alongside holiness, but as the form of priestly holiness. Responsible activity in the service of [humankind] and intimacy with God are not in competition with each other. The service of others is the articulation of one's being-consumed for God, of one's being grasped by Him, of one's being-with-Him.[101]

This chapter's movement away from prevailing monastic underpinnings for the spiritual life of priests is a means of emphasizing that nourishment in and for ministry comes from its foundations in a commitment to Christ and in union with his life and ministry. It is in the exercise of their ministry that priests find the fullness of life and holiness.

Section 1: The Vocation of Priests to the Life of Perfection

The new emphasis in this chapter and in *Presbyterorum Ordinis* 12 in particular is the realization that the essence of priestly spirituality is the mission to ministry. In their ordination priests are "made living instruments of Christ the Eternal Priest." This is not an activist approach to ministry, which loses the sense of the connection with the ministry of Christ, but the ministry of those who act "as ministers of him who is the head." The union between the priest and Christ the High Priest gives direction to all that the priest does in service of and toward the fulfillment of the reign of God. "I can preach the Gospel only if I live in the Gospel. Conversely when I proclaim the Gospel, my preaching is directed not only to others, but always at the same time to myself."[102] This is the human shape that the call to perfection takes in the life of the priest. The call to proclamation in pastoral or missionary terms to all people adds a new dimension to the understanding of priestly identity developed here.[103]

In commenting on the call to perfection and to explanations contained within the article, Alberigo comments on both their unity and their restrictive character. Their unity is derived "from the fact that ordination fundamentally makes the priest a representative of Jesus Christ in a more powerful way than baptism makes Christians generally."[104] Thus the priest's daily ministry to the people of God is the means to the holiness and fullness of life to which he is called. "Unless the priest involves himself in people's lives and interprets their conditions of life under the influence of the Spirit and by means of the discernment of spirits, how can he become aware of the duties of his office and find the way to a fulfilled life for himself?"[105]

In this comment Alberigo reminds the reader of the earlier emphases in *Presbyterorum Ordinis* on the changing circumstances of priestly ministry alongside the unexpected and often unpredictable situations in which the people of God may be finding themselves. Precedents are not always present for priests in the changing environments of life and relationships. How they are to establish a balanced and informed response to ministerial challenges remains a question. It may be argued, then, that the tensions and the circumstantial angst that may dog the life of the contemporary priest surely form an integral part of his priestly spirituality. Perhaps these are the means by which his faith-fulness, hope, and love will become purified in the crucible of his min-isterial experience.

A priestly asceticism is encouraged and based on the realization that it is "the Spirit of Christ" which "gives life and direction" to ministry. The perfection that is urged is one of service: "those who exercise the ministry of the spirit and of justice will be confirmed in the life of the spirit, so long as they are open to the Spirit of Christ, who gives them life and direction." *Presbyterorum Ordinis* 12 affirms that as priests en-gage wholeheartedly in ministry, the Holy Spirit will be with them, leading them "in that holiness which Christ endows." This is a holiness that is integral to "an internal renewal of the church, of the spread of the Gospel in every land and of a dialogue with the world of today." This transforms the abstract notion of perfection into the reality of daily choices and lifelong commitment to God and God's people.

Presbyterorum Ordinis 13 continues with a reaffirmation of the teaching, sanctifying, and shepherding role that is integral to the inner life and to the pastoral ministry of priesthood. The threefold ministry is made concrete in its connection to the human circumstances of con-temporary life, by "daily celebration of Mass," their "greatest task," their faithfulness to the Divine Office, and in the administration of the sacraments. In all these tasks they are following Christ "under the di-rection of the Spirit of Love, which breathes where it will." This article has nothing of the paternalism or separation that is found in some other sections of the document.

The understanding of priestly spirituality will no longer be sought for through an idealistic or abstract perfection apart from the priest's routine ministry. The spirituality developed in the decree has moved from the prevalent model of an imitation of the monastic life or the priest's efforts to find the necessary unity and harmony of his pastoral life "merely by an outward arrangement of the works of the ministry or by the practice of the spiritual exercises alone" (*PO*, 14). In *Presbyterorum Ordinis* the priest's spiritual exercises are no longer regarded as those practices that are interrupted by the distractions of pastoral work. It is the integration of the preaching, ministering, and pastoral care with the formal and informal times of liturgical celebration and personal prayer that is the substance of priestly spirituality.

The movement through *Presbyterorum Ordinis* 14 connects priestly ministry with the struggles and problems all people face in their lives. Priests share the same struggles and "involved and constrained by so many obligations of their office," they have to find their own ways "to coordinate and balance their interior life" and their "outward activity." Such a balance can be arrived at only "by following the example of Christ our Lord in their ministry."

There is a contemporary claiming of an authentic spirituality for the diocesan priest who engages actively with the world, which the genuine priest must be aware of rather than reject or despise. The strength that nourishes this engagement is drawn from the priest's inner life. "Priests through prayer continue to penetrate more deeply into the mystery of Christ." Past emphases on the necessary separateness of the priest from the world are absent in this decree. This section closes with the reminder that the priestly vocation is not a private but a public one. Priests collaborate "in a strong bond of union with their bishops and brother priests."

Section 2: Special Spiritual Requirements in the Life of the Priest

This section addresses the evangelical counsels in the priestly life. The priestly spirituality proposed in earlier sections of the chapter is applied in *Presbyterorum Ordinis* 15, 16, and 17 to the priest, his pastoral activity inspired by charity, his intimate union with Christ, and his devotion to God's will as revealed in the mission of the church. That the section covers controversial understandings of the spiritual requirements for priesthood is attested to in the multiple changes to the title as well as to the section's content.[106] The heading "Perfect Chastity and the Other Evangelical Counsels" was dropped, as was "On the Formation of the Priest's Life According to the Norms of the Gospel." The intentional movement away from a monastic spirituality for active apostolic life can be seen in the decision to exclude the term "evangelical counsels" in the final title.

Presbyterorum Ordinis 15 opens with a discussion of humility and obedience. The meaning and purpose of priestly obedience proposed in the decree are found in "the hierarchical union of the whole body."

Priestly ministry is for the whole church, and the priest places himself in service to the people of God entrusted to his care. It is an obedience that will enable the balance aspired to in the graced tension between the priest's pastoral and personal spiritual life.

Commentators on this section point out that obedience as addressed here leaves several critical problems unmentioned. A weakness of the decree is that it speaks only in terms of "edifying generalizations" of the obedience of the priest to his bishop without any reference to "the right use of authority" or "the reciprocal relation between subordinates and superiors."[107] Wulf argues that it is not appropriate to say that these issues will be addressed elsewhere as so often happens in the discussions about ecclesiastical authority. Priestly obedience to the bishop implies obedience to the church and above all to Christ.

That the document refers only to the obedience of the priest to the bishop without reference to the obedience expected of the bishop is particularly problematic, "since it is only in the correlation of obedience on the one hand and the rightful use of authority on the other that a full understanding of obedience is possible."[108] The moral theological questions about the rights and duties of superiors as well as of subordinates, most of all the question about the limits of authority, along with the anthropological questions about the mature obedience of adults, which alone leads to "the freedom of the children of God," are scarcely ever asked. Today this is no longer feasible.[109] The final section of this article addresses the spirit of ministerial obedience in conformity to the life of Christ "who emptied himself taking the life of a servant."

Presbyterorum Ordinis 16 addresses the contentious area in the conciliar debate, that of priestly celibacy. The present statement appears to have resulted from the volume of discussion and the uneasiness expressed in both the council and the public arenas when the earlier revised text was being presented. At one period, the decision was not to address celibacy at all.[110] The resultant outcry from the bishops led to the inclusion in the second draft of the 1965 text a section that seemed to be a compromise that suited neither side and offered little support to priests.

Polarization occurred between those who wanted mandatory celibacy dropped because of the ministerial pressures in their dioceses and those who wanted the present law to be reconfirmed and reinforced. The bishops were stopped from working on a deeper theological reflection on celibacy as a group, not only because of the internal division, but also because of pressures from the media, which exaggerated the debate and virtually generated "an assault on celibacy."[111]

While there was an insistence on the importance of the need to discuss celibacy among the Latin American bishops, there was little interest shown by the European bishops. The question was exacerbated by the fear among the council members that such a divisive issue would lengthen the council. Some observers were also in support of the decision not to address the issue in council. "The council receives so much publicity that the discussion of celibacy would be given a disproportionate amount of attention."[112]

The final text evidences a careful concern to affirm the congruence between celibacy and the priestly life and the decision to maintain the status quo. Celibacy is a gift to esteem and embrace, "a sign and a stimulus for pastoral charity and a special source of spiritual fecundity in the world." It was assumed that although the council would not take up the debate, that there would be "a simple transfer of the subject from the general congregation to a more suitable venue, since, among other things, the problem did not seem to affect all the episcopates to the same degree."[113]

The concern not to offend the Eastern Church, which did not impose clerical celibacy, influenced the eventual reworking of the text, which reaffirms the traditional discipline but does not describe it as essential to priesthood. "[Celibacy] is not demanded by the very nature of the priesthood, as is apparent from the practice of the early Church and from the traditions of the Eastern Churches."[114] The final section of the article addresses the law of celibacy. It is approved and confirmed by the council which, "fully trusting this gift of the Spirit so fitting for the priesthood of the New Testament," exhorts both priests and laity to pray that God "will always bestow this gift upon his Church."

The problematic aspect of celibacy was as significant at the close of the council as it was during it, and although it was no longer openly discussed it remained a polarizing issue, mainly because of its implications for ministry. This was particularly the case for many Latin American bishops. Even though there was obedience and acceptance from the bishops in response to the papal intervention, they still had to return to their dioceses, to their few priests and the priestless communities.

In *Presbyterorum Ordinis* 17 priests are encouraged to live the asceticism of the evangelical counsel of poverty. They are to strive for the "freedom and docility" that nourish "spiritual discretion in which is found the right relationship to the world and earthly goods." What this notion of "docility" might mean to bishops, and what it might mean to the priests themselves, are not addressed. That "created goods" are to be appreciated but not overprized connects with the evangelical counsel of poverty. Church property is to be used in accord both with church law and with effective mission and ministry. Voluntary poverty is to be esteemed for the sake of Christian witness and "pastoral charity." That this is a personal decision rather than a communal mandate means that the poverty of the diocesan priest is somewhat different from that of religious clerics.

Section 3: Aids to the Life of Priests

Intrinsic to the image of priestly spirituality in this section is the combination of monastic asceticism and pragmatic concern. Exhortation to "docility" in relation to priestly spirituality, as mentioned in *Presbyterorum Ordinis* 17 above, does not seem to give a priority to the encouragement of priests to work for a just society or to the concern for the poor. Yet these are important Christian values that were actively promoted in the council. The endorsement of a spiritual life for priests that could remove them from facing and being involved in the ordinary vicissitudes of life rather than one that promotes priests' ability to develop an apostolic spirituality appears to be implicitly expressed here. "The double table of the Sacred Scripture and the Eucharist" along with the sacraments and spiritual reading are unquestionably important sources of spiritual nourishment" (*PO*, 18). However, this section seems removed from the interplay of daily concerns that do appear in other sections of the decree.

Earlier emphases on changing circumstances and the difficulties of dealing with contemporary pastoral ministry find some resolution in the aids discussed. Scripture study and pastoral knowledge are to be pursued, along with studies of social sciences and also sacred sciences that have progressed. So "priests are urged to suitably and without interruption perfect their knowledge of divine things and human affairs and so prepare themselves to enter more opportunely into conversation with their contemporaries" (*PO*, 19). It is a daunting and demanding task for priests in parishes to try to engage in such as pursuit of knowledge "without interruption."

The recommendations to participate in meetings, courses, and further theological and pastoral studies "that they may strengthen their spiritual life and mutually communicate their apostolic experiences with their brothers" are important to what is described as the common life of priestly ministry. The suggestions are practical, and bishops are encouraged to facilitate these further studies for all priests and also to provide opportunities for specialized studies for those priests whom the bishop may wish to involve in seminary formation.

The importance of material support, remuneration, and accommodation to relieve unnecessary anxiety about the future is placed as a priority for bishops. The importance of annual vacations and of equitable support across varied forms of priestly ministry is addressed. A new initiative in the decree is seen in the recommendation for financial planning that will sustain a balance between the various parishes and that will enable pastoral works to be effectively undertaken.

It is hoped that insofar as is possible in individual dioceses or regions there be established a common fund enabling bishops to satisfy obligations to other deserving persons and to meet the needs of various dioceses. This would also enable wealthier dioceses to help poorer ones, that the need of the latter might be supplemented by the abundance of the former. These common funds, even though they should be principally made up of the offerings of the faithful, also should be provided for by other duly established sources (*PO*, 21).

While all possible help and support for the well-being of priests is to be provided within dioceses, the concluding sentences of the decree are an encouragement to the priests themselves to "cultivate evangelical poverty more readily and give themselves fully to the salvation of souls."

CONCLUSION AND EXHORTATION

The final article offers a personal message from the council members to priests. It is an expression of support in the difficulties of priestly ministry and life and the struggles with experiences of alienation and loneliness. The "danger of becoming spiritually depressed" is also acknowledged as one of the issues priests have to face.

The concluding exhortation is a reminder that the priestly vocation has its foundations in the faith-based acceptance of God's call, and that as a consequence priests "are never alone, but strengthened by the power of Almighty God, and believing in Christ who called them to share in his Priesthood, they should devote themselves to their ministry with complete trust, knowing that God can cause charity to grow in them."

A note of thanks "to priests of the entire world" follows, with the final reminder that it is God's power at work in all. The conclusion offers understanding of the enormity of the task and recognition of the faith commitment that is foundational to priestly identity along with the note of gratitude to priests.

The key contribution of Vatican II to a contemporary understanding of ministerial priesthood is in the movement forward from an understanding of priesthood that was confined to the sacerdotal ministry in the celebration of the sacraments. *Presbyterorum Ordinis* expands the Tridentine understanding through an emphasis on the threefold office of Christ as teaching, sanctifying, and guiding, and on the threefold mission of the church. That the priesthood of the ordained was reaffirmed within the common priesthood by Vatican II is a unifying means of enabling all the baptized to cooperate and collaborate in the mission of the church, the bringing about of God's reign in God's time.

PART III

IMPLEMENTATION

To address the question of how the points in *Presbyterorum Ordinis* were implemented or blocked from implementation is to examine what developments took place in diverse church documents such as papal statements, letters, and speeches as well as the responses within the community of believers in reaction to the decree. Some key concepts have been the subject of discussion from a variety of ministerial or professional perspectives. These writings have also played a part in the ways diverse issues have moved in the faith community at large.

All those who were involved in the composition of the final decree acknowledged the haste of the composition of the final draft. It is the result of syncopated efforts rather than a developing consistency due to the unsatisfactory nature of the original text and then to the great number of suggestions that were received during subsequent debates and especially in such a constricted and concentrated way in the closing period. The global identity of the church, with its range of local and national, historical, sociocultural, economic, and political backgrounds, made a unified pastoral ecclesial response to the decree enormously difficult, in spite of all the good will of the conciliar members.

THE PRIESTHOOD IN THE MINISTRY OF THE CHURCH

A major concern of Vatican II in the constitution on the church and in the decrees on bishops, on the ministry and life of priests, on ecumenism, and on the laity was to open up an understanding within the Catholic community of the two forms of priesthood, the common and the ordained. There was a clear definition of the order of the priesthood and of its purpose and function. However, the intended clarity of

the decree broke down in the attempts to implement it across dioceses
and parishes in the years that immediately followed the closing of the
council.

The Vatican II emphasis on the two forms of priesthood had unexpected impacts within the communities both of the ordained and of the
laity. Even during the council itself there was some confusion as a consequence of information released by the media about possible changes.
Catholics had been well taught over many decades about the unchanging nature of their church and its faithfulness to the gospel mandate to
preach and witness to God's saving mission fulfilled in Christ Jesus.
They knew their place in the hierarchical structure.

It is interesting to note how many pedagogical tools of the 1960s
and earlier that were used to describe the church were pyramidal in
shape, with the pope at the apex and priests and religious in the lowest
segment. The laity were often not even included in the diagram. The
concept of the "common priesthood of the baptized" to people well cat-
echized in the pre–Vatican II narrow understanding of church was a
shock to many such people, even to priests and religious.

In the pre–Vatican II era, Western Catholics had defined themselves as separate from other Christians.[115] Particular symbols and devotional practices indicated Catholic identity in their own and in the
larger sociocultural context. The use of Latin in liturgy was a primary
symbol of the importance of the constancy of this language as an expression of faithfulness to the tradition. Although as a "dead" language
it was seen to be a language that enabled liturgy to be experienced in a
universal way, there was an irony in the fact that ordinarily it was a language of only a certain elite within the church. Candidates for ordination had to learn Latin, but it was the *lingua franca* of only a select few
rather than the many, even among bishops and priests. Over the centuries the boundaries between bishops, priests, and their people had
been clearly delineated in ritual, in relationships, and in opportunities
for theological and ministerial education.

Preaching, catechesis, and religious education had been directed
toward the claiming of a Catholic identity, its worldview and its values.
As changes in boundaries and in relationships were being promoted by
this pastoral council, priests who had been formed to pass on the dogmas, doctrines, beliefs, values, and practices to their people as they
themselves had been taught were uncertain about the implications of

the changes for their own identity and ministry in parish and diocese. In 1965 it was being claimed that the council was "becoming aware of its mission. This entire council is doctrinal, because its aim is to make the presence of the gospel real through and in the church."[116] This was the task that priests and religious, along with all involved in the educational and pastoral ministries of the church, had to undertake.

It was incumbent upon diocesan priests in particular to communicate the new understanding of priestly order and relationships to their people. Workshops and renewal programs were set up in the years following the close of the council so that people could get a sense of the developing worldview, community identity, and relationships that were being promulgated in the council documents. Yet who were these priests on whom both the burden and blessing of renewal rested? In fact, while church membership was increasing, the number of Catholic priests had already begun to diminish by the end of the 1950s. Parishes were growing but priestly vocations were falling.[117] The task of communicating the vision and the new developments was up to these men, many of whom had a limited formation and, because of the growing complexity of their ministry and the expectations of their congregations, had minimal continuing educational opportunities to update themselves.

The admonition to priests in *Presbyterorum Ordinis* 19 to continue pastoral studies was an important one. An indication of the need for this might be seen in the comment by U.S. Catholic politician Daniel Moynihan that the Catholic clergy were not keeping up the standards of education of their Catholic communities.

Is there any way to bring our bishops and pastors to see this? Surely there must be. The great task of the educated laity at this moment is to begin to ask, even to insist on a share of judgments of this kind, on an opportunity to bring into the life of the Church the standards of taste, and rigor and excellence as they are experienced by the best minds and spirits of the age...

Protest is in order. The time has come to walk out on sermons that are so puerile as to threaten the very bases of faith, or at least to arrange gestures of mass inattention... The time has come to suffer mediocrity less than gladly and to make known to those who try harder that we appreciate it more than

they may have sensed. ("Art-less Catholics. 'What Kind of
Faith Built the National Shrine?'" *Commonweal* 84 [July 1966]:
408–9)[118]

This was the tensive world of priest-lay relationships that characterized
much of the Western world of Catholicism in the 1960s and 1970s.

The laity were becoming increasingly well-educated, personally
and professionally, while priests generally were receiving a limited formation for a ministry with roots in a medieval ecclesiastical worldview
that had long been transcended by the secular culture. Yet the formal
and informal church and media communications about Vatican decrees
and documents continued to feed into the community at large. Parish
priests had to deal with the new information, address the changes, and
cope with the diverse reactions of parishioners to the best of their own
abilities and interests. It is not surprising, then, that the "fortress mentality" of aggression and closure behind the walls of religious orthodoxy
was seen by some bishops and priests as the safest defense against a laity
that sought to be actively involved in the life of their church, in parish
and diocese.

Within the institutional church itself, the rules for implementation
of the decrees *Christus Dominus*, *Presbyterorum Ordinis*, *Perfectae
Caritatis*, and *Ad Gentes* were issued by Paul VI in the form of a skele-
ton law in the apostolic letter, *Ecclesiae Sanctae* (*ES*) of August 6, 1966.
Alberigo points out that in July 1966 Cardinal Ottaviani, as head of the
Congregation for the Doctrine of the Faith, wrote a letter listing ten
areas of "abusive interpretations" of the council. This was an impetus
for the apostolic letter to be written. The governing of the church

> demands indeed that new norms be established and that new
> adjustments be made to meet relationships introduced by the
> council and which will be more and more adapted to the new
> goals and areas of the apostolate which through the council
> have been opened up to the Church in the modern world. (*ES*,
> par. 1)

That the implementation might be more effective, the particular norms
addressing *Presbyterorum Ordinis* initially dealt with the importance of
consultation between bishops and priests.

In the government of the dioceses entrusted to them, however, the bishops have necessary helpers and counselors especially the priests—whom they should be willing to hear, in fact consult, preserving all the while the bishops' power to act freely, in setting down methods of procedure and norms and in making laws in keeping with the awareness of their obligation and the principles of Church government (cf. Dogmatic Constitution *Lumen Gentium*, No. 27). (*ES*, 1)

This section is followed by a reference to *Presbyterorum Ordinis* 10 on distribution of clergy and aid to dioceses. The consultation process recommended in both *Presbyterorum Ordinis* and in *Ecclesiae Sanctae* has been unevenly sustained in dioceses. Where bishops were themselves trained to function fundamentally in regulatory mode, and without real communication skills, then an autocratic and unilateral defensiveness rather than consultation or dialogue has been the operative mode of leadership.

The concern to have priests who could lead their parish communities in the renewal was of high importance. Bishops were also reminded of the need to foster pastoral and scientific training of their priests, with the suggestion that some priests be given leadership in study centers and other avenues of pastoral and scientific training of priests (*ES*, 7; *PO*, 19). The remuneration and provision of social security for priests was also to be implemented (*ES*, 8; *PO*, 20–21) as was the council of priests and the pastoral council. Bishops were to appoint

a group or senate of priests who represent the body of priests and who by their counsel can effectively assist the bishop in the government of the diocese. In this council the bishop should listen to his priests, consult them and have dialogue with them on those matters which pertain to the needs of pastoral work and the good of the diocese. (*ES* 15.1; see *PO*, 7)

The implementation of these norms was primarily concerned with the relations between bishops and diocesan priests. Religious clerics were mentioned only in a minor way in terms of their inclusion in diocesan councils. The importance of bishops and priests devoting time to listen to each other's concerns and to engage in dialogue with regard to pastoral needs was made explicit. The relationship between priests themselves and with laity was not the explicit subject of this apostolic letter.

In both diocesan and parish contexts, the changing expectations of ministerial relationships were being felt at all levels. The conciliar affirmation that the episcopate was the fullness of priesthood was not an issue for the majority of people. The line of ministry from the apostles through to bishops was accepted with few questions. That Christ's mission from the Father was handed on to the apostles, through them to the bishops, and through the bishops to the priests was consonant with the lay acceptance of hierarchical authority as it had been handed down to them. In contrast, those priests whose spirituality and priestly identity[119] had formed them to see the priest as an *alter Christus* found their role instead as that of adjuncts to their bishops who had received the fullness of priesthood. "Priests, as co-workers with their bishops, have the primary duty of proclaiming the Gospel of God to all" (*PO*, 4). This experience of an apparent downgrading of their own priestly status, with an increase of responsibility to communicate the changes to an up-graded laity, had an impact on their priestly identity.

One of the difficulties in carrying out this new task was the issue of the communicative competence of both priests and their bishops. Seminary formation warned priests against the dangers of intimacy; it had inculcated in them a sense of the importance of the sacerdotal separateness of their ministry; and it had encouraged them to believe that communications skills were subordinate to the ontological change that would enable a graced reception of their ministry. The notion that the preaching of the word of God and their sacramental status as priests would transcend personal or relational limits in their ministry was part of the training of the pre-conciliar period. In practice, their formation had not prepared them for the recognition of their need to continue to develop skills to communicate and relate effectively rather than unilaterally in their ministerial practice.

In his discussion of the relation of the priest-presbyter to the bishop, ecclesiologist Richard Gaillardetz points out that "any authentic theology of the ministerial priesthood must take into account the post-conciliar shift from a theology of ministry based on power (e.g., ministries being distinguished by the powers they can exercise) to a theology of ministry based on relationships."[120] The relative personal isolation of the pre–Vatican II priest, apart from the people, has been to some extent reconfigured in this decree to a more communal relationship, with the priest ministering within the community of the faithful. That the decree carries the recommendation of a "common life" for priests adds another new transition from the more individualized role that had previously characterized their pastoral leadership to one of mutual support and shared pastoral concerns.

> In order that priests may find mutual assistance in the development of their spiritual and intellectual life, that they may be able to cooperate more effectively in their ministry and be saved from the dangers of loneliness which may arise, it is necessary that some kind of common life or some sharing of common life be encouraged among priests. (*PO*, 8)

Yet, because of the previous training, which had taught them to work outside of any community structure, and the distinction between the communal life of the religious priest and the more individualistic diocesan priestly ministry, those priests who did try to develop a "common life" might have found themselves under some scrutiny from other priests and perhaps even from their bishop.

The constant use of the plural "priests" in the document is a reinforcement of this shift from priest as individual to priest-in-relationship. The collegial identity of bishops has its equivalent in the collegiality of the presbyterium, but their collegial identity differs. In writing of the achievements of Vatican II, one of the theological consultants present, Edward Schillebeeckx, commented on the difference in the level of collegiality that exists between bishops and that which exists between priests, whether diocesan or religious. He pointed out that priests are essentially dependent on bishops in their pastoral mission. It is a "coordinated cooperation" that is rendered feasible by priestly representation in general pastoral planning processes.[121] The "fullness" of the episcopal priesthood is not an individualistic identity. It is one that both *Presbyterorum Ordinis* and *Ecclesiae Sanctae* present as participatory, inter-relational, and collaborative with other Christian ministries.[122]

The concept and interpretation of collegiality had been the subject of polarization in the council hall. The relation between papal primacy and episcopal collegiality was debated at length, because it had ramifications for the relations between bishops and priests. Fear of a restoration of "episcopal monarchy," with complete control by the bishop of priests and religious in his diocese, was countered by the idea of establishing an "episcopal senate."[123] Episcopal conferences were affirmed as a concrete means of engaging such collegiality.[124]

These new hierarchical relational models required a reworking of priests' understanding of priestly "order" in relation to the bishops at the same time that the common priesthood was under discussion.[125] It was expected that the new relationship of priests with their bishops would be implemented by the bishops, but simultaneously with this change, priests' relationship with the laity became increasingly complex as parishioners began to exercise the voice that they believed they had been given by the council. Initial post-conciliar implementation of and education on these new relationships put increased pressure on priests, many of whom were questioning their vocation.

In the period between 1968 and 1974 an influx of requests for laicization indicated loss of confidence in priestly identity and ministry.[126] The drop in priestly vocations between 1966 and 1968 was about 40 percent in major seminaries of France, Spain, Germany, Austria, Belgium, Canada, and Brazil.[127] Some major causes suggested for this drop were the impact of secularization on young people, the involvement of the young in social justice activities that seemed not to be of importance in the institutional church, the image of priests who seem out of touch with the demands of modern life, their absence of freedom, and the obligation of priestly celibacy.[128] In those early post-conciliar years, conflicts between bishops and priests were being experienced globally.[129]

Part of the confusion that flourished among priests in the early post-conciliar period was due to the change in emphasis from the sacerdotal identity of priesthood that had been the basis of priestly formation and ministry from the post-Reformation to the present period. The man set apart from the people, "on a pedestal" as described by some, in terms of celebration of the sacrifice of the Mass,[130] of sacramental practice, and even of his clothing, was moved to the position of a "servant-leader," a man among the people.

The mystique of the priest as the man apart from the people was steadily receding into the background in the late 1960s and early 1970s, while the vitality and new life in parish congregations was expanding as people were increasingly invited and enabled to exercise various leadership roles in worship and other services. Team leadership of priest and parish workers brought new life into many parishes in the 1970s, but not all priests were comfortable with the changes they were being asked to initiate. The conciliar endorsement of the priestly threefold office of preaching, sanctifying, and leading the people brought about a new place for both priests and people to find themselves in, with both loss and gain for all.

The 1970s also ushered in a number of conflicting reactions and initiatives in response to the issues raised by the documents with regard to priesthood and ministry. The consequent upheaval in ministry that was taking place in dioceses and parishes was not lost on the Catholic hierarchy. There was so much unrest that the Council of the General Secretariat recommended a synod of bishops on the ministerial priesthood.[131] This was accepted by Pope Paul VI, and ministerial priesthood with the need for further guidelines in implementing the council's mandate was the subject of the 1971 Synod on the Ministerial Priesthood.

A primary purpose of this international synod, held so soon after the council, was to counter what were seen to be problematic interpretations of the council. The synodal document, "The Ministerial Priesthood" (MP) acknowledges that there are variations globally in relation to changes but the purpose of the synod was to offer "some principles of the church's teaching on the ministerial priesthood which are at present more urgent, together with some guidelines for pastoral practice."[132] Yet part 2 of this document has the title, "Guidelines for the Priestly *Life* and Ministry," a not-so-subtle rejection of the conciliar decision to put primary emphasis on the priest's ministry as a means of understanding his life.

That the synod itself held importance beyond the church can be seen in the fact that two issues of *Time* magazine had front-page headlines and major articles on it. On May 10, 1971, there was a report on the problematic relations between the U.S. bishops and the clergy:

> Like most other establishments, the Roman Catholic hierarchy of the U.S. has had some hard times lately. Just three weeks ago, a $500,000 study of the priesthood commissioned by the bishops themselves concluded that a "serious and potentially dangerous gap" existed between them and their clergy.[133]

On October 11, 1971, the reporting on the synod continued with a discussion of the number of international representatives and the need to address key issues affecting relationships between bishops and priests: "Of the 210 delegates, the majority (136) are from Third World countries, where the issue of social reform is compelling."[134] An interesting comment on the documents that come from such collegial bodies is made by Francis X. Murphy, the writer of the various journalistic reports from the council.

What tradition seems to indicate is that frequently the solutions arrived at in such gatherings are not half as important as the fact that the problems troubling the church should be honestly debated, and that their implications be thoroughly investigated by the residential bishops involved in the pastoral conduct of the church.[135]

The discussion itself can then become a means of authentic dialogue and unity between bishops from different global regions so that greater understanding of cultural diversity and its consequences for ministry and church life can be achieved.

This does not seem to have been the case at the 1971 Synod. What Thomas Reese has described as "a showcase of unity"[136] at the expense of genuine dialogue may be a more appropriate description of the discussions that took place and that took permanent shape in the document on ministerial priesthood. The tensions being experienced between the pastoral and the sacerdotal leadership roles of the priest, along with the renewed concern for global justice and peace, had a significant impact on priests' self-understanding and on their relationships with other priests. This was a major concern for the bishops at the synod.

In the effort to balance or, in some quarters, to correct the image of priest, the final document on the ministerial priesthood reinforced the sacerdotal focus to some extent, at the expense of the threefold ministry. In addressing the issue of mission and sacramental life, a section from *Presbyterorum Ordinis* 3 is quoted,

Priests of the New Testament,[137] by their vocation and ordination, are in a certain sense set apart in the bosom of the People of God. However, they are not to be separated from the People of God or from any person; but they are to be totally dedicated to the work for which the Lord has chosen them. They cannot be ministers of Christ unless they be witnesses and dispensers of a life other than earthly life. But they cannot be of service to men if they remain strangers to the life and conditions of men. Their ministry itself, by a special title, forbids that they be conformed to this world; yet at the same time it requires that they live in this world among men. (*PO*, 3)

Yet this is precisely the tension that characterized the struggle of priests to respond to the vision and purpose of priesthood that they received from the new ecclesiology of Vatican II, and instead of the support for this, the ground seems to have moved. In many ways priests carried the consequences of much of the upheaval of the council because they were at the grassroots level of implementation. Eminent Swiss theologian Hans Urs von Balthasar,[138] on the occasion of this 1971 Synod, expressed the conviction that the clergy today is "the clear trouble spot of the Church."[139]

Accusations of autonomy at the expense of obedience and of lack of orthodoxy in liturgical practice were leveled at priests when they were among those suffering most from the struggle to find their new place in a mediating relationship with bishops and laity. This document on ministerial priesthood does attempt to address the situation of priests and address the questions they face, but it reemphasizes the sacerdotal image while endorsing the wide range of pastoral activities of the priest. This was not an immediate help to the diocesan priest who was trying to find his way in and through the ecclesiology of Vatican II.

During the synodal period of 1967–1971, while there were "in-house" efforts to address contemporary questions related to ministerial priesthood, the church was also aware of the context in which mission and ministry are exercised. Bishops from Asia, Latin America, and Africa were presenting the problems of injustice that were impacting their dioceses and their Catholic communities. The issue of justice and peace was also a focus of the synodal meetings. The synodal statement, "Justice in the World" also arose from the meetings and deliberations that took place during three meetings in Rome in 1967, 1969, and 1971. This statement was accepted as setting the justice and peace agenda for the 1970s. Thus the issues of ministerial priesthood and of justice and peace were joint issues that mutually informed and concerned the bishops in those years.

The decade of the 1970s was also the period in which ecumenical activities were taking place. These in turn impinged on the implementation of the conciliar documents on ministry and interchurch relationships. At the close of the 1973 General Convention of the Episcopal Church, the presiding bishop commissioned a book of essays to help deal with the divisive issues in regard to ordination. Titled *To Be a Priest: Perspectives on Vocation and Ordination*, the book surfaced those issues that were problematic across the Christian denominations. The ecumenical complexity is highlighted in a chapter on what is described as the "neuralgic" issue of "The Meaning of Ordained Priesthood in Ecumenical Dialogues."

> In contemporary theology there is no question more difficult, more controversial or more urgent than the meaning of the ordained ministry. The difficulty arises not only from the pastoral aspects of the question but from the different decisions that the Christian churches have made in the course of history to assure that in differing cultural and political circumstances the life of the Gospel be lived meaningfully, Christ's message preached intelligibly and the saving mission which Christ received from the Father and entrusted to his Apostles be carried out faithfully in the Spirit.[140]

Various ecumenical study groups have been continuing the discussions between the Christian denominations, with a number of statements coming from commissions of the World Council of Churches, the Anglo–Roman Catholic, and the Lutheran commissions of churches in their dialogue on the movement toward mutually recognized ministry. Yet while so much of the research and so many of the discussions have taken place among ecumenical specialists, it is at the level of parish community interaction that both the frustration and the fruit of such interaction are experienced.

Efforts at dialogue with various interfaith and secular groups are also most problematic and promising at the diocesan and parish levels. But in those early post-conciliar years, after centuries of Roman

Catholics defining themselves against, rather than in relationship with, other Christian denominations and religious belief systems, it was difficult to get either balance or depth when such initiatives were undertaken as a response to the council. Again, it was at the local level that such tensions were experienced and suspicion engendered or, on the contrary, where peace and harmony reigned in local ecumenical communities and interfaith gatherings. The local priest carried much of the burden of these dialogical initiatives.

The spiritual formation of pre–Vatican II diocesan priests has been described as one that centered on the sacerdotal or Tridentine identity of a man set apart, and it was influenced by their training to be careful of relationships with lay people (usually perceived explicitly or implicitly to be of inferior status). This type of formation did not enable them to be aware of the reality of their own sexuality, or even of their sexual identity.[141]

The theological vision of such priests was dualistic, unrelated to the natural world and elitist both in the understanding of their own status (demanding a respect for the "Roman collar") and in relation to ministerial practice. The focus on what was described as their ontological change as priests, rather than on the community that it was their vocation to serve, promoted a spirituality of regulations, appearance, and performance.[142] Such a spirituality for the diocesan priest is totally at odds with that of Vatican II.

The problems of this style of spirituality for an understanding of the vision and pastoral direction of *Presbyterorum Ordinis* were many. A major issue was that many priests were unable to understand or interpret the decree outside their own experience of formation and ministerial practice. They had been inducted into a role of priestly ministry based primarily on performance and practice, and they were unable to bring themselves to review their training or to adapt to the new relational demands of the decree.

Change was as inimical to the well-trained and unquestioning "system-priest" as it was to many of his parishioners. While priests who were embedded in the priestly ministry and liturgical leadership of the past chose either to ignore the changes or to slow-track them, some parish members began to look for a church where they might find a community with which they could identify. The freedom that such parishioners felt in their efforts to find a worshiping community in which they felt at home meant that priests were often set up against each other at a diocesan level and the fraternal relationships encouraged by the council had little hope of being developed. Pockets of alienation and isolation began to grow in communities of diocesan priests as a consequence of the cultural and ecclesial changes that accompanied the 1970s.

It was twenty years after Vatican II that the division within the church with regard to implementation of the council vision and practice was a subject of public discussion. A 1982 article by Andrew Greeley on the failures of Vatican II published in *America* magazine caused wide-ranging reactions and responses.[143]

Among the many respondents, Archbishop John May, a recognized leader in the post–Vatican II church, particularly in regard to race relations and the role of women, and who had served terms as president of the National Conference of Catholic Bishops and the United States Catholic Conference, had been asked to formally reply to Greeley.[144] In his response May described the struggles experienced by many priests and bishops in their efforts to implement the changes of Vatican II. He wrote of the

> vigilante mentality which, in the name of "defending the faith," actually undermines the faith of untold thousands of laity and clergy alike. Operating from a static, two-dimensional view of faith that totally disregards Vatican II's "hierarchy of truths," these misguided zealots attack theologians whose writings they have never understood...Every bishop in the country could describe the wounds which these heresy hunters inflict on Christ's body.[145]

What May described in 1982 is still a factor in the present Catholic Church in many countries. It is an echo of the "intransigent" faction at the council, an echo that is still resounding in the present church.

It was at the local diocesan and parish levels that the efforts to implement the key points of *Presbyterorum Ordinis* were most problematic. Attempts to move toward the Vatican II understanding of the priesthood and of priestly order and relationships were a source of division in many parish and diocesan settings. Bishops and priests were being put under the scrutiny of those fearful Catholics who (as a consequence of parental training, catechesis, or child-centered religious education programs that communicated a rigid and punitive "God" and that taught them too much, too soon, and outside the level of their understanding or experience) saw themselves as watchdogs of righteousness. In fact, such Catholics were casualties of a catechetical program that promoted fear of God rather than love of God, and mistrust rather than trust.

Because these people were unable to cope with change, they saw those church leaders who were implementing the changes as betrayers of the Catholic faith as they had understood this from childhood. Archbishop May described the "bitter fruit" of such "faithfulness" as an inability to discern between the significance of "central dogmas of faith, theological opinions, disciplinary rules and pious customs." The religious fervor of these people, usually only a minority in parishes, stirred and disturbed the efforts of those priests who were trying to bring change of any sort into the parish. Among priests themselves there was division and misunderstanding.

Reports sent to ever-higher authorities of perceived "betrayals" by priests and bishops who encouraged the implementation of the conciliar vision were, sadly, often received by such higher authorities, in Rome or by individual bishops or bishops' conferences, as evidence of unfaithfulness without any further investigation or opportunity for rebuttal or reply by those who had been accused. In some cases, where the conciliar understanding of priesthood was resisted among members of the hierarchy, these reports and reporters were given a credibility they did not deserve.

One of the problems of the religiously faithful whose understanding of their faith is the two-tiered construction described by May is that such individuals are often the victims themselves of what has been described as a "precocious faith conversion."[146] Because they have been the subject of catechesis or religious educational initiatives that told stories of a punitive god, of hell-fire and heaven, reward and punishment, or given oversimplified understandings of good and evil before the age of reason, they have internalized this two-tiered world deep in their imagination. Their rigid inner world holds them captive, and their fears, along with their convictions of their own righteousness, fuel the fires of their vigilante activities.

Even those adult Catholics who have had little or no religious education beyond elementary school not only can hold whole communities hostage to their narrowly circumscribed worldview of religious faithfulness and loyalty but can also become arbiters of an orthodoxy that enables them to pass judgment on bishops and priests, theologians and ministerial educators. Such people have enormous energy and conviction, and they can exercise an influence that is frightening in its consequences at all levels of church life and leadership. When their religious fervor is backed by wealth and social or political influence, the power of such vigilantes of their own normative orthodoxy can be even more destructive in its consequences for the church, both locally and globally.

In contrast to churchgoers of such rigidity of worldview and purpose are those Catholics described by Andrew Greeley as "do-it-yourself" or "individualistic" Catholics who questioned the credibility of the institutional church as a consequence primarily of *Humanae Vitae*, the 1968 papal encyclical of Paul VI that is best remembered for its prohibition of artificial contraception.[147] For these, the impetus toward a deeper understanding of their membership of the common priesthood legitimated their personal responsibility for their life choices.

Greeley pointed out that 80 percent of Catholics who attended church and received communion on a weekly basis also rejected papal teachings on birth control.[148] This is where the pressure is placed once again on those priests who have followed the mandate of *Presbyterorum Ordinis* to take the ordinary circumstances of their Catholic community and their contemporary problems seriously (*PO*, 4). Catholic women's disillusionment with the church as a consequence of what they perceive and experience as the church's discrimination against them was also discussed by Greeley.

Compassionate pastoral care of these groups of adults can generate illness-causing tensions in the lives of faithful priests. Various research studies and papers confirm that "admitting the seriousness of the problem of stress in the life of a priest today is the first step toward an answer...The problem of stress in the lives of priests is one that bishops and priest must face together."[149] The majority of priests and people can and do offer mutual support in the promotion of authentic Christian community where there is a diocesan ethos of effective communication and trust. Where this is missing, morale breaks down in communities and in individuals. Christian community life is eroded by such leadership failures.

In considering other factors that have affected the implementation of the conciliar approach to the threefold ministry, it is necessary to note the fact that the writings, public addresses, and in particular the Holy Thursday letters of John Paul II have played a major part. The pope expressed his deep concern for the crisis of priesthood that increased rather than abated in the post-conciliar decades. Rather than stay with the more inclusive approach of the preaching, sanctifying, and leadership thrust of *Presbyterorum Ordinis*, John Paul II focused particularly on the priestly image of the man set apart from the people, and on the uniqueness of the ordained ministry. Donovan points out the number of times the pope used sacerdotal language rather than that of presbyter in his relatively brief letter of 1987: sacerdotal language is used forty-three times, *sacerdos* twelve times and presbyteral language only three times.[150] This is an indication of the pope's apparent shift back to the emphasis on the Tridentine model of priesthood.

The concern to clarify the relationship between the common and the ordained priesthood characterizes many of the pope's communications. The importance of each category functioning according to its own gifts and place in the church is emphasized: "The church develops organically according to the principle of the multiplicity and diversity of 'gifts'" (Holy Thursday Letter to Priests, 1989, 4).

In his 1992 apostolic exhortation, On the Formation of Priests in the Circumstances of the Present Day, the pope spoke of presbyters as

> a sacramental representation of Jesus Christ, the Head and Shepherd, authoritatively claiming his Word, repeating his acts of forgiveness and his offer of salvation, particularly in Baptism, Penance and the Eucharist, showing his loving concern to the point of a total gift of self for the flock, which they gather into unity and lead to the Father through Christ and in the Spirit. (15)

The thrust in the document is almost entirely toward the sacerdotal leadership of the priest, and where the common priesthood is mentioned it is in terms of the priest's action on behalf of the people. This resonates with the pope's affirmation in his post-synodal apostolic exhortation, *Pastores Dabo Vobis* (*PDV*), "I will give you shepherds after my own heart" (Jer 3:15; *PDV*, 1), that it is a particular aspect of Christ the Priest that the priest represents.

Christ stands "before" the Church and "nourishes and cherishes her" (Eph. 5:29), giving his life for her. The priest is called to be the living image of Jesus Christ, the spouse of the Church. Of course, he will always remain a member of the community as a believer alongside his other brothers and sisters who have been called by the Spirit, but in virtue of his configuration to Christ, the head and shepherd, the priest stands in this spousal relationship with regard to the community. "Inasmuch as he represents Christ, the head, shepherd and spouse of the Church, the priest is placed not only in the Church but also in the forefront of the Church." (*PDV*, 22)

In March 1993 the pope began a series of addresses on the role of the ordained presbyter. His conviction was that priests stand in specific relationship with and to the people of God, and this understanding remains on the plateau of the sacerdotal image where the priest is separate from, and leading from a distance, rather than in the midst of the faithful. The opening of John Paul II's 2005 Holy Thursday letter reminds his priests that this is "the day when Christ's love was manifested 'to the end' (cf. Jn 13:1), the day of the Eucharist, the day of our priesthood." In this letter the *in persona Christi* emphasis reinforces once again the exclusivity of the Christocentric model of priesthood that has characterized John Paul II's understanding of priesthood. The notion of the priest operating *in persona ecclesiae* appears to be at best a subordinate element in these letters.

The implementation of the priestly spirituality of *Presbyterorum Ordinis* has also been affected by the pastoral model promoted by John Paul. The emphasis on the "vertical dimension" of the priest's relationship with his God focuses on the eucharistic spirituality of the man set apart in worship and in ministry from the community he leads. This emphasis is continued in other church documents. It is "a climate of friendship with the Lord" that is encouraged in the 1994 *Directory on the Ministry and Life of Priests* (39). The text of the International Symposium on the Thirtieth Anniversary of the Conciliar Decree of *Presbyterorum Ordinis* appears to leave aside the ministerial spirituality of *Presbyterorum Ordinis* in the section on "The Means of Spiritual Perfection." Rather, it is a reinforcement of the earlier monastic spirituality that is given primary emphasis.

Being aware of the urgent need for intimate union with God, the priest must set aside time for personal prayer, spiritual reading and for the Rosary. Regular use of the Sacrament of Reconciliation and of spiritual direction is indispensable for growth in one's own spiritual life. The contemplative aspect of adoration and profound intimacy with the Lord in the Eucharist and in the Sacred Scriptures are also requirements. (1)

An instruction, "The Priest, Pastor and Leader of the Parish Community" (August 4, 2002), contains a section on the "Central Elements of the Ministry and Life of Priests."

Priestly identity is three dimensional: pneumatological, Christological and ecclesiological. This primordial theological structure of the mystery of the priest, who is a minister of salvation, can never be overlooked if he is adequately to understand the meaning of his pastoral ministry in the concrete circumstances of the parish. He is the servant of Christ. Through Him, with Him, and in Him, the priest becomes the servant of mankind. His very being, ontologically assimilated to Christ, constitutes the foundation of being ordained for the service of the community. (5)

The integration of the pneumatological, Christological, and ecclesiological developments is a reminder of the eschatological mission of Christ that is carried out in contemporary times through the ordained and the common priesthood, although the latter are essentially subordinated in the instruction.

The increasing emphasis in recent Vatican documents has been described as having the tendency to over-dramatize and over-sacramentalize the ordained minister at the expense of the directions of the documents on the church and *Presbyterorum Ordinis* to affirm "the Church as sacrament of Christ alive in the world."[151]

PART IV

THE STATE OF THE QUESTION

What direction priesthood might move in the future will surely depend on the balance established between those who want the present movement toward the Tridentine model to be continued until that model takes precedence and those whose vision of priesthood is more in terms of a priesthood that is both *in persona Christi* and *in persona ecclesiae*. Both the mission of Christ and the relation of the priest to the people of God are important to a contemporary theology and practice of priestly ministry. That we are in a time of transition in our church is without doubt. We are on the cusp of change, but regarding the direction in which the church will move there is still some doubt. The horrendous stories and unprecedented scandals that have beset the church in terms of the sexual predators and the administrative abusers among priests and hierarchy have indelibly affected Catholic communities, even though the vast majority of priests and bishops have struggled over the years to serve their God and the congregations with and to whom they minister in faith, hope, and love to the best of their abilities.[152]

The clerical culture that has persisted in hiding the perpetrators of criminal offences and pastoral betrayal has been under assault since the 1990s. But it is a strong fortress that protects its interests. Contemporary writers who have a love for the priesthood suggest that topics such as the inclusivity or exclusivity of the ordained priesthood, the status of women, celibacy, and the appointment of bishops cry out for further exploration and education so that priesthood can be genuinely understood and appreciated by priests themselves and by the people of God.[153]

Statisticians remind church leaders that the numbers of priests in active ministry are decreasing. Some commentators describe the reality of a priestly community that gives evidence of priests being divided among themselves—young versus old, those who have lived through Vatican II and those whose ordination was subsequent—of low morale and a struggle to claim a status through their identity.[154] One of the consequences of this movement is the "protestantization" of the Catholic Church. The sacraments are being denied to the many for the sake of a few. At the expense of a church which is truly eucharistic in leadership and identity, an exclusively sacerdotal model of priesthood will be preserved for a dominantly European or Western urban minority. This is a dilemma that must be faced in the future by those whose vision has its foundations in a narrow view of the past that does not take the broad sweep of the development of ministries in the global church into account.

While there is a movement toward bringing priests from nations where there is a high ratio of priests to people to those places that suffer from a lack of priests, this initiative has also been the subject of research that cautions the enthusiasm of those who look to such short-term solutions for priestly ministry. In an analysis of the issue of international priests in America, founder of the Mexican-American Cultural Center Virgil Elizondo comments that, "In many cases, simply bringing in a Spanish-speaking priest disrupts a very active and dynamic lay apostolate... Simply because a priest speaks Spanish does not prepare him to work well with Spanish-speaking Americans."[155] Where priests from other cultures and with little language competence have been brought into already-functioning lay-leadership of parishes, simply to provide sacramental ministry, then conflict, confusion, and community break-down may be the consequence. The last state is often worse than the first.

The term "international priests" is rejected in this context by Elizondo, who describes such priests as missionaries to the United States. He asks whether the key issue is one of lack of priestly vocations or the "healthy growth and development" of the United States Catholic church.[156] Many dioceses are putting resources into providing vocation directors and working intentionally toward an increase of priestly vocations. In addressing the issue of the increasing proportion of laity to priests, some researchers point out that unless some changes are made in the present systemic structure of the priesthood and hierarchy, such initiatives will not succeed.[157]

In addressing the present problem of priestly ministry, pastoral psychologist, former seminary rector and vicar for clergy and religious Donald Cozzens compares the approach taken by the hierarchy of the institutional church to that of corporate giants such as General Motors, IBM, and other major American corporations. He laments the fact that just as the CEOs and boards of such transnational giants were so locked in their past successes that they failed to see the changing nature of the world in which they were operating, so too "Vatican officials and church leaders appear to be in denial of the Church's own data."[158]

Cozzens' concern is that there is a myopic reluctance to address the fundamental issue of the dearth of priestly vocations because of "fear of solutions that would alter long-standing church traditions and disciplines. Discussion and study about married priests and the role of women in ministry is discouraged and in some cases forbidden."[159]

The effort to increase priestly vocations is admirable, but some changes must surely be made if these efforts are to bring the results that are hoped for, and in some dioceses they are desperately needed. In contrast to this situation, research and experience indicate that while vocations to the ordained priesthood are diminishing, lay ecclesial ministry is blossoming.

Departments of theology and ministerial studies find that the numbers of applicants for degree programs in pastoral ministry are growing. There has been a 30 percent plus increase in the number of lay ecclesial ministers from 1996 to 2004, with more than thirty thousand lay people actively involved in their parishes and dioceses.[160] This indicates the response to Vatican II that has characterized the people of God in their growing recognition of their own identity as the common priesthood. It is the present reality of ministry. The council took both the historical and the contemporary contexts into account in their decision-making processes and in their affirmation of the collegial and communal priestly identity presented in *Presbyterorum Ordinis* 2 and 3. They were aware of the past, they had a sense of the changing present, and they recognized their accountability for the future. This was the basis for the new approach to priesthood in the decree on priestly ministry and life.

The challenge for the continuity of both the ordained priesthood and the common priesthood that Vatican II laid down for the church of the present and future is to believe that the two can engage collaboratively in carrying out the mission of Christ in today's world. This challenge, affirmed in the present reality and fruit of lay ministry in the contemporary church, is surely in contrast to the patronizing stance represented by theologian Hans Urs von Balthasar:

The lives of the laity will always be directed towards goals proper to themselves and ... any attempt to burden them with an ecclesial ministry ... in imitation of those in the states of election will soon prove to be impossible not only because of the practical differences involved but also because of the realistic boundaries that separate the lay state from the states of election.[161]

In contrast to von Balthasar, Thomas O'Meara OP,[162] one of the prolific writers in the area of theology of ministry, has proposed an alternative and generative vision of these two priesthoods working together, a vision that surely has its source in the hopes of many of the council members. Drawing on the writings of Yves Congar, O'Meara describes a model that would replace the present polarized divisions of clergy and laity.[163] He proposes a circular model, with Christ and Spirit as ground or animating power upon ministries in community. This can also be extended to the relation between community and pastor or bishop.

The communal leader stands not over against or in competition with other ministries, but as a leader who enables ... The other ministries themselves are not all the same, but they are all truly ministry: the ordained and those working full-time in a church along with all kinds of part-time ministers, volunteers and assistants in the parish. It is best not to try to find their identity fully in the linguistic division into "lay" and "ordained." We live in a time when simple linear divisions into two groups are not adequate, and all Christians are basically enabled for ministry through baptism.[164]

This is the collaborative network that is integral to the decree and summed up in *Presbyterorum Ordinis* 9.

Priests, therefore, must take the lead in seeking the things of Jesus Christ, not the things that are their own. They must work together with the lay faithful, and conduct themselves in their midst after the example of their Master, who among men "came not to be ministered unto, but to minister, and to give his life as redemption for many" (Mt 20:28). Priests must sincerely acknowledge and promote the dignity of the laity and the part proper to them in the mission of the Church. And they should hold in high honor that just freedom which is due to everyone in the earthly city. They must willingly listen to the laity, consider their wants in a fraternal spirit, and recognize their experience and competence in the different areas of human activity, so that together with them they will be able to recognize the signs of the times. While trying the spirits to see if they be of God, priests should uncover with a sense of faith, acknowledge with joy and foster with diligence the various humble and exalted charisms of the laity. (*PO*, 9)

It may be helpful to conclude this section with an example of a diocese that has taken Vatican II ecclesiology and its priestly and ministerial directions seriously, and where the concentric collaborative and cooperative network of O'Meara can be seen in a practical pastoral reality. The Archdiocese of Los Angeles has over six million Catholics with an estimated growth rate of at least one million every five years into the foreseeable future.

The Catholic population of the archdiocese is richly multicultural and quite diverse. Every Sunday, the Eucharist is celebrated in over 50 languages in parishes all across southern California. There are still large numbers of parishioners whose origins are European; however, now there are larger numbers of parishioners from Asia and Africa, while the majority has roots in Mexico and Latin America, and a vast number of our population is immigrant and poor.[165]

Cardinal Mahony, in his Holy Thursday, April 20, 2000, letter to the Priests of the Archdiocese of Los Angeles, *As I Have Done For You*, sketched two typical Los Angeles parishes, one in 1955 and the other in 2005, to illustrate the enormous changes that have taken place in those fifty years. The consequences for priests, people, and parishes are radical and they are still being experienced.

Mahony's approach has been influenced by the 1997 Los Angeles archdiocesan assembly in which bishops and priests together explored "the nature of the ordained priesthood in light of the challenges we must face in the Church of today, as well as in the Church of tomorrow in offering a vision for the future."[166] At that assembly there was a clear recognition that mere adjustment and small shifts in practice would not suffice to deal with the changes. It was recognized that what was needed was "a major reorientation in our thinking about ministry as well as in our ministerial practice."

Four things were seen to be essential for such a major reorientation to take place. The first was a recognition that lay ministry rooted in the priesthood of the baptized must not be seen as a stopgap measure. "It is in the nature of the Church to be endowed with many gifts, and these gifts are the basis for the vocations to the priesthood, the diaconate, and the religious life, as well as for the many ministries rooted in the call of baptism." The second was the need for "greater collaboration and inclusivity in ministry." This requires the effort to work together to raise consciousness and to be open to the new understanding that this demands. "Third, there is a need for a clear understanding of the nature of lay ecclesial ministry on the part of the baptized and those who have received the sacrament of Holy Orders." The final essential thing was the recognition of the need for "a common foundational theology as the basis for the formation of seminarians, deacons, religious and lay persons for ministry, as well as for the development of more collaborative skills on the part of the ordained, so that one and all can exercise their ministry in a collaborative fashion."[167]

That the connection between this archdiocesan initiative is used as a practical example of concentric circles can be clearly seen in "Part IV: Planning for the Future: Toward a Collaborative, Inclusive Ministry," which offers four specific exercises toward consciousness-raising and action for parish-based groups, pastoral councils, and other groups within the archdiocese as they seek to strategize ways to meet ministerial needs of the church of tomorrow. The basis for the praxis approach to an understanding of the common and ordained priesthood is given in the concluding section:

Ministry in this new millennium will be more collaborative and more inclusive in its exercise. The Body is endowed with many gifts. Authentic collaboration is rooted in the conviction that all of the baptized are given a share in Christ's priestly ministry, and that one and all are necessary for the fulfillment of the

Church's mission. True collaboration requires an appreciation of the distinction and differentiation of roles and responsibilities in the Body of Christ, together with a clear recognition of the fundamental equality of all the baptized, ordained and nonordained. For effective collaboration to occur, each one must believe that he or she has something to offer, and have trust in the gifts that others bring to our common task. Above all, we must be willing to admit that we can achieve something together that we cannot achieve alone.

While lay ministry differs from the ministry of the ordained, it too is a participation in the priestly ministry of Christ and so appropriate in its own right. Only with this realization is true collaboration between ministries ordained and nonordained possible.[168]

This is a means for discovering, through the communal discernment processes and the empowering of the Holy Spirit, an understanding of priesthood that is faithful to the past, is responsible and generative in terms of the present reality, and offers hope for the future.

SECTION II
ON THE TRAINING OF PRIESTS

Optatam Totius

PART I

THE DOCUMENT[1]

The history of the document on priestly ministry and life is complex, and that of the training of priests is no less problematic and conflictual. The atmosphere in the council hall during the debate on this document was described as one of tensions.[2] Questions of faithfulness to past seminary training processes and adaptation to the changing circumstances of the present and possible future were at the basis of the bishops' concerns in relation to the document.

Yet, just as the attention to priests as primary mediators of the spirit and praxis of the council was important to the council members, so also was the concern for future priests a primary issue. Cardinal Suenens was reported as saying, "Now the moment has arrived for a searching examination. Vatican Council II must create a new kind of seminary in line with the needs of today. If there is one place where Pope John's *aggiornamento* is needed, it is here."[3] The reason for the need for "a new kind of seminary" can be seen when we consider a necessarily brief overview of the history of seminaries.[4]

Historians point out that no comprehensive history of seminaries on an international basis has been written and that the documentation that has survived over the millennia is composed largely of pious and edifying reports about the ideal espoused rather than the reality lived.[5] What is known about seminary training is that before the time of Augustine (354–450) there was no formal institution for the education of candidates to the priesthood. In the post-persecution period of the Western church, seminary training primarily involved mentoring and apprenticeship. The earliest local synods, such as one in Carthage in the late fourth century, called for a priestly training that produces priests "who know scripture, can preach, understand church laws and are upright in their personal behavior."[6] Those aspiring to priestly ministry were connected to a particular church and they assisted the bishops and priests in caring for that church. In the process they were taught scripture and trained to prepare candidates for baptism and to administer the sacraments. [7]

More formal training took place under Augustine, but diversity still existed in terms of length of training and the process. Priestly formation gradually took shape through the process of minor orders. A life of prayer, discipline, and study began to take shape and monastic and episcopal schools for priestly formation developed during the period from the seventh to the thirteenth centuries. These schools were located near cathedrals. Lateran Council III (1179) mandated that a priest be appointed to the cathedral and that he be responsible and remunerated for the formation of local clerics. Lateran IV (1215) made the further requirement that this priest be a theologian who would teach the scriptures and pastoral theology.[8]

It was in the twelfth and thirteenth centuries that the seeds of present formation structures were sown in the university programs provided for candidates for the priesthood. Most monastic, cathedral, and palace schools "probably trained few parish priests, especially for the countryside. They produced elite ministers for high society, and not all their students proceeded to orders. They do not bring us much closer to understanding how the average parish priest learned to be a priest in the Middle Ages."[9]

The current divisions into academic, pastoral, and spiritual formation have their origins in the style of training received by those students who were specially selected by their bishops to attend university.[10] These students lived in what may be described today as residential colleges where the daily routine was usually that of a rigid and demanding asceticism, with compulsory attendance at liturgy and pious devotions. The formational life of the candidate had little or no relation to the demands or routine of life after ordination. However, the majority of those in priestly formation in this period were not sent to such colleges; they simply stayed in their family homes and did their training in the style of apprentices. This style of formation was dependent on the parish priest to whom they were apprenticed.[11]

The fifteenth and sixteenth centuries were starting points of the existing seminary system as it was known at Vatican II. In 1408 Jean

Gerson, a University of Paris chancellor and leader at the Council of Constance (1418), recommended separate theological schools in each diocese for the training of parish priests. However, he also had faith in the apprenticeship system as a means of priestly training.[12] During the years preceding the Protestant Reformation, clerical formation in general lacked a solid and well-balanced intellectual and moral foundation and a practical preparation for ministry.[13] The Council of Trent represented a major change in seminary training in terms of its reform of the diverse and inconsistent types of formation for ordination that had prevailed globally over the centuries. In 1546 Trent amended the Lateran conciliar requirements by mandating that a theologian must teach scripture in the cathedral and collegiate churches. This proposal led to the Tridentine decision that colleges be established solely for priestly training.[14]

The Tridentine decree came out of and belonged to the world of counter-reformation. It sought to isolate and protect priestly candidates from the dangers of the world, to educate and form priests who would serve the church and keep their parishioners away from the aberrations of the era. The intention of the entire Tridentine Decree on Seminaries was to protect "endangered youth" by removing them from the world and to fortify them in their priestly vocation.[15] In its reformation of the seminary system of the period, Trent returned to the much earlier practice of grouping candidates around their bishop, and having them formed morally and intellectually under his supervision.[16] The system of separate places for priestly training was solemnly confirmed as the form of education for the clergy on July 15, 1563, in the twenty-third session of the Council of Trent. These schools would provide adequate learning and the spiritual discipline to become a parish priest. However, there was still considerable variation in priestly formation well into the twentieth century.[17]

One of the fruits of Trent was the founding of several important seminaries, especially those that had their origins in, or were inspired by, that of Charles Borromeo, Archbishop of Milan (1538–1584). By 1593 Borromeo had established three seminaries for his diocese, based on age distinction: a minor seminary for younger boys, one for adolescents, and a major seminary for older men.[18] This "three school" pattern, modified by the French during the seventeenth century, took root in the church as the formal seminary system. Pius IV established the Roman College, attached to the Roman Seminary in 1565, as a Tridentine model for all dioceses.[19] However, not all clerical students attended the theology classes at the college attached to the seminary; and an interesting feature of the college was that, within a few years, the number of lay students enrolled in its classes far exceeded that of clerical candidates. The interest in theology was not confined to intending clerics even in the sixteenth century! In 1639 the proportion was 130 lay students to 40 clerical students.[20]

Trent required that candidates have an education of sorts before they joined the seminary, and preference was to be given to poor boys. They were to receive the tonsure and clerical dress on entry to mark their new status in the church. The responsibility for the clerical candidates was in the hands of local bishops and it was expected that the candidates would receive moral training, through the study of cases of conscience, and the development of basic liturgical skills.

By the seventeenth century, the formation and spirituality of the diocesan seminary was fundamentally shaped by the French model of the Sulpicians and Vincentians. The founders of this approach were Cardinal de Bérulle, Jean Jacques Olier, Vincent de Paul, and John Eudes; it was only later that the influence of the Benedictines and Jesuits was felt.[21] The theological and ascetical training for diocesan priests was based on the model of the Risen Christ as priest and victim. The emphasis on priestly vocation that prevailed in this model was less that of service to the people than of an inner call to life in Christ. The monastic approach to priestly vocation and formation influenced much of the writing on the spirituality of the diocesan priest even until Vatican II.

This Sulpician understanding was in competition with the idea that the priestly vocation consisted in the external call to service issued by the prelate of the candidate, an idea that had been confirmed as the traditional interpretation of priestly vocation as late as 1912.[22] Formation was divided into six years of minor seminary with major seminary training consisting of two years of philosophy and four years of theology. The approach to seminary formation that dominated seminaries globally from the seventeenth century to the 1960s was "more reminiscent of the cloister than it was of a school for clerics intended for an active parochial ministry."[23]

The earlier opportunities for laity as well as candidates for the priesthood to engage in theological education together had been lost in the more isolated approach to formation of the Sulpician model. In his analysis of the intellectual formation of American Catholics in general and of American priests in particular in the pre–Vatican II era, acclaimed historian and critic of the American intellectual life John Tracy Ellis argued that "the ideals of the spiritual life likewise far more befitted the monk and the friar than they did the parish priest," [24] and those priests who had isolated themselves from the secular world in which they ministered were often presented by the hierarchy as model clergy.

The emphasis on authoritative and disciplinary aspects of Catholicism in the post-Tridentine era meant that by the twentieth century priests were "a corps of loyal, obedient men trained spiritually and intellectually to form the type of Catholic called for by the rigorous spirit and letter of the Council."[25] However, some church leaders in the 1950s and 1960s recognized that this was an era in which intelligent and committed priests were needed to exercise initiatives to lead their Catholic communities into important critical engagements with their culture.

The anti-communist and polarized Western world of the mid-twentieth century was one where industrial affluence, an expanding mass media that opened up the information channels for the general populace, and movements toward independence in colonized countries were shaping the Catholic identity. While educated Catholics were looking for inspiration and support from their priests to help them exercise leadership in their own life circumstances, they found instead, from the majority of their priests, a predominantly defensive attitude toward the world and even toward education.[26] This was a consequence of a spiritual formation for priesthood which was monastic rather than diocesan and a church which was ghettoist in its stance toward the world. Catholicism at this time was rendered immobile by its certainties.[27] This was the world where the plea of Cardinal Suenens for a new kind of seminary in line with contemporary needs was responded to by the council in the document "On the Training of Priests."

THE DEVELOPMENT OF THE DECREE

To trace the development of this decree is to recognize the enormous amount of working and radical revisions from 1960 to 1965 that went into the six drafts and that resulted in the final text. The training of priests was initially seen to be an "in-house" regulatory issue, rather than one of major concern to the world. When the initial questionnaire was sent out at the beginning of the council, the bishops' responses in regard to seminary training were passed on to the curial Commission for Seminary Studies and Catholic Education (Commission on Seminaries), which was chaired by Cardinal Pizzardo.[28] Benedictine Father Augustine Mayer, rector of the Pontifical Athenaeum of Saint Anselm, was appointed as secretary.[29]

The task given to this commission was to develop a schema addressing the furthering of vocations to the church and the training of seminarians. The questions of the nature of ecclesiastical vocations and how to promote them, of the spiritual and pastoral formation of priests, and of Catholic schools, were all areas that came under consideration in the preparatory work.[30] Special attention was also to be given "to the integrity of the doctrine in submission to the magisterium and to the teaching of scripture. Similarly the question of clerical discipline should include a rejection of recent errors that promote a certain specious 'autonomy.'"[31]

The commission worked together from 1960 to 1962 under some difficulties due to the large size of the group (thirty-nine members with thirty-two consultors) and the distance from Rome of several of those involved.[32] To facilitate the process, the plenary commission was divided into twelve sub-commissions that met regularly; the whole commission met six times in plenary sessions. Six sub-groups were to explore priestly formation, two were to examine the question of vocations, and one each was to work on spiritual formation, on discipline, on the nature of priestly studies, and on pastoral formation. Their collaboration resulted in two documents comprising six texts: the first was "On Forming Seminarians" (*Schema Constitutionis de Sacrorum Alumnis Formandis*) and the other was "On Fostering Ecclesiastical Vocations" (*Decreti de Vocationibus Ecclesiasticis Fovendis*). The latter contained a series of exhortations that bishops, priests, and their communities should do all they could to foster vocations.

The influence of Cardinal Pizzardo and other curial members was prominent in the approach, structure, and content of these documents.[33] The first text provided sets of general laws, principles, and criteria which would need to be accommodated to various times and places. The chapter on the course of studies required that seminarians be given at least as good a general education as the laity receive (an interesting requirement that supports the evidence of the growing gap between priests and laity educationally, in contrast to earlier centuries when the priests were educated and the laity unlettered); that they be trained in Latin; that in a two-year course they be taught scholastic philosophy according to the principles and methods of Thomas Aquinas and learn how to analyze and reply to contemporary philosophies; that their four-year theology curriculum also follow Aquinas's principles; that they study scripture according to norms given by the council; that they become acquainted with separated Christian communities; and that they learn enough about modern religious errors to be able to show the erring the way to truth.[34]

These texts were passed on to the Central Preparatory Commission (CPC) in early 1962. The number and volume of documents already submitted by other commissions meant that the texts were returned to the Commission on Seminaries for condensing into one shorter document. In July 1962 the revised document was given to the CPC for presentation to the bishops. It is important to note that during this period of preliminary work there was already much concern within the commission itself about the fact that there had been a significant decline in vocations prior to the council. This problem they ascribed to the de-Christianization of the world (basically the Western world), the smaller size of Catholic families, and the failure of church leaders to encourage vocations. That these factors, along with so many other socio-ecclesial problems, were subsequently attributed to the Vatican Council as a cause of the present crisis of the church can be seen to be both historically inaccurate and an example of blaming the council for all sorts of church problems, and using this as a reason for regression to the past.[35]

The compartmentalized thinking of the past, along with the lack of a coherent or common understanding of the aim and purpose of priestly formation within the commission was apparent, even in the way the document was sent to the CPC. Chapter 4 on the program of studies was submitted, along with the schema on vocations on February 26, 1961, four months before the other five chapters of the schema on formation arrived in June 1962. Since chapter 1, on the general organization of seminaries, contained the description of the aim of seminary formation, it appears that the aim described had not greatly influenced the chapter submitted earlier on the program of seminary studies. The past approach was simply repeated and slightly updated.

In the complete schema there were some good cross references linking one aspect of formation with others, for instance, the importance of theology and liturgy for the spiritual life with the insistence on the parallel development of pastoral and intellectual formation. However, the general impression was that separate elements had been included without any evidence of their internal unity and general coherence.[36]

The four distinct parts to the training of seminarians: the spiritual, the disciplinary, the intellectual, and the pastoral, had their foundations in the Tridentine model. The treatment of disciplinary formation began in typical scholastic style: description, definition, and errors, with the errors given prominence.[37] These sections obviously came in response to episcopal complaints about the self-indulgence, autonomy, and insubordination of priests and seminarians.[38] In regard to the curriculum of studies, the traditional division between the two years of philosophy and the four years of theology, and the separate consideration of theology and scripture was unchanged. The language remained wordy and repetitive.

Commentators on the document recognize the significant contribution made by the commission in the recognition of the importance of the role of local hierarchies in shaping the seminary curriculum. Another important contribution was the insistence on the proper training of seminary staff. Some flexibility in terms of the length of the training period was introduced through the provision of two reasons for allowing seminarians to interrupt their studies. Where there was a need for seminarians to dedicate themselves more intensely to spiritual formation rather than to simply keep up their academic work, approval for interruption could be given. It was also recognized that in order to exercise the diaconate before priestly orders, formal studies might need to be put aside for a period.

The commission also made a cautious and carefully sanctioned recommendation for seminarians to be initiated into the pastoral life through the practical experience of apostolic work. In describing this recommendation Archbishop Hurley of Durban, South Africa, a member of the Commission on Seminaries, commented, "The old conviction still shone through that the best way to train a man for a job was to keep him away from it for as long as possible."[39]

The second draft came as a consequence of the reduction of the two schemas to one by the Central Preparatory Commission in 1962. The schema on Vocations now constituted the first chapter of Formation of Candidates for the Priesthood. The commission had also prepared three other schemas, one on Catholic schools, one on academic studies, and a third on the reverence due to the magisterium of the church in the teaching of sacred subjects. The first two were blended into the Declaration on Christian Education and the third was dropped.[40]

As reports were being received from bishops and planning was moving along, some of the commissions were being reconstituted. In this process a new Conciliar Commission on Seminaries, Studies, and Catholic Education (CSS) had been constituted by the pope with both appointed and elected members. Commission members included Archbishop O'Boyle of Washington, former chancellor of the Catholic University of America, who was elected almost unanimously by all the factions represented at the council.[41] Bishops from Chile, Spain, Germany, and Belgium were then elected, each of whom had exercised leadership in seminaries or in Catholic education. The next group elected represented Poland, Canada, Italy, Paraguay, South Africa, France, and Brazil. In addition to these elected members, the pope appointed members from Brazil, Portugal, Spain, Australia, and the United States. Professor Mathijs Lamberigts, dean of theology at the Catholic University of Louvain, in his research on the document on seminary formation, points out that no bishop from Asia or "black Africa" was either elected or appointed to this important commission for global priestly formation.[42]

At the first meeting on December 30, 1962, commission members discovered that they had nothing to work on until the approved schema had been discussed in the council. There were more significant schemas than that on priestly training up for discussion; however, the issues generated in the debates concerning the church, liturgical reform, and the place of scripture were to be significant for this commission.

The text did not come up for debate during the first session of the council in October 1962, but bishops sent in written comments and suggestions to the newly formed CSS throughout this session.[43] On January 30, 1963, the commission was informed that the schema was one of those listed for discussion at the next session, but in the meantime the text was to be shortened once more. The third draft, which involved abridgment of the schema to about one-third of its original length, was produced by Fr. P. Dezza, SJ, a consultor to the CSS. Described by Hurley as a masterpiece of brevity, Dezza's rewrite was also abstract and dry, which masked its depth.[44] The decision was made to drop all questions related to clerical orders other than the priesthood because these were dealt with in other areas. This abridged document was the subject of debate at the plenary CSS meeting in preparation for the second session of the council.

This draft was titled "The Aim of Formation and the Organization of Seminaries." The influence of the progress of the debates on other related documents, such as that on the church, *Lumen Gentium* (*LG*) and that on priests, *Presbyterorum Ordinis* (*PO*), was evident in this draft. The aim of pastoral formation as expressed in this schema was to train priests for the threefold function of the priesthood explicitly formulated as: the ministry of the word, the ministry of worship, and the pastoral ministry strictly so-called.[45]

With this clarification of the goal, the internal structure became clearer and more consistent. The earlier chapters were expanded to a preface and five sections: Ecclesiastical Vocations; The Aim of Formation and the Organization of Seminaries; Spiritual Formation; Studies; and Post-Seminary Formation. Formation was now more clearly related to both intellectual and pastoral formation and the correlation of philosophy and theology had been more strongly emphasized.[46]

The program of studies was designed to give candidates training that offered a scriptural foundation and model for priesthood and that integrated theology and philosophy into a ministerial framework. The place of spiritual formation was debated in the CSS. The previous primacy of its place in formation needed to be contextualized into the understanding of diocesan priesthood. However, the commission decided to leave it in its present position. Seminary discipline came under discussion and the decision was made to address it under spiritual formation rather than in a separate chapter as in the first draft.

In this schema, seminary discipline was dealt with in terms that, while taking account of the concerns of the bishops in their responses, generally used the language of expectations rather than lamentations.[47] This was a positive move. The new draft was accepted by the CPC, approved by Pope John a month before his death, and distributed with the other schemas to the council fathers in the fourth volume of the council documents, *Schemata Constitutionem et Decretorum* (209–275) in May 1963.[48] The schema did not come in for much criticism at this stage, due mainly to the preoccupation of the bishops with the far more contentious topics of revelation and the Dogmatic Constitution on the Church. However, a significant number of amendments were sent in by individual bishops and by some national and regional conferences.

During the second session of the council in October–November 1963, the CSS decided to work on submissions that had arrived after the due date. Within the CSS there was some misgiving about this, as the revised schema had already been approved for debate and there did not seem much point in discussing further alterations before the debate took place. There were debates about both the content and direction that sometimes became quite heated.[49] However, commission members gave time to all the amendments received and formulated appropriate changes in the hope that permission would be given to incorporate them in a new text before the debate in general congregation. These changes affected style and emphasis rather than the substance of the schema. This became the fourth draft.[50]

The reactions to this draft during the second session were negative. Many bishops found it either completely or partly unacceptable. It did not make sufficiently radical changes in the seminary system, nor did it make enough allowance for the important and legitimate differences and expectations in seminary life in different parts of the world. It failed to stress the need for the seminarian's personal responsibility for his intellectual, spiritual, and pastoral formation, as it also failed to emphasize the importance for the seminary director to move from "passive obedience to obedient initiative" in his leadership role.[51]

Many complained of the dry, juridical, and somewhat pessimistic tone of the document, and some argued that seminaries were no longer necessary.[52] In its attempt to make sure that the concerns of all bishops were on record, the CSS again asked those episcopal conferences that had not yet commented on the schema to make suggestions for the improvement of the text.[53] All these revisions were to be included in the next revised text submitted to the CPC. Then, on November 29, 1963, new instructions were issued by the CPC concerning those schemas that had not been discussed in the council hall up to that date. But before

these instructions could be acted upon, there were further developments that affected the submission of the text as it stood.[54]

Urgent meetings of the CPC held after Christmas 1963 resulted in
what appeared to be a rushed decision, either because of the deteriorat-
ing health of the pope or the increasing volume of material emanating
from the various commissions. On January 23, 1964, the instruction came
from the CPC to the CSS that they were to reduce the whole schema on
the training of priests to short propositions that would be voted upon but
not discussed in the council hall.[55] This reduction to a series of votable
propositions had to be completed by the end of March 1964.

The CSS members returned to Rome to participate in the recon-
struction from March 3 to 9. The successive reworkings of the text am-
plified the difficulties that had cropped up consistently within the
commission itself. In these condensed meeting times two alternative
drafts of the propositions were constructed by sub-committees; from
these two the CSS plenary commission would choose one as the basis for
further discussion. An 850-word summary of the 1963 schema, presented in the form of twenty propositions, was chosen. Further revisions
were carried out and the propositions were expanded to twenty-two.[56]
This draft was sent to the CPC on March 11, 1964, under the title, "The
Training of Priests."

These propositions were organized into seven chapters:

1. Responsibility of Each Country for Priestly Formation"
   (no. 1), which gave primary responsibility to the local
   episcopal conference
2. "Promotion of Vocations to the Priesthood" (nos. 2–3),
   which included the topic of minor seminaries
3. "Major Seminaries" (nos. 4–7)
4. "Spiritual Formation" (nos. 8–12)
5. "Ecclesiastical Studies" (nos. 13–18)
6. "Pastoral Formation" (nos. 19–21)
7. "Formation after the Seminary" (no. 22)

The new additions to the draft were the articles on the minor seminaries (article 3) on celibacy (article 10), and on the method of higher
studies (article 17). Extended articles addressed the vocation of the
priesthood, theological studies, and pastoral training.

Three positive achievements balanced the heavy debit of reduction. The first was the opportunity for local hierarchies to adapt seminary training to their own circumstances. This was given a primary place and was the backdrop for the understanding and implementation of the other propositions. Second, seminary discipline was integrated into the section on spiritual formation.[57]

A third feature of this fifth draft was that creditable psychological and pedagogical principles were integrated into the formation structure and content, while the importance of study was emphasized and attention was given to the human sciences as well as the other fundamental disciplines.[58] Amendments to the previous text were published side by side with the original, a report on the work of the commission was provided, and amendments that had not been accepted were dealt with in an appendix. This revised schema was distributed to the bishops in a booklet containing the earlier schema of propositions, the two texts printed in parallel columns along with notes on the changes, and a report from Bishop Carraro, of Verona, Italy, spokesman for the CSS.

The third session convened on September 12, 1964. In the first several days petitions were submitted both by episcopal conferences and by individual bishops requesting that all those schemas that had been reduced to propositions be given discussion time in the timetable. One of the major contributors to the critique and development of this schema was Cardinal Suenens, of Malines-Brussels, primate of Belgium. At a public lecture at the Pan-African Secretariat on the theme of priestly formation, before any debate on the revised schema, he had insisted on the importance of a reform of the studies of philosophy and theology, the need to deepen the pastoral formation of future priests, even if it meant an extra year before ordination, and a lifelong program of ongoing education in the theological and pastoral sciences for all priests.[59]

The negative reaction of the bishops to the limited nature of the propositions meant that the CSS was given the opportunity to write a sixth draft, which was a compromise between the propositions and the fourth draft and which took the interventions into account. Two thousand words in length at completion, this draft also proposed the new idea of dividing the student body of large seminaries into smaller groups to better provide for their personal formation while retaining unity of direction and scientific training.[60]

On September 25, 1964, it was announced that there would be time for a short discussion of all those schemas that had been reduced to propositions, followed by voting. Only the amendment stage of the procedure was to be admitted. This meant that an immediate jump was made from the debate to the vote, a loss because more detailed explanations and reasoning had to be omitted in the narrow time slot that had been allotted.[61] An atmosphere of unease and tension had prevailed in the council hall before the debate on *Optatam Totius* (*OT*) because of clashes in the earlier debate on religious freedom and because of the intervention by the pope in that discussion, an intervention that was interpreted by many as a concession to the conservative minority who were defensive of the rights of the church, particularly in Italy and Spain, at the expense of the majority. The tension continued into the discussion on *Optatam Totius*.[62]

The debate on the schema took place between November 12 and 17, 1964.[63] As the CSS reporter, Bishop Carraro of Verona, introduced the discussion on behalf of the commission. He expressed his hope that the document would be useful both to the Holy See and to episcopal conferences in preparing the proposed post-conciliar directories and the new Code of Canon Law. He believed that the text reflected "a middle course for the reform of seminaries and a balanced outlook."[64] Henri Fesquet reported Carraro's description of the earlier schema in contrast to the present one as the difference between "a free-flowing river" in comparison to "a walled enclosure" as it was in its present refined status.[65]

The links between this and other schemas, especially that on the church, "which should be considered as the hinge of everything that is being investigated, discussed and decided in the council hall" were also pointed out to the bishops. Indeed, the propositions could be considered, "as it were, certain corollaries that derive necessarily from this principal constitution of the council." [66] The text was also to be read as "a complement to Trent on the one hand, and as an effort to adapt seminary formation to the new circumstances in which the church found itself on the other."[67]

The five main strengths were in terms of its pastoral emphasis, its adaptation to the times, the provision for local needs on an international scale, its balanced response to the diversity of amendments proposed, and the fact that it took account of appropriate renewal. The propositions aimed at promoting an "organic and vital synthesis" in the education of priests.[68] The schema was Christocentric, with Christ himself as the standard of reference for the updating of seminaries. Carraro hoped that the schema and its subsequent application by episcopal conferences would eventually complete the work of seminaries begun four centuries ago by the Council of Trent. The direction and approach can be seen in the opening article.

> In order that the general rules be adapted to each people and each rite, episcopal conferences will prepare a program for the formation of their priests. This program will be continually brought up to date and submitted for the approbation of the Holy See. Thus priests can receive a formation that will enable them to respond to the spiritual needs of their country. (Article 1)

This proposition gives evidence of the fruit of the discussion on the decentralization that permits each region and country great freedom in adapting the style of seminaries to meet their local requirements. It marks the end of the requirement of a normative European uniformity in non-European countries where seminaries had not been able to adapt to local or regional needs.

Thirty-two speakers responded. The first speaker was Cardinal Bueno y Monreal, Archbishop of Seville, one of the few to speak at length about the document. First he expressed his satisfaction; then he expressed his concern about the vocations crisis and emphasized the need to define priestly vocation more clearly, to distinguish it from the various natural and supernatural callings of the laity, and to recognize vocations as a grace of God. Promotion of priestly vocations needed to be worked at, thus the importance of family and school formation for priestly vocation was recognized. Reports of the discussions on vocation leave some doubt about whether there was any common agreement among the bishops about the nature of a priestly vocation. Some bishops felt that there was already a clear understanding, but others wanted it spelled out more specifically in the text. [69] The importance of taking the initiative and suggesting to a potential candidate that he might have a vocation was emphasized.[70]

The structure and format of the schema were generally praised. Few bishops expressed an interest in expanding the text into a fuller schema as had been requested in the case of the document on priesthood and that on the missions. Eighteen bishops spoke on behalf of large groups of bishops. Five speakers were members of the Commission for Seminaries, Studies and Catholic Education: Staffa (Roman curia) and De Barros Câmara (Rio de Janeiro, Brazil) who were the CSS's two vice-presidents, Colombo, (Milan, Italy), Botero Salazar (Medellin, Colombia) and Hurley (Durban, South Africa).[71] The polarization in the CSS was evidenced in their very different approaches to the schema.

Cardinal Döpfner of Munich, a member of the CPC, commented that this modest expansion of the schema had produced just the right balance in the response to a difficult task. "The propositions...hold on to the rules that have been proved over centuries, but they also openly and courageously introduce new laws appropriate to the changed circumstances of the age."[72] De Barros Câmara of Rio de Janeiro endorsed the "trust in the pastoral prudence of bishops and episcopal conferences," while Gopu of Hyderabad, India, approved of the provision more on account of the diversity of situations, for "seminaries in the missions should not try to imitate European seminaries exactly or slavishly."[73] Only a few speakers warned of the possibility of too much diversity. Cardinal Meyer of Chicago approved of the delegation of responsibility to episcopal conferences but, in view of other bishops' concerns, asked whether the schema paid sufficient attention to those principles that may be recognized as common to all regions and all priests.

Archbishop Garrone of Toulouse, shortly to become prefect of the Congregation for Seminaries and Universities,[74] commented that the structures of this congregation would have to change as a result of the decentralization. In its role of coordinating local institutions with their new autonomy, it would have to "transcend the timeless and rather negative manner in which it has been accustomed to work," and "men from all regions of the world would have to be called to the congregation."[75] As he was speaking on behalf of seventy bishops, his comment carried some weight. Garrone also pointed out that "the congregation lacked a sufficient degree of openness with respect to developments in the theological sciences."[76]

There was real division among the council members, even though serious hostility to the schema was confined to a few members. Cardinals Staffa and Bacci of the curia concentrated their attacks on the treatment of studies, Cardinal Ruffini on studies and other issues, and

Archbishop Méndez Arceo on chastity. Bishop Drzazga (Gniezno, Poland) was the spokesman for Polish bishops who asked for a more concrete formulation of the new orientation, which they felt should not be left to the local bishops' conferences, because the basic problems were everywhere the same and the conferences required firm and specific norms. This was the only group that had wanted a total reworking of the schema.[77]

While most of the debate concentrated on major seminaries, their need and their value, Drzazga stressed the importance of minor seminaries. Cardinal Döpfner and Bishop Weber of Strasbourg, France, in contrast, argued against them because family life and schools often produced better or mature vocations, "more in conformity with human nature."[78] There was general acceptance that seminaries should continue to provide the basic formation for priests.

Only one speaker took up the schema's paragraph on older candidates and suggested the establishment of special interdiocesan seminaries for them. Benavent Escuin of Malaga, Spain, proposed an apprentice-style preparation for priestly ordination with a diaconate of at least two years after the seminary and before priestly ordination during which time the deacons would work alongside the priests and live in common with them. "Further they should be familiar with the world of the young and with the social doctrine of the church, which is the projection of the Gospel adapted to our times."[79] He also wanted seminarians, at least during vacations, to live among the poor and to help them deal with their problems.

In agreement with this position, Bishop Sani of Den Pasar, Indonesia, suggested that seminarians live at home and help their parish priests during vacations and that there be a year's pastoral or practical work after the seminary before priestly ordination. He also welcomed the provision of an extra year for spiritual formation, which he saw as a kind of novitiate, especially necessary in mission countries where the seminarians' parents were often non-Christians or recent converts and lacked grounding in the Christian heritage. Various suggestions were also made for a more pastoral and missionary approach, for more contact with the laity, implying life and work outside the seminary. However, there was no consensus on the proportion of pastoral work and studies to be engaged in during seminary years.

There was general agreement about the balance of the schema in terms of preserving the old and introducing the new as well as of integrating the various aspects of formation—spiritual, pastoral, and intellectual. However, different emphases were proposed, some bishops thinking the document had gone too far while others argued that it had not gone far enough.

Döpfner praised the schema's call for a better integration of philosophy and theology, as well as within the various disciplines of theology, and for its emphasis on the study of scripture, "which ought to be as it were the soul of all theology." Suenens thought the pastoral dimension of formation needed greater emphasis. Diocesan priests are not monks; rather they are "called by the love of God to the service of souls in the world" and with this mission in the world they should not be formed outside it.[80]

The bishops were clearly divided on such questions as the place of lay faculty in the seminary and of the importance of Thomas Aquinas. The issue of philosophy and theology studies was a particularly vexed one. A minority led by Ruffini, Staffa, and Bacci was anxious about the innovations that had been proposed and they expressed great regret that Aquinas had not been accorded a position of preeminent authority, especially in philosophy. In contrast, a number of the more progressive bishops desired to see the basic lines of the new directions in seminary discipline and courses of study made even more clear.

As a member of the commission, Hurley took a middle position in this debate. He agreed with Suenens on the need to review philosophy courses in seminaries, but he also thought that Scholasticism could not be brushed aside. There was a need for seminarians to develop their philosophical ideas in light of the growing arenas of human knowledge and to express their ideas in modern language so that dialogue would be possible.

Ruffini, however, speaking as one who had spent thirty years in seminaries and seventeen as secretary of the Congregation for Seminaries and Universities, urged the value of more traditional seminary discipline and piety; old ways should not be forgotten with the rightful introduction of new ideas. He argued:

> This schema has a defect: it does not mention Thomas in connection with philosophical formation. He is mentioned very

timidly in connection with theological formation. But Saint Thomas remains the master and guide of scholarship. He is the very doctor of the church. He is more useful than ever in fighting against modern errors.[81]

Other conservative voices supported Ruffini.

In opposition to this, Cardinal Léger argued that the term that was being used in the debate, "philosophia *perennis*," is ambiguous.

> What does it apply to, since there are several radically different Scholastic philosophies?...It is the nature of philosophy to begin with an investigation into reality and not into authority. It is evident that if the council imposes the teaching of Scholastic philosophy, it will seriously inconvenience non-Western countries. Anyway, the council has no business imposing a particular philosophy.[82]

Although applause was not permitted in the council hall, commentators record that there was "thunderous applause."[83]

Archbishop Staffa, secretary of the Sacred Congregation of Universities and Seminaries, and described as a ruthless spokesman for the official line on Thomism,[84] stated that he was speaking on behalf of bishops of both the West and the East. He "indignantly and categorically rejected the imputation of Cardinal Léger that St. Thomas was not all the Thomists had claimed him to be."[85] Staffa argued that "no progress is possible if we are more concerned with what is new than with the truth... The church decides what is good in philosophy... St Thomas is not a milestone but a beacon. Let us at all costs keep the fundamental principles of Saint Thomas contained in the encyclical *Humani Generis*."[86]

Cardinal Bacci, speaking as a member of the curia, expressed "surprise and pain" at the comments made about Aquinas during the debate.

> Surely no one wishes to weaken the role of the Angelic Doctor, even indirectly, since ninety pontifical documents have made the importance of this philosopher clear. If anyone opposed this teaching—which I do not believe—it would mean that the council is not only above the popes but against them as well.

This is unimaginable... Some have suggested that a new com-
mission should be created to deal competently with seminaries.
This is surprising since such a body already exists, the Sacred
Congregation of Universities and Seminaries.[87]

Various speakers disagreed with Bacci's arguments, including Archbishops Colombo of Milan and Hurley, both members of the CSS, and,
most vigorously of all, Cardinal Léger. In response to the Thomist
issue, Léger summed up his argument:

> Beware of the man of one book! Beware too of the church of
> one doctor! Rather than imposing Saint Thomas, we might
> propose him as a prototype of the scholar, as a master and
> model who knew how to turn the learning of his time to the
> service of the Church. It is well known that Saint Thomas in a
> way baptized Aristotle, who until then had been considered ab-
> solutely incompatible with Christianity. For several decades, a
> great number of theologians have dialogued only with the
> philosophies of the Middle Ages. This has its disadvantages.
> Let lay experts be invited into the seminaries to compare secu-
> lar and religious kinds of philosophy.[88]

There was another bout of applause when Cardinal Léger also
roundly criticized morality as it had previously been taught in the seminaries. "Our manuals do not correspond with the adult mind of modern man. The morality taught in seminaries suffers from several defects.
It is too preoccupied with casuistry and legalism."[89] He argued that as
it had been taught it was neither principally nor fully Christian.

In agreement, Suenens supported the efforts of the CSS to integrate theology and philosophy and to have the foundations of priesthood located in holy scripture and centered on the love that sums up
the threefold mission of Christ. He commented that it is not enough for
contemporary priests to be holy; they must also be trained to adapt
themselves to ministry and life in their own times and circumstances. In
Belgium, Suenens had undertaken the reform of seminaries. He urged
a formation that was authentically based on a diocesan spirituality. It
should be totally centered on the apostolate, and he suggested that the

order of studies be reversed: first scripture and theology, and then (or at the same time) philosophy.[90]

The tension in the council hall that permeated this part of the debate on seminary formation was caused by the inevitable showdown between philosophy, theology, and morality. This was because "the intellectual and pastoral renewal of the church, so much desired by the majority and so much feared by the minority, depends on these three fundamental disciplines."[91] The minority group remained both polarized and influential to the end. Hurley commented that it would have taken "the wisdom of Solomon to reconcile them."[92] As journalist and observer, Henri Fesquet perceived that the Roman church appeared to be locked into Thomism and he wondered whether the council or the church itself subsequently would ever really be able to bring about the change that had been recommended in the schema and that resounded strongly among the bishops in the council hall.

The issues of ongoing formation after the seminary and of later formation received little comment. Bishop Fernández-Conde of Cordoba, Spain, thought the spirituality of seminaries had been too "angelic" and insufficiently human, based on ideals rather than reality. He praised the insistence in the schema that:

> The students should be accustomed to work properly at their own development. They are to be formed in strength of character, and, in general, they are to learn to esteem those virtues which are held in high regard by men and which recommend a minister of Christ. Such virtues are sincerity of mind, a constant concern for justice, fidelity to one's promises, refinement in manners, modesty in speech coupled with charity. (Article 11)

Cardinal Meyer spoke in support of the greater integration of all aspects of formation and quoted Pius XII, "You need in a sense to be a perfect man before you can be a perfect priest."[93]

Various speakers urged the importance of the human and psychological development of seminarians. Bishop Colombo of Milan spoke of two principal weaknesses in the formation of seminarians that the schema attempted to address. There was a lack of integration of the various types of formation—spiritual, intellectual, pastoral, and disciplinary—

that operated in mutual ignorance of one another and remained isolated. Also, he commented that when many seminarians left the seminary they were immature and passive in character. He believed this was
a consequence of the defensiveness of seminary training, noting that
those in charge had been too exclusively concerned with protecting
seminarians from "the contagion of the world and cutting them off
from a society which they will one day have to evangelize."[94]

Colombo also denounced the pressures exerted on those candidates
who were too immature to be able to function effectively in the situations in which they are placed in their seminary formation. He also supported the respect in the schema for the rules of healthy psychology,
and those that promote maturity.

> The norms of discipline are to be applied according to the age
> of the students so that they themselves, as they gradually learn
> self-mastery, may become accustomed to use freedom wisely, to
> act spontaneously and energetically, and to work together har-
> moniously with their fellows and with the laity. (Article 11)

No economic, family, or ecclesiastical pressure should be brought
to bear on vocational discernment. The bishops were also reminded
that the fact that some candidates might leave the seminary should be
considered as something quite normal. The seminary must be characterized by an atmosphere of total liberty, so that anyone who feels he
must leave should not be embarrassed by his decision.[95]

Cardinal Döpfner thought the treatment of celibacy in the schema
was too negative because it concentrated too much on dangers to
chastity. Psychology and anthropology should inform the understanding of human sexuality taught in the seminary and then seminarians
would learn how they might integrate their bodily and physical powers
more fully into their whole personality and so learn to become more authentic in their way of living and ministering.

Other bishops with experience in seminary leadership also wanted
a more positive treatment of celibacy. Bishop Charue of Namur saw isolation as a fundamental problem in celibate living. To resolve this problem, he encouraged a "profound and austere" spiritual formation so that
all traces of infantilism were eradicated.[96] Rather than viewing celibacy

as an unwelcome renunciation, seminarians should be encouraged to recognize it as an undertaking for the reign of God in service of people, following the example of Jesus.

Bishop Pawlowski of Poland emphasized the importance of confession and obedience to a spiritual director to help fidelity to celibacy. Bishop Rivera Damas thought the schema went too far in requiring a "clear knowledge" of marriage before the choice of celibacy could be made properly. He also urged a firm and correct discipline to be imposed, rather than the autonomy that seminarians claimed and which some seminary directors placated.

Although the pope had reserved the question of priestly celibacy for himself, Archbishop Méndez Arceo of Mexico argued that celibacy should be the result of a free decision. He was a most severe critic of the schema's treatment of celibacy. There was too much emphasis on dangers and a legalistic approach. He wanted bishops to have the power to dispense priests from the obligation of celibacy and thereby to return them to the lay state.[97]

Priestly formation "should be carried out in accordance with the age of the students and local conditions, and with the prudent judgment of the bishops, methodically and under the leadership of men skilled in pastoral work, the surpassing power of supernatural means being always remembered" (article 20). The importance of the revision of seminary studies and of the integration of those studies was endorsed by several speakers. To this end, up-to-date books as well as good professors and moderators were essential.

Bishop Añoveros Ataún of Cadiz, Spain, noted that those in authority in seminaries are often clever but immature, "without pedagogical formation and ignorant of pastoral practice, who confuse the difficulties of youth and puberty with the lack of a vocation, with disastrous consequences."[98] Bishop Sauvage of Annecy, France, and others urged the importance of unity between seminarians and staff. Sauvage particularly supported the pastoral predominance of seminary training and endorsed the spirit of Paul VI's encyclical on the church, *Ecclesiam Suam* (1964) by calling for dialogue to be exercised between teachers and students as well as exchange of knowledge about non-Christian modern philosophies.[99] He also asked that seminaries correspond more with the aspiration of the seminarians themselves so greater hospitality might foster vocational fidelity.

Disunity in the teaching body was described by some bishops as a problem of the faculty rather than of the seminarians.[100] The proposal to establish institutes to help seminary staff was welcomed.

> Since priestly training, because of the circumstances particularly of contemporary society, must be pursued and perfected even after the completion of the course of studies in seminaries, it will be the responsibility of episcopal conferences in individual nations to employ suitable means to this end. Such would be pastoral institutes working together with suitably chosen parishes, meetings held at stated times, and appropriate projects whereby the younger clergy would be gradually introduced into the priestly life and apostolic activity, under its spiritual, intellectual, and pastoral aspects, and would be able, day by day, to renew and foster them more effectively. (Article 21)

The importance of inculturation in the seminary training and experience was emphasized by several bishops in missionary lands. Seminarians need to know and to be able to adapt to the cultural, social, and religious conditions of the people to whom they will be sent, since priests are not sent to people "in the abstract" but to the people of their time and culture.[101] The personal formation of clerics received attention because the life can be so remote from the world and so artificial. Professional degrees should be part of their studies so that if they leave the seminary they will be educated for employment. The necessity of contact with both lay people and their world during the seminary training period was affirmed. The seminarian "will discover that the non-Christian man is not a spiritual nothing."[102]

The pressure of time in the third session meant that a number of bishops were prevented from speaking because of the decision to close the debate. In addition, sixty-two individuals and four groups presented written submissions. Alberigo comments that many of the major conciliar protagonists made speeches and that the debate with its polarized positions on seminaries could be seen as a microcosm of the council and a summary of the state of conciliar theology. It seemed that the preconciliar emphasis on morals, virtues, and juridical obligations was giving way in these debates to an approach based more on evangelical life and biblical spirituality.[103] After reading about the division and the heat of the Thomistic debate it is surprising perhaps to read that Carraro, in a brief concluding speech, thanked the bishops for the "serene and constructive manner" in which the debate had been conducted and for the generally favorable reception.[104]

An unexpected event occurred during the closing of this debate in the third session. When the final report from the commission had concluded, the floor was given to a parish priest, Father Marcos of Madrid, Spain, who had been invited to be present as an observer. Instead of delivering a polite cameo piece expressing gratitude for the honor of his invitation to speak at the council, he spoke out passionately and articulately on behalf of priests everywhere.

> He called for emphasis on the idea of a diocesan *presbyterium* in the schema on the priesthood, that is, the notion that bishops were to govern with the advice of their parish clergy. More specifically, he wanted wider permission to be granted to parish priests to confirm, as clergy of the Eastern rites were able to do, and for greater flexibility in the hearing of confessions, at least within the confines of one country."[105]

There is no record of the way this unexpected intervention was received by the council members.

The bishops accepted the recommendation that the schema had accomplished its task and it was put to the vote. It was carried by a vote of 2,076 to 41; the "intransigents" remained locked in their position throughout the debate and the voting. The text was then sent back to the CSS for its final revision. The CSS was bound by these favorable votes and therefore could make only minor changes in its subsequent revision of the text. This was a compliment as well as a disadvantage for the commission. The vote was as much a dismissal as it was an expression of approval; no further time could be given to the decree. More important schemas required attention. The bishops had done as much as they could in view of the entrenched divisions within the CSS itself as well as in the council hall.[106]

The commission met in Rome from April 26 to May 4, 1965, to apply the finishing touches in light of proposed modifications for presentation at the final session. Hurley comments that during this time the battle over St. Thomas flared up again, and the CSS ultimately compromised by being rather vague about a "philosophical patrimony which is perennially valid" (article 15); it was slightly more specific about the leadership of St. Thomas in systematic theology (article 16).[107] The explicit mention of the necessity of major seminaries was added to the schema to clear up any doubt that might have come as a consequence of the diverse opinions expressed about them among the bishops. The treatment of formation for celibacy was elucidated in its eschatological dimension.

The final voting on the schema took place during the fourth session of the council from October 11 to 13. Again, *Optatam Totius* (On the Training of Priests) was well-received, although with some minor misgivings. But they were not serious enough to hold up the decree. It was promulgated on October 28, 1965. In the vote to decide on voting for the schema in detail, 2,076 were for, and 41 against. In the voting on each separate section, again the bishops were significantly in favor of the revised text. For example, on the need for seminaries (article 4), votes for numbered 2,038, against 88, invalid 1; on celibacy (article 10), the votes for numbered 1,971, against 16, invalid, 2; on seminary discipline, human maturity, and personal responsibility (article 11), the votes for numbered 1,975, against 6.[108]

However, although the great majority supported the decree, a strong and powerful rejection of it remained in some quarters of the church. In a footnote to the history of the decree, Alberigo notes that Cardinal Antoniutti, prefect of the Congregation for Religious, wrote a letter to the rectors of institutes of study and religious colleges in Rome, stating that they were forbidden to allow their seminarians "to participate in any conferences and public debates of the experts of the council, in order that they might not be disturbed by the novelty of certain opinions."[109]

This letter was published in October in the Spanish-American review of ecclesiastical sciences of the Missionaries of the Heart of Mary, with the comment that some experts had expressed some extreme and doubtful ideas about priestly formation, and it was also reprinted in *Le Monde* at the beginning of November.[110] This letter is recorded in Fesquet's French publication of his journal of Vatican II, but not in its English translation.

Another important indicator of the response of the conservatives to the decree is the unusual fact that Archbishop Staffa, while being vice-president of the commission, was one of the most vehement critics of the decree it produced, the product of his own commission, and of the voting of the great majority of the council members.[111] The decree had been approved by the council, but its future had to be under question in light of the powerful but small lobby of its enemies. There were mixed reactions all round. Alberigo commented that the decree was "poor and destined to be forgotten."[112] However, Giuseppe Dossetti, while criticizing the lack of impact of the reforms mentioned in the schema, and the emphasis placed on the role of major seminaries, regarded as extremely important the principle that the episcopal conferences were given responsibility for developing their own programs. "If this decentralization is really carried out, many of the drawbacks of the decree itself will become unimportant" (Dossetti, "Per una valutazione," 80).[113]

PART II

MAJOR POINTS

When reading this decree in light of its history, it is obvious that *Optatam Totius* is notable not only for the major points it makes about priestly training, but also because of what the commission chose not to include, as well as the style of the document. It is in sharp contrast with the juridical and isolating asceticism of early drafts and approaches. The emphasis on the importance of taking account of both the local circumstances and the person to be formed in the seminary is a major movement from the past, as is the integrative approach to the program of priestly studies.

The emphasis on decentralization is an affirmation of the local episcopal conferences and of their commitment to nurturing the Christian community through the encouragement of vocations, of those in formation and of those who are involved in all aspects of the educational process. This is not a document that eschews the world; rather, it embraces the best of contemporary natural and social sciences in the training of priests for ministry in the world. The importance of a seminary and of diversity within seminary life also represents a significant move toward training priests in the present reality so that they may minister in more effective ways to the communities in which they serve. Adaptability has been recognized as a major criterion for mental health.[114] This is a document that takes the capacity for adaptability and a certain flexibility seriously in the formation of its priests.

Fundamentally the major contribution of this decree is its clear statement that the primary aim of priestly formation is simply to train the seminarian for priestly ministry in his own context. This training must be an integrated training of the whole human being. All earlier fragmentations of formational processes into spiritual, intellectual, and moral categories can no longer be allowed.[115]

Priestly training in the past suffered because of the juridical approach to priesthood in which the bishop had the fullness of the threefold ministry and the priest became "a depository of the sacramental powers."[116] *Optatam Totius* affirms the humanity of the priest. It stresses the relational context of seminary training and the responsibility of the bishop to adapt the program of studies to the particular local needs of personnel and ministry.

The contribution of *Optatam Totius* can also be summed up similarly in the principles of integration and concurrence that are prescribed for the threefold aspects of ministry: teacher, priest, pastor.[117] Forty years after the decree was promulgated, Lamberigts proposed that foundational to the decree are

1. Respect and appreciation for the past
2. Conformity with the decisions of the council
3. Attention to the new historical situation in which the church found itself.[118]

The decree is responsive to the concerns of the council members for a formation that is in continuity with the past, adaptable in the present context, and responsible for the future. It has to be understood in the context of the prevailing ecclesiology and worldview that permeated the council in its deliberative processes. The opening paragraph offers both continuity and the promise of the new.

PREFACE

The opening lines of the preface are "Animated by the spirit of Christ, this sacred synod is fully aware that the desired renewal of the whole Church depends to a great extent on the ministry of its priests." Priestly formation is immediately located in the context of the concrete event of the council, in contrast to the introduction of the original schema, which located the training of priests in the dogmatic and juridical context of the priesthood of Christ and his church.

This version states simply that the training of all candidates for the priesthood—for the diocesan clergy, religious orders, and different rites—requires renewal. It recognizes the value of seminaries, and it lays

down certain basic principles by which those regulations that long use
has shown to be sound may be strengthened and new elements that correspond to the constitutions and decrees of the council and to the
changed and changing conditions of our times can be added.

CHAPTER 1
PROGRAM OF PRIESTLY TRAINING TO BE UNDERTAKEN
BY EACH COUNTRY

Chapter 1 highlights the importance of priestly training for the realization of the council's aims. The changes proposed will not take place unless bishops and priests take them seriously and work to bring them
about. It is the primary responsibility of the bishop and the religious ordinary to bring about "a special 'program of priestly training' [which] is
to be undertaken by each country or rite" (*OT*, 1). This first chapter
makes the implementation of the decree the responsibility of the episcopal conference and the religious ordinary.[119]

The decentralization endorsed by the schema means that the universal laws underpinning priestly formation will be "adapted to the particular circumstances of the times and localities so that the priestly
training will always be in tune with the pastoral needs of those regions
in which the ministry is to be exercised" (*OT*, 1). The importance of
human and social development and the dynamic consequences of this
are implicit here.

Reference is made, in accord with the principle of Catholic continuity, to the proven regulations of the past. There is also an implicit acknowledgment of what is owed to the Council of Trent. It was through
Tridentine clerical training that the church received inspiration and
legislation.[120] At the same time, reform is needed, and *Optatam Totius*
offers a clear challenge to bishops globally to assume leadership in the
formation of clergy that is equal to the needs of the people they serve
locally. Episcopal conferences are challenged (or invited) to introduce
creative and far-reaching changes in this crucial area.[121]

Variations in the training programs of priests from country to
country and even region to region are called for as concrete circumstances and needs require; bishops are to work out their own seminary
and study system with the help of professional advisors. At the same

time, unity is to be preserved within a nation and regular revision is recommended. Thus Rome should be kept informed of significant changing contexts and developments in the program.

CHAPTER 2
URGENT FOSTERING OF PRIESTLY VOCATIONS

The decree was written with an awareness of the vocations crisis in
parts of Europe, but the bishops probably had no expectations of the
large-scale resignations of priests and the dearth of vocations in the
Western world in general.[122] This section may be seen as disappointing
by many. Articles 2 and 3 deal with vocations, but they say nothing new
and offer little inspiration in relation to the vocations crisis. This chapter represents the compromise between those bishops who wanted the
decree to elucidate "the signs of a vocation" and those who were reluc-
tant to list such signs and who simply preferred to speak of vocation as
grace from God.[123] The latter group argued that the call from God
would become apparent in a young man's life if he offered himself with
the right disposition.

The approach to vocation has to be understood in light of *Lumen
Gentium*, chapter 5, "On the Universal Call to Holiness," which deals
with vocation in general, with its apostolic aspect, and with particular
vocations to the various states: lay, married, single, clerical, religious. [124]
Optatam Totius recognizes that vocations to priesthood and religious life
flourish where Christian marriage and families thrive. "The principal
contributors to [vocations] are the families which, animated by the
spirit of faith and love and by the sense of duty, become a kind of initial
seminary, and the parishes in whose rich life the young people take
part" (*OT*, 2). Disappointing though this section is in many ways, an effort has been made to balance the human and the divine in the allusions
to what a vocation is.

In the fostering of vocations, article 2 takes into account the importance of "all the traditional means of common effort, such as urgent
prayer, Christian penance and a constantly more intensive training of
the faithful by preaching, by catechetical instructions or by the many
media of social communication that will show forth the need, the nature and the importance of the priestly vocation."

Ascetical and devotional practices are to be informed by good psychology and an understanding of the human person. Contemporary communication and technological techniques and approaches are to be used in vocations promotion. "No opportune aids are to be overlooked which modern psychological and sociological research has brought to light." The final paragraph in this section opens up wider boundaries and works against ghettoism or territorialism. This presents a new perspective in the approach; the needs of the global church are to be recognized in the allocation of priests:

> The work of fostering vocations should, in a spirit of openness, transcend the limits of individual dioceses, countries, religious families and rites. Looking to the needs of the universal Church, it should provide aid particularly for those regions in which workers for the Lord's vineyard are being requested more urgently. (*OT*, 2)

Underlining this chapter is the twofold conviction that God will never cease to sow the seeds of priestly vocation and that these seeds will be brought to full flowering for the people of God.[125]

Article 3 is a more difficult section for some cultures than for others. That minor seminaries are included here is mainly due to two different conceptions of what they meant among the bishops. For those in Latin countries such as Spain and Italy, the minor seminary was as much a seminary as the major seminary. With a relatively long history and identity in the Catholic community, these seminaries prepared boys for the priesthood. In non-European countries the minor seminary formed boys for the priesthood in a way that was conducive to the possible development of a priestly vocation. Entry into these "juniorates" did not assume that the decision to become a priest had been finally made. *Optatam Totius* follows the latter approach and indicates that the purpose of the minor seminary is to foster "the seeds of vocations."

Minor seminaries are accepted but not imposed. During the discussion on this issue in the third session, a number of bishops were concerned that life in minor seminaries might result in the foreclosure of the boys' human development. However, for some Latin episcopal conferences that minor seminaries were seen as an option rather than being given an unqualified endorsement was a revolutionary stance. Article 3 represents the compromise position.[126]

> Under the fatherly direction of the superiors, and with the proper cooperation of the parents, their daily routine should be in accord with the age, the character and the stage of development of adolescence and fully adapted to the norms of a healthy psychology. Nor should the fitting opportunity be lacking for social and cultural contacts and for contact with one's own family. (*OT*, 3)

The natural family setting is preferable, and it is only where this is not possible that boys should be admitted to minor seminary. The general education provided should enable boys to move into further education for professions or a career if they decide they do not have a vocation. The idea of late vocations is simply mentioned but not developed.

CHAPTER 3
SETTING UP OF MAJOR SEMINARIES

"Major seminaries are necessary for priestly formation" (*OT*, 4). This stark opening statement is in response to those bishops who believed that the major seminary was no longer a viable form of training. A number of bishops saw the major seminary as protective and isolating from the world and its reality. Other bishops argued that the seminary could provide a congenial atmosphere for authentic priestly training and spiritual growth.

The aim of pastoral formation is "the formation of true shepherds of souls after the model of our Lord Jesus Christ, teacher, priest and shepherd" (*OT*, 4). Theirs is to be the ministry of the word, of the Eucharist, and of pastoral service. The chief aspects of priestly education are drawn from the threefold office of Christ, and these are the basis of the Christocentric orientation that is characteristic of the council's approach to priestly ministry. The priest is consecrated not in order to enhance his status in the church, but in order to realize in service and self-sacrifice the saving mystery of Christ in his community.[127]

This section addresses the importance of the organic unity of the training with the integration of spiritual, intellectual, and pastoral formation: "All the forms of training, spiritual, intellectual, disciplinary, are to be ordered with concerted effort towards this pastoral end" (*OT*, 4). The call for the incorporation of the different aspects of formation precedes the specific details of the training because it is the integration that is foundational to the approach endorsed in the decree. This is probably the most urgent need of seminary training, and "to attain it all the administrators and teachers are to work zealously and harmoniously together, faithfully obedient to the authority of the bishop" (*OT*, 4).

Close cooperation between those in charge of the seminary as well as seminary staff is essential. All involved should be qualified not simply in their field, but also in their capacity to collaborate and communicate effectively with other staff and students. That staff members be able to work under the direction of the bishop is essential. This of course takes for granted the effective and mutual communication between the bishop and those involved in the formation process.[128]

Priestly formation is dependent not only on "wise laws" but, "most of all, on qualified educators," thus all involved administratively and educationally "are to be carefully prepared in sound doctrine, suitable pastoral experience and special spiritual and pedagogical training" (*OT*, 5). The concern is no longer to protect seminarians from harmful socio-cultural influences but through the balance of a disciplined lifestyle, an appropriate program of studies, and a relational and communicative competence to provide the necessary training for their pastoral work as priests.

The conciliar criticism of previous seminary education as too legalistic and theoretical is addressed in this article. The communal and collaborative aspects of seminaries emphasized in the varied submissions find expression in article 5. Effective relationships between faculty themselves and with students are an important aspect of seminary training.

Administrators, however, and teachers must be keenly aware of how much the success of the students' formation depends on their manner of thinking and acting. Under the rector's leadership they are to form a very closely knit community both in spirit and in activity and they are to constitute among themselves and

with the students that kind of family that will answer to the
Lord's prayer "That they be one" (cf. John 17:11) and that will
develop in the students a deep joy in their own vocation. (*OT*, 5)

To achieve and sustain their high level of academic learning, relational skills, and their own lifelong formation, the faculty themselves
need to take the recommendation for ongoing education seriously.
"Institutes, therefore, should be set up to attain this end. Or at least
courses are to be arranged with a proper program, and the meetings of
seminary directors are to take place at specified times" (*OT*, 5).

The sabbatical and study leave for seminary staff that will enable
them to continue their own development in "sound doctrine, suitable
pastoral experience and special spiritual and pedagogical training" is
not an option but an obligation if their responsibilities are taken seriously. The integration of all these intra- and interpersonal relational as
well as academic competencies are a counter to the legalistic, isolating,
and compartmentalized priestly formation programs and personnel that
were lamented in early drafts by many bishops.

The understanding of the seminary as "the heart of the diocese"
means that it needs to be supported by other priests and by the bishop,
"a true father," as well as being closely connected to the whole life of
the local church. Local clergy should feel at home in and be ready to
help in the seminary, and it should not be remote from the families and
communities related to all involved there. This section offers broad
outlines rather than specific details, which are the responsibility of
those in the local context.

Article 6 describes the "watchful concern" and "inquiry" that requires effective communication and discernment according to the age
and stage of the candidate. Firmness is essential, but this is tempered by
an informed discernment process. Each man's "spiritual, moral and intellectual qualifications," and "his appropriate physical and psychic
health—taking into consideration also possible hereditary deficiencies"
—need to be addressed, that the genuineness of his intention and any
obstacles to freedom of choice can be uncovered.

No matter how few priests there may be, there must be no pressure
for seminarians to remain if their vocation is in doubt. Along with the
seminary courses, university studies are recommended. These provide

candidates with the opportunity for an alternative career if their priestly vocation is not real. There is also a mandate for bishops to take serious interest in ex-seminarians, to help them in their future life and career, and there was strong support for this from bishops in the council.

The importance of various regions working together in setting up seminaries is another concern of article 7. Adaptation is integral to this article. Canon law desires a separate seminary for every diocese. This is obviously not possible in small dioceses or mission countries, so the setting up of regional or national seminaries is recommended in this section. The cooperative and collaborative establishment of such inter-diocesan seminaries is no longer to be under papal authority as before. Instead their statutes are to be drawn up by particular bishops and approved by Rome.[129]

Another new aspect of *Optatam Totius* is in its recognition of the importance of the size of the seminary. There must not be so many students that "the personal formation of each" is problematic. In this case, in order to reduce regimentation and foster responsibility, students can be organized into smaller living groups so that seminarians can run the discipline in their own small groups. Both large institutions and smaller group living are endorsed in this section. The emphasis is on training seminarians for full responsibility. The general principles for these options are proposed in the decree, but the process for groups to be formed and integrated into seminary life is to be in the hands of the seminary administrators.

CHAPTER 4
THE CAREFUL DEVELOPMENT OF THE SPIRITUAL TRAINING

The necessary spiritual formation of the seminarian into the mystery of Christ is addressed here. Article 8 draws on a genuine Christian ontology and authentic Christian mysticism for its sources. This was missing in the formation approach that many bishops were concerned to leave in the past.[130] The article expresses the conviction that this priestly formation cannot take place in monastic seclusion, nor can it be dissected into disparate parts for simpler implementation. Rather, personal formation must be integrated with intellectual and pastoral instruction and pastoral praxis.

The spiritual training should be closely connected with the doctrinal and pastoral, and, with the special help of the spiritual director, should be imparted in such a way that the students might learn to live in an intimate and unceasing union with the Father through His Son Jesus Christ in the Holy Spirit. (*OT*, 8)

The goal of seminary training is the formation of the whole person combining theological education with opportunities to develop intra- and interpersonally, in relation with one's God and with one's community in one's pastoral work.

Essential elements of a scriptural and Christocentric spiritual life are expressed in terms of internal attitudes, "They should so live His paschal mystery themselves that they can initiate into it the flock committed to them." Development of a Trinitarian perspective is important; seminarians should "learn to live in an intimate and unceasing union with the Father through His Son Jesus Christ in the Holy Spirit." Devotions such as the recitation of the breviary, contemplation of the Word of God, and veneration of Mary, along with the ministerial praxis of finding Christ in the needy together nourish a gospel way of life.

The priestly spirituality sanctioned in article 8 is clearly not an emotional piety but one directed toward developing an authentic spirituality for ministry.[131] While specially trained spiritual directors should be provided, an education in developmental psychology is also needed in case seminarians develop "only a religious affectation." The priestly role can be learned at the expense of forming a priestly identity that is integrated to the identity of the seminarian. The importance of "sound psychology and pedagogy" discussed later in article 11 is relevant here if an understanding of the development of the emotions in the formational process is to be grasped.[132]

The theological foundations of both articles 8 and 9 reflect the profoundly Christ-centered and ecclesial basis of the decree. Seminarians "should learn to take part with a generous heart in the life of the whole Church in accord with what St. Augustine wrote: 'to the extent that one loves the Church of Christ, to that extent does he possess the Holy Spirit'" (*OT*, 9). To understand this section, the ecclesiology of *Lumen Gentium* is vital. The church is "mystery." It is the community "in whose social structures and activities God is actively present."[133] If priests view their relationship with their institutional church in human terms alone then they are selling the priesthood short. The mystery of the church is the mystery of salvation in which ecclesial community and cooperation are an expression of Augustine's affirmation that in the life of the church we have the spirit of Christ.[134]

Although the decree takes the developmental and sociocultural aspects of the human person seriously, it takes the ascetical and transcendent aspects of the spiritual life even more seriously. The evangelical counsels are an essential part of the formational commitment. Seminarians are to be "formed in priestly obedience, in a simple way of life and in the spirit of self-denial that they are accustomed to, giving up willingly even those things which are permitted but are not expedient, and to conform themselves to Christ crucified" (*OT*, 9). It is mandatory that the radical self-giving that is required for the priestly life be made clear. "The students are to be made clearly aware of the burdens they will be undertaking, and no problem of the priestly life is to be concealed from them."

The core of article 10 is the eschatological aspect of celibacy, its witness to the reign of God present and yet to come, along with the striving for an undivided and self-transcending love. The concern here is to present celibacy not in legal terms but as gift of the Spirit. This is the reason priests "embrace the Lord with an undivided love altogether befitting the new covenant, bear witness to the resurrection of the world to come (cf. Luke 20:36), and obtain a most suitable aid for the continual exercise of that perfect charity whereby they can become all things to all men in their priestly ministry" (*OT*, 10).

Seminarians are not to dedicate themselves to celibacy without due consideration of "the duties and dignity of Christian matrimony, which is a sign of the love between Christ and the Church." Dangers to celibacy are to be addressed and the students should, with "suitable safeguards, both divine and human...learn to integrate their renunciation of marriage in such a way that they may suffer in their lives and work not only no harm from celibacy but rather acquire a deeper mastery of soul and body and a fuller maturity, and more perfectly receive the blessedness spoken of in the Gospel" (*OT*, 10).

To appreciate the structure and content of this article, it is essential to see it in the context of the conciliar discussions and processes. The original succinct section on priestly chastity had to be expanded at the request of the bishops who wanted something more substantial. They knew that their seminarians would face the contemporary questioning and doubts about the value of such a vow.

Requests that a scriptural dimension be offered that would place celibacy beyond the juridical level, for its expression as a charism of priestly service and for an ecumenical aspect to be acknowledged, played a part in the development of article 10, which provides a multi-faceted presentation of celibacy. It offers both a positive and a practical education for chastity that would enable seminarians to be helped by "suitable safeguards, both divine and human" so that it would not be a negative experience but one that would enable them to "acquire a deeper mastery of soul and body and a fuller maturity, and more perfectly receive the blessedness spoken of in the Gospel."

In order to espouse the evangelical counsels of poverty, celibacy, and obedience that have been described in the decree as integral to the spiritual formation of seminarians, an effective educational model must be used. Article 11 states that the "norms of Christian education are to be religiously observed and properly complemented by the newer findings of sound psychology and pedagogy." Maturity and responsibility are important goals that involve all aspects of the human person. Emotional, intellectual, developmental, and physical well-being must be addressed explicitly in seminary programs.

As the way to maturity is always through an inevitable immaturity, in order to come to the "self-mastery" and "strength of character" that are endorsed in the decree, counseling may be an important option within the seminary program. Seminary discipline is united with spiritual formation to develop a lifestyle that will sustain priestly commitment, responsibility, and initiative in the exercise of ministry. "The whole pattern of seminary life, permeated with a desire for piety and silence and a careful concern for mutual help, must be so arranged that it provides, in a certain sense, an initiation into the future life which the priest shall lead" (*OT*, 11).

Contemporary psychology and pedagogy are recommended, not so much for study in themselves as disciplines, but as foundational for informing and developing all aspects of the formation program, its structure, process, and content. Seminary staff should be able to communicate effectively and ready to contribute to the communal discipline of a common life shared, rather than allow it to regress to the exercise of authoritarian discipline.

Education to full human maturity is integral to priestly formation. A conciliar criticism of seminary training was its insufficient development of human qualities and strengths. Thus seminarians are to esteem and to practice the virtues of "sincerity of mind, a constant concern for justice, fidelity to one's promises, refinement in manners, modesty in speech coupled with charity" (*OT*, 11).

To some extent the time-span of formation is negotiable. Article 12 mentions three special periods that a bishop may require his student to go through. It does not insist that the decision relating to them is the matter of the episcopal conference, even in principle. However, it is obviously desirable to maintain some degree of uniformity in a country or region.

A spiritual period that enables a "more intense introduction to the spiritual life" is required. This may come at any time in the student's formation. Also, a bishop may decide to use a different environment to test a candidate's fitness. This can be an introduction to pastoral work. The bishop may also raise the minimum age for ordination, or require that ordinands spend more time in diaconate before priestly ordination.[135] All of these are dependent upon the local circumstances and they are recommendations only.

This whole section on spiritual training can be critiqued for its lack of emphasis on the Holy Spirit and on the love that seminarians should be trained to reflect in their lives. Although love is referred to in the decree, it is primarily in terms of "charity," which distances it from its important relational dimension. This section can be effectively understood only in conjunction with article 5, in connection with the formation of "a very closely knit community both in spirit and in activity" fostered by seminary staff and responded to by the students who pass through the seminary.[136]

CHAPTER 5
THE REVISION OF ECCLESIASTICAL STUDIES

Chapter 5 focuses on the revision of ecclesiastical studies. The section opens by establishing that the educational standard expected of the seminarian is that of university entrance. Seminarians are required to know the liturgical language of their rite and enough Latin to read ecclesiastical documents;[137] scriptural languages are recommended. It is up to each bishops' conference to decide on the obligatory nature of biblical languages, though a knowledge of these is to be encouraged.

Both academic and pastoral courses should be oriented toward priestly ministry. Article 13 proposes that "before beginning specifically ecclesiastical subjects, seminarians should be equipped with that humanistic and scientific training which young men in their own countries are wont to have as a foundation for higher studies." The mystery of Christ and the history of salvation must be central in these studies, which also consider the realities of the contemporary world. The innovation in this section is the introductory course, flexible in its duration and content, recommended in article 14:

> That this vision be communicated to the students from the outset of their training, ecclesiastical studies are to be begun with an introductory course which should last for an appropriate length of time. In this initiation to ecclesiastical studies the mystery of salvation should be so proposed that the students perceive the meaning, order, and pastoral end of their studies. At the same time they should be helped to establish and penetrate their own entire lives with faith and be strengthened in embracing their vocation with a personal dedication and a joyful heart.

All studies during the seminary years should be undertaken with an awareness of the current ecumenical efforts taking place in the local and global church.

Article 15 addresses the vexed question of philosophical studies. The position taken in the decree is clear.

> The philosophical disciplines are to be taught in such a way that the students are first of all led to acquire a solid and coherent knowledge of [the human person], the world, and of God, relying on a philosophical patrimony which is perennially valid and taking into account the philosophical investigations of later ages. This is especially true of those investigations which exercise a greater influence in their own nations.

In the past, seminary professors identified a system of thought with a method of teaching rather than with the apostolic requirements of young men studying for the priesthood.[138] The exclusive use of Scholasticism was no longer an appropriate way to train seminarians for contemporary ministry. Because of the number of renewals that sprang up in the church—biblical, patristic, catechetical, liturgical, and apostolic—there came a questioning of the scholastic method.[139] Theology and philosophy had been too distinct and dualistic in implication. The "over-intellectual treatment of out-of-date and abstract problems can no longer have a place in the curriculum."[140]

The effort to develop an integrated approach to academic and pastoral formation is well presented in this article:

> In the very manner of teaching there should be stirred up in the students a love of rigorously searching for the truth and of maintaining and demonstrating it, together with an honest recognition of the limits of human knowledge. Attention must be carefully drawn to the necessary connection between philosophy and the true problems of life, as well as the questions which preoccupy the minds of the students. Likewise students should be helped to perceive the links between the subject-matter of philosophy and the mysteries of salvation which are considered in theology under the higher light of faith. (*OT*, 15)

There is here no attempt to address the question of teaching philosophy on its own or in conjunction with other studies. This has been left open. However, the separate study of philosophy in a period and program distinct from the theology is not supported by the decree.[141]

Where the introductory course is well done, solid foundations for the other courses, academic and pastoral, will have been laid. Seminarians will have acquired a fairly good general idea of what their priestly ministry involves. "Into this can be integrated an acquaintance with philosophical thinking and a broad understanding of what it means to be human, of the universe, and of God."[142] This article doubled its length as a consequence of the number of submissions and interventions received during the conciliar debate.

Article 16 is proposed as the high point of the decree.[143] It expresses the spirit of the decree most clearly.

The theological disciplines, in the light of faith and under the guidance of the Magisterium of the Church, should be so taught that the students will correctly draw out Catholic doctrine from divine revelation, profoundly penetrate it, make it the food of their own spiritual lives, and be enabled to proclaim, explain, and protect it in their priestly ministry. (*OT*, 16)

Seminarians must develop their understanding of Catholic doctrine by drawing from these sources and not simply be satisfied with derivative formulae. They must fully understand the doctrine, not simply memorize it, because it must inform them as they face the problems of their world. They have to make it fruitful for their lives.

Faith and reason are needed for priests to understand their vocation and mission most effectively. Seminarians are to study not only for their own personal development and understanding of church teachings but also for others, so that they can communicate and minister in the embodied service of the word. Scripture is affirmed as the "soul of theology" and the theological tradition is to be presented in the context of the history of the church.

Dogmatic theology should be so arranged that these biblical themes are proposed first of all. Next there should be opened up to the students what the Fathers of the Eastern and Western Church have contributed to the faithful transmission and development of the individual truths of revelation. The further history of dogma should also be presented, account being taken of its relation to the general history of the Church. (*OT*, 16)

This is to be the source of effective ministry as, through their studies they "learn to seek the solutions to human problems under the light of revelation, to apply the eternal truths of revelation to the changeable conditions of human affairs and to communicate them in a way suited to men of our day" (*OT*, 16).

In their training they learn to experience the liturgy and life of the church as the expression of the mystery of Christ that is alive and at work in church and society. They are to be trained to translate theology into concrete terms of life and place human problems in the context of the saving mystery of Christ. Canon law and the history of the church are to be presented as expressions of church life. Ecumenism and instruction in non-Christian religions, especially those the seminarian is likely to meet in ministry, are to be engaged in. They are to be taught the positive elements in these religions.[144] The ideal is expressed here in a most comprehensive way, but how it should be done is the task of faculty to discern.

Article 18 emphasizes the importance of personal integration of studies. It is not so much the transfer of knowledge that is the issue here, but rather the transformation of the seminarian in the transmission process. It is not "a mere communication of ideas" but "a true and intimate formation of the students" that is at the core of the chapter. The important thing is that students take their own education seriously; "an excessive multiplication of courses and lectures" is to be avoided if it detracts from the formational purpose.[145]

In article 18 the obligation is laid on bishops to see that promising students are given an opportunity for more advanced study in either the sacred sciences or other fields. A threefold qualification is proposed. It is through the criteria of "temperament, virtue and ability" that the selection for further studies must be made. The importance of priests being able to communicate with the rapidly increasing number of educated people in the world is emphasized once again.

CHAPTER 6
THE PROMOTION OF STRICTLY PASTORAL TRAINING

Chapter 6 insists on pastoral training as an integral part of formation through the use of modern methods and with the provision of practical experience. Article 19 states that the spiritual and intellectual formation that seminarians have received during the seminary years must be given its practical expression in ministry. They must "be diligently instructed in those matters which are particularly linked to the sacred ministry, especially in catechesis and preaching, in liturgical worship and the administration of the sacraments, in works of charity, in assisting the erring and the unbelieving, and in the other pastoral functions."

This pastoral training could start in the first year and continue throughout. However, practical training must be given in all the priestly functions. For the ministry of the word, they are to be trained in catechetics and preaching; for the liturgy of the word, through appropriate liturgical training; for the office of pastoral guidance, through training in works of charity and the lay apostolate, "in assisting the erring and the unbelieving," and in the art of spiritual direction, with special reference to religious men and women.[146]

An important aspect of this pastoral formation is to develop in the seminarian the art of listening and those attitudes and skills that are integral to dialogue. The formation described in the decree has its fruit in the priest's capacity to help Christians in their own journeys. Priests are called to deepen their capacities for human relationships in the concrete circumstances of the ever-changing as well as the constant aspects of the lives of those to whom they minister, in whatever mode of priestly ministry they are called to exercise.

In order to communicate the faith and to minister effectively in the varied ways demanded by life, "they should also be taught to use the aids which the disciplines of pedagogy, psychology, and sociology can provide, according to correct methodology and the norms of ecclesiastical authority" (*OT*, 20). Seminarians should be aware of the cultural and societal pressures on the laity in their life situations so that they can engage more effectively in their education. It is essential, therefore that they be aware of some of these pressures in their own lives; otherwise their lack of self-understanding will impede their capacity to be aware of and to attend to the concerns of others.

The article reminds seminarians of the need to train for future ministry, even in vacation periods, "by opportune pastoral projects." Practical training is not to be limited to the acquisition of techniques within the seminary. Experience must be gained in the field, subject to the judgment of the bishop and under the guidance of those skilled in pastoral work. Seminarians are encouraged to engage in pastoral work beyond the narrow circle of their own immediate sphere of activity and to look beyond "limits of diocese, nation or rite" to the whole church, to engage in collaborative initiatives and to be encouraged in developing a missionary awareness in their ministry. Practical norms are presented in terms of their pastoral projects:

> These should be carried out in accordance with the age of the
> students and local conditions, and with the prudent judgment
> of the bishops, methodically and under the leadership of men

skilled in pastoral work, the surpassing power of supernatural means being always remembered. (*OT*, 20)

There is a "rather dry caution at the end of [the section on] pastoral formation."[147] It calls attention to the overriding importance of the supernatural. Hurley questions the value of this. He believes that the word "supernatural" is never inspiring.

> But we have to live with it until we find a better word. The reality does deserve a better word, for the reality is all we mean by union with Christ—his presence with us and our striving to know him and the power of his resurrection, that we may share his sufferings, becoming like him in his death so as to attain the resurrection from the dead (Phil. 3:10–11).[148]

CHAPTER 7
TRAINING TO BE ACHIEVED AFTER THE COURSE OF STUDIES

The final mini-chapter of just one short article reminds episcopal conferences that priestly formation is an ongoing process and that provision must be made for continuing studies for all priests.[149] Article 21 reminds bishops of those critical years just after ordination. The newly ordained can be confronted with new and unpredictable problems, especially given the rapid progress in theological and pastoral sciences. Ongoing pastoral opportunities are essential for "younger clergy." The provision of pastoral institutes, regular meetings, courses, and workshops is implicit in the decree and it is the responsibility of episcopal conferences to provide such opportunities that address the organic unity of spiritual, intellectual, and pastoral influences to help the newly ordained grow more authentically into their priestly ministry and life.

CONCLUSION

This conclusion came as a consequence of the bishops' recommendation that there should be a means of drawing all the articles together into a concluding summary.

The Fathers of this Holy Synod have pursued the work begun by the Council of Trent. While they confidently entrust to seminary administrators and teachers the task of forming the future priests of Christ in the spirit of the renewal promoted by this sacred synod, they earnestly exhort those who are preparing for the priestly ministry to realize that the hope of the Church and the salvation of souls is being committed to them. They urge them also to receive the norms of this decree willingly and thus to bring forth most abundant fruit which will always remain.

The hoped-for renewal of the church and the effectiveness of its work in the world are bound up with the proper training of priests. Trent knew this, as did Vatican II; hence directors and professors of seminaries along with seminarians and priests themselves are reminded of their responsibility to contribute to the developing understanding of their own priesthood and of the priesthood of Christ in the spirit of the council's renewal.

PART III
IMPLEMENTATION

Key areas in *Optatam Totius*—of adaptation and decentralization, of the importance of priestly identity, of seminary re-visioning, vocations, pastoral formation, and training—were much more potentially demanding on all those involved in the training of priests than might have been recognized when the decree was promulgated. At first it was enthusiastically received. One of the first people to speak in support of *Optatam Totius* was not a bishop but one of the Protestant observers, Oscar Cullmann, professor of New Testament at the Universities of Basel and Paris.[150] In his summing up of the council at a German press conference at the end of the fourth session in 1965, Cullmann singled out this text as one of the best and most important. The primacy of place given to the study of scripture was a key issue for him. He believed that this decree had the greatest potential to influence the implementation of the new directions of the council. He also saw it in terms of the ecumenical cooperation that was not simply desirable but essential for Christian churches if renewal was to take place.[151]

The positive evaluation of the schema was primarily related to the fact that through the debates and deliberative processes the commission had been able to construct a reasonable balance between respect for tradition and adaptation to a new and changing context of priestly ministry and life for which training programs needed to be developed. The inclusion of the human sciences, the integrating approach to the teaching of philosophy and theology, along with the emphasis on the human person and on the personal formation of seminarians bore witness to the fact that this part of the council's proceedings was intended to renew the church and to bring seminary training up to date.[152]

The opportunity for each bishop to adapt priestly formation to his own diocesan context was seen by most council members as the major contribution of the decree. In writing about the achievements of Vatican II, council expert Edward Schillebeeckx singled out *Optatam Totius* for its innovation in regard to the curriculum. The foundation of salvation history, "a kind of overall saving-historical picture of the redemptive ministry in which we are living"[153] is integrated with the teaching of philosophy and theology. These studies are centered in humankind, in the world, and in God.

Contemporary philosophy is to be taken into account along with scholastic philosophy and "attention drawn to both the difference and the connection between a person's philosophical appraisal and their religious outlook."[154] The biblical and patristic foundations for theological studies open up new directions for a ministerial response to the needs of the modern world. "New also is the fact that this arrangement of the curriculum is not regarded as a definitive rule but incorporates the principle of continual *aggiornamento* in the rule itself."[155] New directions and greater flexibility in seminary training programs and lifestyle were recognized as a major benefit for episcopal conferences.

In their reviews of the first decade following the council, commentators point out that the document seemed to meet some of the formation needs and continued to be reasonably well accepted at the local level. However, there was some backlash initially with regard to the use of Latin in liturgy in seminaries. As soon after the council as January 1966 the Congregation of Seminaries published a decree requiring the use of Latin as a liturgical language in all seminaries of the Latin rite. Many seminaries had been using English in the liturgy for some time and the new decree seemed to be a step back to the past. Apparently this decree had actually been drawn up before the end of the council.[156]

Implications of the broadening of seminary faculties in terms of employment of qualified laity, men and women, caused some uneasiness among the curia. Cardinal Ottaviani, secretary to the Supreme Sacred Congregation of the Holy Office, is reported to have said in an interview with a curial official that he was "concerned about overboldness on the part of the laity" and he expressed the opinion that "some of them might overreach themselves and try to dominate the clergy, judging from what they were already saying" (*The Catholic Transcript*, December 24, 1965).[157] Such comments from members of the hierarchy surely carried ominous overtones for future collaboration between the members

of the ordained and common priesthood and for inclusiveness of training programs and of personnel employed.

In the years that followed the council it became obvious that, while
the decree dealt directly with the training of the diocesan clergy, much
more needed to be done in relation to the training of clerical religious
candidates. *Optatam Totius* had been intended for all rites, Eastern as
well as Western. Members of the Eastern rites and of Asian nations
were able to argue that not much consideration had been given to their
traditions and outlooks because the decree is thoroughly Western in
style and thought. As a member of a religious order, and as a CSS member himself, Hurley's response to such comments was that people would
need to go beneath the Western thought categories and style for the reality that was being addressed in the decree.[158]

Over the past forty years, at both the international and national levels, a significant amount of writing and research has addressed both the
theological foundations and practical principles and practices for priestly
training that are integral to *Optatam Totius*. Each decade has made its
own contribution to the developing understanding of the importance of
the decree within its own ecclesial and sociocultural framework.

VATICAN AND OTHER CHURCH DOCUMENTS
ON THE TRAINING OF PRIESTS

The decree has generated a number of additional documents from the
Roman curial level and from national or religious congregational levels
that refer to its contents and its implementation. A number of general
plans and specific programs have come from these two sources.[159] In
January 1970 the Sacred Congregation for Catholic Education issued
the *Ratio Fundamentalis Institutionis Sacerdotalis* (*Ratio Fundamentalis*)
concerning priestly formation. In this document the term "seminary" is
used in terms of "institution organized for the formation of priests."
This usage is symptomatic of the beginning of what has been described
as "the erosion of the distinction that had been drawn between diocesan and religious order institutions."[160] The two are conflated into one
approach in which the normative understanding appears to be that of
the diocesan seminary. This is a consistent approach in most subsequent
Roman documents.[161]

The foundational document of 1970 was followed by a set of guidelines from the Sacred Congregation for Catholic Education, "The Basic Plan for Priestly Formation." The "Basic Plan" takes up the recognition of major seminaries that was explicit in the decree in the single sentence: "Major seminaries are necessary for priestly formation" (*OT*, 4). The Plan describes as primary the role of the seminary as community and way of life rather than as an institution. It does however emphasize some "institutional" aspects of the seminary: professors, superiors, and courses of study. It also deals with spiritual formation and pastoral ministry, both as essential components of seminary life.[162]

In the closing section of "The Basic Plan for Priestly Formation" there is a recommendation in support of the extra spiritual preparation recommended in *Optatam Totius*.[163] It is a suggestion that the congregation would like "to be followed and gradually to become part of the normal seminary practice in a solid and lasting way."

> Experience shows that a period of preparation for the seminary, given over exclusively to spiritual formation, is not only not superfluous but can bring surprising results. There is evidence from seminaries in which the number of candidates has suddenly gone up. In these the people responsible attribute this to such a brave initiative. This period of spiritual apprenticeship is welcomed by the students. It appears that it is the diocesan authorities who are rather opposed to this spiritual propaedeutic period. This seems to come from a lack of priests and a view that it would be foolish to institute such a practice. In reality, were it tried they would soon become convinced of its benefits. Permit us to insist, in conclusion, that this suggestion be tried.[164]

During the next decade, the Congregation for Catholic Education issued five documents that addressed specific aspects of the "Basic Plan." In 1972, in relation to philosophical formation, the Congregation published "The Teaching of Philosophy in Seminaries"[165] (chapter 11 of the "Basic Plan"). This document defended the need for philosophical studies as formative of the type of thinking that is competent to deal with theological problems, and as a means for real dialogue with non-believers. It gives guidelines for the teaching of philosophy in the modern world which shuts itself off "always more and more to the problem of transcendence" and "is becoming more adverse to authentic philosophical thought, particularly to metaphysical speculation which alone is able to reach absolute values." It gives an example of the integration of philosophy and theology, and shows how they can be connected with the social sciences.

That a document such as this was thought necessary may be due to the fact that while Thomas was "rediscovered" as an important theologian at the beginning of the sixteenth century, he had an uneven popularity over the centuries. In the late seventeenth and eighteenth centuries he faded once again into relative obscurity. His "second 'rediscovery' in the nineteenth century had to do primarily with the fact that the Catholic Church was looking for a viable alternative for the Enlightenment. Bearing this in mind, the waning of interest in Thomas that is evident from the mid-1950s should not elicit much in the way of surprise."[166] The relationship of twentieth-century philosophy with postmodernism certainly put scholastic philosophy under further pressure in the seminary as well as in the academy.[167]

In 1974, the congregation published a document entitled "Guidelines for Formation for Priestly Celibacy."[168] The concern once again was to support the stance taken toward celibacy in *Optatam Totius* and to give seminarians guidelines for receiving the "precious gift which God gives to those he calls" (chapter 8). These guidelines also offer a theological explanation of the meaning of celibacy in priesthood, and the document outlines three goals of seminary training in light of this: human, Christian, and priestly maturity. These guidelines do not deal with issues of intimacy or sexual expression. There is little evidence in them of any input from the social sciences to help to understand the meaning of the vow. In these guidelines "reason and rationality are to reign supreme... where emotional expression and affective intimacy are ignored as if non-existent."[169] The atmosphere conveyed is that of a community of "cool, rational people... capable, no doubt of social niceties but [they] keep their emotional and sexual distance."[170]

The abstraction of the approach taken by these guidelines gives the expectation of ignorance, or even psychological repression, rather than one of a community of adults capable of authentic interaction and mutual relationships. This colors the response to the practical guidelines that are proposed to help in fostering celibacy in seminary life. The problem is that, as in most of the ecclesiastical documents on priestly formation, the basis of the human, intellectual, and spiritual training is focused almost exclusively on ascetical aspects of formation at the expense of social sciences and an understanding of developmental implications for genuine human interaction and personal and communal growth.[171]

"The Theological Formation of Future Priests"[172] was published in 1976. This document is parallel to the former one on philosophy. In the contemporary world, where materialism is rife and technology can seduce people's worldviews, theology must be taught so as to be comprehensible and enticing to contemporary men and women who are more familiar with the intricacies and "alternative" realities of cyberspace and of cyber games, for example, than with the mysteries of a transcendent God. This fifty-page document describes the problems of forming seminarians in a time of "deep cultural and theological changes." It addresses the tasks of formation in such a complex context and the importance of theological research and training. It also addresses the nature and function of theology and its relationships with the magisterium, with philosophy, and with the human and natural sciences.

Two documents appeared in 1979, "Instruction on Liturgical Formation in Seminaries"[173] and a circular letter "Concerning Some of the More Urgent Aspects of Spiritual Formation in Seminaries." The instruction treats both the theoretical and practical aspects of liturgical formation and describes the liturgical topics to be discussed in seminary courses: the nature of the liturgy, including its instructive and pastoral dimensions, and its history; the Mass and the sacraments. This four-part, seventy-five-section document "offers suitable directives and norms so that the liturgical life and the study of the sacred liturgy in institutions of priestly formation might be better adapted to modern needs."[174] The circular letter elaborates on the "Basic Plan" in four fundamental areas: prayer, Eucharist, penance, and Marian devotion.

Another document which followed from the congregation was the "Instruction on the Study of the Fathers of the Church in the Formation of Priests" (1990). Seminarians are reminded that "to follow the living tradition of the fathers does not mean hanging on to the past as such, but adhering to the line of faith with an enthusiastic sense of security and freedom, while maintaining a constant fidelity toward that which is foundational." [175]

The recommendation in *Optatam Totius* for the training of seminary educators is followed up in another document, "Directives Concerning the Preparation of Seminary Educators" (1994).[176] The congregation recognized the shortage of seminary educators and that the task had become even more difficult than before. The document examines the qualities of seminary staff along with the allied roles of those involved in the formational community. The place of lay men and women and their contribution to the training program is affirmed. The world in which the laity live and relate is an important backdrop to the "didactic and pedagogic" task in the seminary. The need for formation personnel to collaborate with personnel of other dioceses and regions, especially in regard to sharing personnel, is recommended.

INTERNATIONAL SYNODS AND THE FORMATION OF PRIESTS

The decade immediately following the council was a crisis period for priests and therefore for those in charge of or working in seminaries. Questioning abounded and certainties were becoming fewer than ever before.[177] From 1969 to 1971 preparations for a synod of bishops on issues related to the ministerial priesthood took place. On November 30, 1971, the synod issued a document titled, "On the Ministerial Priesthood," in which church teachings on the ministerial priesthood were reaffirmed. In this document the bishops describe both the strengths and the struggles of priests in the present era. The purpose of the document is "to set forth briefly some principles of the Church's teaching on the ministerial priesthood which are at present more urgent, together with some guidelines for pastoral practice."[178]

While some of the issues the bishops address, such as the presbyteral and sacerdotal identity of the priest, are more related to *Presbyterorum Ordinis* than to *Optatam Totius*, it is in the section on guidelines that both conciliar documents seem to be under reassessment and even revision. The title of the section "Guidelines for the Priestly Life and Ministry" has changed the emphasis from ministry to life. It is

an all but deliberate repudiation of the development at Vatican II which finally led to the formulation, *de presbyterorum ministerio et vita*, (On the *Ministry* and Life of Priests). The phrase, the ministerial priesthood, by itself seems to make the priestly cat-

egory again the central, if not exclusive, one for understanding
the ordained ministry. The breadth of the threefold office and
especially the focus on the pastoral as a unifying factor for the
ordained ministry disappear. The situation becomes more confused when "ministerial priesthood" is used interchangeably
with "the priestly ministry."[179]

Commentators on synodal documents and the guidelines have expressed their concern for what they believe is a loss of the prophetic and
pastoral dimensions of the Vatican II understanding of priesthood in
both *Presbyterorum Ordinis* and *Optatam Totius* in subsequent decades.[180]

It was in 1971 that the United States edition of the *Program of
Priestly Formation* (*PPF*), in accordance with the *Ratio Fundamentalis*
and the "Basic Plan," was published by the National Conference of
Catholic Bishops. This set of guidelines for priestly formation then became normative for all U.S. seminaries and, as mentioned earlier, clerical religious institutes have also accepted it as such. Described as "a
living document,"[181] it has been revised over the years through the input
of those involved in the formation process and through subsequent documentation received from the Vatican on seminaries.[182] This reviewing
process has taken place on a regular basis until the present time.[183]

In the first edition of the United States' *Program of Priestly
Formation* there was a section dedicated to religious clergy, "The
Religious Priest's Formation." There is a preface that indicates that the
Conference of Major Superiors of Men agreed to accept the *Program of
Priestly Formation* as the recommended program for the formation of
religious priests, if a short section which they had prepared on religious
life were included (part 4). This was once again, an apparent consequence of the earlier conflation of documents in the *Ratio Fundamentalis*. It is notable that "within the short period between the
publication of the *Ratio* and the publication of the first edition of the
PPF, 'seminaries' of the orders and congregations found their training
for the first time in history seeming to require episcopal approval."[184]
This is surely a significant change for religious orders, and it also has
ramifications for the effort to develop and maintain a distinct spirituality for diocesan priests which is not dependent on the monastic heritage
of the Tridentine era. It certainly has important implications for clerical religious.

A noteworthy aspect of part 4 of the *Program of Priestly Formation* was its focus on an ascetical spirituality associated with religious or monastic life and on the evangelical counsels of poverty, chastity, and obedience at the expense of any sense of ministerial activities that identified the religious cleric apart from diocesan priests.[185] The third edition dropped the section on religious priests altogether because they share "an increasingly pluriform priesthood" and their training needs do not differ. Any sense of a spirituality that is integral to the ministerial priesthood itself is absent from the *Program of Priestly Formation*.

A further insight into the effect of this emphasis is the statement at the opening of the fifth edition of the *Program of Priestly Formation*, 2006, in which the Conference of Major Superiors of Men indicate that "the committee which drafted this revision of the document has included sections dealing with religious life." In looking at the list of contents, this inclusion is not readily obvious. The statement then adds, "Although academic requirements may be similar for both religious and diocesan priests, the religious priest will understand the ordained role and ministry as reflecting the charism and spiritual tradition of his religious institute."[186] While most religious clerics have their own training programs, which may build on and add to that of the diocesan priest, the absence of references to these in this context leaves the question of pastoral formation open to misinterpretation as it stands.

Again, a reading of the various chapters in this document does not immediately evidence any application to religious clerics. The primary reference is to diocesan seminarians, with just a few inclusions of references to religious ordinaries or religious governance, with no further elaboration apart from their inclusion. Section 19 treats of "Priesthood: Diocesan and Religious" but primarily it points out the similarities between the two, "though they can appear to be very different." The specific mention here seems to be to remind clerical religious that they are "subject to the same formation laid out in this program of *PPF*." This was particularly the case in the sections on human, spiritual, and intellectual formation where some sense of the difference might have been alluded to.[187]

Although a separate treatment of novitiates was included in the first edition, in the 2006 edition the period of preparation for training in spiritual life does not include novitiates.[188] There is no mention of novitiates in the headings or index, but in the "Stages in Preparation for Theology" (141–63) there is a mention of high school and college seminaries.

The significant post–Vatican II changes that have taken place in clerical religious orders in terms of ministry and lifestyle are more obvious than the *Program of Priestly Formation* might indicate in terms of implementation of Vatican II directions. One example might suffice to explicate this: religious order schools "have relocated in urban areas and abandoned their freestanding status by establishing important relationships with similar institutions and sometimes with prestigious universities; these actions plus the decline in vocations have led to the amalgamation of institutions and even to the closing of many."[189]

The new self-understanding that seems to be a consequence of the Conference of Major Superiors of Men's stance with regard to conflation of priestly and religious identity, which does not appear to have been challenged or systematically argued in any major way, is a point that surely invites further consideration by both bishops and major superiors. The council members were forthright in their resistance to the monastic style of priestly formation and spirituality for the diocesan priest. One can only wonder what has happened to this insistence subsequently, especially in light of the formation programs endorsed in the various editions of the *Program of Priestly Formation.*

In 1990 another international synod of bishops took place in Rome to discuss "The Formation of Priests in the Circumstances of Today." The synod addressed issues such as the identity and mission of the ordained priesthood and the consequent implications for seminary formation. The preparation period for this involved a number of global consultative processes on the question: What is the identity and mission of the ordained priesthood and what are the implications for priestly formation?[190] It was a diverse cultural and historical context that influenced the direction of the synod. Dedicated to "the formation of priests in circumstances of the present day," the purpose of the synodal discussion and subsequent document, "The Formation of Priests in the Circumstances of Today" was to put into practice the council's teaching on this matter. It was to offer an up-to-date and incisive understanding of the priesthood in present circumstances, twenty-five years after the council itself. "The purpose of the synod was to summarize the nature and mission of the ministerial priesthood as the church's faith has acknowledged them down the centuries of its history and as the Second Vatican Council has presented them anew to the people of our day" (John Paul II, *Pastores Dabo Vobis*, 11).

In this post-synodal apostolic exhortation, *Pastores Dabo Vobis* (*PDV*) 1992, John Paul II spoke of the work of the church in forming candidates to the priesthood and priests themselves.

> The Church feels called to relive with a renewed commitment all that the Master did with his apostles—urged on as she is by the deep and rapid transformations in the societies and culture of our age; by the multiplicity and diversity of contexts in which she announces the Gospel and witnesses to it; by the promising number of priestly vocations being seen in some dioceses around the world; by the urgency of a new look at the contents and methods of priestly formation; by the concern of bishops and their communities about a persisting scarcity of clergy; and by the absolute necessity that the "new evangelization" have priests as its initial "new evangelizers." (*PDV*, 2)

Pastores Dabo Vobis has been a key document in relation to the implementation and interpretation of *Optatam Totius* in the 1990s and onwards.[191] This document is a reaffirmation of the essential interconnectedness of human, intellectual, spiritual, and pastoral formation for priesthood. It asks priests in formation to be aware of the unique situation of their particular church. There is an implicit connection with diocesan spirituality in the pope's concern that seminarians and priests be attentive to local ministry.

> The essential content of this pastoral charity is the gift of self, the total gift of self to the Church, following the example of Christ. "Pastoral charity is the virtue by which we imitate Christ in his self-giving and service. It is not just what we do, but our gift of self, which manifests Christ's love for his flock. Pastoral charity determines our way of thinking and acting, our way of relating to people. It makes special demands on us." The gift of self, which is the source and synthesis of pastoral charity, is directed toward the Church. This was true of Christ who

"loved the Church and gave himself up for her" (Eph. 5:25), and the same must be true for the priest. (*PDV*, 23)

The gift of self is of the essence of priestly ministry, but it is a gift that is located in the circumstances of a particular church in a particular socio-ecclesial context.

> The priest needs to be aware that his "being in a particular Church" constitutes by its very nature a significant element in his living a Christian spirituality. In this sense, the priest finds precisely in his belonging to and dedication to the particular Church a wealth of meaning, criteria for discernment and action which shape both his pastoral mission and his spiritual life. (*PDV*, 31)

This recognition of the spirituality of the diocesan priest in terms of finding God in all the circumstances and responsibilities of priestly ministry and life is an affirmation of the approach of *Optatam Totius*.

It is the particularity of the church in which he ministers and the socio-ecclesial demographics and context, along with the presbyteral relationships that are operative within the priest's ministerial context, that shape his spirituality.[192] This is not always a harmonious relationship, as an "immature relationship with the diocesan bishop and other presbyters can cause excessive dependency which can lead to a loss of self-worth, over-emphasis on personality and loss of focus for ministry in a particular community."[193] That the priest lives in a particular parish context, and in collaboration with a network of presbyters and laity, indicates that his spirituality will be shaped by these influences. But change is constant, even in the apparent consistencies of everyday living.

> Most diocesan priests have been formed in other "spiritualities" which have been tried and true in the past but might not be appropriate in the face of the expectations, demands, and challenges presented to a priest today... there is no one model but many for the spirituality of the diocesan priest. All need to be developed in the light of consecration and ministry, in the local church in union with the bishop and other presbyters.[194]

This is the context of ecclesial ministry and of spiritual development that requires the lifelong formation proposed in *Optatam Totius* and endorsed by John Paul II.

> The Church responds to grace through the commitment which priests make to receive that ongoing formation which is required by the dignity and responsibility conferred on them by the sacrament of holy orders. All priests are called to become aware how especially urgent it is for them to receive formation at the present time: The new evangelization needs new evangelizers, and these are the priests who are serious about living their priesthood as a specific path toward holiness. (*PDV*, 82)

Pope John Paul II addresses the ministerial formation issues raised in *Optatam Totius*, but there is often a renewed emphasis on the sacerdotal emphasis over the prophetic and leadership aspects of the threefold ministry endorsed at the council.

> "Live the mystery that has been placed in your hands!" This is the invitation and admonition which the Church addresses to the priest in the Rite of Ordination, when the offerings of the holy people for the eucharistic sacrifice are placed in his hands. The "mystery" of which the priest is a "steward" (cf. 1 Cor. 4:1) is definitively Jesus Christ himself, who in the Spirit is the source of holiness and the call to sanctification. This "mystery" seeks expression in the priestly life. For this to be so there is need for great vigilance and lively awareness. Once again, the Rite of Ordination introduces these words with this recommendation: "Beware of what you will be doing." In the same way Paul had admonished Timothy, "Do not neglect the gift you have" (1 Tm. 4:14; cf. 2 Tm. 1:6). (*PDV*, 24)

This sacerdotal emphasis is also a characteristic of the pope's Holy Thursday letters to his priests.

In his 1980 letter, "to all the bishops of the church on the mystery and worship of the eucharist" John Paul II writes in article 41 about the impact of the eucharistic mystery on priestly ministers.

There is a close link between this element of the Eucharist and its sacredness, that is to say, its being a holy and sacred action. Holy and sacred, because in it are the continual presence and action of Christ, "the Holy One" of God, "anointed with the Holy Spirit," "consecrated by the Father" to lay down His life of His own accord and to take it up again, and the High Priest of the New Covenant. For it is He who, represented by the celebrant, makes His entrance into the sanctuary and proclaims His Gospel. It is He who is "the offerer and the offered, the consecrator and the consecrated."[195]

It is in this statement that the pope makes explicit what may be implicit in the traditional understanding of *in persona Christi*.

The ordained minister's Eucharistic and other sacramental activity is not performed as by the delegate or representative of an absent Christ. Rather it is performed in sacramental representation of Christ, thus making Christ sacramentally present and active as the "offerer" and as the "consecrator," *in and through* the presence and action of the minister.[196]

This is a favored pastoral emphasis of John Paul II in his letters and in other documents. In *Pastores Dabo Vobis* he explains and expands on his conviction about "the way in which the ordained minister acts "in persona Christi."[197] This then is a ministry for the whole church.

For the sake of this universal priesthood of the new covenant Jesus gathered disciples during his earthly mission (cf. Lk. 10:1–12), and with a specific and authoritative mandate he called and appointed the Twelve "to be with him, and to be sent out to preach and have authority to cast out demons" (Mk. 3:14–15). (*PDV*, 14)

Pastores Dabo Vobis then presents the ordained minister as a sacramental figure in its fullest sense. It is the sacerdotal ministry that is at the forefront. This emphasis of John Paul II has had further influence on subsequent developments of the ecclesial and ecclesiastical understanding of priesthood in and for the church and for priestly formation and ministry. The exclusive aspect has been endorsed at the expense of the Vatican II affirmation of common priesthood and of collaborative ministry.

In 2001 the U.S. bishops published their own "Basic Plan" for the ongoing formation of priests as recommended in *Optatam Totius*.[198] This is a comprehensive document that encompasses the commitment of the bishops to support this plan for ongoing formation, an outline of the plan, formation at different ages, and the ongoing formation of an entire presbyterate. There is an appendix that addresses the doctrinal understanding of the ministerial priesthood.

This is obviously an "in-house" document. Apart from a few references to the Association of Theological Schools, all references are to Vatican documents.[199] This national plan may have provided an opportunity to integrate the social sciences with the wisdom of the church, especially as mid-life issues and aging are explicitly addressed and expanded on in the text, yet there are no references to developmental sources that do address these issues explicitly and in the context of the contemporary culture. An integration of ascetical and psychological disciplines may have enabled this document to have a more significant impact on priestly formation, but such an approach seems to create difficulties in such documents.[200]

This is evidence that additional work on the inclusion of the social sciences in research into the understanding of priestly vocation and formation, as recommended in *Optatam Totius*, needs to be carried out in seminaries, especially in relation to the changing ages and stages of vocational choice and commitment.[201]

In 1967 the United States had thirty-six diocesan and eighty-six religious high school seminaries, seventeen junior college seminaries, and thirty-eight combined high school and junior college seminaries. In 2005–2006 there were 1,297 seminarians enrolled in thirty-seven college-level priesthood formation programs, with 173 pre-theology students in college seminary programs. Such institutions provide Latin, Greek, and other subjects for seminary studies. Of the high school seminaries, in 2005–2006, only nine active high school seminaries remain, with a combined enrollment of 763 students.[202] Initial and ongoing formation programs at such institutions need to include the recommended conciliar approaches in regard to faculty, seminarians, and prospective candidates.

SEMINARY VISITATIONS

Among the factors that affected the implementation of *Optatam Totius* were the two apostolic visitations of seminaries that were announced in 1981 and in 2002. The first visitation was mandated by Pope John Paul II in June 1981. The purpose of that visitation was to provide "an opportunity for seminaries to do some intensive self-assessment and to be evaluated by a team of bishops and seminary personnel."[203] The visitation was supervised from Rome by Cardinal Baum, prefect of the Vatican Congregation for Catholic Education, and coordinated in the United States by Bishop John Marshall of Burlington, Vermont. The norms for this visitation were provided in the 1981 *Program of Priestly Formation*. The reaction to it was mixed.

> The announcement of that visitation was greeted with alarm in some quarters and considerable anxiety on the part of some engaged in priestly formation, but once it became apparent that the visitation would have clear criteria for the study and that those engaged in it would be familiar with the process of priestly formation, some of the uneasiness began to recede. After a number of the visitations were successfully concluded, the word spread quickly that this was a useful and productive exercise that truly advanced the cause of priestly formation. By the end of the first year, disquiet and uncertainty had given way, for the most part, to appreciation and support.[204]

That this visitation had an impact on seminaries from the time of its announcement until its close in 1986, and that it offered some strong cautions along with an affirmation of the good service of the church meant that this experience would have left the seminary faculties and bishops with varied reactions. Each visit included a self-study by the seminary, an almost weeklong visitation by the team with interviewing of faculty, students, alumni, and board members, and observation of seminary life and worship. A preliminary report presented to the bishop and seminary administrators on the last day of the visit was followed up by a written report in 1986 from the team to Cardinal Baum and to the bishops responsible for seminaries, with a letter from the cardinal to all bishops on the subject of priestly formation in U.S. seminaries.[205]

This letter expressed Cardinal Baum's concerns about the need for a clearer understanding of priesthood, of priestly identity, of the importance of having a significant number of priests on the faculty, and of the specialized nature of priestly formation in U.S. seminaries. The role of rector needed to be reviewed, as many were being asked to cover too many areas of responsibility, from fund-raising to recruitment.

Cardinal Baum emphasized his concern for those seminary programs that allowed lay students to be educated with seminarians. He was also concerned for what were reported as "instances of dissent from the magisterium in the teaching of moral theology." Yet he noted that "confusion about the magisterium is a more common phenomenon than dissent."[206] The conclusion of the visits to religious order seminaries resulted in a joint letter from Cardinals Baum and Hamer (of the Congregation for Institutes of Consecrated Life and Societies of Apostolic Life). This repeated the same themes but also called for clear demarcation lines between the various authorities at diocesan and religious order level in the varied theologates and seminaries.

During the period of seminary visitation, the leaders of men's religious orders and bishops met at an assembly of rectors and ordinaries in Mundelein, Illinois, in 1983 and at Seton Hall University in 1986 to discuss seminary formation especially in light of the visitation. Questions addressed concerned formation for ministry in the multicultural church especially in regard to adaptation of the formation program for multicultural seminarians and the preparation of all seminarians to serve in a multicultural church. Issues of candidate screening and selection were also key concerns.[207]

The need for diocesan seminaries and religious orders to work together was recognized, as was the importance of continuing education programs for priests. The theology of holy orders, priestly identity, and ministry were recurrent formation issues mentioned.[208] Conflict areas were seen as having been caused by different ecclesiologies and understandings of church and its mission within seminary faculties.

The divergence from some of the directions of *Optatam Totius* continued to surface in terms of the polarized positions of faculty members within some seminaries, and also because of the pressures that were being felt in the seminaries, with some seminarians whose expectation of seminary education was one of foreclosure on ideological interpreta-

tions of some doctrines rather than disclosure of the developing understanding of the tradition.[209]

When the 2002 seminary visitation was announced at the meeting
of the U.S. cardinals in Rome on April 23–24, 2002, there was mixed
reaction within the seminaries.[210] The burden of the problems of sexual
abuse scandals that had shocked the church was being felt among the
clergy and laity in varying degrees.[211] The failure in accountability at
the leadership level over decades was having its consequences at all levels of priesthood and priestly training.

The leaders of various Vatican offices understood that sexual abuse
is not a problem confined to the United States, but a worldwide problem for the church. While some members of the hierarchy were complicit in the protection of the priestly predators, others acquired
insights into a terrible and hidden problem that has plagued the church
for a very long time. Church processes for dismissing guilty clergy from
the clerical state and for making official visitation of seminaries and religious houses of formation were eventually established.[212]

The recent scandal involving the repeated sexual abuse of minors by
clergy and the administrative betrayal in their subsequent reassignment
to pastoral ministry was given as the reason for the seminary visitation.
According to Donald Wuerl, in an article published in *America* magazine,

> The focus of the visitation is therefore much more narrowly
> defined than the earlier one. Nonetheless the desired outcome
> would be a renewal described by the pope as one "rooted in a
> deepened awareness of the sacred character of the priesthood
> and of the priestly ministry" . . . [the study will be based] "on the
> criteria found in *Pastores Dabo Vobis* (1992)." Since the visit will
> focus "on the question of human formation for celibate
> chastity," the norms for judging the effectiveness of any partic-
> ular priestly formation program are already clearly spelled out
> and available to all.[213]

Arising from this article were some pertinent questions posed subsequently in letters to the editor, such as why, if the vast majority of sexual abuse cases are among clergy who were ordained more than
twenty-five years ago, is there a seminary visitation? What direct link is

there between the current sexual abuse scandal and present seminary formation? As a key issue related to the abuse is the reassignment of abusive priests, what does that have to do with seminary formation? Surely the sole responsibility is with the bishops rather than the present seminary faculties and programs.[214]

It is interesting to read psychiatrist and priest James Gill's comments on this visitation, which focused on two key issues: "the need for fidelity to the church's teaching, especially in the area of morality, and the need for a deeper study of criteria of suitability of candidates to the priesthood."[215] Many seminarians were fearful that it would turn out to be a "witch hunt," while various formation personnel were making public the precise steps they had taken to deal more effectively with sexuality in a frank and comprehensive way that until recently was unthinkable in their institutions. Gill describes some of the concerns of seminarians and staff in relation to issues of sexuality and his own concern for the fruit of the visitation process.

> Regrettably, anyone who has been in close contact with many American seminaries in recent years knows that there are a number of aspects of these institutions that call for urgent attention … So when visiting teams look closely at what is being provided by seminaries to help prevent sexual abuse on the part of priests in the future, it will be important for them to determine just why the Vatican-mandated preparation of seminary personnel has failed to be taken seriously in relation to the specific need they have in the area of sexuality. Without competent help to attain deep and accurate knowledge of themselves as unique sexual beings, too many seminarians are likely to go on approaching celibacy and chastity in a highly intellectualized and personally detached way, and abusive behavior can thus be expected to continue.[216]

Optatam Totius had emphasized the need for seminarians to work on their understanding of their sexual identity. This was recognized as essential for all young adults and no less for candidates to the priesthood. Yet, the subsequent Vatican documents give little evidence of their concern for, or even understanding of the psycho-sexual component of celibate commitment.

As most young candidates for ordination are still developing their sexual identity, and their understanding of this in terms of their life commitment, these developmental tasks need to be addressed in seminary programs and in the provisions for counseling in the seminary. Gill points out that one of the problems that has affected seminary life is homophobia. Because this has been rife in Western cultures, and because of the punitive consequences of homophobia, it is not unusual for some young men to have come to adulthood without real resolution of their sexual identity. Religious commitment to celibacy may then become a means of escaping sexual identity rather than a means of growing in self-acceptance, and in love of God, self, and others. The careful attention to conformity and to meeting the expectations of seminary life can subvert the responsibility to develop the capacity to relate to and collaborate with others. In the "good" seminarian, the lack of the capacity to relate may go unnoticed, or it may even be seen as virtue.

The retention rate of seminarians at theologates is steadily dropping, although the number of laity engaged in theological undergraduate and postgraduate programs is increasing exponentially. In 2002–2003, the retention rate of seminarians in studies was 85 percent but present statistics indicate the retention rate for the class of 2005–2006 throughout their four years of study to be 67 percent.[217] Issues of priestly image, morale, and stress are growing in significance for seminarians and the newly ordained.[218]

The increasing numbers of documents from the Vatican and from episcopal conferences give evidence of the concern to continue to promote vocations and to give priority to the training of priests as expressed in *Optatam Totius*. The irony is surely that the number of such documents, with their many references to the wisdom of the sacred sciences at the expense of the social sciences, may be seen to be almost in inverse proportion to the number of priestly vocations.

The question must surely be asked whether the commission that drew up *Optatam Totius* and subsequent Vatican documents might have paid more attention to the question of vocation to the ordained priesthood in the contemporary context. To reflect on the amount of material on formation for priestly ministry and on the multiplicity of references they contain from other ecclesiastical documents at the expense of psychosocial resources is to ask oneself to what extent those Vatican writers have taken into account psychological, psychosexual, sociocultural, and developmental factors that influence vocational identity and commitment.

The hard questions asked by some writers as to whether ordained priesthood would continue, and under what conditions, does not seem to have been a feature of the ecclesiastical worldview of the past or the present.

> If all other factors remain constant, in the course of the next century the Catholic priesthood might almost disappear. A decade ago anyone who would make that assertion would be thought to have taken leave of [their] senses. In the intervening ten years, however, the alarming decrease in vocations to the priesthood, the rising tide of dropouts from the seminaries, and the well-grounded suspicion of an increasing number of defections from the priesthood itself, have given [this] somber prediction a note of reality in the mind of thoughtful Catholics.[219]

This was written in 1967, and the comment is still applicable forty years later. The concerns expressed in the 2002 visitation and in the subsequent meetings of rectors and ordinaries were in terms not simply of the numbers of vocations but also in the quality of vocations. There has been a growing concern about the type of young men who have been presenting themselves for priestly candidature.

While both *Optatam Totius* and *Pastores Dabo Vobis* affirm the importance of the four dimensions of seminary training—human, intellectual, spiritual, and pastoral—there still seems to be, in some diocesan seminary programs, a greater concern for the intellectual and ascetical at the expense of the human and the pastoral. Many priests who have been asked to evaluate their seminary training have requested greater diversity in the pastoral experiences offered in the seminary. "An older priest ordained in 1972 and currently serving an East Coast diocese, said, 'My seminary gave me theory—so to speak—without integration, it was pretty useless for all priestly life.'"[220] The pressure put on seminaries at both visitations as a consequence of the 1986 visitation report and letter from Cardinal Baum and the scandals of sexual and administrative aberration along with the scapegoating of homosexuals in priesthood and seminary life still seemed to focus more on theological orthodoxy and much less on the developmental or relational and collaborative aspects of seminary life.

Questions about hierarchical authority, celibacy, ordination issues, and the place of women have been alive and fermenting in the *sensus fidelium* if not in the magisterium. These are issues that must be addressed in the training of seminarians, not simply in the content of courses, but in the seminary lifestyle itself. The apprenticeship style of learning of earlier times may still have something to offer in terms of priestly formation. But the seminary itself must surely be a place where there are opportunities to work with lay men and women, married and unmarried, to learn from them and to have opportunities to relate to them. Earlier models of seminaries where seminarians and laity studied together may well be an important approach for both discerning and discovering ministerial vocations in the future. A "performance-based" seminary of clerics alone will not provide the necessary challenge, and the opportunities to learn how to minister in a context that is a microcosm of the parish will be lost.

Those cultures that prize personal liberty, the emancipation of women, and work on behalf of the marginalized in society appear to be speaking with their feet and making choices about identity and ministry. There is no evidence of *Optatam Totius* having any influence in the vocational impasse that is afflicting the Western world. Yet it is obvious that such issues must be addressed in some way if the next forty years are to be different from the previous in regard to issues of ordained priesthood and priestly ministry.

PART IV
THE STATE OF THE QUESTION

The church of the twenty-first century is confronted by a growing Catholic population and a diminishing number of vocations to the priesthood. Contemporary understandings of priesthood, training for priestly ministry, and the question of ordination are surely the most urgent and vexed issues for the church to address. Statistics indicate that in the United States the discrepancy between the numbers of priests in parishes and the size and numbers of parishes is putting pressure on bishops, priests, and Catholic communities.

From 1965 to the present, the changing dynamic between priests, parishes, and the Catholic population has been dramatic. The impact of these statistics on Catholic identity and community life has not yet been assessed.

U.S. DATA	1965	1975	1985	1995	2000	2005	2006*
Diocesan priests	35,925	36,005	35,052	32,349	30,607	28,702	28,299
Religious priests	22,707	22,904	22,265	16,705	15,092	14,137	13,495
Total priests	58,632	58,909	57,317	49,054	45,699	42,839	41,794
Priestly ordinations	994	771	533	511	442	454	431
Parishes	17,637	18,515	19,244	19,331	19,236	18,891	18,584
Parishes without a resident priest pastor	549	702	1,051	2,161	2,843	3,251	3,405
Catholic population	45.6m	48.7m	52.3m	57.4m	59.9m	64.8m	64.0m

Center for Applied Research in the Apostolate (CARA)
*The 2006 numbers do not include the Archdiocese of New Orleans, due to Hurricane Katrina.[221]

The world situation is just as traumatic, if not more so, in the consequences for those countries that have not had access to ordained priests in their communities for decades. We are living in the midst of an implosion of priestly ministry and have already begun to see the consequences. The system appears to be destroying itself from within, in spite of all the goodwill and good intentions that are expressed at all levels of church life.

WORLD DATA	1970	1975	1980	1985	1990	1995	2000	2004
Diocesan priests	270,924	259,331	257,409	253,319	257,696	262,418	265,781	268,041
Religious priests	148,804	145,452	156,191	150,161	145,477	142,332	139,397	137,409
Total priests	419,728	404,783	413,600	403,480	403,173	404,750	405,178	405,450
Diocesan priestly ordinations	4,622	4,140	3,860	4,822	5,938	6,444	6,814	—
Parishes	191,398	200,116	206,503	212,021	215,805	220,077	218,196	219,655
Parishes without a resident priest pastor	39,431	46,074	50,469	55,343	57,664	60,705	55,729	—
Catholic population	653.6m	709.6m	783.7m	852.0m	928.5m	989.4m	1.045b	1.114b

Center for Applied Research in the Apostolate (CARA)[222]

What we are experiencing is that there are now around 15,000 fewer priests serving the same number of parishes as forty years ago. Further, the number of parishes without a resident priest has increased over those years from 549 to 3,405.[223]

To address these issues in relation to *Optatam Totius* and the future training of priests in particular, we will look at several questions in relation to future ministry, lay and ordained, and the situation of women in regard to ordained ministry in the future. Issues related to parish size and population mix as well as the relationship between the Vatican and semi-nary studies in the global context will be explored. We will also reflect on issues relating to celibacy. Cultural attitudes to celibacy and to sexuality have changed radically during the past forty years. Priestly ministry itself has undergone tremendous pressures in terms of expectations of parish leadership and team ministry. Finally, a critical matter that is "in the face" of Christian communities today is that of ordination. What are some of the key questions in relation to ordination, and how do we educate seminari-ans, priests, and the people of God to be attentive to the directions in which the Holy Spirit is surely calling us in such a way that we are accountable to both the past and the future in the way we live in our present time?

The problem of a dearth in priestly vocations brings up the issue of ministry and in particular of women and ministry. In 1980, in *Called and Gifted*, the U.S. bishops wrote that they welcome the gift of lay persons who have prepared for professional ministry in the church. Such people serve as pastoral associates, directors of religious education, and school principals, as well as in youth, liturgical, and music ministry and numer-ous other roles.[224] Commencing in 1995, a subcommittee of the Com-mittee on the Laity focused its attention on the theology of lay ecclesial ministry, the preparation and formation of lay ecclesial ministers, and their identity and relationship within the church.[225] The consequence of this was the call for church leaders, ordained and lay, to become more intentional and effective in ordering and integrating lay ecclesial minis-ters within the ministerial life and structures of dioceses.

In 2004 and 2005, in the United States, more than 2,000 lay per-sons ministered in the name of the Catholic Church in hospitals and health care settings, on college and university campuses, and in prisons, seaports, and airports. Today, 30,632 lay ecclesial ministers work at least twenty hours per week in paid positions in parishes. An additional 2,163 volunteers work at least twenty hours per week in parishes.[226]

Although priestly vocations have been diminishing consistently since the 1950s, there has been an extraordinary burgeoning of lay ministry. And, even though a significant number of parish lay ministers have not found their salaries adequate for their needs, in keeping with the work and expertise required of them, or "at-or-above average" relative to com-parable positions, they have stayed in their commitment to ministry.

The numbers of women have consistently far outweighed the num-bers of men, and in the past few years, women enrolled in lay ministry formation programs have outnumbered men by a ratio of nearly two to one. This burgeoning of lay ministry, and the number of women involved, means that seminarians must be trained to deal with the laity, and particularly with women, in ways that are neither paternalistic nor closed in clericalism. Openness to inclusiveness and to mutuality in ministerial teams and parish leadership roles and structures is essential for the priest of the twenty-first century.

> Ordained ministers, then need to forswear attitudes and presuppositions such as "gender-defined and shame-based rules of order" and the lack of respect for "internal, personal authority" which are the hallmarks of "the typical ecclesiastical official." In facing the contemporary challenges that orbit around "ministry," the goal is to express the church as a communion of all the baptized.[227]

This surely impinges on the consciousness of all involved in priestly formation, at all levels, including that of episcopal leadership.

The bishops of the United States have made significant efforts to include women as equals in the mission of Christ, but inequality and discriminatory practices must be addressed in the future if not at present. At the level of ecumenism, this has been an issue of concern for women and men. At the Presbyterian and Reformed–Roman Catholic Dialogue held in October 30, 1971, the following statement was made:

> Of the many injustices of our age, the injustice inflicted upon women is surely one of the most massive, for it affects one-half of the human race—and one-half of the Churches' membership! The unjust conditions under which women are (often subtly) compelled to live affect adversely the personal development of men as well as women. No human being is truly and fully free as long as even one other human being is in bondage. "More and more women today feel strongly that they wish to share fully with men in all human responsibilities" ("Ministry in the Church," Draft paper of the Theological Section of the Roman Catholic/Presbyterian and Reformed Consultation, Richmond, October, 1971). This aspiration of women today is

frustrated by the accepted status of women in society and the Church. We judge this status quo to be sinful and immoral.[228]

As ecumenical and interfaith collaboration necessarily develops in the future, the treatment of women is not going to remain simply an issue of concern, but a scandal.

In 1975 two initiatives within the Catholic Church influenced the question of women in ministry. The U.S. bishops formed an Ad Hoc Committee on Women in Society to implement Vatican II directives in relation to women's role in the church. At the USCC-NCCB annual meeting, the question of the ordination of women surfaced quite strongly. Cardinal Bernadin's response was that there seemed to be solid evidence against women's ordination but that the matter could not be closed to discussion: "Even matters that have been solemnly defined continue to be studied so that our knowledge of them can be deepened or refined."[229]

In October that year the Canon Law Society of America's Committee on the Status of Women in the Church reported that the 1917 Code had failed to recognize women's human dignity and placed limits on women's role in the church.[230] "Many canons place women in an inferior position and demonstrate either protectiveness or paternalism or defence against sexual provocation on the part of women." Further, the church had made "only perfunctory, sporadic and uncoordinated efforts to examine its own practices and attitudes towards women."[231] These initiatives had both explicit and implicit ramifications for the publication and reception of subsequent church documents on priesthood and ministry at all levels of the Catholic community.

Consequences of women's exclusion from ministry have been experienced in parishes and in seminaries; tensions have built up in relation to priestly identity and ministry, and in some places a regression to the defensive approaches of the past began to surface in the renewal of Tridentine emphases and approaches. Certainly the issue of ordination became an increasingly painful one at all levels of church. The place of women in ministry has caused polarization in communities as well as some negative consequences for ecumenical dialogue. The Pontifical Biblical Commission had studied the role of women in the Bible to help clarify the issue. The result was that the commission considered that the

New Testament could not be used to settle the question of women's ordination.[232]

On October 15, 1976, the "Declaration on the Admission to the Ministerial Priesthood: *Inter Insigniores*" was promulgated by the Congregation for the Doctrine of the Faith (CDF). This document opens with the affirmation that "the Catholic Church has never felt that priestly or episcopal ordination can be validly conferred on women." This conviction is elucidated with theological and scriptural substantiation and comes to closure with an affirmation for women:

> Women who express a desire for the ministerial priesthood are doubtless motivated by the desire to serve Christ and the Church. And it is not surprising that, at a time when they are becoming more aware of the discriminations to which they have been subject, they should desire the ministerial priesthood itself. But it must not be forgotten that the priesthood does not form part of the rights of the individual, but stems from the economy of the mystery of Christ and the Church. The priestly office cannot become the goal of social advancement; no merely human progress of society or of the individual can of itself give access to it: it is of another order.[233]

As the numbers of women involved in ministry increased, and as other Christian churches ordained women, the issue continued to be discussed. Pope John Paul II put out a further statement in his apostolic letter *Ordinatio Sacerdotalis* (On Reserving Priestly Ordination to Men Alone).

> Although the teaching that priestly ordination is to be reserved to men alone has been preserved by the constant and universal Tradition of the Church and firmly taught by the Magisterium in its more recent documents, at the present time in some places it is nonetheless considered still open to debate, or the Church's judgment that women are not to be admitted to ordination is considered to have a merely disciplinary force.
>
> Wherefore, in order that all doubt may be removed regarding a matter of great importance, a matter which pertains to the

Church's divine constitution itself, in virtue of my ministry of confirming the brethren (cf. Lk 22:32) I declare that the Church has no authority whatsoever to confer priestly ordination on women and that this judgment is to be definitively held by all the Church's faithful.[234]

In discussing this issue in his history of ecclesiology through the centuries, Bernard Prusak asks the question,

How did the Congregation for the Doctrine of the Faith and the pope arrive at their conclusion? Vatican II taught that the bishops dispersed throughout the world can teach infallibly when, in communication with one another, they unanimously concur that a particular teaching on a matter of faith and morals must be held conclusively (*LG 25*). Invoking that text, the CDF, in 1995, declared infallible the teaching that women cannot be ordained; this teaching is a matter of faith, and the Congregation asserted that it has always been the ordinary, constant and definitive teaching of all bishops through the world. The Congregation further concluded that Pope John Paul II's letter, *Priestly Ordination* had confirmed, or handed on, this same teaching by a formal declaration, thereby making explicit what is always and everywhere to be held by all as belonging to the deposit of faith.

It should however, be noted that the congregation's declaration is itself noninfallible, and was proclaimed without prior consultation to verify whether that is the de facto position of all bishops serving today. These are the crucial issues that are still being debated and questioned by theologians studying the Vatican's statements, and more discussion is likely to develop in the years ahead.[235]

Prusak's concern is one that is shared at many levels of church life. The statement is still having ramifications in church and society.

In the "Afterword" to *Creative Fidelity*, Francis Sullivan gives a helpful and wise illustration in regard to the current issue of women in ministry. He comments that "when a doctrine has been infallibly defined, or when it is certain that it has been infallibly taught, it is irreversible." But then, as a historian of Catholic doctrine, he reminds his readers of some propositions which "seemed to be the unanimous teaching of the whole episcopate, and yet as a result of a further development of doctrine, is no longer the teaching of the church." He gives an example:

> The bishops gathered at the Council of Florence in 1442 no doubt expressed the common teaching of the whole episcopate at that time when they said that all pagans and Jews would certainly go to hell if they did not become Catholics before they died. This is certainly not the doctrine of the modern Catholic church. Other examples of doctrines that had a long tradition but were subsequently reversed concerned the morality of owning slaves and exploiting their labor, and the obligation requiring rulers of Catholic nations to prevent the propagation of Protestantism in their countries.[236]

Sullivan continues to examine the ways in which the tradition has remained constant and he also continues to contextualize the statement of the Congregation for the Doctrine of the Faith in terms of the establishment of Catholic doctrine.

However, the immediate issue, in relation to the key elements in *Optatam Totius*, is the importance of a seminary training that is attuned to the present and future needs of church and society.

> The formation of future priests, both diocesan and religious, and lifelong assiduous care for their personal sanctification in the ministry and for the constant updating of their pastoral commitment is considered by the Church one of the most demanding and important tasks for the future of the evangelization of humanity. (*PDV*, 2)

Optatam Totius opens with the statement, "Animated by the spirit of Christ, this sacred synod is fully aware that the desired renewal of the whole Church depends to a great extent on the ministry of its priests." What the research on priestly formation in the present indicates is that this ministry must be inclusive, collaborative, communal, and responsive to the signs of the times as well as to the richness of tradition if there is to be a viable priesthood ministering in the spirit of the gospel of Christ in the future.

The growing awareness of the contribution of women in church and society is one of the signs of the times that is moving within Christian denominations, in other religious traditions, and most certainly in civic society. This will come to the surface as a justice issue in the future; it is to be hoped that for the sake of the mission and ministry of the church it will not be too long in coming.

The next question takes the importance of celibacy into account. What sort of man is presenting for ordination at present? What self-knowledge does he bring in terms of his own sexual identity and what sort of priestly "brotherhood" might he expect? Donald Cozzens has addressed issues of sexual development and formation in seminaries at some depth.[237] Some candidates for ordination may be sure of their identity and of their sexual orientation while others may be unclear. Selection processes do not always surface developmental immaturity, which can be masked by many disguises learned from childhood. The sexual orientation of both students and faculty members can be a divisive and complex issue in seminaries. Much work needs to be done on this issue in the present and future.

> In most (but not all) seminaries, a screening process involving professional interviews, psychological tests and careful inspection of the candidate's sexual history has been adopted. Courses on human sexuality have been established, along with discussion groups where sexual orientation, chastity, celibacy, the need for interpersonal boundaries, ways of coping with temptations and spiritual motivation are led by men and women (including laypersons) dedicated to helping their seminarians reach full psychosexual and moral maturity.[238]

But the culture of silence is still present; it is prohibitive and it can be and has been destructive, particularly in light of the shifting of blame to homosexuals when abuses are more commonly related to pedophilia or ephebophilia (the sexual attraction of adults to pubescent adolescents).

> What sustains the silence and reinforces the closet is fear, whether the fear of the gay priest about his own orientation

and possible discovery, the fear of the straight priest to see what he really does not want to see and to incorporate this knowledge into his understanding of clerical culture, or the fear of the ambivalent priest who suspects, to his own horror, that he may be gay.[239]

In the American church of the present decade, church leadership may be seen as complicit in the problems that are being faced within the priesthood in general and in seminaries in particular. Many bishops know that celibacy is not universally practiced by their clergy, but, just as pedophilia and other forms of sexual abuse were swept under the episcopal carpet with such a devastating impact on all members of the Catholic community for many decades, it is still having an impact.

Some members of the hierarchy "deny overwhelming evidence that celibacy is not being practiced because it might lead to questions about the wisdom and viability of mandatory celibacy for the Latin rite."[240] The mandatory nature of celibacy is obviously no longer applied to all priests of the Latin rite, because married men ordained in another denomination, who convert to Roman Catholicism, can be ordained for the Roman Catholic Church. Many Catholic authors are writing about celibacy and the priesthood not simply because of the public aberrations of some clergy but because they see the need for the issue to be addressed when there are numbers of apparent injustices that have been a consequence of the acceptance of married priests from other denominations into parish leadership roles, and when they see some of the more effective priests in their church leave the priesthood because of this disciplinary issue.

Celibacy is a charism, a gift from God, which is clearly not given to all. It is a "graced ability" that has to be grounded in natural gifts. For those so gifted, the celibate state is simply "the right way to live out their lives . . . the deeper their love for God, the greater their capacity for human love and friendship."[241] This relational invitation in celibacy is not always recognized or understood and it takes great courage and trust, and the willingness to sometimes make mistakes and to learn from them.

One of the untold stories of the priesthood at the close of the twentieth century is the large number of life-giving, joyful,

loving friendships between celibate priests and their committed friends. Both straight and gay priests have sustained celibate relationships of real grace and depth...In spite of the
confusion and ambiguity that sooner or later surfaces, in spite
of the suffering that inevitably touches all human love and
friendship, priests blessed with celibate, loving intimacy give
thanks for the wonder of it all. In the process, they believe they
have grown as men of God, as men of the church.[242]

The tragedy is that, while the successful integration of celibacy has
been a characteristic of priesthood for so many centuries and across diverse cultural and ethnic contexts, it is a minority group—those for
whom a celibate life has been a cover for predation on the unwitting
and defenseless—that receives public notoriety and causes the devalu-
ing of celibacy in the church.

Professionals from a variety of backgrounds are commenting on the
scandalous failures in celibacy that are calling for more than a reaffirmation of ascetical foundations for celibacy, a reaffirmation that ignores
contemporary psychological research into sexual development. The
Research Study by the John Jay College of Criminal Justice on "The
Nature and Scope of the Problem of Minors by Catholic Priests and
Deacons in the United States" reported on the crisis that has already
cost the United States Catholic Church more than a billion dollars (including $85 million in Boston and $60 million in Los Angeles) in set-
tlement to victims. [243]

Another response to the scandal from the U.S. bishops was the establishment of the National Review Board, which called for better formation in clerical celibacy and showed that most cases of clergy sexual
abuse occurred decades ago and that relatively few cases had been reported since 1990.[244] The National Review Board "did not believe that
either homosexuality or celibacy was a cause of the sexual abuse crisis."
Their emphasis was on "the need for screening, for formation for the
training of seminarians in celibacy."[245] Unfortunately, there are no psychological tests that can, at the present time, flawlessly identify future
offenders.

Only an awareness of what is transpiring within their minds
and bodies can signal seminarians that it is time to talk with

someone about their sexuality and its bearing on their vocation. Providing such readily available and skillful help is one of the most valuable and essential services their spiritual and formation directors can offer them.[246]

Attentiveness to seminarians and their relational competencies and development during the seminary years, and also priests' recognition of the importance of presbyteral relationships will sometimes offer indications that priests may be in need. Ongoing diocesan formation programs can be another means to review the needs and circumstances of priests.

Most Catholics recognize that the vast numbers of priests are "sincere men of God who serve in love and were and are exhausted by their pastoral work."[247] This is the comment of Jack Dominian, a British psychiatrist who has worked with many pre– and post–Vatican II priests. He reflects on his experience and describes some of the more problematic priests he has had to deal with as "sacramental technicians, pouring out ill-digested Thomistic theology and emphasizing rules, sin and guilt."[248] He points out that these were not the norm; they were the minority, and a problem minority. While he sees that there are priests who "truly identify with Christ's priesthood" there are candidates who come forward for ordination who are "rigid conservative personalities who are attracted by the current atmosphere in the official Church."[249]

In his affirmation of bishops and priests with whom he has worked, Dominian acknowledges their effective leadership of their congregations: "they look forward, are focused on Christ and so have the evangelization of their people as a priority. The trouble with all of them is they are faced with so much bureaucracy that they are forced to spend much of their time with maintenance instead of mission."[250] When the complexity of priestly relationships is exacerbated by lack of numbers and distance factors, then the identity of priests will need to be strong, as will their support structures.

In his presidential address to the U.S. Conference of Catholic Bishops after the 1990 Synod, Archbishop Pilarczyk, then chairman of the Committee on Doctrine for the U.S. National Conference of Catholic Bishops, commented on the "time of testing," of "special challenge" that priests and those in formation were facing. He described priests as "hard-working, hard-praying, self-sacrificing men who have a demanding job to do and who do it generously."[251] Pilarczyk spoke about the recurrent theme of priestly identity and priestly holiness that was heard in bishops' comments about seminary formation and young priests.

> Our priests are fewer and more is being demanded of them than ever before. Suspicions have been raised about their faithfulness to their commitments. There have been sad lapses, publicly known, touching even our own bishops' conference. There are consequent moral problems among some of our priests, perhaps even among some of us. But this is not the whole picture ... I know that by and large, our priests are happy in their ministry and that they are deeply appreciated by the people they serve ... They are men who have given their lives to the exclusive service of the Lord and his church.[252]

Just over a decade later, Bishop Wilton Gregory in his presidential address had to acknowledge once again the problems priests face in light of the public image of the priesthood. "In our own Church, as well, we have had to face the criminal and sinful sexual abuse of children and the mismanagement of those violations by some Church leaders."[253] The complex image of the priest in the Western world is one that must be addressed in seminary formation, and those who are forming priests must have done their own personal work in terms of their personal and priestly identity or they will fail the seminarians and their brother priests. This is the lifelong task of ongoing formation that *Optatam Totius* mandated.[254]

A number of research studies on the priesthood have been engaged in by Dean Hoge and his colleagues. In his study of the first five years of priestly life, Hoge states that his research was undertaken in response to the reports about the pressures on newly ordained priests and the unacceptable rates of resignations that are occurring. He investigates some of the issues and points out that there is

> a growing polarization of students along ideological lines. The main battlegrounds are the nature of the priesthood, liturgy, devotions and adherence to orthodoxy (Schuth, 1999, 78). A portion of Catholic seminarians today are firm in their loyalty

to Pope John Paul II, their adherence to all church teachings about sexual morality and contraception, and their preference for tradition and formality in ritual and priestly roles. They feel comfortable wearing cassocks in public...The polarization of seminarians extends to the priesthood; there is more polarization among priests than there was twenty years ago.[255]

Indications of appropriateness for priestly ministry should surely be recognized in the seminarians' response to faculty and in their relationships with each other and with those they meet in their pastoral ministry. Rigidity, focus on external trappings of priestly status, and ideological self-righteousness must be taken seriously as indicators of the lack of the capacity to minister effectively in contemporary Christian communities.

Along with issues such as polarization among seminarians and faculty members are the cultural changes already described and Hoge's concern is to discover which of these most affect seminarians and newly ordained priests. He postulates that there are three trends that have caused changes and stress in ministry. The first is that the laity have a preference for "more participatory church structures." The next is that many Catholics are taking a more personal approach to decisions of conscience and to religious authority. The third trend is related to the relaxation of sexual mores in regard to premarital relationships and cohabitation. Hoge offers the insight that the movement of the popular culture away from Catholic moral teachings makes the task of pastoral leadership more difficult.[256]

The aspects of the research by Hoge that are pertinent to *Optatam Totius* indicate that celibacy was a major reason for priestly resignation. "Our study was suffused with talk about celibacy, loneliness, desire for intimacy, and homosexuality—more-so than we expected...the frank talk about homosexuality is something new."[257] "A major complaint expressed by resigned priests is that their theological training did not prepare them well for coping with problems of loneliness. They were also critical of their preparation for celibate life."[258] The issue of priestly overwork is another factor (and one that has consequences for faithfulness to celibacy) that was an issue for the priests who resigned. As the demographics show, this issue is not going to be resolved—and is in fact more likely to be exacerbated—in the next several years.

Another problem that priests posed as an issue for seminary training was that of alienating relationships with bishops or superiors.[259] The priests themselves proposed that "making seminary programs more practical" was an important issue for them. Time management, living conditions and burnout avoidance were also areas that they wanted to see addressed.[260] The commentaries included in the study by Gill and others offer important information for those involved in seminary formation. Perhaps the fact that there was "alarming evidence of the too numerous ways in which stress that is preventable is being encountered by priests today"[261] calls for a more thorough examination of formation personnel and programs.

Formation personnel need to enable seminarians to be in touch with their human needs and to find appropriate ways to help them deal with these. Cozzens describes this as a quality of "realism." He takes it as a given that formators are "both knowledgeable about human sexuality and comfortable discussing issues related to sex."[262] A number of priests commented that in their seminary years "few attempts were made to help the seminarian learn how to deal with people."[263] Issues of intimacy, of effective relating skills, are surely a necessity for the priest of today, and they need to be addressed in the living context of the seminarians, in their interactions with each other and with outside faculty, and in their pastoral commitments, not simply in workshops.

This leads to the further question of the sort of man who presents himself for ordination and what sort of "brotherhood" he might expect in terms of the emphasis in *Optatam Totius* on the fraternal life of the priest.

When the celibate, all-male clergy lost sight of their primary identity as disciples and over-identified with their ministerial priesthood, a caste system evolved that psychologically isolated them from the non-ordained and insulated them from the everyday struggles of most believers. A culture of control, secrecy and superiority emerged. Only the authentically humble escaped the arrogance and elitism of this clerical culture.[264]

Such issues of a clerical culture, its elitism and its arrogance, need to be addressed explicitly in seminaries, among faculty and students.[265] Related to this must surely be the issue of image and esteem in the priesthood. Issues of esteem and image are listed as important for priests. If candidates for ordination are looking toward enhancing their status and public image through ordination, this is contributing to the clerical culture that is destructive of the fraternity that was endorsed in *Optatam Totius*. Although the council's decree recommended that older and younger priests collaborate, this does not seem to be a feature of the diocesan priesthood today. How related this intergenerational issue is to image and status questions versus gospel mission and ministry needs to be addressed in episcopal conferences. Hoge and Wenger discovered different generational patterns of concerns, of needs, and of relationships. Older priests were more open to reassessment of their understanding and experience of priestly life than were younger priests. The young seemed to be concerned with issues of their image as priests. But in particular the differences are summed up as follows: "The younger priests want more discussion of their work conditions, and the older priests want more discussion of central church rules and disciplines, including celibacy, the ordination of women and the process of selecting bishops."[266]

If seminarians are not intentionally engaged in developing their understanding of their inner world, of their desires and their needs, they may well repress them and fall into the trap of clericalism as a means of escaping their own identity. Their energies may well be expended as a consequence of meeting the expectations of formation personnel or of church leaders who seem to sum up the qualities of the role they aspire to. The focus is then on performance at the expense of self-knowledge. "Clericalism arises from both personal and social dynamics, is expressed in various cultural forms, and often is reinforced by institutional structures."[267] Seminary personnel can be unwittingly caught into supporting such behavior as it does not ordinarily disrupt the seminary ethos and it can have the appearance of a benevolent and docile conformity that belies the inner reality of the seminarians.

The next question for the future is what style of training is appropriate for seminaries in this decade when the focus is on the ever-increasing size of parishes and of parish clusters? In his preface to the analysis of trends and transitions in seminaries and theologates, Msgr. William Baumgartner, a diocesan priest with decades of experience of seminary training programs, proposed that there have been three

phases in seminary training. The pre–Vatican II phase of the founding
and failure of seminaries, along with the context of staffing of and conduct in seminaries in the post–1918 Code of Canon Law period, as one
which was "strictly controlled, quasi-monastic, and the dominant concept of priesthood" in the pre–Vatican II years was "that of the seventeenth century reformer."[268] The majority of priests trained in this
mode have either retired or died. There are however, some contemporary seminaries that have maintained such an approach, and they constitute part of the present community of the ordained priesthood. They
seem to be meeting the expectations of a certain theological orthodoxy
at the expense of dealing with the contemporary needs and circumstances of parish life by maintaining a narrow ecclesiology and ghettoist
seminary lifestyle.

Phase two represents the direction taken by Vatican II in terms of
priestly training. Episcopal conferences and individual bishops altered
the traditional seminary context radically in directing that candidates
for priesthood should be educated in ways that enable them to relate
and minister more effectively to the people they serve. The "priest
apart" became the "priest in the midst" of the parish community. For
nearly forty years many bishops and the faculties of their seminaries
have committed themselves to interpret and implement faithfully the
directives of *Optatam Totius* and the many international and national
documents that have come from the hierarchy. They have tried to serve
their church and their people according to the best of their resources.
Seminary programs at graduate levels have been developed, often in
conjunction with other tertiary institutions. In the development of
these programs, accountability to the diocese, to the magisterium, and
to the spirit of Vatican II, has been of utmost concern.

Baumgartner then describes a third phase that seminaries were
faced with as they moved into the new millennium. This he sees as pos-
ing "a challenge of accountability to the church and her mission in the
postmodern world with its emphasis on pluralism and otherness, and on
the regional and local churches. The new context may be threatening,
but it may also help us deepen our understanding of the gospel."[269]

The movement has been from a seminary training where the expectation was that the priest should have just enough formal learning to administer the sacraments, to the current situation where the leadership is
of educated people who are both questioning and committed to their

identity, and claiming their place in *their* church. The future of church and ministry as discerned by priests and people who are committed to worship and work in their Catholic community is one in which both a pluralistic and multicultural society is taken seriously.

The diversity of the Catholic community itself needs to be taken into account. This diversity includes not simply sociocultural, inter-generational, racial, and ethnic differences, but also ideological differences and the connected issues of fundamentalism and conformist and dependent developmental levels of many communities (and of ministers, ordained and lay). The diversity of needs in terms of evangelization, faith formation, and social welfare also need to be addressed in terms of future training of priests for ministry in such contexts. Finally, the collaborative possibilities of ordained and lay ministers, and the promotion of lay Catholic leadership, not simply in ministry, need to be taken seriously.[270]

At a meeting of the Federation of Asian Bishops' Conferences (FABC) in January 2002, Bishop Claver, SJ, vicar apostolic emeritus of the Vicariate of Bontoc-Lagawe, Philippines, and former chairman of the Episcopal Commission for Indigenous People, described his experience of the changes in parish life in the Philippines as a consequence of Vatican II. He experienced the priestly life as one that became more participatory and more directed toward social transformation.

> The distinctive note of such a Church, one soon realizes, is sharing—and sharing is but another name for charity, the essential message of Christ's Gospel and the effective bond of unity in a Church of Communion. A Church that is fully participatory is thus a most powerful and living sacrament of Christian charity in act.[271]

The church of the Philippines has become a more consciously "lay" church. This has generated new ways of working together in the training of Catholic leaders.

> If at this time the concentration of efforts is on the formation of lay leaders, it is so in the understanding, unspoken but real nonetheless, of the fact that participative communities cannot be fostered without a participative leadership. A new kind of

leadership in the Church, in other words, or perhaps better, a
new way of exercising leadership (not only by lay people but by
clergy and hierarchy as well) is being consciously created and it
is geared towards encouraging participation in the Church by
the rank and file of Christians beyond merely attending church
and giving financial support for its pastoral programs.[272]

Bishop Claver points out that this training of lay leaders is not simply for lay ministry that is primarily concerned with liturgical matters,
but "other areas of Christian community living—economic development, social justice, communal action on problems of consequence for
the good of society at large, the integration of faith *and* life."[273]

The impact of the universal call to holiness and of the common
priesthood of the faithful of Vatican II is still reverberating in churches
and in communities of committed lay Catholics. Bishops today must ask
questions about the impact, not simply of the rapidly changing cultural
context, but also of the changed and changing identity of the lay faithful on the preparation and program provision of both ordained and lay
leaders ministering in a church in a multicultural and pluralist world
that is growing in membership while experiencing diminishing numbers of ordained ministers.[274]

In Asia this is an issue that was addressed by the Federation of Asian
Bishops' Conferences at a meeting held in Japan in 1986, as the visitation of U.S. seminaries was being concluded. The Asian bishops described their experience of "a deep crisis in every sector and a threat to
human life and dignity" and their response is directed toward developing a more participative church and ministry for ordained and lay ministers collaborating in serving church and society.

Ministerial formation is needed for those who enjoy the
charisms for stable ecclesial service. The clergy, who have the
responsibility to encourage, welcome and help these charisms
prosper for the benefit of Christian Churches and their mission
in the world, must offer assistance in accordance with what is
needed. By reason of the lay character, formation should be
done on the basis of the laity's own experience of the realities
of the world. A secular context and a job-oriented formation
must be encouraged. (4.7.2.3 C.)[275]

If the "clergy, who have the responsibility to encourage, welcome and help these charisms prosper for the benefit of Christian Churches and their mission in the world" are going to be able to exercise such responsibility, then the opportunities to collaborate must be provided in training programs for priests. This is an urgent global issue in the Catholic Church of the present.

A participatory church is a sociocultural as well as an ecclesial challenge at all levels of church life and across all nations, although it is experienced uniquely in each national or regional setting.

> Preparing for ministry in the Church in the United States is a complex undertaking. The entire society is undergoing tremendous transformation, the Catholic population is growing rapidly and becoming increasingly diverse, and Church personnel and structures are in the midst of massive evolution.[276]

The fundamental issue of the changing sociocultural context of parishes in a mobile and often transitory population confronts seminaries in ways that require a dynamic rather than a static response or program. The 2006 *Program of Priestly Formation* does take account of both internal and external pressures on seminaries, but it does so in a way that is more attuned to the Western ecclesiastical voice than that of the multicultural and pluralist context in which ministry is exercised.[277]

> Parishes in the future will be characterized by more interaction and inclusiveness, and so it will be even more essential to teach skills that prepare ministers to work collaboratively; faculty and administrators will be making adjustments in the design and content of programs accordingly.[278]

The web of relationships is spread wide in the changing size and structuring of parishes and their ecumenical, interfaith, and agnostic contexts.

What is true at the local or regional level is more complex at the global level. When documents are sent out from the Vatican to the global church, it is not always clear that there are quite diverse approaches and understandings that are necessarily involved before any national response can be made. Pope John Paul II, in his apostolic letter

Tertio Millennio Adveniente, 38 (November 10, 1994), voiced his intention to convoke a special assembly of the Synod of Bishops for Asia in 1998.[279] The Vatican sent an initial outline, a *Lineamenta* (working, or preparatory document), to the bishops of the forty Asian conferences in September 1996.

The response of the Japanese bishops indicates something of the difficulties that non-Western Catholic communities might face in receiving such a document.

> *Opinions of the Bishops concerning the questions of the Lineamenta themselves:* Since the questions of the *Lineamenta* were composed in the context of Western Christianity, they are not suitable. Among the questions are some concerning whether the work of evangelization is going well or not, but what is the standard of evaluation? If it is the number of baptisms, etc., it is very dangerous. From the way the questions are proposed, one feels that the holding of the Synod is like an occasion for the central office to evaluate the performance of the branch offices. That kind of Synod would not be worthwhile for the Church in Asia. The judgment should not be made from a European framework, but must be seen on the spiritual level of the people who live in Asia.[280]

The Japanese bishops point out that their specific response represents what the Catholic Bishops' Conference of Japan "gathered from the valuable opinions sent from throughout the entire nation, and [they] sincerely hope it will be a useful contribution to the discussion at the Special Assembly for Asia of the Synod of Bishops." In fact, these bishops came up with a list of their own issues and questions, and the fruit of their collaborative consultation resulted in the proposal of a synod more in tune with Asian realities.

These are the global issues of diversity and of the need for inclusive participatory processes that are reproduced in some ways in microcosm at the local level. Parishes have been growing in their own diverse ethnic and generational identities over the past decades and the needs and circumstances of the people have been changing accordingly. As seminary faculty hear from the priests whom they have trained, it will be surely incumbent on them to begin to structure new programs according to the feedback they receive; hopefully there will be feedback from representative parishioners as well.

At the FABC Plenary Assembly in Thailand in 2000 the issue of continuing education for priests was a major matter for discussion. Internship and apprenticeship training workshops and experiences for newly ordained were discussed, while the needs and circumstances of mid-life and "golden years" priestly veterans were also given special attention. The concluding comment of the workshop discussion guide for the bishops summed up the importance of ongoing formation:

> Becoming fully human and fulfilled priests of our God to [God's] people is an on-going and lifetime process. The moment of sacerdotal ordination was only a simple genesis of an earnest desire to attain the perfection of their vocation. As priests traverse this path, they inevitably experience their finiteness, needs and challenges to become more cogently effective and responsive individuals and part of a community of presbyters of our Lord.[281]

This was recognized as an important need for priestly formation at the council in both *Presbyterorum Ordinis* and *Optatam Totius*, but it is an even greater need at the present time. There is so much sociocultural and racial diversity, with "differing (and often competing) theologies, worldviews and models of what the church is and ought to become."[282] Ethnic diversity is a characteristic of most social contexts at the present time. There are few nations where racial, ethnic, and some religious diversity does not exist.

In the United States the diversity is unprecedented, and while there may be clusters of ethnic or cultural groups, the size of parishes will make the homogenous parish a rarity. Even within the one apparent group there can be a wide range of ethnic backgrounds. In what may be simply described on the surface as Hispanic, Asian, European, or African communities, appearances can be misleading. Members of a Hispanic "community" may be native-born Americans or first-generation immigrants; they may be from any of the twenty Latin American nations. There is no unified Asian-American subculture, regardless of whether it is labeled as such by outsiders. Even within a so-called African-American parish community there may be members who are from African nations with radically different cultural and worshiping backgrounds.

In the complexity of such cultural diversity within a worshiping community in the United States, the individuals "encounter not one but two major threats to Catholic identity: the threat to unity posed by ethnic, generational, and class diversity; and the threat to religious belief itself posed by a consumerist society that has attained unprecedented affluence for some while remaining mired in moral and material poverty.[283] This puts further pressure on parish communities and surely demands collaborative and participatory ministerial structures and approaches in ordained and lay ministerial leadership.

Another additional factor in the mix is the issue of intergenerational diversity. Researcher Scott Appleby describes three generations of possible members of a Catholic community. He describes the first as the "Old church—smells and bells" variety of Catholic. These have been brought up in an aura of mystery in their church; in Catholic school they were taught to be obedient and, generally speaking, to have their priests on a pedestal (1920–1960). Then there are those whose faith was formed during Vatican II and its aftermath (1960–1980). These are the "people of God," or a "pilgrim people." They are usually individualistic in their obedience to church law and ecumenical in their relationships. Described as "baby-boomers," and "justice-activists," most members of this age cohort were born into a "culture of narcissism" in an era of national affluence where there were wide gaps between the rich and poor. They did not know their catechism as well as their parents, their world was less dualistic, and personal conscience was a value.[284]

The third generation grew up in the period from the 1960s to 1980s and is generally described as Generation X, "who lack a recognizably Catholic moral and religious vocabulary."[285] One description of "Generation X" indicates something not only of the struggle that a priest might have in working with Generation X Catholics, but also what difficulties the Generation X seminarian might find in adapting to seminary formation programs. "We are a multicultural generation, racism still affects our relationships...sexism still works subtly...the roots of homophobia still run deep and run religious. We inherit homelessness, illiteracy, spousal abuse, drug abuse, and a hypersexual culture from our parents."[286] This is the generation out of which contemporary vocations will come. This is the generation that is in need of ministry. What formation programs can attend to this age cohort to enable effective evangelization within and for their generation?

The next generation, Generation Y, born between 1976 and 1994, is moving into the young adult group. This is the new catchment area from which vocations must be drawn. Businesses are taking account of both Generation X and Generation Y young adults, and working on ways to connect with them for marketing purposes.[287] It is to be hoped that seminary staff and vocations personnel are also aware of possible ways of connecting with this generation for ecclesial and evangelizing purposes. Such people will represent the whole panorama of the search for meaning—religious, spiritual, and agnostic. They will be bringing their own personal and generational worldview into their efforts to find meaning and purpose for living and loving authentically.

There are not simply diverse groups within Catholic communities, but there are also divisions and fragmentation within these communities that are alive and active. Catholic culture wars are still taking place inside and across parish communities. There are prevailing ideologies, supported in various media sources that delude believers into thinking that they are following the truth when it is their (or someone else's) interpretation of their faith as they remember it. Such adherents are held bound in static (rather than stable) ties of loyalty and pseudo-faithfulness rather than a commitment to the Trinitarian God as Ultimate Truth.[288] People can be held bound by a falsely remembered "orthodoxy" of the past as much as they can suffer from rigid or "laissez-faire" pastoral approaches of the present. The contemporary ministerial and experiential diversity of Catholic identity and belonging in a worshiping community is enormous.

> The assortment of professional interpreters and expositors of the faith—the religious, the lay and clerical theologians, the public intellectuals of the church, the catechists and directors or religious education—[is] split into "liberal" and "conservative" camps, with reforming movements of spirituality and activism such as Call to Action, Womanchurch, and Pax Christi positioned on the left and Cursillo, Catholics United for the Faith, and Opus Dei, among others, occupying the right half of the ideological map.[289]

Not all these groups have the same power of voice or influence, but the divisiveness is present at both the macro and micro levels of Catholic community life.

Polarization permeates such communities. This must be a factor that influences the pedagogical practice within seminaries. If the seminary faculty cannot deal constructively themselves with the factions in church and parish life, and the history of *Optatam Totius* gives evidence of such divisions at the highest level of church governance, then how can they educate seminarians to deal with the rifts in their parishes?

In terms of the expanding size of parishes and of parish clusters, Schuth comments that it is seminaries that are in "a unique and critical position to promote effective ministry of priests who are asked to serve more than one parish.[290] Seminary researchers such as Schuth, with an interviewing model of over one thousand priests, are reporting results indicating that the demands that such demographic shifts are making must surely bear fruit in new programs and approaches for the training of future priests.

Research has shown how extensive multiple parish assignments have become. Phenomena such as parish clusters make team leadership and communication skills almost mandatory. Research indicates that priests report the real need for "field education experiences with pastors serving parish clusters" to be integrated into seminary training.[291] But Schuth points out that almost no sharing of priests from one diocese to another has taken place. As long as priestly formation and spirituality are directed toward a "lone ranger" or cultic and separated style of priestly ministry, the future must seem bleak, not simply for the priests themselves in these ever-larger ministerial contexts, but also for the communities to whom they minister, and those other ministers, priestly and lay, with whom they are presently, or will be, connected on a diocesan or even inter-diocesan level.[292]

A question that must also be asked of church leaders for the present situation must be "Are they willing to consider providing some relief to the dioceses with the greatest need for priests for the sake of providing rural areas with vibrant pastoral leadership and weekly Eucharistic celebrations?"[293] The priests interviewed did not believe that their bishops would be prepared to do this. Schuth offers a variety of strategies for priests who are caught in such constricted ministerial contexts, but perhaps the title of her chapter, "Listening and Learning," sums up the most important attributes and skills that must be taught in seminaries.

Priests of the present and future must be people who are open to learn, and for this to be the case they must be able to listen to what is happening within themselves, to what is happening with their co-ministers, to what is happening with their parishioners, and to what their God is leading them to in these ever-new and ever-ancient contexts of ministerial commitment. For this quality of listening and learning to be developed in seminarians, it must be the way of being-in-relationship that characterizes the community for formators and educators in seminaries.

The purpose of priestly ministry is surely one of evangelization, and formation for evangelization is the mandate of seminaries. Following the 1990 Synod on priestly formation, there was a movement toward priestly formation directed to "the church's evangelizing task." In describing three principles of priestly formation within the context of evangelization, Bishop Derek Worlock of Liverpool, speaking in the name of the Bishops' Conference of England and Wales, said that "evangelization begins with the conversion of the evangelizer to the good news of the Gospel."[294] Worlock emphasized the importance of a deep priestly spirituality and motivation for this to take place. Second, the evangelizing task requires the capacity to work with others, as a co-worker with bishops, priests, and other Christians, "a collaborator and animator with other ministries." Ecumenism in the context of Vatican II ecclesiology was recognized as an essential element in the evangelizing commitment.

Finally, the bishops' conference commented that "encouragement must be offered to all students to move away from the underlying, often unacknowledged, fear of secular society and culture."[295] Priests "ought to be helped to know and love human society which constitutes the church's apostolic work...This requires a basic understanding of the cultural needs of the local community. These will vary in considerable measure between continents, nations, even parts of a nation. The need for pastoral formation is undoubted."[296] But the formation must be imparted in ways suited to the local culture and conditions.

In this case, the priest is truly "a man for others." Thus priestly formation for the twenty-first century requires that the formation program be one of inculturation. This inculturation process must be firmly rooted in the gospel, and Worlock quotes Pope John Paul II in support of this. "We need heralds of the Gospel who are experts in humanity, who have shared to the full the joys and hopes, the anguish and the sadnesses of our day, but who are at the same time contemplatives in love with God."[297] This is the essence of diocesan priestly spirituality, which is always connected with ministry.

During the council, Cardinal Meyer had asserted that "The end ... of all seminary formation is the apostolate, however this apostolate is going to be exercised."[298] The apostolate is always exercised in the present world and in the present circumstances of the people. Thus it requires ministers and their formators to pay careful attention to their culture. Western culture is one that has been changing rapidly during the past century, with the consequence that the experience of disconnectedness is endemic. "We are unsettled to the very roots of our being ... We have changed our environment more quickly than we know how to change ourselves."[299] The impact of the global identity on the previously northern hemisphere church is still being experienced, and its consequences are too close for us to assess.

Surely the faculty appointed to seminary training will be attuned to the culture within which the seminarian will be called to minister when he leaves the seminary. Opportunities to discover strengths and weaknesses in collaborative and cooperative ministry will be surfaced in a formation program offered by a faculty and staff composed of men and women, married, single, and religious, as well as ordained clergy. Interaction between all those involved in the seminary community at all levels of service will then provide a context and a process to assess the communicative and ministerial competence of both the educating community and the individuals receiving and responding to it.[300] This is certainly an essential component of the decree on priestly training. Inculturation and an authentically adult seminary formation are surely essential to the integrated approach recommended in *Optatam Totius*.

In taking account of the local culture and context, it is impossible to ignore consequences of the lack of vocations to the ordained priesthood that are affecting the life and identity of people at the parish level. Commentators are lamenting the fact that the Catholic Church is los-ing or has lost, over decades of parish life without a priest, its eucharistic identity.[301] This is an issue that is important for the whole church to address. Perhaps if the Catholic Church were able to take both the common and the ordained priesthood seriously, and men and women, lay and ordained, were to work collaboratively in various forms of leadership in church and society on behalf of God's reign, then more vocations to the priesthood might be the result.

SECTION III
ON THE ADAPTATION
AND RENEWAL OF RELIGIOUS LIFE

Perfectae Caritatis

PART I

THE DOCUMENT

The simplicity of the term, and often of the image, of religious life belies its complex reality. Many older people, believers or unbelievers, religious or otherwise, have received images such as the "Flying Nun" from the Western world of TV and media, of "Maria Monk"[1] or the nun who leaped "over the wall," from centuries of superstitious horror stories and romanticized tales of hidden beauty lost to the world. Those who have been taught, nursed, or cared for by nuns usually hold the memory of that experience, whether it is a positive or negative one. Younger people rarely have any image of nuns, and little interest in religious at all, unless they have come into personal contact with them. The image of religious women and men today is influenced by stereotypes of the past, misinformation, and, within the Catholic world, polarized and polarizing concepts in terms of attitudes, expectations, and experience. In reading literature of the pre-conciliar period, one wonders to what extent this might also have been the case in the Catholic world that the Vatican Council came to regenerate in the 1960s.

The pre-conciliar and dominantly European world was one where the clerical religious ordinarily had a privileged position in church and society.[2] Religious women were also privileged, in place if not in lifestyle, because of the prevailing worldview that all religious had chosen "the better part." They had been called by their God to a "higher state" of life. The response to this call was in either the monastic enclosure or the semi-enclosed apostolic life of those called to minister in the traditional services of education, health, or welfare. It is not possible, nor is it appropriate to address in this book a detailed history of religious life in the Catholic tradition.[3]

The panorama of history gives evidence of small groups of lay women who, drawn together by their commitment to Jesus Christ,

177

chose to live shared lives of prayer and asceticism in rudimentary apostolic community life in late New Testament times.[4] Along with these instances were more organized, though embryonic, communities of hermits and solitaries of the third and fourth centuries. Through the centuries the movement was made from these early local, and then more expansive, religious communities to the diverse forms of canonical religious life of the twentieth century, which played a part in the approach of council members to constructing a decree on the place and role of religious in church and society of the 1960s.

The expansion of apostolic religious orders in the period of the sixteenth to the early twentieth century in the Western church was unprecedented. Between the eighteenth and nineteenth centuries, more than "600 new religious orders were founded in Catholicism worldwide."[5] As these more active orders grew in number, the vocations to the traditional, more monastic orders declined.[6] While women chose to follow this "higher calling" in religious life, in most cases, their actual experience within the church in terms of lifestyle and ministry created demands that differed from those in monastic models.

In what was a groundbreaking book at the time, *The Nun in the World: New Dimensions in the Modern Apostolate*, Cardinal Suenens of Brussels proposed a new approach to religious women ministering in the "modern" world. His books, *Gospel to Every Creature* (1957) and *The Nun in the World*, (1962) and the many talks on religious life that he gave in the church of the 1950s and 1960s came out of Suenens's deep concern for what was happening to women religious in the semi-enclosed religious life at the time. He called for the "integration" of nuns into the "new dimensions in the modern apostolate." His proposal was not "a heavier load for their already-overcrowded time-tables [but] a pruning of them and proper attention to the scale of values. A proper balance must be obtained between the essential and indispensable components of the religious life and the priorities of what God expects of us."[7]

The absence of religious women with their giftedness "from the main spheres of influence at the adult level, spheres where they have a right to be and where their talents are called for and their presence is needed" was lamented by Suenens.[8] The fact that so many religious women in Europe seemed to function only in relation to children and to the sick and elderly was a matter of concern to him. He wanted religious women's influence to be with those who "run the world, create the climate of opinion and the atmosphere we all breathe . . . The adults who in their turn will form, or deform, the coming generation."[9]

Suenens understood the historical circumstances for the ecclesiastical repression of those women who had endeavored to engage ministerially in the ways he was proposing. Women like Angela Merici in the sixteenth century,[10] Mary Ward in the seventeenth, and Frances Xavier Cabrini in the nineteenth century,[11] had been forced to accept the regulations of monastic or semi-monastic enclosure in order to follow their vocations to minister to those on life's margins. Suenens describes the situation of the religious enclosure and the strictures imposed on apostolic women and men through the centuries. He points out that "religious constitutions did not escape the spirit of their times and were marked, as other church institutions were, by the ideologies and deficiencies of their epoch."[12]

His concern was for the liberation of women for themselves as women, and in terms of their unrealized potential for ministry simply because they were women. To support his position about the anti-feminism alive in the church, he quotes an eminent Roman canonist, consultant to the Congregation for Religious Affairs:

> It is not surprising that canon law long reflected the common conviction of woman's weakness and her incapacity in many matters. From this came the dominant concern to protect her and supply her deficiencies by men. A typical case is that concerning the enclosure of nuns. For centuries the adage *aut maritus aut murus* (a husband or a wall) was the accepted principle. To defend woman against the attacks of a brutal and not very well organized world there was no other solution conceivable: a wife was protected by her husband, if need be by cold steel; but an unmarried woman concerned for her virtue had to be shut away. True, a woman is still exposed to danger, but in our modern society immorality is less open and it is easier to avoid it behind the protection offered by the regular constabulary and an ever-alert police.[13]

Suenens adds that anti-feminist attitudes in the church are to be found among canon lawyers and spiritual writers, even in the 1960s. Another influential voice on behalf of religious in the 1960s was that of Bishop

Huyghe of Arras, France, who worked in preparation for the 1959 regional congress of apostolic religious committed to nursing and social work.

Religious vocations had been declining in numbers for some time. It was in the mid-1940s that secular institutes had begun to grow.[14] These institutes did not require their members to take vows, but they offered some of the benefits of communal identity and ministry. This was also the time of the World Congresses for the Lay Apostolate which were convened in Rome in 1951 and 1957. The identity and place of the laity in the church were coming to the fore. Lay people were beginning to claim their baptismal identity.

Against the rise of awareness of alternatives to religious life and the developing role of the laity in the church of the 1940s and 1950s, religious were struggling with their own identity and with ministry. Huyghe points out that while congregations were diminishing in numbers, their houses and ministries were reacting by asking fewer people to do more work. In one congregation there was "a decrease of 30% in the number of sisters engaged in the same works over a period of ten years; yet not a single house of the institute was closed."[15]

Another aspect of the lives of religious men and women over the 150 years before the council was the increasing centralization of religious orders as the authority of Rome was being exercised more directly on world-wide orders. "The centralization was not an isolated phenomenon but simply an instance of the increasing centralization of the Church under the authority of the Holy See from the French Revolution all the way up until Vatican II."[16] The same period had more formal communications in terms of encyclicals, decrees, solemn declarations, and briefs from the Vatican than in any previous five-hundred-year period.[17]

Increasingly bishops and heads of religious orders turned to Rome for sanctioning of their various issues and concerns. The centralization process was confirmed both implicitly and explicitly by the movement of superiors general and their administrative teams to Rome, and their tendency to then defer to Rome for decisions and direction. "More and more the Vatican offices took on such legislative activity. All of this culminated in the Code of Canon Law of 1917, one of the most impressive, ordered, universal, legislative codes, civil or religious, ever put together."[18]

The religious orders were thus complicit in the centralization of their own leadership structures, with the blessings and burdens that were a consequence of their move to Rome. At the time, many religious institutes were staffed by elderly, overworked religious who were suffering from the tensions between their ever-increasing ministerial demands and their efforts to live their religious lives according to the rigid structures of a juridically regulated semi-monastic timetable and lifestyle.[19]

Huyghe's lamentations about religious women extend to their habits and their demeanor. Their clothing—cumbersome head-dresses, voluminous and heavy robes that hid all evidence of a feminine identity (no matter what the weather)—was accompanied by training in deportment that suited earlier eras. All these practices left religious as living anachronisms rather than witnesses to an authentic Christian lifestyle.

> Many religious congregations offer the last example of artificial mannerisms that prevailed amongst upper middle-class ladies of the nineteenth century. Even the parlors with their waxed floors, their primly covered upholstery, their walls decorated with portraits of ancestors (or of deceased superiors general) recall a bygone civilization. This uniformly reserved and even solemn demeanor is adopted, not only with laymen and the clergy, but even with religious of other congregations.[20]

While these concerns about religious life, its decline in numbers, its rigidity and isolation, were being expressed at the diocesan levels in the European context, they were also a concern for the whole church.

During Pius XII's papacy and then into the 1960s, the Congregation for Religious Affairs was communicating to religious leaders its recommendations for updating. Many religious women suffered greatly.

> It is unfortunately true that there are convent communities which are nearly dying of hunger, neglect and privation; and others which, because of material difficulty, lead a very painful life. There are other communities which, without living in need, often decline, because they are separated and isolated from all the others. Moreover, laws of the cloister, often too strict, frequently provoke great difficulties.[21]

In fact, the first draft of the Vatican II schema on religious life is almost a compendium of the state of the questions about religious life as Pius XII and the Sacred Congregation had perceived them in the pre-conciliar period.[22] It is interesting to note that all the criticisms of religious life in terms of declining numbers of vocations, aging and overworked religious, ministerial burnout, and loss of an authentic religious spiritual life that were laid at the feet of Vatican II, were issues of concern to the church hierarchy in the first half of the twentieth century.

In contrast, however, to the European church of that period, American religious life was alive and flourishing, though also experiencing the pressure of outdated regulations. Some religious leaders had listened to the exhortations of Pius XII in regard to updating and renewal for the sake of authentic ministry to the people of God. In pointing out the "necessity of adapting to the present," Pius XII reminded religious that it was their duty,

> to use, as far as this is possible, all the progress in knowledge and techniques for the advantage of religion. Let the dangers and the trials which today so overwhelm the human race seem to religious as so many means of bringing back the souls of the faithful to the practice of the precepts of the Gospel; let them show that they are capable of responding to the multiplicity of their needs.[23]

There was little understanding at that time of the local implications of the renewal and adaptation that were being proposed in Rome. In 1922, when a group of American Benedictines representing a core group of seven monasteries submitted their constitution to Rome,

> they were faced with the need to represent their lives in a way that more clearly fit definitions of Benedictine life under European cultural circumstances reaching back through the modern into the medieval world. When they could not match Roman expectations of how Benedictine nuns should live with the demands of immigrant life, their Benedictine authenticity was questioned...No place existed in the ecclesiastical consciousness of the time for the concept of development within a living tradition or of cultural adaptation to new circumstances.[24]

The European ambivalence toward the new world was evident in its treatment of religious orders that endeavored to carry out their Christian mission and ministry in a world that did not carry the medieval or reformation context or identity issues. "Conflicting self understanding and expectations were woven into the fabric of American Benedictine women's history."[25]

Formational and educational initiatives such as the Sister Formation Movement were flourishing in the United States particularly. Publications of the Sister Formation series extend from 1954 to 1970 and range across a variety of topics from "The Mind of the Church in the Formation of Sisters" to issues of formation in juniorates and spiritual and intellectual formation.[26]

There was a series of workshops in 1968–69 at Woodstock College, Maryland, under the titles of "Prayer, Person and Community" and "Incorporation into the Community." From these came regional meetings of the Sister Formation Conference in 1969 on "Prayer and Renewal." In this particular conference there was a panel on "Adjustment Problems of Black, Mexican-American, Indian and Rural Candidates to the Religious Life."

New issues that were arising from the changing culture of U.S. religious life were being addressed at national and regional levels through the Sister Formation Movement, and this was an initiative that was also taken up in Canada.[27] The Canadian Religious Conference also engaged in renewal and adaptation initiatives through consultations and workshops.[28] The North American response was not received by the European leadership with unqualified recognition or appreciation. Perhaps the most significant aspect of the background to the Vatican II mandate for religious is the ambivalence that characterized the relationship between the Vatican and religious men and women. Religious of the old and new worlds were struggling with different issues in terms of the communities in which they lived and for which they were called to serve, and with juridical requirements that were not in keeping with the diverse demands of their ministries or their circumstances.

With regard to religious women there was always a tension between those who heard the call for renewal and adaptation and saw ways in which their mission could respond with vision and courage, and those who were locked into a commitment of conventional subordination and the acceptance of an obedience that reduced religious ministry and lifestyle to a unity expressed in conformity and submission.

> Soldiers of God they had always been, but their appearance and their way of life (in the early period) generally had more in common with lay women than with clerical men. Now the characteristics of an army on active duty—their uniform dress, their disciplined manner, their common mess, and their barrack-like quarters—set them apart from lay women and marked them as part of the clerical force.[29]

However, they ranked in the lowest levels of church life, as they had none of the power of the clergy.

The transition of the place of religious in the church was a radical one, requiring a movement away from dominant past perceptions of women and men religious as "an ecclesiastical job corps" or "an exotic spiritual subculture" or even "a comfortable lifestyle enclave for the religious elite."[30]

THE HISTORY OF THE DOCUMENT

To understand *Perfectae Caritatis* (*PC*), the Decree on the Adaptation and Renewal of Religious Life, it is essential to see it in the context of the other conciliar documents, particularly those on the church, *Lumen Gentium* (*LG*) and *Gaudium et Spes* (*GS*), and on missionary activities, *Ad Gentes* (*AG*). The doctrinal foundations for the decree are to be found, not in the decree itself, but particularly in chapter 4 of the Dogmatic Constitution on the Church. The opening sentence of the decree acknowledges this. "The sacred synod has already shown in the constitution on the Church that the pursuit of perfect charity through the evangelical counsels draws its origin from the doctrine and example of the Divine Master and reveals itself as a splendid sign of the heavenly kingdom" (*PC*, 1).

In July 1960 the Commission for Religious, which was chaired by Cardinal Valeri, a member of the Sacred Congregation for Religious, with Fr. O. Rousseau, a member of the Oblate Congregation, a clerical religious order, as secretary, began to gather and arrange material for its work.[31] The commission was composed mostly of religious, thirty-five of whom were resident in Rome, and half of its members were affiliated with the Roman curia.

From the beginning, the commission was under the influence of the Sacred Congregation for Religious and this was evident at all stages in the formation and presentation of the document.[32] Most meetings took place in Rome, and in the preparatory stage they were usually held twice a week. The material for discussion had been gathered from the responses to requests sent out by the preparatory commission to bishops and major superiors of clerical religious orders. They had been requested to consult with "prudent and enlightened advisers" before replying. An indication of the amount of consultation that went into these responses may be indicated by the response of one major superior: "I have written these few notes in the presence of God." Alberigo's wry comment is that the superior obviously consulted no-one![33]

The commission had been asked to address five key areas in their document: the renewal of religious life, the union or the federation of religious institutes, the exemption of religious, and the religious habit. By early November 1960, twenty topics had been identified and accepted at the first plenary session of the commission. Studies on these topics were sought from members and consultors. Responses were synthesized into a preparatory draft of thirty-two chapters in two sections that presented church doctrine on the nature and character of religious life and practical suggestions for its renewal. There were two hundred articles and numerous footnotes in the first text. The text was delivered to the Central Preparatory Commission (CPC) in eleven installments in early 1962.

The doctrinal dimension of the text was not theological in character but juridical. The theological aspects of religious life had been left to the theological commission to address.[34] Friedrich Wulf's comment that there was little unity in the document, or in the commission itself, is evidenced at this early stage of the different approaches to, and understandings of, the religious life in this large commission.[35]

The strength of the document was perhaps in its substance. To read the documents cited from this draft would enable one to reconstruct almost the whole of the teaching of Pius XII on the religious state, and his efforts to adapt this state to modern times as well as similar efforts made during the previous twenty years by the Sacred Congregation for

Religious.[36] That there were five drafts presented to the council and a number of title changes is another indication of the tensions within the commission, the problem of presenting an acceptable text, and the concern of the council members to have a document that might adequately represent the renewal and adaptation that was so obviously required.

The title of the first massive text, itself modeled on the approach taken to religious life at the Council of Trent, was "Questions Concerning the Life of Religious."[37] The text had a tone of defensiveness, of combating errors of naturalism and activism, which had already been condemned by Pius XII. The "naturalism" under discussion implied a neglect of supernatural motivation for religious life, and "activism" implied the lack of prayerfulness, brought on by a concern for social justice issues, that could prevent a return to the authentic spirit of the founders.

The concept of renewal foundational to this first schema was a restoration of what belongs essentially to the nature of religious life itself, and to the intentions of the founder, and the adaptation was directed to meet the changing circumstances of time and place. However, no renewal or adaptation could be undertaken without the approval of the Holy See. The criteria for both adaptation and renewal in this schema were virtually the same, "fidelity to the intentions and spirit of the founders and respect for the historic patrimony" of the order.[38]

This first draft, like the four that were to follow, was rejected by the CPC as needing revision before discussion by the council. In March 1962, Cardinal Suenens wrote a criticism of all those preparatory texts, including the draft on religious life, which were the stuff of law rather than renewal and which failed to address the pastoral renewal that had been called for. In response, the commission met to rework the rejected text and by April the commission delivered a further text, "States That Aim at Perfection," reduced at this stage to one hundred pages, to the Central Preparatory Commission for council debate.

In October 1962, Cardinal Döpfner, as member of the Central Preparatory Commission, was appointed as the reporter to work in liaison with the Commission on Religious Life. Because of the volume and depth of material to be dealt with by the council, the instruction for many of the reconstituted commissions, including the Commission on Religious Life, was to abbreviate their schema. The reconstituted commission, under the leadership now of Cardinal Antoniutti, a member of the Sacred Congregation for Religious, and described as a member of the faction described as "zealots," received on January 30, 1963, the instruction to abbreviate the text.[39] Commission members were given concrete suggestions for abbreviations as well as a list of topics which had to be discussed.

The religious life was the responsibility of two commissions, the one led by Cardinal Antoniutti, and the other the doctrinal commission assigned to handle doctrines that dealt with issues related to the church and religious life, especially in terms of the universal call to holiness. A theological approach to religious life was therefore the task of the doctrinal commission. The Commission on Religious Life was concerned with addressing juridical aspects of the various forms of religious life and secular institutes in the church. From these two groups a few members were selected to form a new sub-commission, described as a "mixed" commission, to work on the chapter on the religious vocation in the schema on the church.

Commentators on this decree point out the difficulties in doing justice to the development of the schema on religious life, to the conciliar commissions involved in the drafts on religious life in the council, and to the debates on the decree itself.[40] Early in 1963 the mixed commission had worked on chapter 4 of the schema on the church and they had composed a revised text that should have then been sent for approval by the full doctrinal commission. But instead of doing this, the mixed commission bypassed both the doctrinal and religious life commissions and submitted their text directly to the Central Preparatory Commission. This bypassing of the doctrinal commission prompted it to reject not only the revised chapter but also the mixed commission itself, and instead, on its own authority, the doctrinal commission appointed an entirely new writing group chaired by Bishop Charue of Namur, with no reference at all to the Commission on Religious Life. Charue had exercised an important role of both leadership and mediation between factions in the council on other issues and he played an important role in this new sub-commission.[41]

The new "Charue draft" was completed in some haste, and it was accepted by the doctrinal commission for submission to the CPC, again bypassing the Commission on Religious Life. The CPC duly accepted the Charue document on religious life. On July 4, 1963, the newly elected Paul VI accepted the decision of the CPC and ordered the immediate sending out of the Charue version of the chapter, which signaled its new approach in the title: "The Call to Holiness in the Church."[42]

The Commission on Religious Life had been totally ignored in this process and it denied that the issues related to religious life had been authentically represented by the few religious chosen by the doctrinal commission to work with Charue in developing the theological foundations for religious life. Having been cut out of the process, the Commission on Religious Life was hostile to this chapter of *Lumen Gentium* and its treatment of religious life. Commission members found the content of the new draft unacceptable, and they immediately alerted many bishops from religious orders about their exclusion from the discussion on this section on religious life and about the action of the doctrinal commission.

The religious order bishops were a formidable group in their own right, and they knew how to exercise their influence in the voting process. The count of religious bishops varied from 1,050 to 800, according to different criteria used.[43] (It is perhaps of interest to note that, while the 300,000 male religious were represented by these more than 800 clerics, there was no woman's voice to represent the more than one million women religious serving the church).[44] The religious order bishops and leaders offered their support to the members of the Commission on Religious Life against the direction of the Commission on Doctrine. This was a reason for the division among the council members in general in regard to the acceptance of the revised draft of the schema when it came up for discussion in the second and third sessions of the council.

At this point it may be useful to address the actual issues that were under debate in each of the two commissions, the doctrinal and the religious life commissions. A major factor in the debate was the understanding of religious life. The Commission on Religious Life made no attempt to define religious life theologically, believing this to be the mandate of the doctrinal commission. However, the issue that was fundamental to both commissions was that of the call to perfection expressed in and responded to by the evangelical life lived according to the counsels, in particular, by chastity, obedience, and poverty.

To understand the relationship between the two groups it is important to look at the theological foundations of chapter 6 of *Lumen Gentium*. The doctrinal commission chose to propose a definition for religious life in the church. Unlike the Commission on Religious Life, it moved away from the language of "call to perfection," from the emphasis on the following of the counsels, and from the traditional scriptural call of the rich young man (Matt 19:16–22). Contemporary biblical studies and theological updating no longer allow such a proof-text approach to the call to live a more "perfect" life as a religious.[45]

The ecclesiology of Vatican II affirmed the baptismal call as the call to perfection, a call to all Christians, no matter what their life commitment. Thus the evangelical counsels are addressed to all Christians, the entire church, not simply to religious. The universality of Christ's call to holiness was the subject of the debate on the different states of the Christian life, and this formed the content of what were ultimately chapters 5 and 6 of *Lumen Gentium*. To follow Jesus, to do God's will, and in this following to be enlivened by the power of the Holy Spirit is the baptismal mandate and promise. This is of the essence of the ecclesiology that permeated all the conciliar documents. The concern was to determine how to define religious life in such a way that the result was not a setting up of "grades" or "classes" of Christians. According to chapter 6,

> the religious state of life is not an intermediate state between the clerical and lay states. But, rather, the faithful of Christ are called by God from both these states of life so that they might enjoy this particular gift in the life of the Church and thus each in one's own way, may be of some advantage to the salvific mission of the Church. (*LG*, 43, par. 2)

The emphasis in this chapter is on the stable form of life that is integral to religious life. Elitism or the superiority of one calling over the other is deliberately omitted.

The notion of community is a complex one, because the secular institutes and other non-communal forms of the consecrated life are included in the draft. "These religious families give their members the support of a more firm stability in their way of life and a proven doctrine of acquiring perfection" (*LG*, 43, par. 1). However, because the majority of religious do live in community, the most common expression of a stable form of life integral to the ecclesiology espoused in this document is community life.[46]

The Christian who belongs to a religious order differs, therefore, from other Christians, not necessarily because [he or she]
is seeking a more intense following of Jesus—this may be
sought also by Christians in the world—but because, in reply to
a call [he or she] has chosen to do this in a community designed
to facilitate and promote this quest...What is specific about
religious communities is that they have been instituted by the
Church for the express purpose of intensifying the following of
Christ.[47]

Chapter 6 of *Lumen Gentium* defines religious life in terms of both
the intensity of, and the intimacy in, the following of Christ. By their
"profession of the evangelical counsels" of poverty, chastity and obedience, religious are "more intimately consecrated to divine service" (*LG*,
44, par. 1).[48] The essential choice for the aspirant to religious life, then, is
the commitment to join a community in a public ecclesial commitment.

The vows, their number and definition, are a canonical question. What counts is the commitment of a person to lead the
Christian life in a religious community (or some other stable
form of life) devised to intensify communion with Christ. It follows that the definition of religious life given in the *Constitution
on the Church* provides great liberty for the future unfolding and
development of religious life in the entire Church.[49]

Theologically, the baptismal fellowship of religious, and its intensifying
of one's relationship with Christ, enables a new opening up of relationships toward other Christians, and to the world in which they live.

The Tridentine rejection of the world, which had its place in the
adversarial context of the period, is not the context of Vatican II ecclesiology. Those regulations which were a consequence of the rejection of
the world can no longer be operative. Instead, a solidarity between all
Christians is a baptismal responsibility, and the living out of their specific charism determines the apostolic outreach of religious.

The evangelical counsels which lead to charity join their followers to the Church and its mystery in a special way. Since
this is so, the spiritual life of these people should then be de-

voted to the welfare of the whole Church. From this arises
their duty of working to implant and strengthen the Kingdom
of Christ in souls and to extend that Kingdom to every clime.
This duty is to be undertaken to the extent of their capacities
and in keeping with the proper type of their own vocation.
This can be realized through prayer or active works of the
apostolate. It is for this reason that the Church preserves and
fosters the special character of her various religious institutes.
(*LG*, 44, par. 2)

Religious discipline and lifestyle is in accord with this mission in the
contemporary world.

The location of the religious vocation in the context of the universal call to holiness is an affirmation of the union of all the baptized in
Christ and in his mystical body.[50] This means that the Christian commandment to love God and one's neighbor is a single commandment.
"Christian life may not be described as a quest for the love of God, and
after some progress has been made in this, also a quest for the love of
neighbor."[51]

There is an eschatological dimension to Christian witness and ministry in and through religious life.

The profession of the evangelical counsels, then, appears as a
sign which can and ought to attract all the members of the
Church to an effective and prompt fulfillment of the duties of
their Christian vocation. The people of God have no lasting
city here below, but look forward to one that is to come. Since
this is so, the religious state, whose purpose is to free its members from earthly cares, more fully manifests to all believers the
presence of heavenly goods already possessed here below.
Furthermore, it not only witnesses to the fact of a new and eternal life acquired by the redemption of Christ, but it foretells
the future resurrection and the glory of the heavenly kingdom.
(*LG*, 44, par. 3)

This commitment extends across all the various forms of commitment
of religious orders, apostolic and monastic, and of the various forms of
secular institutes recognized by the church.

The tendency to dichotomize the apostolic life and the interior quest for holiness is corrected when the document on religious life is read in the context of *Lumen Gentium*'s chapters 5 and 6 particularly. When the universal call to holiness is grasped, then the unity of love of God, of neighbor, and of the created world take on a new dimension.

> The older viewpoint that the primary purpose of religious life is the seeking of personal perfection and the secondary purpose is to serve the Church in the apostolate, can no longer be defended. These two ends of religious life are so intimately connected that they cannot be classified as primary and secondary.[52]

Religious profession, according to Vatican II, is an intensifying of the commitment made at baptism to love and serve Christ in and through his mystical body.

Because after Vatican II the Decree on the Adaptation and Renewal of Religious Life was not always read in light of the church documents, the significance of religious life itself came under question. The universal call to holiness seemed to many religious to be an undervaluing of the currency of religious life and of its place in the church. It is made clear that religious are not part of the hierarchical structure of the church: "The state which is constituted by the profession of the evangelical counsels, though it is not the hierarchical structure of the Church..." Even the second part of that sentence, "nevertheless, [it] undeniably belongs to its life and holiness" (*LG*, 44, par. 4), did not seem to carry any real weight in the scheme of things.

The asceticism and the apostolic demands of religious life in the past had been heavy, but the sense that religious were called to a higher state, or were living a more perfect life had given some support to religious struggling with their vocation. Now the question that came to them, and to those who may have thought of joining religious life, was whether in the following of Christ the religious life had any greater significance than the lay state. The value of religious life in itself was the subject of new questions and concerns.

In addressing the theological foundation for religious life in chapters 5 and 6 of *Lumen Gentium*, Baum comments that

> Becoming a member of a religious community signifies an enduring commitment to follow Christ more intensely as part of a family dedicated to his service. In this quest the religious is aided by the community and (they in turn aid each other).[53]

The strength and support of the community enable the religious to undertake tasks that would be impossible or at least daunting to the lone Christian without communal backing. Members of religious communities are a sign in the church of the transcendence of the reign of God and of the complete commitment to mission to which Christ invites all Christians in baptism. As such, religious share in the prophetic mission of their order. Their lives become a visible sign "inviting other Christians to follow Christ more faithfully, a more visible sign than it could be if [they] followed Christ in the world. Through religious profession, the Christian enters more fully into the mystery of the church's ministry of reconciliation."[54]

As the council progressed, tensions grew among the council members and in the commissions. The contextualization of religious life in the universal call to holiness did not fit easily with the more juridical approach of some of the members of the Commission on Religious Life who were resistant to the new directions the council was taking. Other members were determined to present a schema that was attentive to the mandate for a pastoral council, and to the new circumstances in which religious lived and ministered. The Commission on Religious Life stayed focused on the notion of three evangelical counsels and with the states of perfection in their early drafts. Religious life was described in the earlier drafts as a special charism that enables religious to witness and minister to Christ and the people of God in a way in which other Christians are not called to minister. "It is a gift of God granted primarily for the sake of the Christian community... The charisms which the one Spirit grants in the Christian church are many and diverse."[55]

The diversity of approaches, statutes, organizational forms, and the lifestyles into which the world of the religious was broken up was a further cause of the complexity of the task on which the Commission on Religious Life was working. At the same time, the increasing pressures of debates about the episcopate and the local church, the increasing interest in and emphasis on the lay apostolate, along with the

unprecedented attitude of openness to the world with the inevitable
impact this would have on the regular religious life, were at best dis-
concerting to the conservative but powerful minority and to their followers among council members.

The task of abbreviation of the schema on religious life had been
undertaken by a subcommission of the Commission on Religious Life
under the chairmanship of Archbishop Paul Philippe, a member of the
Dominican order and a representative of the Holy Office, and the secretary of the Commission for Religious, a Cistercian monk, Fr.
Compagnone, both strong defendants of the work of the initial commission. They worked together with consultants they had selected for
the task.[56] Their draft was accepted by the plenary Commission on
Religious Life at its meeting in February–March 1963 and handed to
the CPC on March 9 for approval. As was to be expected, the draft contained nothing new in comparison with the pre-conciliar draft; but, in
accord with the pastoral orientation meanwhile declared by the council, all condemnations were avoided. The draft was sent out to the
council members who were asked to send back comments by July 1963.
Bishop Huyghe, a member of the Commission on Religious Life, commented at the time that the glimmers of light in the commission discussion shone through rarely.[57]

As their liaison and CPC member responsible for the Commission
on Religious Life, Cardinal Döpfner commended the work for its abbreviation (from 100 pages to 35 pages) and its attention to requested
changes. This text recognized that the apostolic life of religious was
now valued rather than seen as a danger. But the CPC was not in favor
of the title of this draft, "On Religious," because it was too narrow and
not applicable to the secular institutes, nor did they approve of the frequent use of the term "state of perfection" in regard to the religious life.

The CPC also objected to the fact that there was too little attention
given to the Christological and ecclesiological concept of religious life
associated with the counsels. The narrowness that has plagued the official ecclesiastical concept of the religious state especially since the nineteenth century was in evidence in this text.[58] The absence of biblical and
theological support for the presentation of religious life was remarked
upon and needed to be attended to in the next draft.[59]

As both conciliar historian and member of the Commission on
Religious Life, Wulf describes in some detail the dissension in the

commission with regard to the traditional doctrine of the evangelical counsels, which had been such a decisive feature of religious life in the past, and its place in contemporary ecclesiology. "Counsels were too much severed from the perennial activation of God's loving will. They were materialized and regarded as objective moral performances, to some extent as a superstructure above the commandments that bound everyone."[60]

The response of council members to the reworked draft was notable for its volume and for its diversity. The approach was too dualistic in its division between the interior life and the apostolic life for many members of the council to accept. The harshest reaction was from the English and Dutch bishops. This text was seen to be simply a repetition of earlier Vatican documents and statements on religious life without any connection to the conciliar context. There was no explanation or development of an understanding of religious consecration, or of the connection between religious life and the gospels, or the pastoral character of religious communities.[61] Many of the bishops disapproved of the title, "On the States that Aim at Perfection," and the text was criticized on the grounds of being too juridical and not genuinely pastoral in its approach.

There was nothing said about the collaboration of religious orders and episcopates. Some felt that there was a Latinized uniformity in the presentation of religious life. There was little understanding of, or even attention given to, the diverse geographical contexts in which religious life was being lived. The deeper problems of adaptation and renewal from the perspectives of theological, anthropological, psychological, and sociological angles were not addressed at all.

Commentators on this decree point out that in spite of the amount and type of radical criticism that was made in council and even underlined in the CPC Minutes of the Report of March 27, Philippe considered that the text had been approved with only minor corrections required. He made the unilateral decision to cancel the next scheduled plenary session of the Commission on Religious Life and proposed that the amendments requested be undertaken by a sub-committee for completion before the third session of the council in October. There was dissension about this decision among the members, but it was ignored, so, as a member of the commission himself, Huyghe sent in his own suggestions for renewal of contemplative orders for consideration by the sub-committee.

Because of Döpfner's status, and the fact that his amendments in the council hall had been noted in the CPC minutes, about half of his suggestions were incorporated into the next draft and the reasons for the omissions of the others were included in numerous footnotes. Huyghe's proposals were discounted and omitted on juridical grounds. The amended 1963 draft was approved by the CPC and distributed to the council members on April 22, 1963. The polarized approach to religious life that had characterized the Commission on Religious Life from its beginnings remained operative throughout the council. "Unanimity was found only in the view that the renewal demanded by the Church and recognized as necessary required a return to origins as well as an accommodation to the needs of the world."[62] But the control for interpreting this view was in the hands of Philippe and his curial colleagues.

This 1963 draft did not come to the council for discussion because the discussion on the document on the church, subsequently *Lumen Gentium*, had taken a month. The Commission on Religious Life received a letter from the CPC requiring a further abbreviation of the text and greater attention to the pastoral intention of the council. A letter dated January 23, 1964, was sent to the Commission on Religious Life informing it that the revised and abbreviated schema was to state only the essential points of religious life in the form of propositions, of short guiding principles—essential points—of appropriate renewal of religious life.[63] This schema would then be presented in the third session without any debate, and a vote would simply be taken. The Commission on Religious Life worked on this task during two sessions in early 1964. The text was reduced from fifty-one to nineteen articles in a four-page document that was sent out to the bishops on April 27.

Wulf points out that there was little response to this amended 1963 draft, and what response there was indicated the prevailing polarization of viewpoints. He notes that there were only two bishops who rejected the entire schema, and they did so for completely opposite reasons. Cardinal Heenan considered that the draft in its truncated form said so little and was so disappointing it ought not to be published. Jesuit superior general Fr. Janssen, (who died in October 1964) thought that "the draft was so loud in its call for an *aggiornamento* that it encouraged a dangerous weakening of the essential elements in religious life of obedience, poverty, chastity and love."[64] There were also quite diverse reactions to the specific articles, especially those related to the monastic orders. A fear was expressed by some bishops that the monastic and contemplative lives were being devalued in the conciliar discussions. Major superiors of apostolic orders felt that their ministerial works were being overlooked.

The tensions between the juridical approach to the unity between the contemplative and apostolic dimensions of religious life and its lived reality were the subject of heated discussion. This was most evident in the discussions on articles 5 and particularly 6 in the final text.

> Let those who make profession of the evangelical counsels seek and love above all else God who has first loved us (cf. 1 John 4:10) and let them strive to foster in all circumstances a life hidden with Christ in God (cf. Col. 3:3). This love of God both excites and energizes that love of one's neighbor which contributes to the salvation of the world and the building up of the Church. This love, in addition, quickens and directs the actual practice of the evangelical counsels. (*PC*, 6)

The complaint of modern congregations was with "the theological characterization of the active religious life" which, as it was "conceived in monastic terms, obstructed rather than encouraged the characteristic spirituality of the apostolic religious life. In these orders, apostolic work is of the essence of their religious lives; it is their way to holiness."[65] The superior general of the Missionary Society of Scheut[66] formulated the statement which was incorporated almost totally in the final text of the decree. In addressing apostolic communities it is noted that

> apostolic and charitable activity belongs to the very nature of the religious life, seeing that it is a holy service and a work characteristic of love, entrusted to them by the Church to be carried out in its name. Therefore, the whole religious life of their members should be inspired by an apostolic spirit and all their apostolic activity formed by the spirit of religion. (*PC*, 8, par. 2)

Among the further amendments which were made that also became part of the text were articles 2 (c) on participation in the life of the church and renewal initiatives; 18 on lifelong formation and personal development; 19 on fresh forms of religious life; 20 on the missionary spirit.

Two extra articles on chastity and obedience were proposed and accepted as supplements to the existing articles on these topics because of the number of requests from the bishops. Wulf notes that these supplements were derived from a speech of Paul VI to religious congregations in May 1964.

> This demonstrated how reluctant people were to depart from the material produced by the Preparatory Commission, and to open the door to new stimuli and new perceptions. It required the energetic intervention of some of the members of the Commission to change the too negative style at least of the article on chastity, and to introduce a more positive and apostolic horizon, at the same time pointing out the psychological side of education for the free acceptance of celibacy. (The original had been made up of warnings and exhortations.)[67]

Although the document appeared to be locked into the curial approach of the first draft, commentators were aware of the progress that had been made, considering the initial document and the polarization that still prevailed in the Commission on Religious Life itself.

One of the factors in the debate on the religious life text and in the eventual acceptance of the decree was the tension that had been generated in the discussions on the chapter on religious in *Lumen Gentium*. In the second session of the council, Cardinal Döpfner had called for an end to the debate on whether to have a separate chapter on religious. Some bishops in support also argued that the Commission on Religious Life document had become superfluous in view of the protracted debates that had taken place on religious life and the universal call to holiness that resulted in *Lumen Gentium* chapters 5 and 6, but their numbers were not among the religious. In contrast, a number of religious order bishops and major superiors felt that they had been badly treated by the moderators.[68] This was a strong and forceful group who were in support of the fourth draft of the Commission on Religious Life schema on religious life. This draft, with a new title, "On the Adaptation and Renewal of Religious Life"

(*Perfectae Caritatis*) had been completed shortly before its scheduled public discussion of November 10–12.

An interesting feature of the third session at which the religious life schema was to be discussed was that women and particularly women religious were invited to be present at the council for the first time. The process of the invitation of female observers is itself an indication of the opposing viewpoints among the council members, at all level of attendance. On September 8, 1964, less than a week before the third session resumed, Paul VI, addressing a large group of women religious, made the following announcement:

> We have made arrangements so that some qualified and devout women can be present, as auditors, at some of the solemn rites and some of the general congregations of the upcoming third session of the Second Vatican Council; we mean those congregations that will be discussing questions of particular interest to women. Thus we will have, perhaps for the first time, present at an ecumenical council, a few (obviously) but significant and as it were symbolic women representatives; they will represent you women religious, first, and then all Catholic women's organizations so that women will know how much the Church honors them in the dignity of their existence and their human and Christian mission. (*Insegnamenti*, II, 529, Caprile, II, 492)[69]

Both Fesquet and Alberigo point out that this has all the appearances of a last-minute decision by the pope and one that was apparently not well received by all the council members, especially among the curia.

On September 12 Cardinal Cicognani informed Archbishop Felici (secretary of the CPC) of the pope's decision and sent him a list of the new lay auditors and of the lay and religious women whom the pope had named. Felici was responsible for the organization of this matter, and it was his task to make the appropriate contacts. He did not do this until September 18, four days after the opening speech in which Paul VI had included a greeting to the women auditors, none of whom was present! The letters of invitation were signed and mailed on September 21.

Eight women religious (including Mother Mary Luke Tobin, superior general of the Sisters of Loretto and president of the Conference of Major Religious Superiors of Women's Institutes of America) and seven lay women were invited. The pope had indicated that the women were welcome to attend those sessions which were relevant to their particular interests. Alberigo notes that Mother Mary Luke Tobin, when told that her pass enabled her to attend sessions of interest to women, replied, "Good, then I can attend them all."[70] So women, and particularly women religious, were in attendance when the decree on religious life was to be debated.

The new text, consisting of twenty short paragraphs (between four and ten lines each) was presented in booklet form with the reasons for the acceptance or rejection of written amendments submitted. Bishop McShea, of Allentown, Pennsylvania, was appointed by the Commission on Religious Life to introduce the document. He gave an overview of the points contained and justified the brevity of the text in view of the demands made by the CPC, and showed that the document was concerned to present the means to "an appropriate renewal" in conjunction with the goal of the council. The attendance in the council hall was high, as was the participation in the debate.

Following the rules of precedence, Cardinal Spellman spoke first. He approved of the schema as it stood but urged that caution be exercised in planning renewal. He believed that superiors of women religious were themselves fearful that the council was imposing an active apostolate on them that would diminish their religious life. He was referring particularly to the suggestions made by Cardinal Suenens about new apostolates, and of his encouragement to women religious to work with adults rather than children. Spellman argued that it was sufficient for religious to do what they had always been respected for—nursing, teaching, or the contemplative life. He was worried on behalf of women religious about a possible move toward activism at the expense of their interior life.

There were two obvious factions in the debate that ensued over the next two days. There were those who favored a more expansive understanding of the religious life. They wanted the present text rejected because they saw it as too conservative and too narrow. The representative speakers of this group were the European Cardinals Richaud, Döpfner, Suenens, and Bea, Bishops Charue and Huyghe, and Fathers Buckley, superior general of the Marists, and Lalande, superior general of the Congregation of the Holy Cross. This group represented the majority voice of council members.

The other faction was either in favor of the text as it stood or at least strongly opposed to any drastic alterations in religious life. The representative speakers of this group were Cardinals Ruffini of the curia, Landázuri-Ricketts of Lima, Fathers Fernandez, master general of the Dominicans, Anastasio, master general of the Discalced Carmelites, and Perantoni, former minister general of the Franciscans. This was the minority voice, but they were able to marshal supporters to their side from many of the religious order bishops.

Cardinal Döpfner was most outspoken in his criticism of what he described as a weak schema full of pious old formulae. He argued that its deficiencies did not arise from its abbreviation, as Bishop McShea had proposed, but because it had failed to come to grips with the basic problems of religious renewal, of the accommodation of religious life to modern times, of the preparation of religious for their vocation, and because it took too restricted a view of religious institutes.

Like many of his faction, Döpfner was concerned for the pressures on women religious who often found themselves torn between the demands of a semi-monastic community lifestyle and a heavy apostolic workload. He spoke against the institutional narrowness that was a feature of many contemplative communities in particular.[71] He pointed out that what had been described as a "crisis of obedience" was a matter for superiors as well as for subjects because the obedience required should be that of the mature adult, not a child or servant.

Cardinal Suenens reaffirmed the points he had often made in his controversial book on women religious in the modern world.[72] He was concerned that many people, including the hierarchy, treated nuns as children or minors rather than as adults. He urged a freedom for them to engage in apostolic work that had significance for the present time. He lamented the lack of an appropriate spirituality for active religious and asked theologians to work on developing a "spirituality of the active life for them," so that they could get away from "the traditions and mentality of the cloister."[73]

Suenens wanted the religious apostolate to be more directed to the work of "evangelization," with more frequent contacts between religious and laity. He envisaged that the role of religious should be to help inspire the laity in their apostolate. Religious should be encouraged to work in cooperation with others in ministry.

We should give up the habit of treating nuns as minors, an attitude so typical of the nineteenth century, which is still found in many religious congregations today. This emphasis on infantilism is matched by another disgraceful trait: the exhibition of maternalism on the part of mother superiors. Let us abandon these customs which perpetuate a feeling of inferiority among women religious. They are based, not on consideration for the requirements of religious life, but on outmoded ideas about society. As for cloistering active orders, this serves for the most part as an obstacle to their effectiveness; it prevents nuns from being the leaven in the loaf which they ought to be.[74]

He lamented the absence of reference in the schema to the poverty of Christ as well as to his chastity and obedience. He called for canon lawyers and competent religious women to work together to develop rules for a more balanced organization of religious orders; for a change in the system of electing superiors; for general chapters to be more truly representative of the order; and for the abandonment of outmoded forms of garb, anachronistic customs, and the like. His conclusion was that the text should be rejected and a new one drawn up. This was seconded by Bishop Moors of Holland.

Several speakers, such as Jesuit Cardinal Bea (a major contributor to the documents on ecumenism and Christian unity) referred to the "crisis" in the religious life now being experienced. It was not sufficient to urge, as the schema did, a renovation primarily in the juridical sphere. Cardinal Bea was concerned because there was little in the schema for the 300,000 male and 1,200,000 women religious who were presently serving the church. He proposed that there should be an introduction to the schema that laid a theological foundation for religious life.[75] The text should point out that the consecration of the religious regarded not only the individual Christ, but the whole Christ, that is, the church, as described in *Lumen Gentium*.

The debate between the factions was heated and lively. Huyghe, speaking as a member of the commission, criticized what he described as a barren text. Finally, he made a remark much appreciated by some and deplored by others: "The commission should consult superiors general of women's orders, especially those who have been invited to the council as auditors."[76] He noted that it was unfortunately customary for legislation regarding religious to be drawn up by men only. It was a matter of concern to him that no woman religious had been consulted by the Commission on Religious Life, even to the extent that male lay auditors and experts had been consulted on the document on the apostolate of the laity.[77]

Several speakers spoke on behalf of large groups of bishops. Rynne commented on what he perceived to be particularly outstanding interventions delivered by Fathers Buckley and Lalande, who pointed out that while the conservatively oriented Congregation for Religious had been "pushing" for the adaptation of religious orders since 1950, nothing important had been done and the present text, which was intended to accomplish this purpose, was completely inadequate as it stood.[78]

With the tensions between religious orders and bishops being obvious in these discussions, not least because of the delicate issue of exemptions for religious, Buckley asked that a gesture of friendship toward the diocesan clergy be included in the new draft.

> We religious may be worried about the greater authority that bishops want to have over us; but we ought to face up to the fact that some of our habits irritate the diocesan clergy, such as our tendency to talk as if we were the only ones in the state of perfection. The sound spirituality of diocesan priests should be recognized. In fact religious priests of the active life are closer to diocesan priests than to contemplative religious. The canonical distinction, while necessary, should not be insisted on in practice, for what unites us is more important than what separates us.[79]

He asked that the distinction between orders and congregations be dropped and joined with Döpfner and Suenens in requesting a contemporary understanding of obedience. He commented that "today's young people don't swallow archaic formulas like 'the will of the superior is exactly the same as the will of God.'"[80]

Those bishops who had defended themselves against the prickly subject of the exemption of monasteries and convents from episcopal jurisdiction, and of the nature of privileges connected with religious profession, made few interventions in the debate, and their language was discreet, although some did argue that the maintenance of exemption was a key issue for religious.[81] As time was drawing to a close, McShea made his concluding speech in which he defended the schema against almost all the objections, because, he argued, they referred to the third redaction, or they were excessively minute, or they were matters to be dealt with in the proposed new code of canon law, or because they were the concern of *Lumen Gentium* or *Christus Dominus*.

Wulf summed up the debate: "Some saw the draft as a sufficient basis for further study, even if requiring improvement and expansion on certain points, others categorically rejected it and demanded, often with great passion, a complete revision."[82] When a commission approved its own schema, as the Commission on Religious Life had done with *Perfectae Caritatis*, the tendency was for the bishops to vote in approval.[83] Felici called for the vote on whether to proceed to detailed voting and the votes were 1,555 in favor, 882 against, and 5 invalid. The high number of disapproving votes meant that further revision would have to take place. There would be a vote on the separate propositions two days later.

A factor in support of *Perfectae Caritatis* was the massive concerted and consistent action on the part of the many conservatively inclined bishops and religious who had been called on when there had been a sense of threat to the traditional understanding of religious life in the earlier debates on the church. They regarded this schema as a means of claiming lost territory and a safeguard against too much reform.

Cardinals Döpfner and Suenens were aware of this and they marshaled support for their intention to reject the schema as it stood, so that when the individual propositions were put to the vote, articles 1–13, representing the weakest portion of the text, were not carried because of a large number of "approved with reservations" votes (*iuxta modems*). Articles 14–20 were approved by a two-thirds majority, with only minor amendments. In this way the majority of bishops, rather than the minority of conservatives, forced the commission to give consideration to their demands and come up with a more radically revised text than would otherwise have been the case.[84]

The Commission on Religious Life had to go back to revise the text and deal with the record number of 14,000 amendments proposed, the highest number for any schema.[85] But because of the divided nature of the commission, everything depended on the composition of the subcommissions that would be allotted particular articles for revision. In working on reducing the amendments for the revision, the factional nature of the amendments was obvious, with the polarized positions of each group evident.

At the commission meeting, the president, Cardinal Antoniutti, expressed his indignation at the treatment the schema had received. He had worked out an approach that would enable his own priorities to be maintained. However, Bishop Leiprecht of Rottenburg, the elected vice-president of the Commission on Religious Life, spoke on behalf of a number of commission members against this procedure and Antoniutti's plan was rejected.[86] From mid-December 1964 until early January 1965 the commission worked on the integration of the amendments and the revision of the text. Inflexibility of positions continued to be experienced in the meetings of the Commission on Religious Life, but the work of experts in the sub-commissions under the leadership of Philippe enabled the foundations of a new and acceptable draft. This was accepted at the April 27 to May 11 meeting of the plenary commission.

Two other issues that again reinforce the awareness of the difficulties of this commission can be seen in the action of Antoniutti and of the appointed vice-president, Archbishop Perantoni. In frustration at the direction the commission was taking, Perantoni had decided to act unilaterally. He wrote to Paul VI complaining about the commission's unprecedented approach to the role and identity of lay brothers in religious institutes, and particularly of the commission's recommendation in support of their possible ordination if this seemed desirable. This latter had been an initiative requested by some teaching brothers and supported by some bishops. Perantoni was totally opposed to the idea. The pope simply returned the letter to the Commission on Religious Life to be dealt with.

Antoniutti had been approached on behalf of members of secular institutes who wanted to influence the wording of the schema in their regard. In early October, a letter was written to the Commission on Religious Life, apparently with the approval of Paul VI, with the proposal that the text include the statement, "Secular institutes, *although they are not religious institutes*, do *nevertheless* involve a true and complete confession of the evangelical counsels in the world, a profession that is recognized by the church."[87] (The italicized words are those of the amendment). This letter was sent to Antoniutti, who again, on his own cognizance, made the insertion without reference to anyone in the commission. This was met with "surprise and grumbling" by commission and other council members.[88]

The fifth and final schema, no longer in propositional form and almost twice the size of the previous one, was presented, with the new text parallel to the 1964 text and detailed comments on the treatment of the amendments. This schema was printed in time for the final session. The voting on the revised schema was carried out on October 6, 7, 8, 1965, and it was accepted with an overwhelming majority, receiving only four negative votes.[89]

Alberigo's comment on both the religious life and priestly training documents was that "they were poor and destined to be forgotten."[90] Wulf is less harsh and in discussing the significance of the decree he believed it did lead back to the sources that took religious life beyond the legalism and asceticism that had characterized the pre–Vatican approach. The decree led to a movement of religious life

> towards the bedrock of the gospel, the imitation of Christ, a sharing in the way and fate of Christ and in the work of preaching and redemption. Never before in the history of the orders has their close theologically, or rather, Christologically based link with the church come so clearly to light as at this council.[91]

This was the understanding of religious life that Vatican II passed on to the church and the world of its era.

PART II

Major Points

To understand the history of the document is to understand the reason for the council's commitment to a document that is conservative in its stance, compromising in tone, but with a new commitment to a gospel lifestyle. The Commission on Religious Life's decision not to present the doctrinal positions on religious life proposed in *Lumen Gentium* means that the potential structure for renewal and adaptation that the universal call to holiness, and chapters 5 and 6 in particular, would have provided is absent.[92] A significant contribution of *Lumen Gentium* is the movement away from grades and "states of perfection" to an acclamation of the baptismal call to holiness that implies a life open to personal transformation. In this context religious life is one of "the many ways" of responding to the call of Christ. The charisms, or gifts of the Holy Spirit, given in baptism and throughout life are many and diverse. This is the understanding of religious life that was recommended by the majority voice led by Cardinals Döpfner and Suenens. *Perfectae Caritatis* simply refers to *Lumen Gentium* in the opening paragraph.[93]

The title itself expresses a movement away from the earlier, more static and abstract titles and endorses the double dimension of adaptation and renewal. It is a return to the sources of the gospel and to the spirit of the founder. This responsiveness to the sources is foundational to the decree and it needs to be accompanied by the constant effort of religious, through attention to the signs of the times, to offer a contemporary witness to God's reign, now and to come.

A GOSPEL-BASED RENEWAL

Article 1 provides the extended preface that resulted from Cardinal Bea's request for a theological context for the decree. Because the theological questions had already been addressed to some extent in chapter 6 of *Lumen Gentium*, the focus of this decree was on the "life and discipline" of religious. The immediate link with *Lumen Gentium* is made in the opening sentence, and the connection with the evangelical call to holiness through the three counsels is mentioned explicitly, as is the eschatological dimension in the reminder that religious life is "a splendid sign of the heavenly kingdom" both now and in the life to come.

However, the link between "the pursuit of charity through the evangelical counsels" with the "doctrine and example of the Divine Master" is not meant to imply that the three counsels of "chastity, poverty and obedience" can be traced to the teaching and example of Jesus.[94] The new emphasis in *Perfectae Caritatis* is the hearing of a call to "a radical and unconditional imitation" of Christ's life that invites some of the baptized to leave all and to follow Christ in a public witness and life commitment to the mission of Christ. The vocation to religious life is this sort of commitment, a following of Christ according to the gospel.[95] Yet it can also be argued that all Christians are called to "the pursuit of charity through the evangelical counsels" and that the dedication referred to applies to all the baptized.

The second paragraph introduces the charismatic element in the following of Christ and links this with the inspiration of the founders of religious institutes, as well as with the Christological and ecclesial character of the religious state. Once again, the emphasis on the close following of Jesus through the practice of the evangelical counsels in this section reinforces the ascetical dimension of religious life. This section was included as the result of an amendment proposed by a number of bishops who wanted to make sure that the ascetical dimension of religious life would not be lost or downplayed. Yet the importance in this section of the reference to "the inspiration of the founder" cannot be overlooked. It is the inspiration of the Holy Spirit that the founder is following that will be the source of renewal and adaptation, not simply a return to the rules and regulations of the early life of the institute. On this point there is a distinct change of course from earlier drafts and approaches to religious life. Precedence is given to the living spirit that the members will attune themselves to in their contemporary mission and ministry.

In the third paragraph the reference to those who respond faithfully to God's call can be traced back to an amendment that spoke of Christ having desired to redeem and sanctify mankind through his poverty, virginity, and obedience to death on the cross. Wulf comments that such an idea could scarcely be stated theologically in just those terms of the amendment. Paragraph 3 was the compromise statement that encompassed the inspiration behind the amendment. The first article closes with a favored description of the religious life in the decree, "a life consecrated by the profession of the counsels and its necessary mission." The reminder is added that the decree is always general in its approach because the diversity of the religious communities and secular institutes that are being addressed require inclusiveness rather than particularity. The "norms for the proper explanation and application of these principles" were contained in the 1966 apostolic letter of Paul VI, *Ecclesiae Sanctae*.[96]

Article 2 sections (a) to (e) spell out the approach to adaptation and renewal. "Since the ultimate norm of the religious life is the following of Christ set forth in the Gospels, let this be held by all institutes as the highest rule" (a). There is clearly no greater rule than that of the gospel. The gospel overrules all those regulations that have become unnecessary accretions of religious life as orders took shape under different leaders and historical contexts and changing needs. It is not unimportant that the decree uses the term "following" rather than "imitating" Christ. This is another affirmation of the importance of religious life being lived in the present tense although finely attuned to the past and the future that is theirs, in and through the creative inspiration of the Holy Spirit. The council's stress on the continuity of the charismatic character of the order is a reminder that renewal does not remain focused on the origins of religious orders.

Baum analyzes the implications of article 2 in a way that addresses the contemporary religious in the 1970s as well as those of the present time. He uses the example of congregations engaged in discernment of their founders' inspiration and aims as a source of renewal in the present. "The particular aspect of the Gospel the founder[s] wanted to emphasize and the particular service to the Church [they] wanted to realize in [their] foundation—this is what the communities are asked to retain."[97] For many congregations this is not a problem, but for others, difficulties did arise in the discernment process.

Baum then refers to those orders that set up hospitals for the sick and indigent in periods when there was no such provision by the government. What was a past need for religious ministry may no longer be the case, and health care may be well provided for across the social spectrum.

> What does renewal demand of these sisters? Should they insist that their founder intended the congregation to serve the sick and thus remain in their hospitals, or are they justified in abandoning hospital work which is done well by secular nurses and turn to social services to the underprivileged for which one needs the special kind of dedication religious communities provide? In such a situation being faithful to the inspiration and plan of the founder means to serve the needs of contemporary society, especially of the poor and underprivileged, just as the founder in his [or her] day served the poor and underprivileged in ways proper to the society.[98]

It is interesting to note the increasing complexity that religious congregations have had to face over the decades when governments have moved into greater social responsibility for health, education, and welfare, when non-government agencies are giving dedicated service, and when litigation can turn charitable aid into a web of confusion, loss of purpose, and even cases of deception and greed. The situation of renewal of the founding charism is a far more complex issue for some congregations in both the short and long term.

The subdivisions within article 2 on adaptation and renewal develop some specific aspects by which the life of the counsels can be distinguished from the general calling of the Christian to follow Christ. But article 2 needs to be read in harmony with chapter 5 of *Lumen Gentium* (*LG*, 44). In this way it brings out the essentially ecclesial aspect of the religious state: "All institutes should share in the life of the Church" and their renewal initiatives integrate "the founders' spirit and special aims" with "the Church's undertakings and aims in matters biblical, liturgical, dogmatic, pastoral, ecumenical, missionary and social." Article 2 (b) and (c) integrate the apostolic work of specific religious orders into the life of the church. The broad spectrum of church ministry moves to the importance of adaptation that is conditioned by understanding of the "social conditions of the times they live in and of the needs of the Church" (d) so that more effective ecclesial ministry may be undertaken.

Article 2 places the vocation to religious life in a global, historical perspective, and only incidentally describes the life itself in (a) and (b). The third section, (c), takes up the topic of the call to follow the evangelical counsels and briefly indicates the marks of the life regulated by the counsels. This is reinforced and made more explicit in article 3, where it is adaptation of lifestyle to "the modern physical and psychological circumstances of the members" as well as ministry carried out according to "the nature of each institute, to the necessities of the apostolate, the demands of culture, and social and economic circumstances" that is recommended.

THE ECCLESIAL CONTEXT OF RENEWAL

The renewal initiative that is integral to *Perfectae Caritatis* has to be understood in the context of all the renewal initiatives recommended by the council. *Perfectae Caritatis* is located in an ecclesial context; this is the emphasis of chapters 5 and 6 of *Lumen Gentium*, and it is the reason why the renewal of religious congregations is also to be understood in the context of the document on the missions, *Ad Gentes* (*AG*), as part of the missionary endeavor of the church. Here there is another new understanding of religious life that the council has given to congregations and to church and society. "The ecumenical, missionary and social movements will influence the attitudes of the religious orders toward the larger communities to which they belong."[99] The awareness of the seven separate areas of renewal, "biblical, liturgical, dogmatic, pastoral, ecumenical, missionary and social" offer some indications of the foundations for renewal that can inform religious orders. Their ecclesial responsibilities rest in their accountability to the whole church, those with whom they work ecumenically, societally and in mission contexts, and the "approbation of the Holy See or of the local ordinary... where necessary and according to law" (*PC*, 4).

Another significant contribution of the decree is in terms of the importance of the renewal and adaptation initiative. Those major superiors who simply deferred to Rome to ascertain the specific directives for recommended adaptive and juridical directions for their congregations were acting against both the letter and the spirit of *Lumen Gentium* and *Perfectae Caritatis*. The recommendation for "adequate and prudent experimentation" entails internal discernment of "all the members of the institute" (*PC*, 4).[100] It requires a communal and collaborative context for reconnecting with the founding charism and identifying the present needs of church and society and it is carried out "under the inspiration of the Holy Spirit and the guidance of the Church" (*PC*, 2). A caution against mistaking quantity for quality is added in the rider to article 4: "the hope of renewal lies more in the faithful observance of the rules and constitutions than in multiplying laws."

BAPTISMAL AND RELIGIOUS CONSECRATION

The constant reminder that the consecration of religious has its foundations in the baptismal consecration is one that has taken time, for all church members, to understand and absorb in terms of implications not simply for the identity of religious but for the ways in which they live their mission and ministry. Articles 5 and 6 address the key elements of renewal in the context of the consecrated life. Article 5 offers a biblical context for the following of Christ as religious. The total dedication of their lives to God and the service of the church is expressed in "a special consecration, which is deeply rooted in that of baptism and expresses it more fully." This article appeared only in the final text. The intention was to have the decree address those elements that are common to all communities before moving on to discuss the different forms of religious life and secular institutes in articles 7–11.

The opening profession of the counsels as response to God's call and the choice to live for God alone in "renouncing the world" is followed by a more scholastic explication of the counsels in relation to religious life in the rest of article 5 and in article 6. Wulf comments that this scholastic interpretation of the vowed life was open to dispute at the council and, as it stands in the decree, it could be seen by many as still open to dispute.[101] The ecclesiology of Vatican II explicitly moved away from a renouncing of the world in general as can be seen in this article.[102]

> Religious have handed over their entire lives to God in their consecration. By doing this they do what all Christians must do, but they do it through the symbolic tangibility of a life of celibacy, poverty and obedience, which leaves them completely free in the church and for the church.[103]

That the article implies that the consecration to God by religious is accomplished by the vowed commitment can be questioned theologically, because it is God's initiative to which those called make their response. The strict sense of the vocation to the consecrated life is always understood as God's loving action toward the person, which enables even the most virtuous human response.[104]

The final paragraph of article 5, endorsing the contemplative and apostolic elements of religious life, is a reminder that the goal is not an individualistic or isolating way of living "for God alone." The God who has called humans to participate in the saving mission of the world is present to all people in Christ, and the love of God and love of neighbor cannot be separated. Christ meets people in each other. This is the foundational ecclesiology that informs the contemplative and apostolic mission and ministry of Christians in the world and of religious in particular through their public profession of following Christ. The church affirms and endorses this public profession to a communal, or stable, life.

> This love of God both excites and energizes that love of one's neighbor which contributes to the salvation of the world and the building up of the Church. This love, in addition, quickens and directs the actual practice of the evangelical counsels. (*PC*, 6)

Wulf comments that today it would be the other way around. Rather than the love of God and of neighbor gained through contemplation giving "life and direction" to the practice of the counsels, it is ordinarily "the distress of the neighbor who needs our help, the worldwide concerns of the church, the helplessness of so many nations facing catastrophe, these are things that bring evangelical counsels to mind and reveal afresh their urgent necessity."[105] This is ordinarily the basic dynamism of the apostolic religious life.

The next two paragraphs of article 6 brought a new understanding of spirituality to the post–Vatican II church. The real sources of Christian spirituality are the reading and study of scripture, liturgy, and the Eucharist. The same sources that nourish the church as a whole are the source of nourishment for religious. The pious prayers and practices that had become devotional accretions of so many religious orders have been displaced in article 6. Contemporary Christian spirituality can be found in the word of God and the sacramental liturgy of the church. The constitutions on the liturgy and on divine revelation are foundational to an appreciation of article 6. This is the source of the cultivation and practice of prayer that the article recommends. Present-day spirituality is marked by a simplicity and transparency that is a return to scripture and the liturgy for the essentially ecclesial identity of the religious.

The closing sentence of the article, which affirms that religious "living and thinking ever more in union with the Church, dedicate themselves wholly to its mission," can be seen as having a link with the issue of religious exemption from the jurisdiction of the local ordinary because they are under a pontifical jurisdiction. This was an issue at the council, and the article is an endeavor to remind religious of their need to be "ever more in union" with the church.

THE DIVERSE FORMS OF RELIGIOUS LIFE

Articles 7–11 deal with the various forms of religious life: contemplative, apostolic, monastic, lay members of orders, religious sisters and brothers, and secular institutes. The concern for the contemplative orders expressed at the council is the reason for priority of place being given to communities "entirely dedicated to contemplation, so that their members in solitude and silence" recognize that their special place in the church is confirmed (*PC*, 7). There is a reworking of the understanding of such communities so that what may have been seen in a pre–Vatican II world as an individualistic ministry, totally removed from the world, is now moved to a new arena of "secret apostolic fruitfulness" through their lives of "solitude and silence, with constant prayer and penance willingly undertaken" on behalf of the Mystical Body of Christ. But the article calls for a renewal and adaptation so that "the manifold results of their holiness" can in some way be a public sign in such a manner that "the people of God" can be "inspired by their example" and thus these communities may gain "new members by their apostolate which is as effective as it is hidden."

Article 8 is addressed to the "very many communities, both clerical and lay, which devote themselves to various apostolic tasks." It is not clear to whom this article refers. Wulf points out that while it could be mendicant orders, he is certain that the general nature of the introduction will lead to controversy.[106] But it represents an affirmation of the multiplicity of charisms that are alive in the church. It is important to remember that neither *Lumen Gentium* nor *Perfectae Caritatis* attempted to give a specific definition of the religious life because of the diversity of the groups encompassed by the term. However, in these articles on religious life it may be useful to remember that *Lumen Gentium* refused to accept the idea of religious life as a quest for personal holiness because greater communion with Christ is accompanied by a greater love of the people of God.[107] In article 8 this is developed in the reminder that "apostolic and charitable activity belongs to the very nature of the religious life, seeing that it is a holy service and a work characteristic of love, entrusted to them by the Church to be carried out in its name."

The particular contributions of the various forms of monasticism and the ministries historically connected with it are affirmed in what may be described as the monastic ideal: "The principal duty of monks is to offer a service to the divine majesty at once humble and noble within the walls of the monastery, whether they dedicate themselves entirely to divine worship in the contemplative life or have legitimately undertaken some apostolate or work of Christian charity" (article 9). This then will be the basis of renewal and adaptation of monastic life and discipline.

In article 10 there is an acknowledgment of the place and value of lay orders and societies. The "religious life, undertaken by lay people, either men or women, is a state for the profession of the evangelical counsels which is complete in itself." Wulf suggests that there are two reasons for this specific article that could be seen to have been already covered in article 8. The first reason is "to underline the full status of those modern societies"[108] which had only just found a place in new canon law. In this process, the past "distinction between orders and societies, between solemn and simple vows, has fallen into the background."[109] The article also offers the council's support for those lay orders and societies and their contribution to the church.

The notable second paragraph in this article, "that there is nothing to prevent some members of religious communities of brothers being admitted to holy orders by provision of their general chapter in order to meet the need for priestly ministrations in their own houses, provided that the lay character of the community remains unchanged" was the consequence of the request of some orders of teaching brothers. Wulf adds a wry comment, "Whether it will be a success only time will tell."[110] This article was an issue of concern for some clerical leaders.

The canonical distinction between secular and religious institutes is indicated in article 11. The text is drawn basically from two texts of Pius XII on secular institutes, *Provida Mater* (1947) and *Primo Feliciter* (1948).[111] "This profession is recognized by the Church and consecrates to God men and women, lay and clerical, who live in the world." Articles 7–11 stress the importance of the different forms of the communal and stable consecrated life in the church and in doing so affirm that the purpose of such consecration is the completion of the commandments to love God and neighbor in and through these ecclesiastically recognized life commitments.

THE VOWED LIFE

The three vows listed in articles 12–14 are not the means that the council used as a foundation for religious life. Rather, the foundational element in the conciliar approach is in the following of Jesus. It is a public commitment to follow Jesus Christ in a community, or stable form of life, ecclesially recognized, that is confirmed and acknowledged by the church. "Essential to religious life, therefore, is the commitment to a community as a way of intensifying obedience to the Gospel."[112] Articles 12–14 express "the canonical arrangement in which the commitment to the evangelical life in community [is lived] . . . They do not manifest the essence of the religious life."[113] There is in the decree an attempt to express the vowed life in inspirational rather than exclusively juridical terms, as was the character of the early drafts of the schema. The following of Jesus as chaste, poor, and obedient to the will of the Father is the basis of these articles.

Celibacy, or chastity, is the first of the three vows addressed because "in the New Testament it is the most clearly attested charism of the three and the most unambiguous symbol of the religious state."[114] Not all religious take the same vows or even the same number of vows, but celibacy is a defining vow of the canonical religious life. The purpose of the vow, "for the sake of the kingdom of heaven," that religious profess should be counted "an outstanding gift of grace" (PC, 12). It is liberating, so that the religious "may be more inflamed with love for God and for all [humankind]." Religious can, then, be able to "dedicate themselves with undivided heart to the service of God and the works of the apostolate." The meaning of celibacy is found in the Christological, ecclesiological, and eschatological dimensions expressed in paragraph 1: "[T]hey recall to the minds of all the faithful that wondrous marriage decreed by God and which is to be fully revealed in the future age in which the Church takes Christ as its only spouse."

This article is a contrast to pre–Vatican II treatments of celibacy, which were ordinarily phrased in terms of an unqualified and unexplained exhortation to religious to embrace "the chastity of angels." The decree provides an approach that endeavors to take human reality into account. Religious are not to "overestimate their own strength but practice mortification and custody of the senses. Neither should they neglect the natural means which promote health of mind and body." A more holistic and human approach is recommended, along with some form of personal discipline that will support a lifelong commitment.

It is expected that the pragmatic means of ascertaining that prospective candidates are capable of this vow will be achieved through careful testing that shows they possess the required psychological and emotional maturity to publicly profess a celibate life. Another new dimension is also in the mandate that all, "especially superiors, remember that chastity is guarded more securely when true brotherly [or sisterly] love flourishes in the common life of the community." The emphasis on the mutuality of responsibility for authentic love and the special emphasis on the leadership of the superior in this matter is a fruit of the greater awareness of the co-responsibility of all for the common life, and a breaking down of the subordination of subjects as a given in community.

The vow of poverty is also given a contemporary ecclesial significance. "Religious should diligently practice and if need be express also in new forms ... voluntary poverty" (PC, 13). "New forms" implies that religious engage personally and communally with their sociocultural context so that their expression of poverty is a genuine witness to a following of Christ, not an artificial or contrived continuation of past regulatory requirements. The "common law of labor" is a mandate for all Christians, and religious are not exempt from this.

Baum comments that the two marks of poverty in ordinary society are "insecurity and social disfavor."[115] He believes that these are not experienced in the monastery or convent. Yet, to the extent that religious men and women have taken renewal seriously, these are precisely the contemporary experiences of poverty that characterize many of their lives.[116] The choice of many religious today to side with those on the margins who suffer from injustice and rejection is one that redounds on the religious themselves. They have experienced and continue to experience insecurity and social disfavor because of their radical commitment to justice and peace. This stance has not found favor or support with those conservative members of the hierarchy or members of the Catholic community for whom the maintenance of the status quo is of the highest importance.

Article 14 addresses the vow of obedience. "The theme of obedience was tricky from start to finish. It touches the core of religious life and has been the source of increasing difficulty in religious life affecting both the traditional doctrine and the practice of obedience."[117] The problem faced by the commission in constructing an article on obedience can be understood by referring to two amendments, each proposed by significant groups of approximately four hundred bishops after the November 1964 debate.

> 1. At all costs care must be taken that the authentic concept of religious obedience is preserved undiminished. Religious obedience, as it has always been understood in the church does not diminish the dignity of an adult person, but helps it toward full maturity, for it is a sublime total offering (*holocaustum*) through which a man subordinates himself and all that he is, for the sake of the kingdom of heaven, wholly to the will of Christ, whose place is taken by the superior.

> 2. Religious ought to observe the obedience they have promised according to the aims and character of their community, in

a mature personal atmosphere. Superiors ought so to share responsibility with their subjects, that all members of the community look upon the affairs of the community as their own, and are solicitous for the good of all alike.[118]

The polarization that dogged the discussions on religious life had not abated even by the end of the third session. The final text had to emerge from these two contradictory amendments. The inevitable compromise is present in this article: the extremes of a "total surrender" versus a mature mutual solicitude for the common good are implicit. That there are separate paragraphs addressed to both subjects and superiors is an advance over previous approaches to religious obedience.

That article 14 does not place religious obedience in the wider context of obedience to God and church indicates a limitation in the decree.[119] Commentators remind readers that the traditionally praised "blind obedience," often associated with this vow, can no longer be accepted with the same naïveté that preceded the Holocaust and the My-Lai massacre, where obedience was used in hope of exonerating individuals from responsibility for the consequences of complicity in evil.

It is not possible to use religious obedience as a means of evading the social responsibility of every human being. The vow requires an active obedience, but the content of article 14 does not adequately communicate this.

> Religious, therefore, in the spirit of faith and love for the divine will should humbly obey their superiors according to their rules and constitutions. Realizing that they are contributing to building up the body of Christ according to God's plan, they should use both the forces of their intellect and will and the gifts of nature and grace to execute the commands and fulfill the duties entrusted to them. In this way religious obedience, far from lessening the dignity of the human person, by extending the freedom of the sons of God, leads it to maturity. (*PC*, 14, par. 3)

The replacement of "humbly" for the earlier "meekly" is an improvement. Wulf comments that the third paragraph can be interpreted in either the more traditional subservient way, or it can be read in a "salvation-theological" manner because of the emphasis on the service dimension of obedience. "It does however represent substantial progress for the Christologically, soteriologically, and ecclesiologically determined theology of obedience."[120] This "living obedience" was perceived to be the criterion for religious to be able to enter "a new epoch"[121] when community members would all "cooperate with an active and responsible obedience in undertaking new tasks and in carrying those already undertaken" (article 15).

The common life is an integral aspect of religious life. The content of article 15 is substantially scriptural. The communal love that is described here is one based on an ideal of unity that is not measured by uniformity or conformity. "Moreover love sums up the whole law (cf. Rom. 13:10), binds all together in perfect unity (cf. Col. 3:14) and by it we know that we have crossed over from death to life (cf. 1 John 3:14)" (par. 1). This New Testament model of Christian community, *koinonia*, that is proposed has its foundations in the love of Christ that can enable a response that indicates that we have "crossed over from death to life" (par. 1). An expression of such love is in the inclusion of those community members previously described as "lay" sisters or brothers into the common life (par. 2). There is to be no class distinction among religious in post-conciliar religious life.

The first fifteen articles address the task of renewal. The rest of the decree (*PC*, 16–25) is directed toward the task of adaptation of orders to the needs and circumstances of present-day living. The decree does not go into great detail, but it does open the door for significant changes.

ADAPTATION

The institutional distinction that had been made in the apostolic constitution, *Sponsa Christi*[122] between purely contemplative and apostolic religious women is now widened in article 16.

> Papal cloister should be maintained in the case of nuns engaged exclusively in the contemplative life. However, it must be adjusted to conditions of time and place and obsolete practices suppressed. This should be done after due consultation with the monasteries in question. But other nuns applied by rule to apostolic work outside the convent should be exempted from

papal cloister in order to enable them better to fulfill the apostolic duties entrusted to them. Nevertheless, cloister is to be maintained according to the prescriptions of their constitutions. (*PC*, 16, par. 1)

With this article the minor enclosure was abolished. However, the impact of this decision on those members of contemplative orders who have lived a rigid enclosure does not appear to have been taken into account in the discussions; nor has the impact on, or circumstances of, extern sisters in those communities been addressed.

The habit, dealt with in article 17, must be retained as a sign of special consecration. A major consideration for religious women in particular is the recognition that a new style of habit "must meet the requirements of health and be suited to the circumstances of time and place and to the needs of the ministry involved."

The Congregation for Religious played a major part in the recommendations for appropriate vocational and apostolic educational training programs, both theoretical and practical (*PC*, 18). For the renewal and adaptation processes to be implemented, the education of young religious is important. This is surely a place where the exhortations and writings of Cardinal Suenens also played a significant part.

> In order that the adaptation of religious life to the needs of our time may not be merely external and that those employed by rule in the active apostolate may be equal to their task, religious must be given suitable instruction, depending on their intellectual capacity and personal talent, in the currents and attitudes of sentiment and thought prevalent in social life today. This education must blend its elements together harmoniously so that an integrated life on the part of the religious concerned results. (*PC*, 18, par. 2)

Ongoing education for religious is also recommended and superiors are to endeavor to provide the opportunities for this. All those who work in religious formation in terms of education or spiritual direction are to be carefully chosen and thoroughly trained for the task.

What in Wulf's opinion is lacking in this article is the specialized education of a new generation of leaders who will be familiar with the problems of religious life in contemporary cultural and ecclesial contexts. Such leaders would be better able to tackle the serious problems affecting the internal life of religious orders. The things that are happening today in the various professions must find their counterpart in the religious orders as well, especially the active orders.[123]

New foundations and the questions and problems they pose have been a perennial concern, and they remain thus in article 19. This is a particular issue for foundations in missionary congregations and countries. Article 20, describing some of the approaches to be taken to adaptation, consolidation, and possible closing of ministries, was originally the matter of article 2 (b). But the final rewriting of the decree required some abbreviation and this article has suffered from this requirement. Issues such as fidelity to origins may need to be addressed to contemplative as well as active orders. The needs of the universal church must be considered, but there is no requirement for the cooperation of religious orders in their apostolic ministries.[124]

The suppression of institutes is dealt with in article 21, while in article 22 federations, reconfigurations, or associations of smaller orders is the solution to the problem that was the concern of some council members, namely the number of smaller orders that were doing the same ministerial works.

More effective communication and collaboration between congregations is the concern of article 23, which recommends the setting-up of conferences or councils of major superiors to achieve this end. That religious congregations might continue is the reason for the statement in article 24 on the "serious efforts to foster vocations" that should be made by priests, Christian educators, and parents. The adaptation section comes to a close with article 25, which encourages continued generosity on the part of religious and also notes that their life is highly esteemed by the church.

> Moreover, their apostolate, most effective, whether obscure or well known, offers this synod great hope for the future. Let all religious, therefore, rooted in faith and filled with love for God and neighbor, love of the cross and the hope of future glory, spread the good news of Christ throughout the whole world so that their witness may be seen by all and our Father in heaven may be glorified (Matt. 5:16). Therefore, let them beseech the

Virgin Mary, the gentle Mother of God, "whose life is a model for all," that their number may daily increase and their salutary work be more effective. (*PC*, 25)

This closing exhortation to religious is significant. Wulf, as participant in the construction of the decree, and in his role as commentator on religious life in relation to both *Lumen Gentium* and *Perfectae Caritatis*, proposes that the essentials of religious life are summed up and the important role of religious in the mission of Christ is acknowledged.

There is an affirmation of religious and the hope and trust that there will always be communities whose rule and way of life continue to make a significant contribution to the life of the church in its service in the world. Wulf concludes his commentary on the decree with the affirmation that *Perfectae Caritatis*, despite its shortness and shortcomings, is a turning point in the history of religious orders, and that it will indeed initiate that turning, the full sweep of which cannot yet be seen.[125]

That the contribution of the decree has been a turning point is without doubt, and that new experiences of unity and division have characterized religious life worldwide over the past forty years is also a reality. Along with all the losses and gains, the presence of the Holy Spirit has sustained women and men religious in their efforts to live religious life in these tumultuous decades. This is clearly evidenced in their mission and ministry on behalf of the people of God.

PART III

IMPLEMENTATION

The implementation of the decree has been as polarizing a process as was its construction. Initial reactions were diffuse. The first five years after the council were alive with congresses, conferences, workshops, and other national and diocesan initiatives throughout the world. Religious familiar with various news items from church and secular media were unsure of what was expected of them. To understand the factors influencing the effective implementation of the spirit of the council, it is important to see the polarized and polarizing reactions to change both from within the Vatican and from within religious orders themselves.

High expectations and deep-seated fears, the familiar and the unexplored, hope and doubt, came into conflict. In some congregations, short-term modifications inadequately thought through defeated the possibility of long-term transformation. The long-standing value of religious life itself was confronted by the euphoric reclaiming of the baptismal rights and identity of the laity. While the place in the church for the priestly ministry of the ordained and of the laity was celebrated, the place of religious was being redefined in the crucible of renewal, adaptation, and apparent downgrading.

Various initiatives had already been taking place in North America.[126] Sisters' conferences and congresses were involved in responding to the challenges held out by Pope Pius XII. The record of a symposium of lectures held in Portland, Oregon, shows the efforts to integrate the apostolic and contemplative dimensions of religious life, the professional status of religious, the place of the individual in community spirituality, and the role of leadership in contemporary religious life.

This symposium was attended by around 350 religious superiors, representing the range of major to local leaders, during the period from 1960 to 1963. While the lectures given covered virtually all the aspects of renewal and adaptation that were endorsed in *Perfectae Caritatis* years later, particular issues in relation to community living received extra attention. In addressing the issue of obedience and group decision-making, the importance of communication and the congruence between equality and obedience were proposed as viable options.

> If we are to have wholesome and effective family, or community spirit, in a modern world where our apostolate requires us to have as much solidarity as can possibly be mustered, then one of the salvific moves toward that end is that we learn to talk openly, to express and exchange opinions, and to have a willingness to modify our views... It is clear that we need to study further the type of leadership that protects essential democratic values and yet makes for essential functioning and a satisfying experience for members in various group situations.[127]

This recognition of the importance of mutual exchange within the community was a notable change for apostolic community life and ministerial commitment. These are perennial issues that were under discussion, but the demands of the communal life and of the ministry have become even more pressing over time and the issues pertaining to effective leadership in the contemporary religious community remain in the foreground even today.

That Vatican II was held "at a point between the decline of the age of ideology and the beginning of the postmodern period"[128] meant that there was a seismic shift in the lives of people who had been educated into a church of stable and sure identity, a church that would not change, with the evidence of this unchanging nature being celebrated by the use of Latin in the liturgy. The grassroots communities of the first half of the century had been well schooled into accepting an unquestioning obedience to hierarchy and to a belief in external criteria for their identity. They knew who they were and what they believed more by their practices than by their understanding of church teachings. Uniformity and conformity were the external marks of fidelity and loyalty. This was the era in which the Bible had been a closed and virtually forbidden book.

Most pre–Vatican II Catholics had been nourished on Bible stories and catechisms and critical engagement with ideas was not a feature of their faithfulness, nor was this expected of them at that time. Yet these were the people who were expected to cope with the post-conciliar transformation of their church and of their local leaders, priests and religious. Those who preached and taught, who nursed and cared for them, had been brought up in the same mentality.

The mediation of the message of Vatican II confronted religious with radical questions about the meaning and purpose of their commitment, and about their role in this new experience of church. It was both a liberating and a fear-inducing task that renewal and adaptation had placed on the shoulders of religious. On the other hand, for those religious who had been hoping for renewal, who had been educated through various programs and workshops such as the Sister Formation initiative in North America and various congresses in Europe,[129] the decree provided opportunities that they had been waiting for and working toward.

An awareness of the importance of systemic change led Edward Schillebeeckx, a Belgian Dominican and council expert, to address the problem of implementation of the spirit as well as the practice of the conciliar contribution to the present and future understanding of religious life.

> The "supreme rule" of a monastic foundation is not its own particular "rule and constitution" but Christ himself; the religious life is based on "following Christ," referred to in the bible; in other words, authentic evangelism. That is where the religious life must find its renewed inspiration. The "adaptation of the religious life" must be first and foremost of its structures. The consequences of this conciliar maxim are more numerous than a superficial reading of it might seem to indicate. The text gives the church an inspiration whose charismatic consequences, I feel, cannot even be surmised at this moment. But eventually this "supreme rule" will break through, without any clashes, we trust, though some may well occur.[130]

Schillebeeckx's faith that the "supreme rule" would break through was tempered by his realization that "unfettered personal conclusions" about renewal would be in some conflict with reclaiming the basic inspiration of the religious order or congregation. "Apostolic monastic foundations in particular must be up to date and show no naïve ignorance about life in the world."[131] What changes would equal voting rights in community bring? What would the complete equality of all brothers and sisters among themselves really mean? How would religious cope with this?[132]

As the council came to a close, bishops and experts who had been involved in the writing processes began to publish their own responses. In 1965 Huyghe gathered together writings and research from renewal initiatives directed toward helping those religious orders that were engaged in the effort to renew and adapt to the modern world as requested.[133] In this publication Cardinal Liénart wrote the preface and went on record in his affirmation of the directions of renewal that were being undertaken at the time.

> Founders, Rules, Constitutions and venerable traditions must take second place to the gospel, and they are only meaningful in so far as they ensure real contact with its life-giving power. It is to the light of the gospel, a gospel lived in the very heart of the church of our own times, that we must consider all Rules and Constitutions, the works of founders and all the different traditions, if we are to see how far they need modifying and adapting in order that authentic religious life may flourish in the midst of the modern world.[134]

Huyghe describes some of the responses that were taking place among European religious orders. They seemed to be following the patterns that prevailed in the council itself.

> Some have completely accepted this new world along with its dangers and hopes. Resolutely detached from the sociological milieu in which former generations lived, they are alert to the needs of the people who now expect a new type of evangelization. Others cling desperately to the earlier forms of religious and apostolic life which, they declare, have stood the test of years; and in the shelter of their institutions which have become for them a sort of artificial Christianity, they do not see

that the world is being formed without them and, unfortunately, without the message of Christ which they should be
bringing to it.[135]

While many congregations were characterized by one or the other
response, there were some congregations that suffered the division
within their ranks. Some were split into two groups, one clinging to the
traditional lifestyle and the other opening up to new possibilities of
gospel lifestyle and ministry.

When such polarized positions were operative within communities,
their efforts at renewal and adaptation were often reduced to simple
cosmetic surface changes and ineffectual compromises that, over time,
reduced energy and produced the inertia that eventually led to their demise. In the 1960s in France there were 118,000 active nuns, with 160
small congregations of less than 200 members. Yet many of these were
described as being "fanatically attached to their traditions and customs."[136] Huyghe commented that, twenty years after Vatican II "we
may conclude that unless there is a complete reversal of trends, half the
religious houses of today will no longer exist by 1980."[137] The reversal
did not take place and one can only wonder what might have happened
in France, or in the Western world, had the option for authentic ministerial engagement with the world been followed through in the context of a collaborative response to the universal call to holiness.

Religious worked to integrate the more holistic approach to religious life and spirituality that was recommended in *Perfectae Caritatis*.
An example of such initiatives in practice can be seen in the efforts of
those religious leaders who worked in their congregations to remove
the false dichotomy between the interior life and apostolic ministry.
Contemporary philosophy and psychology, as well as theology, were
brought into the curricula in initial and ongoing formation programs.

One interesting expansion of the conciliar recommendation for
"conferences and councils of major superiors" (*PC*, 23) was the suggestion to establish such "conciliar" groups within congregations as a
means of increasing responsibility and collaboration and of developing
the practice of subsidiarity, cooperation, and effective communication
throughout the congregation.[138] Some religious orders engaged in federation processes were able to use the committee approach in their
chapter preparation with liberating consequences; "the interchange of

views and experiences enabled the brave to assert themselves and the timid to take heart. Their belief in each other bolstered their faith in the work before them."[139] Community life began to be energized in new ways from within.

In less than twelve months after the conclusion of the council, the apostolic letter *Ecclesiae Sanctae* (August 6, 1966) was published with the essential norms for religious congregations promised in article 1 of *Perfectae Caritatis*. Explications of various norms and recommendations integral to the renewal of religious life were being looked for, especially by many religious for whom the juridical approach was the only one they had known. The opening statement of *Ecclesiae Sanctae* provides the purpose for these new norms. For pre-conciliar religious the regulatory way was the normal way for living out the call to religious life.

> The governing of holy Church, following the conclusion of the Second Ecumenical Vatican Council, demands indeed that new norms be established and that new adjustments be made to meet relationships introduced by the Council and which will be more and more adapted to the new goals and areas of the apostolate which through the Council have been opened up to the Church in the modern world. Because of great changes this world is in need of a shining light and longs for the supernatural flame of charity.

The implementation of the conciliar spirit and practice of religious life was spelled out in detail in *Ecclesiae Sanctae*, particularly for preparation and completion of special and general chapters. The approach taken was an enabling one, for example, where *Perfectae Caritatis* 4 required the "cooperation of all the members of the institute," *Ecclesiae Sanctae* 2 reads, "The cooperation of all superiors and members is necessary to renew Religious life in themselves, to prepare the spirit of the chapters, to carry out the works of the chapters, to observe faithfully the law and norms enacted by the chapters." The choice of the word "members" rather than "subjects" is important in the new movement toward mutuality of responsibility within orders.

The grassroots experience of these early years was described as being characterized by "a healthy dialogue concerning the contemporary interpretation of the views; the witness of poverty; the significance of the habit; the value of cooperative action with lay bodies...There are few communities in which the tension between participation in society and withdrawal from it is not making itself felt."[140]

In 1976, Paul VI's apostolic exhortation on the renewal of the religious life according to Vatican II, *Evangelica Testificatio*, was published. This essentially conservative approach to religious life was greeted with mixed reactions. A critical collection of essays was published in response to this exhortation through the collaborative efforts of the Canadian Conference of Major Superiors and the American Conference of Major Superiors of Women in 1974.[141] In the same year, the theme of the Canadian Religious Conference was "Religious and the Evangelization of the World" and the publication that resulted represents an alternative understanding of religious life to the one that seemed to be implicit in *Evangelica Testificatio*. The three objectives listed in this conference publication encouraged participation in research on the evangelization of the modern world from the perspective of religious vocation; the assessment of religious life in Canada under the headings of prayer, community life, and apostolic commitment; and the discovery of "lines of convergence in the orientations" to be given priority by those who were attending the Roman Synod.[142]

The General Assembly of this North American religious leadership initiative closed with thirty-four workshops, each presenting a resolution, the character of which represented the comprehensive engagement with the chosen contemporary or traditional topic, with the strengths and limits of the worldview of the period. One example of the approach can be seen in the recommendation that: "Every religious community should study the possibilities and take the necessary steps to permit their members to become truly integrated among [the] underprivileged for a more understanding evangelization of this sector of contemporary society."[143] This was an initiative that many religious took seriously in their renewal directions.

Another instruction from the Sacred Congregation for Religious and Secular Institutes, *Venite Seorsum* (On the Contemplative Life and the Enclosure of Nuns) was promulgated in 1969. The concern among many bishops at the council was to affirm the contemplative life as one held in the highest esteem, but this document did not support the equally important conciliar concern for appropriate renewal and adaptation, along with a certain kind of public witness to the value of contemplative life of prayer and penance.

The decade of the 1970s ushered in another era of both tension and change. The gospel approach to religious life was the subject of biblical scholars and theologians who could see the impact of the council on religious, their struggles, and their questioning of their own identity as religious. Even the titles of such texts illustrate the issues under debate.[144] The decade of the 1960s had witnessed the beginnings of the "Death of God" theology, the fruit of the new research was coming from biblical studies, and in the 1970s much of the religious world and the world of the religious had come under empirical and scientific analysis and critique. As a consequence, doubt and confusion flourished alongside new ministerial and religious lifestyle initiatives.

The list of contents of a book titled *The New Nuns*[145] gives a sense of the questions that were fueling the tensions that were blazing forth from unexpected quarters. The contributors were themselves religious who no longer wrote under the pre-conciliar anonymity of congregational authorship such as, "by A Sister of Mercy." The fact that they used their own names was itself an advance on past practices of self-abasement derived from questionable understandings of humility.

Chapter titles such as "Can Sisters Be Relevant?" "Margaret Mead Looks at the Modern Sister," "Freud and Sisters," "Freedom of Expression in the Church," "Asylums: Total Societies and the Religious Life," and "Bureaucratic Dysfunction in American Convents" give some idea of the varieties and expanse of issues and contexts of the discussions that were fermenting in the lively period of the 1970s. The editor of *The New Nuns*, Sister Mary Charles Borromeo, was described as "one of the best-known nuns in the United States" because of her leadership in education and in religious reform. That she left her order of the Holy Cross, resumed her baptismal name of Maryellen Muckenhirn, and went in search of "new secular ways of being celibate, totally available to others"[146] is an indication of the tensions, the breakdowns, and the breakthroughs that characterized many Western religious houses and their communities in their efforts to respond to the council mandate to renewal and adaptation.

At around the same time, religious were scandalized and divided in their allegiances and understandings when the arch-conservative

Cardinal McIntyre of Los Angeles intervened in the Immaculate Heart of Mary sisters' renewal processes in 1968.[147] Changes in five areas, more autonomy in choice of ministry, choice of dress, and issues related to prayer, leadership, and formation were proposed by the congregation. Cardinal McIntyre reacted strongly when he received a copy of the proposed changes and he demanded a more conservative response. The congregational leader, Sister Anita Caspary, protested to Rome about this interference and the cardinal backed down to a certain extent. However, when a further congregational chapter resulted in more policy changes, the cardinal took the actions of the sisters as a defiant stance against his leadership and he gave the IHM congregation the ultimatum that if the decrees were not retracted then withdrawal from the archdiocesan schools would be mandated.[148]

As a result of Cardinal McIntyre's further appeal to Rome, a statement came from the Vatican censuring the IHM changes and classing them as deviations rather than adaptation. The Vatican required compliance with the cardinal's demands and ordered the dissemination of its findings through other religious women's communities. The public conflict that followed resulted in a division in the community, and the eventual decision by the congregation to move to a non-canonical status.[149]

While fifty sisters opted to comply and to stay within the Los Angeles school system, the other four hundred were dispensed from their vows and reconstituted themselves as a lay community in the church. Doubt and confusion followed the highly publicized event within some religious communities and in many dioceses and parishes, yet hundreds of letters of support were sent to the dissenting IHMs. Catholic newspapers published editorials and articles on the scandal. The issue of "appropriate" adaptation was not confined to Los Angeles.

> Wearing a habit as a symbol of consecration (and, therefore, separation from the world) and maintaining institutional works in preference to newer services in the public sphere (again, a curtailment of involvement in the world) were particularly controverted points. Since many American communities besides the IHM sisters had adopted similar provisions, discussions focused specifically on whether religious life was what church law stipulated it to be or what was developing through the experience of communities.[150]

The inconsistency of expectations along with the autocratic response of the cardinal to the leadership of the congregation was a blow to the efforts of those religious leaders and congregations trying to implement the changes recommended in *Perfectae Caritatis*.

Curial member Cardinal Antoniutti, former chair of the Commission on Religious Life, criticized documents from the Leadership Conference of Women Religious proceedings, pointing out "doctrinal inaccuracies" in them. The lack of episcopal support for change was another pressure operating against the implementation of change, particularly if this involved a movement of religious away from established ministries in dioceses. "In 1968 and 1973 letters from the Vatican censured changes in ministry, the absence of superiors in convents, modified clothing, and 'purely collegial' forms of government."[151]

The decade of the 1970s could be described as an irruption of power structures, of religious ideologies and a burgeoning of diverse lifestyles as efforts to renew and adapt took communities and individuals in ways unexpected by ecclesiastical authorities. The processes of renewal, adaptation, cooperation, and consultation that were espoused in *Perfectae Caritatis* were not those that were equally appreciated or understood at the hierarchical or grassroots community levels.

Conferences on religious life generated many publications and there was no lack of workshops or occasions to address issues raised by or consequent to the council in the 1970s and 1980s. Identity was a major question for religious and it was addressed from various disciplines and perspectives. A number of psychological studies and group dynamics approaches explored the possibilities and implications of the personal and communal aspects of religious vocation in the sociocultural context of the period.[152]

One of the consequences for formation personnel was the division between those formators who took the "group" approach and those who had been inducted into the "one-to-one" counseling or therapeutic models. When teams were composed of members who espoused either one or the other model, the formation process was hobbled, especially if the leadership was not open to negotiation about the strengths and limitations of each approach. Those being "formed" were sometimes caught between the two models and their proponents.

The question of the conciliar call to evangelization took on a new dimension in this decade when religious realized that they themselves

were in need of evangelization before they could appropriately evangelize other groups. The International Union of Superiors General at Rome
in 1975 focused on the general area of self-renewal or self-evangelization
of women religious, which was seen as essential for their continuing contribution to church renewal. The topic addressed was that of "Women
Religious and the Task of Renewal."[153]

The first task of self-evangelization for religious was described as
their attention to the concrete circumstances of their lives, their place
in church and society. The position of women religious was depicted as
a "frontier" position and it was noted that they have "as a group in the
church" gone further than any other group "toward grasping the radi-
cality of the contemporary crises in the areas of spiritual renewal and
social justice."[154]

The implications of this position for self-evangelization are three.
The first is the acceptance of the responsibility that has come to religious women, "to a large extent, as goes women's religious life in the
next decade, so goes the Church."[155] This may have been the case at the
time, but it is no longer so. Women religious still have some significance in the contemporary church but it is on a more limited scale than
in the 1950s to the 1980s.

The second is the need for intellectual and spiritual formation, "especially in theology and the social sciences of some members of every
congregation" as resource persons in strategic planning for present and
future ecclesial circumstances.[156]

> The serious formation of our general membership is necessary to
> insure the informed and generous consensus which is the only vi-
> able basis of group apostolic effectiveness in an age in which the
> autocratic use of authority is finally beginning to become obso-
> lete. But the general intellectual formation of all of our members
> and the specialized formation of some of them will only create
> another potential (or actual) oppressor unless it is accompanied
> by a spiritual formation which is increasingly radical.[157]

In the past, such formation was not so easy to get on the global scene,
in spite of the initiatives undertaken in some dioceses and in some religious communities. However, the readiness of some congregational
leaders to offer spiritual and specialized formation and education for

their members has resulted in their taking on significant leadership roles ecclesially and societally. The radical nature of the formation proposed is that which is consonant with the return to the sources that is integral to *Perfectae Caritatis*.

The third implication is that religious cannot wait for others to lead in active commitment to social justice.

> The active and effective commitment of our members to social justice is going to continue to shake up religious congregations as nothing else except contemplation itself can shake them up. Our willingness to risk our very institutional existence and personal well-being in the service of the freedom of our sisters and brothers is the measure of our self-evangelization today.[158]

Religious women and men have certainly made both local and wide-ranging contributions to the social justice initiatives that have offered hope to people on the margins in post-conciliar decades. They have accepted leadership positions in church and non-government organizations to work toward the relief of suffering all over the world. Some have accepted public office in order to extend their ministerial outreach beyond church boundaries, and many of them have suffered greatly as a consequence.[159] The contributions of religious congregations in the ecclesial mission to evangelize were recognized globally in this initiative of the International Union of Superiors General.

The decades that followed the council also saw a development of theologies of religious life beginning to take shape.[160] Sometimes the initiative for these came as a result of the tension between the conciliar call to renew and re-engage with the world and the institutional documents that seemed to retract that mandate. Tensions were still fermenting in religious communities. As the 1980s approached, congregational leaders of men and women religious from Canada, Latin America, and the United States gathered together to address "Religious Life and Our Contribution to Its Future in America."

Such inter-American conferences enabled mutual support, challenge, and expansion of understanding of the social justice initiatives that each leadership team had initiated in their own areas.[161] At a 1978 conference the different experience of the search for justice in the Americas was addressed.

Our commitment with the poor of Latin America today leaves the religious little space for the purely profane or the political. Today we have to carry the hopes of the Resurrection to a people without hope. We must be witnesses of the following of Christ in a society where the name of Christian is used to chastise, to oppress, to torture, to maintain the poor in misery. We cannot be quiet: what is in conflict are two totally different ways of understanding Jesus Christ... The urgency of the situation challenges us in such a manner that one cannot but give one answer: a religious life totally lived.[162]

The dialogue that characterized this conference as depicted in its proceedings is surely that of an intercultural transformation of understanding of religious life and commitment across an expanse of worlds and worldviews.

Sociologists of religion engaged in analyses of orders, communities, and their members, and of the religious life itself in the United States. One study, initially carried out by Maria Augusta Neal, covered the chronological period from 1950 to 1984. The consequences of the promulgation of *Perfectae Caritatis* were under review in her research. Over 139,000 sisters participated in the survey to "determine the readiness of American sisters to implement the directives of the Vatican Council."[163]

Her findings indicated the confusion many sisters and communities experienced in their efforts to interpret the contemporary meaning of the vows in the context of their communal life and ministry. Criticism of the past rigidity of interpretations and the diversity of approaches to the vows in the wave of writing in religious journals and books on religious life in the post-conciliar era meant that many of those who had been inducted into an acquiescence of unquestioning acceptance of an ascetical lifestyle were foundering. The throes of change were unsettling and the re-visioning of the semi-monastic lifestyle meant that the carpet of the security of conformity to the demands of the "better" way had been pulled away.

After completing her research, Neal commented on her findings. In spite of issues such as declining membership, employment and unemployment of sisters, the high costs of living and transport, health care, and ongoing education, she discovered that there was a new sense of the mysterious call of the religious vocation.

> It might seem that as we have moved with the church to this new mission embodying a special option for the poor, we have lost the security that others envied in our lives: the contemplative serenity, a dependable community, care in retirement and something important and significant to do, i.e. relevant work. Yet in reality, all these advantages have been heightened, not lost as we have responded in new ways to the mission of Jesus.[164]

Her final reflection is one of affirmation of religious life in the present and for the future. But the path remains one of mystery. In conclusion, Neal offers her readers the example of Bishop Oscar Romero, a man who was open to a change of heart, and of the four American women who were murdered in Central America, two Maryknoll sisters, an Ursuline, and a lay volunteer. The call and cost of collaborative ministry between lay and religious is a witness to the new direction for the future that was barely hinted at in the council discussions on religious life.

Neal's subsequent book on religious life, *From Nuns to Sisters*, developed the implications of returning to the sources and the decision taken by many religious congregations in the 1980s to take seriously the ecclesial preferential option for the poor and its consequences. The change from past hierarchically structured decision-making processes for religious to one that is more collaborative and inclusive in its ministerial options is explored in the context of religious women's response to renewal and adaptation of ministry. Their exercise of an option for the poor and for justice was lived in such a way that their personal and communal lifestyle was also radically renewed by the necessary changes that inevitably need to be made when collaborative ministry is taken seriously.

Neal's research and experience provide her with an image of religious life in the 1980s, an image of a tortoise that has shed its shell, deliberately vulnerable for the sake of new life. "The composite carapace of an outmoded institutional framework and accumulated customs finally shed, these congregations now allow their members an environment for a more faithful response to their apostolic ministry in the church."[165] The prophetic element was alive in the response of religious to the poor and the suffering, and also in collaboration with the "newly aware and organized poor [who] reach out to take their place in shaping the future of society."[166]

Such transformations were the subject of suspicion and questioning, and this took place at various levels of religious life. The relationship between the leadership of American women religious had been problematic in the claiming of their American identity as religious. In 1972 the decision was made to change the name of the leadership group from the Conference of Major Superiors of Women to Leadership Conference of Women Religious (LCWR). One of the reasons given for this was in order to share power and to move away from the anachronistic name of "major superiors." The decision enabled greater member participation in the election of officers, goal-setting, and governance processes. As a consequence it became a more egalitarian and democratic leadership group with a concern for social reform as primary. "It had framed a role for itself in bringing about 'constructive social and attitudinal change' (By-laws, Article II, section 3)."[167]

The LCWR had collaborated with Canadian and Latin American religious leaders in matters of religious life and spirituality and was outspoken about issues of injustice in society and in the church. The communications channels between the Vatican and the LCWR became problematic, with church leaders becoming the go-between. By the 1980s the Vatican relationship with the LCWR had become "increasingly bitter and punitive."[168] As relations with the hierarchy became more problematic, a more conservative group of religious leaders formed itself into the Consortium Perfectae Caritatis in 1970, an action that generated greater division within American religious life and in relations with Rome.

The polarized situation of the council was mirrored in this situation. In 1992 the conservative group renamed itself the Council of Major Superiors of Women and received official recognition from Rome. This created the anomalous situation of the United States being the only nation with two officially recognized leadership groups of women religious.[169] The LCWR had 90 percent of religious membership, but the minority conservative group had the ear of the hierarchy. The reasons for the ability of the Council of Major Superiors of

Women to supersede the place of LCWR was because religious women were no longer as significant as they had been in education and health care and they were becoming less visible to the American laity who were not aware of the situation. "Finally, the implications of offending a constituency whose median age is almost seventy are obvious to Vatican officials. However upset the LCWR communities may be to be disenfranchised, their outcry will not last too long."[170]

In analyzing what, in the post-conciliar decades, she describes as "The Collapse of an Ideology," sociologist Patricia Wittberg comments on the profound shift in the ways in which religious defined themselves, their place in the church, and their ministries. The open-ended call to renewal and adaptation had come into conflict with the carefully de-fined and ideological structures of pre-conciliar religious life. "Such an ideological transformation would be disruptive in the best of circum-stances, and the 1960s and 1970s were *not* the best of circumstances. Inherent contradictions rendered the adoption of a new self-definition impossible."[171] The result was, in Wittberg's terms, an "ideological limbo" that was the cause of the decline in religious orders over the next decades.[172]

Reports of turmoil within religious congregations and the tensions at the level of diocesan and religious leadership led to an unprecedented intervention by the pope in 1983, which had a significant impact on re-ligious and certainly on their movements of renewal and adaptation. John Paul II had summoned the American bishops to an extensive in-volvement with religious communities in the United States. Archbishop John Quinn, papal delegate and leader of the committee, described the task of the joint committee of the Commission of Bishops and the Committee of Religious for the Study of Religious Life in the United States. It was one of drawing to an end the period of updating and re-newing constitutions in light of *Lumen Gentium* and *Perfectae Caritatis.* The pope had asked the American bishops "to enter into the process in order to support and to second the efforts of the religious to strengthen and renew their communities."[173]

The issue of singling out American religious and the significance of the 1983 document, "Essential Elements in the Church's Teaching on Religious Life as Applied to Institutes Dedicated to Works of the Apostolate" from the Sacred Congregation for Religious and Secular Institutes was seen by Quinn as a papal reminder to American bishops

of their responsibilities to work with religious in their response to the
renewal of their consecration to a life of holiness.

> He reminds us of what so many of us take for granted, the
> enormous contributions which religious have made to the
> church in this country, and he directs us during this holy year
> to render them special pastoral service...The religious have
> been a major influence in shaping the present features of the
> church in the United States...the influence of American reli-
> gious, not only in the United States but throughout the world
> is massive. One gets the impression that [the pope] considers
> them as important for the international church as for the
> church in the United States. This means that the holiness of
> the contemporary church calls very much for the holiness of
> American religious.[174]

The document described itself as "a clarification and re-statement" of
the church's teaching on the essential elements of religious life.[175]

The impact of this 1983 "Essential Elements" document in the implementation of the recommendations on religious life was addressed in
a conference and lecture series on the East and West Coasts of the
United States.[176] A theological response to the document initially
pointed out that this unsigned text from the Sacred Congregation was
described by the pope as offering "guidelines," and the text describes itself as a synthesis of the recent magisterial teachings of the church concerning religious life. After Archbishop John Quinn's experience in
listening to the experience of American women religious at this time, he
commented that "American nuns have been exposed to an unprecedented level of misrepresentation and attack, both from the right and
the left.[177] That American women religious have suffered from misrepresentation and slander cannot be denied.

Yet, although the crisis that religious life has gone through both
globally as well as in America has had some problematic and painful
consequences, there are more positive effects that need to be noted.

> In these United States toward the close of the twentieth cen-
> tury, for the first time in history there is appearing a radically
> apostolic form of religious life for women, which heretofore

had been possible for men only—a life characterized by professional personal ministries, and by small and flexible communities. The regimented conventual routine which used to be
followed by communities of women devoted to apostolic works
is beginning to disappear or to be greatly limited.[178]

The document and the work of the joint commission of bishops and religious can be seen as a discernment process contributing to a deeper
understanding of the mission and ministry of religious women and men,
with religious orders and the church itself mutually involved.

One aspect where there seems to be some difference between the
stance of Pope John Paul II and the Sacred Congregation for Religious
and Secular Institutes in regard to the approach to religious life in
Perfectae Caritatis can be seen in the difference between the letter of
John Paul II to the American bishops (April 3, 1983, no.3) on what is
essential to religious life and the 1983 document from the Sacred
Congregation, "Essential Elements."

In his letter the pope listed the ten essential elements which are
lived in different ways from one type of religious institute to another.

Nevertheless, there are elements which are common to all
forms of religious life and which the Church regards as essential. These include: a vocation given by God, an ecclesial consecration to Jesus Christ through the profession of the
evangelical counsels by public vows, a stable form of community life approved by the Church, fidelity to a specific founding
gift and sound traditions, a sharing in Christ's mission by a corporate apostolate, personal and liturgical prayer especially
Eucharistic worship, public witness, a lifelong formation, a
form of government calling for religious authority based on
faith, a specific relation to the Church. Fidelity to these basic
elements laid down in the constitutions approved by the
Church, guarantees the strength of religious life and grounds
our hope for its future growth.[179]

Yet in the subsequent listing in the "Essential Elements" guidelines
document of the Sacred Congregation there are only nine elements. In
his analysis of this document, John Lozano points out that "While it

treats of vocation in connection with consecration, it suppresses 'fidelity to a specific gift and sound traditions,' as an element in itself and adds in fifth place, 'asceticism' which is not mentioned in the pope's letter."[180] The date of the Sacred Congregation's document is May 31, 1983, almost two months after the papal letter; this is surely evidence of an intentional omission of the element of fidelity to the founding charism and thus a rejection by the Sacred Congregation of the emphasis by John Paul II and by *Perfectae Caritatis* on faithfulness to the founding charism and sound traditions. The dynamic element in the conciliar understanding of ongoing faithfulness in terms of renewal is replaced in "Essential Elements" by the more static notion of the ascetical life.

The treatment of the habit in "Essential Elements" appears at face value to be flexible. "Religious should wear the religious garb of the institute, described in their proper law, as a sign of consecration and a witness of poverty" (no. 37). Yet the issue of the habit was a source of contention in many communities. In women's congregations, after years or even decades of the experience of wearing an identity-defining habit that negated any evidence of womanliness, the varied interpretations of "the religious garb of the institute" divided many religious communities in terms of understanding what was meant by simplicity, uniformity, of casual, working, or professional attire.[181]

> The disheartening aspect of this situation is the untimeliness of the statement. Just when institutes were beginning to heal the wounds caused by battles over dress, the document opens them only to renew the hurt. It is amazing how many women and men alike, outside of religious institutes, sometimes even outside the church itself, are preoccupied with the garb of the religious.[182]

The "Essential Elements" document removes congregational responsibility for reclaiming the founding identity of their religious institutes. It also emphasizes the role of the hierarchy in terms of interpreting the founding charism at the expense of the congregation, and it gives evidence of a move away from the collaborative and dialogical context for renewal and adaptation that was encouraged at the council and was a sticking point for many religious communities.

The report from the Pontifical Commission on Religious Life was more positive in its approach and consequences than might have been expected in view of the Essential Elements document. The highlights of this report list the positive factors in religious life during the two decades following the council.[183]

The concern held in the Vatican for the faithfulness of American religious women, a concern that generated *Ecclesiae Sanctae*, was shown to be without cause.

The report also noted that while less than 6 percent of the world's Catholics were in the United States at the time, "the United States still has one of the highest proportional numbers of religious and religious candidates for religious life of any country."[184]

Another aspect of the effect of the recommendations in *Perfectae Caritatis* for the reclaiming of founding charisms could be seen in some Latin American countries. The influence of the new ecclesiology of Vatican II, and especially of Peruvian theologian Gustavo Gutiérrez (described as the father of liberation theology), who had been in Rome during the council, was being felt in the post-conciliar religious communities. The poor became a starting point for ministry and a new worldview was influencing those who worked with the poor. The Latin American Conference of Religious (CLAR) initiated an in-depth study of religious life in Latin America in light of Vatican II. The ecclesial implications and directions invited review of apostolic ministries and their socioeconomic impact on the people to whom religious ministered.

By the end of 1966 CLAR approved a document on the "renovation and adaptation of the religious life in Latin America and its apostolic implementation."[185] That experience and the impact of the Medellín conference in 1968 generated new levels of awareness and response among the religious.[186] The conclusions of this conference led to a greater stress on the option for liberation and for the oppressed than in any earlier documents on religious life. But there was an apparent discrepancy between the experience of the members of the conference and that of religious generally speaking. For religious,

The Medellín Conference was an effort to rethink Vatican II in terms of the reality of our own continent, and to situate ourselves with the help of conciliar perspectives. The "Message to the

People of Latin America" and the "Introduction to Final documents" point up the basic features of the present day and our contribution as a church...different forms of marginality, extreme inequality among social classes, growing frustrations, growing awareness of the oppressed sectors, internal tensions, external neocolonialism, exacerbated nationalism and so forth.[187]

Yet the document on religious life that came out from the conference was a disappointment to many religious. It offered "no social diagnosis or doctrinal synthesis." It distanced itself from the methodology of the other documents.

Instead it recalls the principles of Vatican II and then tries to examine those aspects of the religious life that are directly related to development and joint pastoral work in Latin America. Instead of rethinking the religious life as a whole insofar as it relates to our continent, the document simply adapts certain aspects of the religious life to our cultural, social and economic conditions. It does not start off from the dominated classes mentioned in the document on peace, and a concern for the socially marginalized classes takes fifth place in its set of recommendations. The document on religious talks about the religious life and the process of humanization. But commitment to this process is viewed as the locale for sign and testimony, not as the focal point from which we must rethink the content and demands of sign and testimony.[188]

The critique of this document is the same as that leveled at *Perfectae Caritatis* from the perspectives of liberation theology. "It lacks theological substance, evangelical inspiration and boldness but...it has the merit of pointing us toward the realm of practice."[189] The point is made that, in the effort to be faithful to *Perfectae Caritatis*, the writers of the Medellín document on religious have been more faithful to a static interpretation of the conciliar document than to the dynamism of Medellín itself.

In the years that followed Medellín, leaders of CLAR continued their engagement with the ecclesial and sociopolitical factors that shaped their identity and ministry in Latin America. They reported that the ecclesiastical institution of the church was more often on the side of the affluent and powerful than on that of the poor. The question had to be asked whether the ongoing renewal of religious life in Latin America could be "deep and strong enough to erase the traditional image of the church as an ally of the powerful and an opponent of social changes... There was much to substantiate the complaints that the 'hierarchy, the clergy, the religious are rich and allied with the rich.'"[190]

The National Brazilian Conference of Religious Men and Women faced the same challenges as their sisters and brothers in other Latin American nations. The issue of the changing identity of religious was significant in Brazil, as was clericalism in the church of the time. Religious women "were both protected and scorned, although things were never called by their proper names."[191] The vocations crisis in Brazil began as early as 1954 when numbers of candidates for the priesthood diminished. Women religious in most parts of Brazil were consistently called to fill in the gaps and "after eight- to ten-hour days of work" they were expected to take responsibility for catechism classes or to exercise ministry at the parish Masses on Saturdays and Sundays. Not to meet these expectations was "interpreted as a lack of 'church awareness' and of sensitivity to the needs of the local church... Religious did everything."[192]

The operative meaning of the religious vocation in the post-conciliar period in Brazil was "one among other apostolic vocations in the church," without qualification or comparison with other vocations. Religious tried "to affirm and live communally God's *absoluteness, graciousness,* and total priority."[193] The life "calls for an unconditional *openness* to the service of brothers and sisters... Its original inspiration is not in this or that specific Gospel passage, but rather in the irreversible dynamics of the Gospel as a whole."[194] But what marks it out is "*the public profession—recognized, legitimized and appreciated by the Church—of the will to live fully and radically the Gospel plan, coherently and as the primary objective of one's life.* This is the only thing that justifies religious life in the Church. This *identifies* the religious among the many vocations in the Church."[195] The charismatic and prophetic dimensions of religious life in the church were seen as essential elements in the role of religious as instruments and renewal of the church.[196] The preferential option for the poor was integral to the vowed communal life. The poor had become visible, but the religious and other lay ministers who worked with them were still virtually invisible to the hierarchy.

The liberation approach that was described as characterizing Brazilian religious life and ministry was not one that transformed the whole nation. "In both present-day Christianity and civil society, the belief about the equality of rights between men and women is affirmed in principle." [197] The problem was that sexual discrimination in the male-dominated church was subtly disguised.

> We are faced with a mission of enormous timeliness, the realization of which affects women religious in the very heart of their being and opens to them new and unsuspected perspectives in the missionary aspects of their work. The discovery and practical realization of the reality of women, in their full equality of rights with men, offers the opportunity to religious, as women, to awaken in others of their own sex the consciousness of their dignity and the scope of their rights. This can make them see in the past, but above all in the present, the most diverse forms of male domination, from a merely instrumental glorification and sublimation to an erotic-sentimental, functional exploitation that continues to keep women enclosed in a patriarchal society. [198]

The implementation of *Perfectae Caritatis* in Central and South American as well as in the North American nations has been and will continue to be limited until serious work is undertaken in liberating women and men from gender stereotyping and from the trivializing and the masked power play in terms of orders of ministry that accompany such treatment in the Roman Catholic Church at both hierarchical and grassroots community levels.

The collaboration between the religious orders of the Americas continued to mutually affect their ways of perceiving their identity and mission and their opportunities to cooperate with each other in areas of apostolic ministry and in the contemplative spirituality that fires this. The 1985 fifth inter-American conference on "The Role of Apostolic Religious Life in the Context of the Contemporary Church and World" continued to contribute to consciousness-raising within religious life itself, within and across cultural divides, and in terms of collaborative ministries in church and society. At this particular conference, a celebration of the twentieth anniversary of Vatican II was held and the conference members affirmed the contribution that they had made to the post-conciliar church in "ecumenical and intercultural dialogue; authentic co-responsibility in the service of our churches; the desire to translate into concrete deeds the prophetic vocation of religious life."[199]

What was happening on the international scale also had an impact on the national level. In her experience of leadership of the LCWR, Margaret Brennan saw that a positive aspect of the refounding call of *Perfectae Caritatis* was that the call to serve the poor and marginalized had led many religious from traditional ministries into ministry for the marginalized.

> The pastoral questions emerging from the ministerial experience of apostolic religious women have been made challengingly clear in the need to consider changes of law and to search for new theological formulations that allow these women to serve the sacramental needs of Christians who call them to this exercise.[200]

The conciliar recommendation to, and the openings for, theological and ministerial education have taken women religious into new spheres of understanding their church and its teachings.[201] The question for most women religious (and for married lay leaders) was then—and remains now—not simply discrimination in terms of the exclusiveness of ordination to celibate males but, much more, the deprivation of so many millions of Christians globally of the opportunity to experience the breadth and depth of the sacramental life of their church.

This was an issue for many of the council bishops. The problem over which they expressed concern then has not diminished over subsequent decades. There are communities of women and men who have been deprived of any eucharistic celebration for the lifetime of all the members.[202] The memory is alive, kept there by those who have taken on leadership roles, but for reasons of gender or because of their married state they are unable to be ordained and so provide the priestly leadership that their communities need and surely have a right to.

While women religious in Western and Eastern churches, for varied reasons, lament the exclusion of women to ordination, it is important not to confuse the issue of ordination with the question of religious life. The forms of the "consecrated life" are recognized as unique and indispensable to the church's life and holiness.[203] Religious life offers prophetic witness in its radical commitment to Christ as well as in the ministries undertaken by religious communally and in collaboration with lay people.

> Religious life belongs to the charismatic life of the church, which means we have a certain freedom to commit ourselves to spiritual and corporal works that are outside the stream of church priorities. A strongly felt and deeply lived corporate spirituality, apostolic creativity, and willingness to invest corporate resources are hallmarks of dynamic religious life. The church will be poorer if religious sacrifice these for the sake of parochial ministry.[204]

The issue of religious ministry needs to be understood as a particular charism apart from ordained ministry. That contemporary religious are able to work collaboratively with lay people in non-government organizations and in other lay contexts means that they are able to respond to calls to mission and ministry with flexibility, freedom, and openness to the changing circumstances of sociocultural need.[205]

The heightened social consciousness of the post-conciliar decades has motivated religious to challenge unjust political and economic structures in North America and in other countries where they have worked or engaged in congregational ministries. As the discernment and collaborative renewal processes continued to have an effect, and as awareness of justice issues in society influenced community living, religious women and men had new opportunities to look more deeply into what was happening within the global situation of Catholic communities.

Issues of marginality or cultural inclusiveness were not addressed in the pre–Vatican II era. People had been taught to conform and to accept their place in the dominant clerical culture. The realization that people were being marginalized because of a variety of experiences of being "different" became an increasing concern for religious ministering during the post-conciliar decades.

In 1978 the comment was made that "there was and still is a lack of aggressive recruitment of blacks for the religious life either among male or female communities...This inclusion of blacks could give real meaning to the notion of interdependent diversity if the special charisms of the black church are used."[206] The situation described here is still a feature of the American church, and indeed of many Western churches where color is an unspoken issue.

> African American, Hispanic American, Asian American, and Native American women have often been rejected or "discerned" unsuited for membership in religious congregations of women and men religious because of unspoken racial or cultural considerations. They were perceived as potential sources of heightened fragmentation in the already tense ethnic-cultural experience of the institutes.[207]

This is an issue for the whole church, not simply for a particular ethnic group, or even for religious. But if religious are not aware of the importance of this priority then their efforts to engage authentically with their world in ministry will surely at best limp, or at worst fail to touch those people who live in a world of ethnic and socioeconomic diversity. The failures in terms of integration of different cultural groups have surely had an impact already on the understanding of religious life among the poor of the world. The document on religious life, along with all the documents, did direct religious to a concern for those on life's margins, but the impetus was lost along the way. Many church leaders wanted religious to maintain their presence in established diocesan ministries, and the failure to do this was seen as a failure of religious women and men to the church.

Thirty years after Vatican II, a three-year study of U.S. religious orders of priests, sisters, and brothers, the Religious Life Futures Project or Future of Religious Orders in the United States (FORUS) was conducted by Vincentian Father David Nygren and St. Joseph of Carondelet Sister Miriam Ukeritis, both psychologists. This study investigated the changes "occurring in the experience and understanding of religious life," and "it is based on the assumption that religious life as a whole, individual congregations and individual priests are in the midst of a transformational process."[208]

Concerns to understand the reasons for the continual decline in numbers and the rising median age were behind the research effort. Questions about the change in understanding the ways in which the vowed life was understood across the monastic, contemplative, mendicant, and apostolic orders, about ministry and aspects of communal living, were addressed specifically. More than ten thousand religious priests, sisters, and brothers participated in the study. A major conclusion drawn was that "Fidelity to the spirit of the founder and responsiveness to critical and unmet human needs are basic to the ongoing mission of religious communities."

The conclusions are themselves an indication of the impact of the Vatican documents on religious life, and of future directions for church leadership and for religious orders themselves, as well as for Catholic communities in general. The recommendations in *Perfectae Caritatis* to return to the sources of scripture and to their founding charisms appear in this study not to have been adequately addressed by most congregations as a whole over subsequent decades, although individual religious have responded and been missioned by their congregations in such initiatives.

> Vatican II called religious to a return to the "spirit of the founder." While most congregations have engaged in much study and devoted great efforts to move in this direction, the absence of corporate commitment to embody the group's response to current unmet needs in light of the Gospel imperatives stands in contrast to the collective vision and action, rooted in God, that marked the birth of most apostolic, monastic or contemplative congregations. Religious as a social institution in American society is at a crossroads. To achieve a desired future, religious as a group, as well as individuals must confront the forces that currently restrain them and reinforce those dynamics that will allow them to in fact be responsive to absolute human need in the context of their particular charism. A future marked by significant revitalization will emerge for those congregations that are rooted in their relationship with God and, in a spirit of fidelity to their founding purpose, and responsiveness to absolute human need, confront the current gap between the Gospel and the culture.[209]

Key dynamics of individualism and vocation, leadership, authority, work and corporate identity, affiliative decline and role clarity, racism and multiculturalism, materialism and the gospel, charism and parochial assimilation are listed as operative factors in varying degrees in those congregations that have engaged in serious renewal initiatives.

As parishes have grown and numbers of priests have decreased, religious have been taking up various ministerial roles and responsibilities in parishes. One of the benefits of this has been the greater opportunities for collaboration with and empowering of lay people who are also working in parish ministries. However, one of the consequences of this change in apostolic ministries is the movement of religious away from the central identity of their congregations so that many religious seem to belong more effectively to the parishes or dioceses in which they serve. In expressing her concern for this phenomenon in the United States, Sandra Schneiders points out that there is a "clericalization" of lay religious as they become more accountable to the parish or diocesan administrative structure.[210]

Religious parish workers may become less available to their congregation than to their parish priest employer to whom they are more immediately accountable. As they grow into their ministerial context over time they "increasingly find their affective and social life centered in the parish and its families rather than their communities."[211] The ability of religious leadership to apply pressure on diocesan authorities in regard to support of their members has radically changed from those days when they ran their own educational, health care, or social services and had some influence in the larger sphere of church life.[212] That communities need the stipends paid to these parish workers increases the dependency. Some congregations experience great hardship because of the rising median age and the retirement of members. Fewer religious are supporting ever-greater numbers of retired members of their congregations.

The "progressive parochialization of ministry in the wake of the Council,"[213] while it has brought benefits to religious in terms of their increased opportunities for working collaboratively with lay people in team ministries, it has "seriously undermined the specificity of religious ministry in the Church and contributed to the identity confusion of religious themselves."[214] Schneiders asks whether the identity of a congregation is as "a source of workers rather than an ecclesial life form."[215] Consequences such as these were not foreseen in the hopes of the bishops at the council to free religious for contemporary ministry and for new forms of collaborative and empowering leadership in church and society. This may be more pertinent in some nations such as the United States. In other situations ecclesially and geographically the mutuality of shared ministry may be beginning to open up new understandings of lay women and men and religious working together.

One of the issues that the FORUS research brought to light is that where orders have been able to hold a clear sense of their corporate identity in terms of their lifestyle and work they are more stable and appear to experience a greater sense of their own ecclesial and ministerial identity. There seems to be less dichotomizing in such congregations. The completion of the FORUS research and the presentation of the findings in 1992 gave some concrete directions for religious leadership teams to work on. In their conclusion the researchers made the important statement that the critical component required for transformation and for growth to occur is for religious orders "to imagine a desirable future" for themselves and to "reinforce that movement by consistency in choices based on values and the traditions of the order."[216]

On March 25, 1996, the post-synodal apostolic exhortation on the consecrated life, *Vita Consecrata* (*VC*), of John Paul II was issued. In this exhortation the concept of the consecrated life was the defining category for evangelical communities. This was in continuity with the approach taken by the council. However, the language used is more in tune with what might be understood as a somewhat elitist understanding of religious life. The synod affirmed that "the consecrated life has not only proved a help and support for the Church in the past, but is also a precious and necessary gift for the present and future of the People of God, since it is an intimate part of her life, her holiness and her mission" (*VC*, 3).

The prophetic element of religious life is endorsed, as are the evangelical counsels as expressed in the vows of poverty, chastity, and obedience. Religious have a particular role to play in their world. "The Institutes of Consecrated Life, through the profession of the evangelical counsels, must be conscious of their special mission in today's Church, and we must encourage them in that mission" (*VC*, 35).

The evangelical role of religious as spreading the gospel throughout the world is confirmed. "The consecrated life inspires and accompanies the spread of evangelization in the different parts of the world, where Institutes from abroad are gratefully welcomed and new ones are being founded, in a great variety of forms and expressions" (*VC*, 2). In reference to evangelical poverty the following of the poor Christ is integral to religious life. This is consonant with the Vatican II emphasis on the church and the poor that has been a consequence of many of the post-conciliar religious initiatives.

The pope points out the importance of the contribution that consecrated religious make to their local churches and in communion with the bishop. This resonates with the discussions on exemption and the fact that many council members were against the rights and privileges of exempt religious. Some bishops felt religious should be more accountable to the local diocese than to the works of the congregation. The relation between the consecrated life and the church's mission and the roots of this life in the mystery of Christ and of the Trinity is emphasized in *Vita Consecrata*.[217]

In conclusion, it can be said that there were significant efforts from church leadership to enable the key aspects of the return to the sources and to the adaptation of religious life that came from the reclaiming of the charism as proposed in *Perfectae Caritatis*. Statements and exhortations gave encouragement and caution. It seemed that American religious were singled out for investigation by the pontifical commission because of their democratic-style responses to *Perfectae Caritatis*. But Archbishop Quinn's irenic and collegial approach meant that his report was a positive and affirming rather than a repressive assessment of the state of religious life at the time.[218]

Within religious orders themselves there has been a deep and wholehearted, though sometimes diffused, commitment to take the conciliar direction seriously. That turmoil, division, doubts, and questioning, personal and communal, were experienced may well be not simply an issue for religious themselves but an indication that they did try to embrace the mandate and spirit of *Perfectae Caritatis* as they had been encouraged to do.

More than forty years after Vatican II it may be forgotten that the 1960s were years of "alternative lifestyles." When religious were called by the council to engage with the world, it was to a world that few council members could have anticipated. Communes were surfacing and protest movements celebrating anti-authoritarian lifestyles abounded. Hippies and radicals were searching for their own new worlds. The phenomena of underground press, liberated art, theater, and literature questioned beliefs and values that had been held sacrosanct and offered extreme perspectives on life and relationships.[219] This was the new cultural context in which religious of the period found themselves confronted by, with little understanding of, the dynamics of the present, and for which their past had not prepared them. Yet they responded to the call to go out to minister in the world rather than to eschew it. Extraordinary concern for people and a commitment to the gospel following of Jesus characterized their ways of relating and ministering, and led religious into the new millennium, though at an enormous price and not without casualties.

PART IV

THE STATE OF THE QUESTION

The question of religious life more than forty years after Vatican II is a complex one. The polarization that existed in the council and flourished subsequently is still an issue in the present church context. However, a major factor in the Western world is that the visibility of religious is less obvious now than in the past. While the religious habit is still a defining feature of religious in most African and Asian nations, it is ministry that defines most religious in the present. Religious, particularly women religious, are known by those with and for whom they work, rather than by the distinctive clothing of the past. This is a return to the sources, because founders and foundresses were concerned to respond to the needs they observed in the world in which they lived rather than to establish a privileged class of ministers, distinctive by grade, by dress, or by walled monasteries and convents.

Those Catholics who are unaware of the origins of religious life, particularly of apostolic religious life, and who lament the apparent loss of religious in the church today are confounded by the change. Those who have lived in the midst of the change, and whose identity and communities have been affected by it, are still working to understand the ways in which the Spirit is alive in all that has been taking place, and is still leading religious to follow Christ in the present and future society and church.

Where do things stand now? What is the future for religious life?

It was theoretically possible for "renewal" to have worked. Why didn't it? Ultimately, the crisis it had to meet was too manifold and too intense; there was too much up-dating, too much renewing to accomplish from a point of departure too far back in other times and mentalities.[220]

This comment sums up the stance of some researchers on the post-conciliar experience of renewal and adaptation in religious life. The impact of that first decade had a concertina effect on the other decades. There was both too much information and too little for those who had been so strongly inculturated into the monastic or semi-monastic lifestyle and commitment to easily comprehend the unpacking and dismantling of past structures and practices within such a relatively short period. Had the hierarchy themselves been more united over the changes endorsed by Vatican II, the story of religious life might have been a different one.

A major issue now is the reality that religious life is no longer simply an exclusively Western or European endeavor; religious life is a global reality. While religious congregations were characterized in the past by Western identity and leadership with small numbers of members drawn from other nations, this is no longer the case. Religious from other nations are increasing their numbers in "Western" or "European" congregations.

It has been difficult to access information about membership and leadership issues in Latin American, Asian, and African congregations in the post-conciliar period, but this is an important issue for the global church to consider.[221] Apart from those international congregations that list the increasing indigenous members in their congregations as a result of vocations in these countries, there is little information available about numbers and situations of the indigenous religious communities in these countries and regions. That there has been an increase in vocations is recorded, but the implications of global religious mission and ministries are still being felt and interpreted.

> Certain parts of the church in Asia have shown a steady increase in the number of vocations during the past decades. While many vocations go to traditional religious congregations and institutes which are Western in origin, in recent years a number of new local religious congregations have sprung up in Asia. In general, the percentage of vocations to the priesthood, the religious life and other forms of consecrated life and missionary institutes is higher than in most other parts of the universal church.[222]

However, there has been a drop in the number of religious priests in every continent except Asia, as well as in the numbers of religious women in every continent except Asia and Africa, where there has been an increase.

The voice of the Asian church is being heard in its own right in a variety of contexts, and it is claiming the importance of being heard apart from the Western hegemonic hold on ecclesial approaches to church in society. One of the new phenomena recorded in the developing church in Asia that is going to have an impact in the present and future church, and in our understanding of the global reality of religious life, is the growing awareness of women's place in society and in church in Asia.

> The phenomenon of women's movements is yet another positive development. They are increasing in Asia, making women aware of their potentialities and resources, challenging centuries of subordination to men, enabling them to claim their rights and participation in public life. The Spirit of God is present in these developments.[223]

In a meeting organized by the Office of Consecrated Life of the Federation of Asian Bishops' Conferences (FABC) in July 2005, bishops, women religious, and laity from twenty Asian countries assembled for a symposium on "The Role of Religious in the Building Up of the Local Church in Asia." In their deliberations they made the resolution to "enhance and strengthen greater knowledge, esteem and promotion of all forms of Consecrated Life and Societies of Apostolic Life, particularly that of Religious Sisters and Brothers."[224] Integral to their deliberations was the expressed importance of mutuality between the various ecclesial vocations in accord with *Lumen Gentium* and the recognition that "Charisms are cultural in that their externalization is always mediated by culture; they are transcultural in that they transcend cultures; they are countercultural inasmuch as they provide criteria against which cultures can be judged."[225] If these affirmations do take hold they will have an impact on the ways in which religious life is lived in Asia and, surely, globally.

Some Asian, African, and Latin American religious are meeting together, both in the Ecumenical Association of Third World Theologians (EATWOT), and in other groupings to share their understanding of church in an environment other than that of the industrialized Western

world. Many of these women religious have a more comprehensive picture of the needs of their church, their society, and religious life than
their local leaders.

Indications of the impact of these new voices in the post-conciliar
discussion are now being seen in a variety of meetings and publications.
One expression of the Asian voice can be heard in a comment by a
Korean religious woman at a meeting of the "Ecclesia of Women in
Asia: Gathering the Voices of the Silenced," which was held in Bangkok,
Thailand, in 2002.[226]

> The Second Vatican council proclaimed the mystery of the
> church to all wo/mankind. The mystery of the church is a sym-
> bol of the deep unity of all the people with God, and it is the
> sacramental sign and instrument of Christ (*GS* 2, *LG* 1).
> However, in 1976 the Vatican Sacred Congregation of Faith
> and Doctrine reaffirmed that women could not be ordained
> priests. The reason why I am discussing the issue of women's
> ordination here is the following. Today, thirty-eight years after
> the close of the Second Vatican council, the issue of ordination
> negates the call of Vatican II for the deep unity of all hu-
> mankind with God ... The church, through a dynamic relation-
> ship with human persons in each age, always establishes and
> transmits new traditions. Just as Jesus broke down prejudices of
> his time, now we must break down the prejudices of our time.[227]

The facts that women comprise more than 60 percent of church congregations, that more than 70 percent of those who are active in the
churches are women, and that they account for around 5 percent of appointed leadership roles in those churches are issues for these Asian
women religious.[228] It is particularly important in the new millennium,
which is described as the age of women, and in a culture where "at least
one family in ten experiences serious violence" and "nearly all married
women experience some kind of violence from their husbands."[229] This
is a necessary concern for religious women in their ministries on behalf
of the church in their time.

While the Korean church is one of the many Asian churches that
are increasing in numbers of both religious and Catholics in general, increase is not the case globally.

The statistics on the decreasing numbers of religious sisters, brothers, and priests gives an indication of the global situation in the post–Vatican II era. With the evident losses, which had begun in the 1950s, concern for the survival of religious life became a priority for both conservative and progressive church groups.

WORLD DATA	1970	1975	1980	1985	1990	1995	2000	2004
Religious priests	148,804	145,452	156,191	150,161	145,477	142,332	139,397	137,409
Religious brothers	79,408	70,388	73,090	65,208	62,526	59,515	55,057	54,620
Religious sisters	1,004,304	968,526	960,991	917,432	882,111	837,961	801,185	776,269

Center for Applied Research in the Apostolate (CARA)[230]

On the one hand, scandals about "defections" of religious worldwide have been blasted across continents, and ultra-conservative writers have reported stories of failures of loyalty and fidelity in religious life. That religious life had been so secret in its enclosure and in its monastic isolation meant that among the general populace there was a prurient interest in almost every change that took place and a doomsday atmosphere was enjoyed by many observers. It was true that mistakes were made and that there were failures. The ultra-conservative faction that caused division at Vatican II was able to all-too-quickly lay blame on the decree on religious life and on religious themselves for those problems that were an issue prior to the council.

On the other hand, the generosity and the commitment of those who were on the frontier of change received little recognition or affirmation. Already heavily committed religious had put countless hours into congregational meetings, strategic planning, writing of position papers, ongoing education, and, in later decades, re-founding and re-configuring conferences, so that the recommendations for renewal and adaptation could be implemented. In most cases these renewal efforts were being undertaken while the religious were still carrying out their regular ministries. All these efforts have taken a toll on individuals and on their congregations over the past four decades. Communities have suffered as members found that they could no longer stay in religious life and as numbers joining congregations consistently decreased. What is obvious in most cases is that in spite of smaller numbers and of changes, congregational and personal commitment and energies for ministry have been sustained.

The number of religious, in the United States in particular, who left religious life, may seem to be catastrophic, but what must be taken into account is that the change of commitment may have been an act of faithfulness and a choice for truth rather than an unfaithfulness to their commitment.[231] The 1987 *Report to U.S. Bishops on Religious Life and the Decline of Vocations* also notes that:

> A study of the statistics published by the Vatican Bureau of Statistics shows that notwithstanding the decline in the numbers of vocations, the United States still has one of the highest proportional numbers of religious and candidates for religious life of any country in the world. Less than 6 percent of the world's Catholics are in the United States yet approximately 27 percent of the world's religious are in the United States and 32 percent of the world's novices are in the United States. Hence, though the numbers are down, they are still representative in the context of the universal church.[232]

U.S. DATA	1965	1975	1985	1995	2000	2005	2006*
Religious priests	22,707	22,904	22,265	16,705	15,092	14,137	13,495
Religious brothers	12,271	8,625	7,544	6,535	5,662	5,451	5,181
Religious sisters	179,954	135,225	115,386	90,809	79,814	68,634	66,608

Center for Applied Research in the Apostolate (CARA)

*The 2006 numbers do not include the Archdiocese of New Orleans, due to Hurricane Katrina.

The steadiness of the fall in numbers is addressed in the report, and cultural as well as other societal and ecclesial factors are listed as causes.

The pervasive change in the nature of the Catholic community in the United States itself over the decades from the 1960s to the present has been a factor in the number of vocations to religious life.[233] The Catholic community has emerged from what was recognized as a cultural ghetto to become an influential force in the mainstream of American society.

> Whereas Catholics through previous decades had lived largely in cultural or ethnic neighborhoods or ghettos, they began, after World War II, to join the move of their fellow Americans to the suburbs. Here they became quickly assimilated into the general population...All this happened just as the American culture itself was undergoing far-reaching cultural shifts.[234]

These factors have had profound effects on people's attitude toward religious life and toward the claiming of the lay identity which religious have also worked to confirm in the post-conciliar decades. A fruitful consequence of this has been the greater understanding and appreciation of collegiality and collaboration between religious and laity in Catholic, ecumenical, and interfaith communities and contexts.[235]

A major consequence and a benefit of the upheaval has been the amount of research on religious life that has been carried out across disciplines and that has contributed to a greater understanding of the "multi-faceted diamond" of institutes of consecrated life. The sociological research was often carried out by religious themselves who were engaged in various renewal programs and who then worked to discern the central ideas of renewal and adaptation in lifestyle and in ministry in their own context and period.

Numbers of writers have critiqued religious life and the ways in which the faithfulness of congregations to their founding charism, or their attempts to respond to the contemporary circumstances of mission and ministry have affected their numbers and ethos. The growth, maintenance, or demise of communities became subjects for both intensive and extensive research.[236]

Whether there would be a future for religious life was a frequently asked question from within and outside religious ranks. The hypothesis of one group of researchers in 1979 was

> that religious life in America was going through a major transition, one that had been underway for at least fifteen years, and which would take another fifteen years to complete its major movements. The magnitude of this transition would be major and significant, and perhaps would be viewed in the future as one of the most significant periods in the evolution of religious life. The transition would effect a deep reorientation in the way that religious would live in community and the way they would be of service to the Church and the world.[237]

This hypothesis has to some extent been validated, and is in continuity with the FORUS conclusions which provide new questions and directions thirty years later.

Among the several elements that sociologists proposed for religious congregations to emerge creatively along the "vitality curve" was an "open system" which offers the greatest possibility for "a revitalized community that is in tune with the spirit of the gospel, the charism of the founder and the signs of the times."[238] What this "open system" and what "revitalized communities" meant in practical terms of congregational identity and ministerial commitment has been evidenced in diverse ways over subsequent decades.

Those monasteries that the FORUS project[239] described as being stable and having a clear corporate identity at the time have also been subjected to the pressures of change and new sociocultural circumstances. The two criteria cited by Nygren and Ukeritis in 1992 as crucial to dynamic religious communities, "fidelity to purpose and responsiveness to unmet human needs" are still seen as significant for community identity in the third millennium.[240] Yet even when these have been adhered to congregationally, numbers have changed little and the median age is still rising. However, what is changing radically is the collaboration of religious and laity in both new and established ecclesial ministries.

The research of sociologist Patricia Wittberg, done from within religious life itself, and carried out over more than a decade, has presented religious leaders with a perspective on the different forces that have continued to influence the shaping of post-conciliar religious life. While her research is necessarily an analysis of the past, it offers some directions and suggestions for the future. Strategies for dealing with change, or at least a means of locating particular orders in the context of the larger systems that have affected their growth and their self-understanding, can contribute to the reworking of their mission and ministry in the contemporary church and societal context.[241]

Wittberg offers sociological data on the impact of withdrawal from the ministry in and leadership of their educational, health care, and welfare institutions on religious congregations themselves. In many cases when religious have so long defined themselves, or been defined by their institutions, the separation from institutional governance has had a significant impact on their understanding of themselves and of their identity as religious. "Each institution was, as one sister put it, 'a living example of our mission and vision statements. It is the place where we put our words into actions, our lives on the line. The institutions were an essential and unquestioned component of the *virtuoso* identity of the sisters."[242] The leadership of the religious women themselves was just as essential and a given dimension of the religious identity of their institutions. Religious have made a significant contribution to Catholic health, education, and welfare and the handing over of their institutions represents a new movement toward apostolic religious life, ministry, and mission in the church and society at large.

Another sociologist from outside religious life, Helen Rose Fuchs Ebaugh, has researched the rapid decline in membership of religious congregations.[243] The far-reaching consequences of Vatican II for religious orders resulted in their loss of "the unique niche they had filled for almost one hundred years in the United States . . . The expansion of parish jobs for nuns, coupled with the eradication of the ghetto mentality of Catholics, eventuated in the decline of parochial schools."[244] Ebaugh, a former president of the Association for the Sociology of Religion, argues that while congregations exhibit aging and diminishment of numbers, they are not following the normal sociological model of organizational decline.

The common characteristics of organizational decline, such as increased centralization of authority, fear of risk-taking, lack of direction, internal conflicts between power groups, low morale, and passivity among the grass-roots community members were not evidenced in Ebaugh's research. "Given the traditional submissiveness of nuns in the Catholic church, it is possible that the council 'fathers' did not anticipate the creativity, readiness and strength of Catholic nuns, especially in the United States, to effect the kinds of renewal that occurred."[245] She comments that, while numbers may be on the decrease, new initiatives are also on the increase.

Ebaugh attributes the new energies and initiatives she observed in religious women's self-perception and self-determination to the rise of feminism as expressed in four areas: (1) their withdrawal from parish work in the ways they had previously been involved and exercised leadership; (2) their involvement in social justice issues related to women's concerns; (3) their articulation of women's issues in mission statements; and (4) the struggle women's congregations face in their dealings with the conservative reactions of the Vatican to renewal initiatives in American congregations.[246]

Her research in the 1990s led Ebaugh to the conviction that while women's religious orders were dealing with the problems of aging and decreasing numbers, non-canonical communities of women and associate programs of religious congregations were on the increase. A surprising factor in her research was the high level of energy for both mission and ministry in congregations that evidenced decline in numbers and had a high median age. Rather than becoming more authoritarian, these groups were becoming more collegial and egalitarian in their structures and relationships. Community members were being released from middle management responsibility such as provincial or regional leadership for hands-on work at grassroots with and for the poor. Their commitment to service was seen as one evidencing high morale and with a strong sense of purpose.[247]

The issue of choosing their identity as canonical or non-canonical congregations is one that some orders have been confronting in order to have greater ministerial freedom. Others are working on reconfiguration or merger issues in accord with the spirit of *Perfectae Caritatis* 21, which states that smaller communities have the option to choose to merge with others which share the same or similar vision and spirit. This has taken on a variety of forms in the past decade or so, and will surely continue in the future.[248]

Reconfiguration can take several different forms. A *union* occurs when two or more congregations each give up their distinct juridic identity to from a new institute...A *merger* occurs when a congregation is completely absorbed by another institute...A *reunification* occurs when congregations who began as one and over the years separated, make a decision to reunite...A *unification* occurs when congregations who claim the same foundress but over the years have been independent of one another, make a decision to unite the independent congregations into one institute.[249]

Issues of belonging and identity are important in such changes, and they are significant for the next decade of religious life. The importance of boundaries is real in the establishment of authentic community, and in those congregations that have made their boundaries more porous by accepting non-vowed associates, both male and female, new questions of communal identity, mutuality, and accountability are surfacing. For example, how porous can a boundary be and still enable authentic communal identity and mission? The response to this question is being discovered in the living out of these new relational and ministerial networks in congregations.

The role and identity of religious in the church is being reclaimed by religious themselves as they live out of their communal and ministerial commitments, and in the changing expression and experience of these. After Vatican II it was clear that religious sisters and brothers are not clerical. But neither are they lay. The status of religious may be canonically clear, but experientially it can be much more opaque in terms of their place in church life. Eulogizing of the consecrated life and especially of women religious does not necessarily mean that religious have a real place in the structured life of the church. That many religious are women appears to exacerbate the issue for the Vatican.[250] Religious brothers are also working to find their contemporary identity and ministry through their continued research on their founders and their founding charism. Many of them are renegotiating their relationships with their lay associates and working toward finding their own corporate mission and ministry in the context of their founders.[251] These corporate initiatives of contemporary religious women and men are resulting in an empowering of lay ecclesial mission and ministry in

the church. The corporate commitment is now becoming more prominent than in the past and it is to some extent validating the conclusions
of sociologists in regard to post–Vatican II religious life.

The significant contributions to a scholarly understanding of religious life from an ecclesiological context by writers such as Sandra
Schneiders, Diarmuid O'Murchu, and Joan Chittister[252] open up new
vistas on the heritage, the present state of religious life, and directions
for the future. Schneiders's exegesis and her construction of an ecclesial
and cultural understanding of religious life invite careful study and reflection. She concludes her second of what is to be a three-volume series with a summary of what she perceives to be the three "intimately
interwoven relationships that constitute religious life as a distinctive
form of life in the church and structure it from within."[253] These three
relationships are described as:

> *commitment* through perpetual profession to Religious Life it-
> self within a particular congregation;
>
> total and exclusive self-gift to God in Jesus Christ symbolized
> by lifelong *consecrated celibacy*; and
>
> affective and effective integration into a specific *community* of
> persons in mission to the world.[254]

Not all contemporary religious might agree with all aspects of Schneiders's
understanding of the vowed life, particularly her insistence on perpetual
commitment, but the careful structuring of her approach enables informed dialogue, questioning, and exploration to continue in terms of implementing renewal and adaptation in continuity with the Christian
tradition and in terms of the contemporary Western cultural context.

Another significant contributor to a contemporary understanding
of religious life that is also an extension of the vision of Vatican II is
Irish Missionary of the Sacred Heart Diarmuid O'Murchu, whose writings on the topic also extend over a decade of researching and living the
life.[255] While Schneiders stays within the evangelical and traditional
model, O'Murchu begins with it and then breaks open an understanding that locates the story of religious life in the context of both the du-
alisms and the unities that seem to have been ever-present in the
development of communities of consecrated commitment.

In addressing the changing paradigms of religious life, O'Murchu describes new understandings and naming of the vows which he "radically redesigns" as expressions of contemporary commitment to God and God's community.[256] He proposes directions for inner growth and he offers new horizons of consciousness and of understanding accountability and connectedness that are lifelong challenges for religious and their collaborators, personally and communally, in the following of Christ.

The vow of obedience is described by O'Murchu as a "vow of mutual collaboration." In this context of vowed mutual collaboration, his emphasis on dialogue is offered as the most appropriate way forward in the life commitment of the religious, "a collaborative endeavor, arising from the people, accountable back to them, and engaging their major concerns at all times."[257] The vocation to religious life, which he reminds his readers is a lay vocation, is one that draws its meaning from its connectedness to the whole human community.

> The vow for mutual collaboration operates out of a new paradigm, not for the sake of being trendy or postmodern, but because the collaborative approach is foundationally more creative for, and responsive to, the mutuality on which creation thrives at every level. By embracing this vow, in this new interpretative vein, religious seek to honor mutuality as a key value of creation and of God's involvement in creation's evolution.[258]

Alongside the theologies of the religious life that have been and continue to be developed is a spirituality that is contemporary, contemplative, and apostolic. Joan Chittister has been a prophetic voice during the four decades following Vatican II. Her contribution to the understanding of Benedictine spirituality, from her early collaborative work *Climb Along the Cutting Edge* through to her own communal and autobiographical contributions on the experience of living monastic life, opens up new vistas for religious life in general and offers an understanding of the vowed life in changing sociocultural and ecclesial contexts.[259] Her capacity to communicate the spirituality of religious living enables religious to keep attentive to the movements of the Holy Spirit in their own religious story.

In her analysis of the spiritual dimensions of communal and congregational transformation through the lens of the Benedictine Sisters of Erie, Chittister provides a case study for those congregations that have struggled with adaptation and renewal both within their communities and in the sociocultural contexts of their times. She points out the temptation to simply *adjust* aspects of religious life rather than to pay the price (or take the risk) of adaptation, and her illustrations of such adjustments to cultural change without authentic renewal may touch sensitive places in most women's congregational stories.

The price that various Benedictine congregational leaders paid to maintain fidelity to church and to their Benedictine heritage is not something that is unique to Chittister's community. However, her recounting of the story of the Erie Benedictines and their experiences of adaptation and renewal through leadership and communal changes would surely add breadth and depth to any congregational historian's analysis of the cultural and communal tensions that are a consequence of the endeavors to live Vatican II with integrity.

What is obvious in her account—and this resonates with the story of many religious orders in the United States—is that in their renewal efforts religious leaders and their communities took the Vatican documents seriously, they stayed faithful to their understanding of religious life, and they acted in fidelity to the church.[260] Erie Benedictine community leaders—and this includes Chittister herself during her leadership period as prioress in her community—worked toward the integration of an active apostolic lifestyle and ministry in faithful response to the Vatican mandate for renewal and adaptation. Chittister recalls the time of her leadership as prioress as a period when the understanding "of the community as a public person, a ministering person, a prophetic person in its own right" came alive in herself and in the Benedictine community of Erie.

> This was no time to preside over a monastic museum, to dig moats around monasteries while they took the poor to the jails and the flop houses and the Salvation Army at night but never thought of asking for help at a convent whose order, we were proud to say, "had saved civilization"...Our monasteries, I was convinced, needed to become havens for the weary, signs of hope to the hopeless, centers of spiritual development for all.[261]

This renewal impetus Chittister described as a movement from renewal and adaptation to "revitalization, the capstone of renewal." Documents from Vatican II enabled "a new kind of an old life" another way of being human and spiritual and engaging in ministry in the name of God.[262] The communal impetus for revitalization and the practical consequences for the religious personally and communally are listed in the final chapters of Chittister's book.

What comes through loud and clear in her writing is a practical example of the living consequences of *Perfectae Caritatis* and of the universal call to holiness in the context of the continuing faith journey of a contemporary religious monastic community. The growth to understanding of the corporate commitment of the Erie Benedictines offers a valuable example to other congregations. The teaching ministry of the Benedictines took shape in the new millennium in the Erie corporate commitment:

> To model the Benedictine charism of peace, Pax, by working for disarmament, ecological stewardship and social justice in solidarity with the poor and oppressed, especially women.[263]

Chittister comments that there may be a great deal that communities such as the Erie Benedictines can offer other religious communities as a way of life and as a microcosm of church and society. Theirs is an example of "what it means to change, to grow, to become what [they were] meant to be but become it differently" from what they had planned. The lesson learned is that "change, conversion and leadership . . . are the anchors, the essence, of renewal."[264]

Within the Commission on Religious Life, and within the council itself, division characterized the debate, but one thing on which all agreed was that the basis of religious life was the importance of living a gospel life. What Chittister has shown in her congregational story, what O'Murchu has presented in his changing paradigms, and what Schneiders has presented in her comprehensive analysis of the gospel foundations for a religious life lived in the context of the contemporary *ecclesia* and culture is the panorama of possibilities and the multilayered foundations for such a gospel response, corporate and personal, in the diverse institutes of religious life throughout the world, and particularly during the four decades following Vatican II.

CONCLUSION

Vatican II's contribution to a contemporary understanding of religious life was made more significant because it was located in the context of the universal call to holiness of *Lumen Gentium* (chapters 5 and 6) rather than in *Perfectae Caritatis* alone. While the decree made some important contributions to contemporary religious life, especially in the emphasis on the gospel following of Jesus and the importance of the return to the founding charism, it suffered from the unresolved polarized and polarizing approach that prevailed among both the commission and council members, particularly in relation to the call to holiness and the common priesthood.

Although the extremely conservative group was a minority in terms of its numbers, its members at the time and subsequently have been consistently powerful in their impact on religious life in the decades following the council. The challenge for religious congregations in the present and in the future is to continue to maintain a corporate faithfulness to their founding vision without being defensive when attacked by the religious right, liberal left, or any fundamentalist or ideological power group.

A decade after the close of Vatican II, Johannes Baptist Metz, one of the most influential post–Vatican II theologians, although not a religious himself, wrote about his conviction of the importance of religious life as a following of Christ. What he said then may still be seen as an affirmation of the Vatican II hope for religious life in the present and the future.

When religious orders conceive their identity in the sense of an open history of following Christ, they obtain decisive significance for the church as a whole and bring their own religious life into the perspective of the entire church. This understanding of their identity and faithfulness towards their own origins does prohibit them from withdrawing into an ecclesiastical and social nature reserve and (if possible by appealing to literal faithfulness to traditional patterns of life) cultivating an escapist idyll—in the midst of an age when the life of the Church is fatally threatened...If the religious orders understand their own identity and continuity in the sense of an un-self-contained family history marked by the demand of living out the follow-

ing of Christ, then they always intervene in the life of the
Church as a whole and remind this church, emphatically and in
an openly radical way, of that law of following Christ under
which it indispensably stands and by means of which it must
renew itself.[265]

What the future will be for religious we do not know. Each of the
researchers referred to, and many other writers and researchers, are
mentors for our growing understanding of the future of religious life.
What we do know is that there is a living and vital affirmation that the
religious life will be a feature of the church, whatever form it might
have taken in our Catholic past or will take in the future. It is present
in our midst. We also know that religious congregations developed out
of a situation of need, the need being responded to by one or several
committed Christian believers who made a commitment to engage in
following Christ, and who then found that others joined them in their
commitment to service.

That religious today exercise their mission and ministry locally and
globally in such diverse lifestyles and contexts means that their outreach
will surely both provide "the capacity to comfort the afflicted and afflict
the comforted."[266] When lived authentically, the religious commitment
has always been both paradoxical and empowering in its public witness
and ministry. Whatever shape their commitment takes, following
Vatican II and in continuity with the Christian tradition, religious are
those who have received and responded to a call from God to commit
themselves ecclesially and publicly to the service of church and world,
in some form of vowed celibate and communal lifestyle based on a
gospel following of Jesus, and in witness to God's loving and transforming presence in this world and in the one to come.

FINAL REMARKS

The call of Vatican II was a call to a new vision of being and becoming church in ways that were accountable to the Christian tradition and open to the future into which the Holy Spirit was calling us. The council itself was subject to the tensions between those whose vision was held by their understanding of the power and richness of the Catholic identity and heritage and those whose concern was to affirm the past by witnessing to the life of the Spirit in the present that the future might be one of unity in justice, peace, and love.

The three documents—on priesthood, on the training of priests, and on religious life—while they suffered from the necessary compromises that had to be made in order to be attentive to the contributions of all council members, offer a vision of mutuality of ministries in the present and for the future. The present world is certainly in need of witness to collegial and collaborative ministries directed to service of church and society. The council call to common priesthood and universal holiness is the context for the exercise of these ministries both globally and locally.

The quote from Dickens with which this book opened is a reminder of the tensions that are always present. These are the best of times and the worst of times, times of light and times of of darkness. We have experienced the winter of despair in the polarization of the church. Now surely the spring of hope is on the horizon as we look to the future of ministry as a means of working together in faith, hope, and love, and in the assurance of God's transforming presence in and through the spirit of Love in the universe.

It is essential to draw attention to the communal dimension of the Spirit's powerful embrace. Though it does touch each individual with creative regard for his or her distinctiveness, the outreaching of God that is the Spirit embraces humans in their relationships to one another, that is, as a community…embraced by the Spirit-power of God, women and men will be able to conquer those powers that would diminish them and instead use beneficent powers to become united with God and one another in the power of the Spirit.[1]

This is surely the future of ministry and of ministers as the mission of Christ is lived out in and through the affirmation that it is the Spirit of Love that empowers us all in our yes to the God who loved creation into being.

NOTES

PREFACE

1. Susan K. Wood comments on the blossoming of lay ministry in the post–Vatican II period. See Wood, ed. "Introduction: The Collegeville Ministry Seminar," *Ordering the Baptismal Priesthood: Theologies of Lay and Ordained Ministry* (Collegeville, MN: Liturgical Press, 2003), vii–x.

2. Charles Dickens, *A Tale of Two Cities* (London: T. Nelson & Sons, 1989; first published in 1859), 1.

3. In reading the history of the documents, it is obvious that interventions from non-Western bishops were having an impact on the understanding of church that was developing. Their pastoral concern for their people led them to stake their claim in the developing ecclesiology of Vatican II.

4. In his research of the history preceding Vatican II, Giacomo Martina points out that research in regard to the stance of church leaders in Europe during the wars is a difficult task because of both the amount and the delicate nature of the material involved, alongside the problems in gaining access to archival material. Giacomo Martina, "The Historical Context in Which the Idea of a New Ecumenical Council Was Born," in *Vatican II Assessment and Perspectives: Twenty-five Years After (1962–1987)*, ed. René Latourelle (New York/Mahwah, NJ: Paulist Press, 1988), 1:40.

5. This was a time when the election of the first Roman Catholic president was making an impact. John F. Kennedy's leadership was prominent, and popular church leaders such as Cardinal Cushing and Bishop Fulton Sheen were influential media figures. In the United States in the post-conciliar years the National Conference of Catholic Bishops increasingly became a force to be recognized and respected, not simply because of the population it represented but because of the issues it was addressing and the expansiveness of its concerns.

6. I have chosen to use the terms "council members" and "bishops" inclusively as a means of describing all those, including heads of religious orders, who were present at the council with the right to vote.

7. Reese gives a comprehensive overview of the history of the councils in relation to Vatican II. See Thomas J. Reese, *Inside the Vatican: The Politics*

and Organization of the Catholic Church (Cambridge, MA: Harvard University Press, 1996), 37.

8. It is interesting to note that Cardinal Cushing made the offer to have simultaneous translation available for all participants at the council, but the offer was refused, as Latin was to be the language in which all were expected to be fluent. Bishops from more affluent countries helped many of those bishops from economically poorer countries with the expenses they incurred through their attendance at the council.

9. See Henri Fesquet, *The Drama of Vatican II: The Ecumenical Council, June 1962–December 1965*, trans. Bernard Murchland (New York: Random House, 1967) and Xavier Rynne's books on the four sessions for racy descriptions of the interaction of bishops as well as for the context and atmosphere of the happenings at the council.

10. See Reese, *Inside the Vatican*, 38.

11. Fesquet, *The Drama of Vatican II*, 12.

12. Francis X. Murphy, "Introduction to the 1999 Edition," in *Vatican Council II*, by Xavier Rynne (Maryknoll, NY: Orbis Books, 1999), x.

13. Yves Congar, *Report from Rome: The First Session of the Vatican Council* (London: Geoffrey Chapman, 1963), 27.

14. Giuseppe Alberigo and Joseph Komonchak, eds., *History of Vatican II* (Maryknoll, NY: Orbis Books, 1995–2006), 5:2.

15. Austin Rock, OP, ed., *Impact of Renewal on Priests and Religious* (Chicago, IL: The Priory Press, 1968), 15.

16. Ibid.

17. Before the council it would not have been possible to use the term "ministry" with regard to the service of the non-ordained. In December 2005 the United States Conference of Catholic Bishops published a document on lay ecclesial ministry, *Co-Workers in the Vineyard of the Lord: A Resource for Guiding the Development of Lay Ecclesial Ministry* (Washington, DC: USCCB, 2005). This document is a formal recognition of the role lay ministry has taken over the past forty years.

18. References to these are at the end of this book, but authors such as Kenan Osborne, David Power, Thomas O'Meara, Donald Cozzens, and Dean Hoge exemplify the various streams.

19. Rock, *Impact of Renewal on Priests and Religious*, 14.

20. Dean R. Hoge and Jacqueline Wenger, *Evolving Visions of the Priesthood* (Collegeville, MN: Liturgical Press, 2003), 114.

21. Quoted in *Council Daybook: Vatican II*, ed. Floyd Anderson (Washington, DC: National Catholic Welfare Conference, 1966), 1:6.

22. Quoted by Thomas O'Meara, "The Ministry of Presbyters and the Many Ministries in the Church," in *The Theology of the Priesthood*, ed. Donald J. Goergen and Ann Garrido (Collegeville, MN: Liturgical Press, 2000), 85.

BACKGROUND TO THE THREE DOCUMENTS

1. For the historical background to the council, to the development of the documents and their analysis, I am particularly indebted to the works of Alberigo and Komonchak, Vorgrimler, Jedin, and Anderson.

2. Until regulatory practices such as Lenten fast and Friday abstinence from meat were changed, it did not occur to many Catholics that these were at best superficial differences from other Christians. For an educational and pastoral review of the impact of these "identity factors" see Thomas H. Groome, *What Makes Us Catholic: Eight Gifts for Life* (San Francisco: HarperSanFrancisco, 2003).

3. Michael Novak, "An Introduction," in *The Drama of Vatican II: The Ecumenical Council, June 1962–December 1965*, by Henri Fesquet, trans. Bernard Murchland (New York: Random House, 1967), xv.

4. Giacomo Martina discusses alienating consequences of the Index of Forbidden Books, and of the need to simplify ecclesiastical protocols and to abolish titles and positions from the medieval era that are anachronisms in the twentieth century. Giacomo Martina, "The Historical Context in Which the Idea of a New Ecumenical Council Was Born," in *Vatican II Assessment and Perspectives: Twenty-five Years After (1962–1987)*, ed. René Latourelle (New York/Mahwah, NJ: Paulist Press, 1988), 1:42.

5. Floyd Anderson, ed., *Council Daybook: Vatican II* (Washington, DC: National Catholic Welfare Conference, 1966), 1:1.

I: ON THE MINISTRY AND LIFE OF PRIESTS
PRESBYTERORUM ORDINIS

1. Georges Bernanos, *The Diary of a Country Priest*, (London: Macmillan, 1937), 1. Though the description is fictional, it was drawn from Bernanos's own experience as a Catholic in Europe and South America.

2. Hubert Jedin, ed., *History of the Church*, vol. 10, *The Church in the Modern Age* (New York: Crossroad, 1989), 336–52.

3. Ibid., 339.

4. E. R. Wickham, "Appraisal," in *Priests and Workers: An Anglo-French Discussion*, ed. David Edwards (London: SCM Press, 1961), 152.

5. See Paul J. Philibert, "Issues for a Theology of Priesthood," in *The Theology of the Priesthood*, ed. Donald J. Goergen and Ann Garrido (Collegeville, MN: Liturgical Press, 2000), 17.

6. Jedin, *History of the Church*, 10:337.

7. Xavier Rynne, *Letters from Vatican City* (New York: Farrar, Straus & Co., 1963), 18–19.

8. For the developing understanding of the terms "clerical" and "clericalism" and their implications, see Kenan B. Osborne, *Priesthood: A History of Ordained Ministry in the Roman Catholic Church* (New York/Mahwah, NJ: Paulist Press, 1989), especially 147–49. Osborne notes that the key characteristics of the *kleros* were a living apart from others, unmarried state, lifelong commitment, tonsure, exemption from civil and military service and civil taxation, and membership in "a separated caste" (148).

9. Giacomo Martina, "The Historical Context in Which the Idea of a New Ecumenical Council Was Born," in *Vatican II Assessment and Perspectives: Twenty-five Years After (1962–1987)*, ed. René Latourelle (New York/Mahwah, NJ: Paulist Press, 1988), 1:42.

10. Ibid.

11. Ibid., 44.

12. Young Christian Workers was a movement begun in Belgium in 1912 by Father (later Cardinal) Joseph Cardijn; it attempts to train workers to evangelize and to help them adjust to the work atmosphere in offices and factories. Organized on a national basis in 1925, Cardijn's groups were approved by the Belgian bishops and had the support of Pope Pius XI. See <http://www.britannica.com/eb/topic-95523/Joseph-Cardijn>; accessed 12/12/2006.

13. Hubert Jedin comments that "the rise of pastoral theology from a practical instruction for the pastor for the individual care of his charges to a scientific discipline is one of the most positive advances of the history of theology in the first half of the twentieth century." Jedin, *History of the Church*, 10:289.

14. Osborne comments on the significant influence of the Council of Trent on priesthood in the Roman church. A major limitation of Trent's approach is "the almost total silence on Jesus' own priestly ministry...Jesus' own ministry as the source of all Christian ministry is never alluded to." See Osborne, *Priesthood*, 277.

15. For an understanding of sacerdotal priesthood that prevailed during the discussions on the priesthood, see Daniel Donovan, *What Are They Saying About the Ministerial Priesthood?* (New York/Mahwah, NJ: Paulist Press, 1992), 3.

16. The term "servant-leader" has been taken up in some of the significant writings on leadership by Robert Greenleaf and his Center for Servant Leadership, which is promoting new models of leadership for the twenty-first century. See <http://www.greenleaf.org>. It may be useful also to note James McGregor Burns's writings on a transforming leadership and his critique of American presidential leadership because it fails to engage the people. James MacGregor Burns, *Running Alone: Presidential Leadership JFK to Bush II—Why It Has Failed and How We Can Fix It* (Cambridge, MA: Basic Books, 2006), especially 198–99.

17. See Richard Gaillardetz, *The Church in the Making* (New York/Mahwah, NJ: Paulist Press, 2006), especially 181–83.

18. Timothy O'Connell, *Vatican II and Its Documents: An American Reappraisal*, (Wilmington, DE: Michael Glazier, 1986), 197.

19. Donovan, *What Are They Saying About the Ministerial Priesthood?* 2.

20. Bonaventure Kloppenburg, *The Priest: Living Instrument of Christ, the Eternal Priest*, trans. Matthew O'Connell (Chicago, IL: Franciscan Herald Press, 1974), 265.

21. Ruud J. Bunnik, *Priests for Tomorrow* (Shannon, Ireland: Ecclesia Press, 1969), x.

22. Rynne, *Letters from Vatican City*, 164.

23. Giuseppe Alberigo and Joseph Komonchak, eds., *History of Vatican II* (Maryknoll, NY: Orbis Books, 1995–2006), 5:457.

24. Joseph Lécuyer, "Decree On the Ministry and Life of Priests: History of the Decree," in *Commentary on the Documents of Vatican II*, ed. Herbert Vorgrimler (New York: Herder & Herder, 1969), 4:183.

25. It is interesting to note the vast difference between the composition of the Vatican I Preparatory Commission that had 9 members, all cardinals, and 8 consultants, with representation from only four nations. The Vatican II Antepreparatory Commission had 108 members, with 27 consultants representing fifty-seven nations.

26. Lécuyer, "Decree On the Ministry and Life of Priests," 183.

27. Jedin, *History of the Church*, 10:102.

28. See Alberigo and Komonchak, *History of Vatican II*, 1:185.

29. Alberigo and Komonchak, *History of Vatican II*, 1:508.

30. Lécuyer, "Decree On the Ministry and Life of Priests,"189.

31. Henri Fesquet, *The Drama of Vatican II: The Ecumenical Council, June 1962–December 1965*, trans. Bernard Murchland (New York: Random House, 1967), 153.

32. Lécuyer, "Decree On the Ministry and Life of Priests," 187.

33. Daniel Donovan points out the significance of the Greek and Latin terms used and the different connotations that they carry in the document. These are lost in the English. See Donovan, *What Are They Saying About the Ministerial Priesthood?* 3–5.

34. Alberigo and Komonchak, *History of Vatican II*, 2:483–84.

35. Fesquet, *The Drama of Vatican II*, 153.

36. Alberigo and Komonchak, *History of Vatican II*, 2:233.

37. Ralph Wiltgen details a number of alliances made between the various episcopal conferences in *The Rhine Flows into the Tiber: The Unknown Council* (New York: Hawthorn Books, 1967).

38. Alberigo describes a group of "intransigent" council members led by Cardinal Ruffini who were against the idea of a pastoral council. See Alberigo and Komonchak, *History of Vatican II*, 2:60–61.

39. Cf. Xavier Rynne, *The Third Session* (London: Faber & Faber, 1965), 151. See also Kloppenburg, *The Priest*, 267.

40. Quoted in Alberigo and Komonchak, *History of Vatican II*, 4:354–55, n.108.

41. See Alberigo and Komonchak, *History of Vatican II*, 4:348.

42. Rynne, *The Third Session*, 86.

43. Ibid.

44. Lécuyer, "Decree On the Ministry and Life of Priests," 192.

45. Floyd Anderson, ed., *Council Daybook: Vatican II* (Washington, DC: National Catholic Welfare Conference, 1966), 2:130; see also Vincent A. Yzermans, *American Participation in the Second Vatican Council* (New York: Sheed & Ward, 1967).

46. Raymond Tartre, *The Postconciliar Priest: Comments on Some Aspects of the Decree On the Ministry and Life of Priests* (New York: P. J. Kenedy, 1966), 11.

47. Quoted in Bonaventure Kloppenburg, *The Ecclesiology of Vatican II*, trans. Matthew O'Connell (Chicago, IL: Franciscan Herald Press, 1974), 265.

48. Lécuyer, "Decree On the Ministry and Life of Priests," 193.

49. The comments are dealt with in detail in Alberigo and Komonchak, *History of Vatican II*, 4:346–53.

50. Alberigo and Komonchak, *History of Vatican II*, 4:351.

51. It is interesting to note that in the October 1963 session Archbishop Edelby of Odessa spoke from the Oriental position: "The vocation of a deacon or priest is distinct from the celibate's which requires a special grace ... Celibacy is an undeniable source of spiritual fecundity, but it is good that it remains the fruit of a personal choice." In Fesquet, *The Drama of Vatican II*, 191.

52. Lécuyer, "Decree On the Ministry and Life of Priests," 191.

53. Anderson, *Council Daybook*, 2:129.

54. See Lécuyer, "Decree On the Ministry and Life of Priests," 198.

55. Ibid.

56. Kloppenburg, *The Priest*, 267.

57. Lécuyer, "Decree On the Ministry and Life of Priests," 194.

58. For a discussion of this, see Fesquet, *The Drama of Vatican II*, 694–96.

59. Giuseppe Versaldi, "Priestly Celibacy from the Canonical and Psychological Points of View," in Latourelle, *Vatican II Assessment and Perspectives*, 3:132. Versaldi comments that this assurance was given as a result of the outside pressures to which the council members were subject.

60. Fesquet, *The Drama of Vatican II*, 695.

61. Cf. Wiltgen, *The Rhine Flows into the Tiber*, 264.

62. Lécuyer, "Decree On the Ministry and Life of Priests," 200.

63. Cf. Tartre, *The Postconciliar Priest*, 12.

64. Versaldi, "Priestly Celibacy from the Canonical and Psychological Points of View," in Latourelle, *Vatican II Assessment and Perspectives*, 3:133.

65. Cf. Wiltgen, *The Rhine Flows into the Tiber*, 266.

66. Cf. Lécuyer, "Decree On the Ministry and Life of Priests," 205.

67. Alberigo and Komonchak, *History of Vatican II*, 5:457–58.

68. Friedrich Wulf, "Decree on the Ministry and Life of Priests," in Vorgrimler, *Commentary*, 4:217.

69. See Wulf, "Decree on the Ministry and Life of Priests," 214.

70. See Joseph Cunnane, "The Ministry and Life of Priests," in *Vatican II on Priests and Seminaries*, by Denis Hurley and Joseph Cunnane (Dublin: Scepter Books, 1967), 23.

71. Joseph Ratzinger, "Priestly Ministry: A Search for Its Meaning," *Emmanuel* 76 (1970): 490.

72. Ibid.

73. M. Edmund Hussey, "The Priesthood after the Council," in *Priesthood in the Modern World*, ed. Karen Smith (Franklin, WI: Sheed & Ward, 1999), 21.

74. Vatican II "communion ecclesiology" is described by Richard Gaillardetz, "The Ecclesiological Foundations of Ministry Within an Ordered Communion," in *Ordering the Baptismal Priesthood: Theologies of Lay and Ordained Ministry*, ed. Susan K. Wood (Collegeville, MN: Liturgical Press, 2003), 33. See also Wulf, "Decree on the Ministry and Life of Priests," 218.

75. The Latin *sacerdos* highlights the movement toward the cultic sense of priesthood. The sense of the priest, *sacerdos*, has its origins in the Old Testament understanding of high priest, and with the life, death, and resurrection of Jesus the great high priest who intercedes on behalf of humankind and the created world. It also carries the sense of the priest as a man set apart from the people.

76. Commentators on this decree have written about the movement from the sacerdotal to the presbyteral model of priesthood at some length. Useful sources are Donovan, *What Are They Saying About the Ministerial Priesthood?* especially chapter 1, and Frank C. Quinn, "Ministry, Ordination Rites, and Language," in Goergen and Garrido, *The Theology of the Priesthood*, 43-66.

77. Alberigo and Komonchak, *History of Vatican II*, 5:459.

78. Kloppenburg, *The Priest*, 271.

79. Wulf, "Decree on the Ministry and Life of Priests," 216.

80. Cf. Donald Goergen, "Priest, Prophet, King: The Ministry of Jesus Christ," in Goergen and Garrido, *The Theology of the Priesthood*, 187–210. See also Wulf, "Decree on the Ministry and Life of Priests," 191. For a summary of the history and an analysis of the threefold ministry of Christ, see Osborne,

Priesthood, 310–13; for the Christological and ecclesiological basis of the three-fold ministry, see pp. 317–24.

81. Osborne comments that the traditional or scholastic doctrine was standard before the council began. It was also the basis for the spirituality of priesthood and the ordination ritual of the period. This was the definition "set aside, changed or modified by Vatican II." The definition was not necessarily rejected but rather enlarged upon because "it was deemed too narrow." Osborne, *Priesthood*, 315.

82. See Wulf, "Decree on the Ministry and Life of Priests," 217. It is important to note that although many people blame the Second Vatican Council for the vocational breakdown and especially the upheaval of pastoral ministry in the 1970s and following, the crisis of the drop in vocations had started in the 1950s.

83. Cf. Susan K. Wood, "Conclusion: Convergence Points Toward a Theology of Ordered Ministries," in *Ordering the Baptismal Priesthood*, 258.

84. Cf. Robert Schwarz, "Ordained Ministry: Sign of Leadership and Unity in the Great Sacrament of the Church," in *Priests: Identity and Ministry*, ed. Robert Wister (Wilmington, DE: Michael Glazier, 1990), 95.

85. Wulf, "Decree on the Ministry and Life of Priests," 214.

86. This is discussed at some length in Alberigo and Komonchak, *History of Vatican II*, 5:460–61, and Philibert, "Issues for a Theology of Priesthood," 29–36.

87. Cf. Wulf, "Decree on the Ministry and Life of Priests," 224–25.

88. Alberigo and Komonchak, *History of Vatican II*, 5:461.

89. Wulf, "Decree on the Ministry and Life of Priests," 225.

90. Osborne, *Priesthood*, 323.

91. Wulf lists the four key marks of the theological image of the priest in *Presbyterorum Ordinis* 2, which distinguish the contribution of Vatican II in contrast to Trent; Wulf, "Decree on the Ministry and Life of Priests," 224–25. Osborne summarizes these points; see Osborne, *Priesthood*, 322–23.

92. Wulf, "Decree on the Ministry and Life of Priests," 228–29.

93. Ratzinger, "Priestly Ministry," 492.

94. Wulf, "Decree on the Ministry and Life of Priests," 242.

95. Donovan, *What Are They Saying About the Ministerial Priesthood?* 12.

96. Ratzinger, "Priestly Ministry," 491.

97. Wulf, "Decree on the Ministry and Life of Priests," 247–48.

98. The section on the training of priests will address the issue of sexual abuse, because it is surely related to approaches to and problems of ministerial formation, certainly in the past, and hopefully not in the present.

99. Wulf, "Decree on the Ministry and Life of Priests," 261.

100. Dean Hoge and Aniedi Okure, *International Priests in America* (Collegeville, MN: Liturgical Press, 2006). This research examines the argu-

ments for and against bringing in international priests and describes some of the varied motivations for priests coming to the United States. This will be addressed in more detail in the section on the present state of the question, and also in relation to the training of priests.

101. Ratzinger, "Priestly Ministry," 500.

102. Ibid., 501–2.

103. Cf. Osborne, *Priesthood*, 337.

104. Alberigo and Komonchak, *History of Vatican II*, 5:463.

105. Ibid.

106. For a listing of and commentary on these changes, see Wulf, "Decree on the Ministry and Life of Priests," 276.

107. Wulf, "Decree on the Ministry and Life of Priests," 278.

108. Osborne, *Priesthood*, 336.

109. See Wulf, "Decree on the Ministry and Life of Priests," 278, 279. This is especially true in light of the scandals associated with those bishops whose conspiracy of silence, described by many as "administrative abuse," contributed to the protection of sexual predators in the clerical ranks.

110. The concern about emphasizing celibacy and also the evangelical counsels came from the intention to maintain the distinction between diocesan and religious clerical identities.

111. See Alberigo and Komonchak, *History of Vatican II*, 5:232. The description of the interaction of the bishops behind the scenes and that of the intervention of Paul VI are described in detail on pp. 231–38.

112. Luke Vischer, "Concerning the Fourth Session of the Second Vatican Council No. 4" (October 22, 1965). Quoted in Alberigo and Komonchak, *History of Vatican II*, 5:234.

113. Alberigo and Komonchak, *History of Vatican II*, 5:234.

114. This is also apparent in the influx of married Anglican priests into the Roman church and the acceptance of their ministry.

115. Catholics in what may be described as non-Christian cultures such as Asia and Africa ordinarily identified themselves as Christians in a world where other religious systems dominated the worldview and meaning-making of the people.

116. M. D. Chenu, quoted in Alberigo and Komonchak, *History of Vatican II*, 5:581–82.

117. The Congregation of Seminaries and Universities revealed that for the years 1959–60 in the thirty-nine countries surveyed, the lay Catholic population increased over 2 percent while the growth in the number of priests was well under 1 percent. John Tracy Ellis, "The Priest and the Intellectual Life," in *Secular Priest in the New Church*, ed. Gerard Sloyan (New York, NY: Herder & Herder, 1967), 187.

118. Quoted in Ellis, "The Priest and the Intellectual Life," 186.

119. The seventeenth-century French school of priestly spirituality influenced seminary formation programs until Vatican II when there was a movement from an essentially eucharistic spirituality to a pastoral one. In discussing the spirituality of the diocesan priest, Denis Edwards describes his own formation in terms of an *alter Christus*, drawn from Abbot Marmion's *Christ the Ideal of the Priest*, a "partial" kind of spirituality that did not integrate the whole priestly life and ministry. Cf. Hurley and Cunnane, *Vatican II on Priests and Seminaries*, 186–87, and Edwards in *The Spirituality of the Diocesan Priest*, ed. Donald Cozzens (Collegeville, MN: Liturgical Press, 1997), 73.

120. Gaillardetz, *The Church in the Making*, 181.

121. Edward Schillebeeckx, *Vatican II: The Real Achievement* (London: Sheed & Ward, 1967), 43–44.

122. See Wulf, "Decree on the Ministry and Life of Priests," 326.

123. Alberigo and Komonchak, *History of Vatican II*, 5:243.

124. Wulf points out that the council itself was a concrete example of episcopal collegiality in action, Wulf, "Decree on the Ministry and Life of Priests," 328. Joseph Komonchak, in a working document on episcopal conferences comments about problems that arose at the 1985 Synod in addressing the issue of collegiality at Vatican II. "Something similar happened at Vatican II, as Joseph Ratzinger observed at the time. The debates on collegiality were being oversimplified because pragmatic concerns were being confused with theological questions, with the result that theological statements were coming close to functioning as ideological supra- or infrastructures. Desired or feared practices were being invested with divine-right status and so exempted from criticism." See Komonchak, "The Roman Working Paper on Episcopal Conferences," in Thomas J. Reese, *Episcopal Conferences: Historical, Canonical & Theological Studies* (Washington, DC: Georgetown University Press, 1989) <http://www.americamagazine.org/reese/ec/ec-6komonch.htm>; accessed 12/15/2006.

125. For a contemporary analysis of the Vatican II understanding of ordained priesthood, of "order" and priestly ministry and its relationship to the laity, and for an overview of the historical developments integral to this understanding, see David Power, "Priesthood Revisited: Mission and Ministries in the Royal Priesthood," in Wood, *Ordering the Baptismal Priesthood*, 87–120.

126. Dean Hoge and Jacqueline Wenger, *Evolving Visions of the Priesthood* (Collegeville, MN: Liturgical Press, 2003).

127. See International Theological Commission, *Report of the International Theological Commission: The Priestly Ministry (5–7 October, 1970)*, trans. Jacques Dupuis (Bangalore: St Peter's Seminary, 1971), 8.

128. *Report of the International Theological Commission*, 1971, 8–9.

129. Ibid., 9.

130. For an analysis of the use of cultic language in liturgy and the implications of the different model of priestly leadership that was a key element in this decree, see Quinn, "Ministry, Ordination Rites, and Language," especially 44–48.

131. For an overview of synods, and their effectiveness, see Thomas J. Reese, *Inside the Vatican: The Politics and Organization of the Catholic Church* (Cambridge, MA: Harvard University Press, 1996), 42–65.

132. An analysis of the 1971 Synod in relation to the understanding of ministerial priesthood and the council can be found in Donovan, *What Are They Saying About the Ministerial Priesthood?* 21–25.

133. From website: <http://www.time.com/time/magazine/article/0,9171,902967,00.html>; accessed 11/05/2006.

134. From website: <http://www.time.com/time/magazine/article/0,9171,903180,00.html>; accessed 11/05/2006.

135. Francis X. Murphy, quoted in Reese, *Inside the Vatican*, 61.

136. Reese, *Inside the Vatican*, 61.

137. While this term was used in this document, there has been much subsequent discussion of the term, from quite polarized positions, and of the question of a "New Testament" contribution to our understanding of priesthood and priestly ministry. See David Power, *Ministers of Christ and His Church* (London: Geoffrey Chapman, 1969), especially 26–29; Donald Senior, "Biblical Foundations for the Theology of Priesthood," in Wister, *Priests*, 11–29; Donovan, *What Are They Saying About the Ministerial Priesthood?* 4–5. Also see Julian Herranz Casado (president of the Pontifical Council for the Interpretation of Legislative Texts), *The Image of the Priest in the Decree Presbyterorum Ordinis: Continuity and Projection toward the Third Millennium* (undated document), 20. See website: <http://www.pcf.va/roman_curia/congregations/cclergy/documents/rc_con_cclergy_doc_23101995_imp_en.html>; accessed 12/12/2006. Also Joseph Cardinal Ratzinger, "The Ministry and Life of Priests," *Homiletic and Pastoral Review* (August-September 1997): 7–18. See website: <http://www.ignatius.com/Magazines/hprweb/ratzinger.htm>; accessed 12/12/2006.

138. Hans Urs von Balthasar (1905–1988) was considered to be one of the most important Catholic intellectuals and writers of the twentieth century. In 1972 he joined with other council experts to form *Communio*, an international Catholic review. See website: <http://www.ignatiusinsight.com/authors/vonbalthasar.asp>; accessed 11/05/2006.

139. Jedin, *History of the Church*, 336.

140. Herbert J. Ryan, *To Be a Priest: Perspectives on Vocation and Ordination* (New York: Seabury Press, 1975). This is a topic that lies beyond the scope of

this book. For some further implications, see Edward Cassidy, *Ecumenism and Interreligious Dialogue* (New York/Mahwah, NJ: Paulist Press, 2005).

141. Gerald Coleman points out that when he did his priestly training in 1964, he used the same books that his priest-uncle had used in 1929. He points out the present awareness of the need for addressing basic psychological factors in seminary training and develops these in the contemporary context of seminary formation. See Gerald Coleman, *Catholic Priesthood: Formation and Human Development*, (Liguori, MO: Liguori Publications, 2006), especially 24–33.

142. Paul Philibert, "Issues for a Theology of Priesthood," 11.

143. Andrew Greeley, "The Failures of Vatican II After Twenty Years," *America* (February 6, 1982): 86.

144. There were several responses from different church leaders in the two issues.

145. John L. May, "The Failures of Vatican II Revisited," *America* (June 12, 1982): 455.

146. This is a term coined by Philip Helfaer and used by James Fowler to describe those adults and children who are locked into a pre-conventional meaning-making system of beliefs, morals, and values. See James W. Fowler, *Stages of Faith* (New York: Harper & Row, 1981), 132.

147. There are Catholics who do not fall under the categories described here by Greeley. Numbers of deeply committed Catholics with informed consciences have made life choices and commitments according to their conscience.

148. Greeley, "The Failures of Vatican II After Twenty Years," 86.

149. The Bishops' Committee on Priestly Life and Ministry, *The Priest and Stress* (Washington, DC: USCCB, 1982), 22–23. For an examination of stress in the diocesan priesthood, see R. Hoge, Joseph J. Shields, and Stephen Soroka, "Sources of Stress Experienced by Catholic Priests," *Review of Religious Research* 35/1 (September 1993): 3–18.

150. Donovan, *What Are They Saying About the Ministerial Priesthood?* 27.

151. Philibert, "Issues for a Theology of Priesthood," 39.

152. Michael Papesh addresses some of the problems and possibilities for transformation of a clerical culture and lists topics that obstruct a deeper appreciation of priesthood for today's church. Michael Papesh, *Clerical Culture; Contradiction and Transformation* (Collegeville, MN: Liturgical Press, 2004). See especially chapter 4. The number of priestly predators is given as around 4 percent of the priesthood.

153. These issues, and the Vatican documents pertaining to them, such as *Inter Insigniores* (Declaration on the Admission of Women to the Ministerial Priesthood), *Ordinatio Sacerdotalis* (On Reserving Priestly Ordination to Men Alone) and *Sacerdotalis Caelibatus* (encyclical of Pope Paul VI On the Celibacy of the Priest), will be addressed in the section on

the training of priests, because they need to be taken into account in formation programs as they concern issues that are significant for present and future priests and their congregations.

154. Hoge and Wenger, in *Evolving Visions of the Priesthood*, describe the polarized situation of the priesthood in detail. Of particular interest is chapter 7, which describes the two basic transitions since mid-century, that of the 1960s and that of the 1980s. A diagram of polarization between those priests who follow the cultic model and those who follow the servant-leader model of the priesthood illustrates the situation in the present. *The U.S. Committee on Priestly Life and Ministry Update* also has statistics on the impact of fewer priests on pastoral ministry and the problems faced by priests as a consequence. (Executive summary, June, 2000) <http://www.usccb.org/plm/index.shtml>.

155. Virgil Elizondo, "Commentary," in Hoge and Okure, *International Priests in America*, 148. This book provides comprehensive research on the advisability of bringing international priests into the United States. The research has implications for other Western countries.

156. Elizondo, "Commentary," 149.

157. Donald Cozzens critiques the present state of the priesthood in the United States. See especially Cozzens, *The Changing Face of the Priesthood: A Reflection on the Priest's Crisis of Soul* (Collegeville, MN: Liturgical Press, 2000), 118. An analysis of the situation in Ireland is found in *A Church with a Future: Challenges to Irish Catholicism Today*, ed. Niall Coll and Paschal Scallon (Dublin: Columba Press, 2005).

158. Cozzens, *The Changing Face of the Priesthood*, 20.

159. Ibid.

160. Committee for Priestly Life and Ministry, (Executive summary, June, 2000) See website: <http://www.usccb.org/plm/index.shtml>; accessed 12/12/2006.

161. Hans Urs von Balthasar, *The Christian State of Life*, quoted in Goergen and Garrido, 84, n.25.

162. See <http://www.nd.edu/~tomeara/topical_biblio.html> for O'Meara's publications on ministry.

163. Thomas P. O'Meara, "The Ministry of Presbyters and the Many Ministers in the Church," in Goergen and Garrido, *The Theology of the Priesthood*, 67–85.

164. Ibid., 80.

165. See Pastoral Letters and Statements of Cardinal Mahony: *As I Have Done For You*, Cardinal Roger Mahony and the Priests of the Archdiocese of Los Angeles. Holy Thursday, April 20, 2000. See <http://www.archdiocese.la/archbishop/letters/ministry/5.html>; accessed 12/02/2006.

166. Mahony: *As I Have Done For You*, Part Three.

167. Mahony: *As I Have Done For You*, Part Two.

168. Mahony: *As I Have Done For You*, Part Four.

II: ON THE TRAINING OF PRIESTS
OPTATAM TOTIUS

1. In addressing both the history of the document and its significance, I am once again particularly indebted to Josef Neuner's study of the document in Herbert Vorgrimler's *Commentary on the Documents of Vatican II*, vol. 2 (New York: Herder & Herder, 1969); Giuseppe Alberigo and Joseph Komonchak, eds., *History of Vatican II*, 5 vols. (Maryknoll, NY: Orbis Books, 1995–2006); and Denis Hurley's "History and Commentary" on the text in *Vatican II on Priests and Seminaries*, by Denis Hurley and Joseph Cunnane (Dublin: Scepter Books, 1967).

2. Neuner, "Decree on Priestly Formation," in Vorgrimler, *Commentary*, 2:371.

3. Frank B. Norris, *Decree on Priestly Training and Decree on the Ministry and Life of Priests* (New York/Mahwah, NJ: Paulist Press, 1966), 13.

4. The focus in *Optatam Totius* itself and in most of the commentaries is on the diocesan priest rather than the religious cleric. Diocesan priestly formation will be the focus here. However, O'Malley has developed a historiography indicating some key contrasts and developments in the formation of diocesan and religious clerics. See John O'Malley, *Tradition and Transition: Historical Perspectives on Vatican II* (Wilmington: Michael Glazier, 1989) and "Diocesan and Religious Models of Priestly Formation: Historical Perspectives," in *Priests: Identity and Ministry*, ed. Robert Wister (Wilmington, DE: Michael Glazier, 1990), 54–70.

5. See O'Malley, *Tradition and Transition*, 225–26.

6. Christopher M. Bellitto, "Priestly Training before Trent: Rethinking Some Evidence from the Long Middle Ages," in *Medieval Education*, ed. Ronald B. Begley and Joseph W. Koterski (New York: Fordham University Press, 2005), 35–49.

7. Papesh comments that for centuries the training was informal, uneven, and problematic. Michael Papesh, *Clerical Culture: Contradiction and Transformation* (Collegeville, MN: Liturgical Press, 2004), 61.

8. Papesh, *Clerical Culture*, 62.

9. Bellitto, "Priestly Training before Trent," 38.

10. These were basically situated in Paris, Bologna, and Rome.

11. O'Malley, "Diocesan and Religious Models," 56, 58.

12. See Bellitto, "Priestly Training before Trent: Rethinking Some Evidence from the Long Middle Ages."

13. James A. O'Donohoe, *Tridentine Seminary Legislation: Its Sources and Its Formation* (Louvain: Publications Universitaires de Louvain, 1957), 15.

14. See Bellitto, "Priestly Training before Trent: Rethinking Some Evidence from the Long Middle Ages."

15. Neuner, "Decree on Priestly Formation," in Vorgrimler, *Commentary*, 2:371.

16. O'Donohoe, *Tridentine Seminary Legislation*, 171.

17. See O'Malley, "Diocesan and Religious Models," 59.

18. But the numbers were not large. There were only thirty-three students altogether in these three seminaries.

19. Papesh, *Clerical Culture*, 62.

20. O'Malley, "Diocesan and Religious Models," 64. Another interesting detail O'Malley provides is that by the time Ignatius of Loyola died in 1556 there was not a single institution in the Society of Jesus where Jesuits studied apart from lay students.

21. John Tracy Ellis, "The Priest and the Intellectual Life," in *Secular Priest in the New Church*, ed. Gerard Sloyan (New York: Herder & Herder, 1967), 189.

22. See O'Malley, "Diocesan and Religious Models," 65.

23. Ellis, "The Priest and the Intellectual Life," 200.

24. See John Tracy Ellis, *American Catholics and the Intellectual Life* (Chicago, IL: Heritage Foundation, 1956), and "American Catholics and the Intellectual Life," *Thought* 30 (Autumn, 1955): 351–88 for a comparison of the intellectual life of Americans in general and that of Catholics in particular. <http://www.bc.edu/offices/mission/exploring/cathuniv/ellis_intellectual_life/>; accessed 10/01/2007.

25. Norris, *Decree on Priestly Training and Decree on the Ministry and Life of Priests*, 14.

26. Ellis commented on the situation that educated Catholics experienced in the pre-conciliar period: "The American intellectual climate has been aloof and unfriendly to Catholic thought and ideas, when it has not been openly hostile, and it places no burden upon the imagination to appreciate how this factor his militated against a strong and vibrant intellectual life among the Catholics of this country." Ellis, "American Catholics and the Intellectual Life." <http://www.bc.edu/offices/mission/exploring/cathuniv/ellis_intellectual_life/>; accessed 10/01/2007.

27. Alberigo and Komonchak, *History of Vatican II*, 1:3.

28. Cardinal Pizzardo, a Roman curial official, was described as one of the group of "intransigent" council members led by Cardinal Ruffini. See Alberigo and Komonchak, *History of Vatican II*, 2:60–61.

29. The Pontifical Athenaeum of Saint Anselm was founded by Pope Leo XIII in 1887. It is an institution of higher learning at the university level sponsored by the Benedictine Confederation.

30. While this commission was concerned with issues of Catholic education, particularly in the earlier stages, the issues relating to Catholic education
are covered by Dolores Leckey in *The Laity and Christian Education* (New
York/Mahwah, NJ: Paulist Press, 2006), so they have not been addressed in
this text.

31. This commission was also required to provide "conciliar statements
on soundness and integrity of doctrine, on the relation between theology and
the magisterium and on the teaching of scripture, particularly in seminaries."
Alberigo and Komonchak, *History of Vatican II*, 1:189.

32. Ibid.

33. Alberigo and Komonchak, *History of Vatican II*, 2:490.

34. Problematic aspects of priestly studies can be seen in the criticisms
leveled at seminarians and priests and their training in the pre–Vatican II
years. While the strengths of the formation programs are acknowledged, so
also the church "has been forced every now and then to live with their
mediocrity." Mathijs Lamberigts, "Optatam Totius: The Decree on Priestly
Formation, A Short Survey of Its History at the Second Vatican Council,"
Louvain Studies 30 (2005): 26.

35. See Lamberigts, "Optatam Totius," 31. Also, in an article "Suddenly
Everyone's a Priest" in *Priest & People* (August 2003) Bishop Kieran Conry of
Arundel and Brighton Diocese in Ireland comments on a series of meetings he
convened to address the decreasing number of priests. He was astounded to discover that one group of Catholics ascribed the loss of priestly vocations and all
the ills of the church, "including, inexplicably, the horror of clerical child abuse,"
to the Second Vatican Council. Reprinted in *The Pastoral Review*, April 2007.
<http://www.thepastoralreview.org/cgi-bin/archive_db.cgi?priestsppl-00089>;
accessed 04/03/2007.

36. See Hurley, "History and Commentary," 172.

37. Ibid.

38. Alberigo and Komonchak, *History of Vatican II*, 1:189. Some of the
comments had not come from the bishops but from a curial commission, the
Congregation on Seminaries and Universities.

39. Hurley, "History and Commentary," 172. Hurley, a member of the
commission, gives in his commentary a careful history of the process of for-
mulating the structure and content of the decree. Before the council met
Hurley had also written on the need to provide unified, pastorally oriented
training for priests. See Hurley, "Pastoral Emphasis in Seminary Studies," *The
Furrow* 13 (1962): 16–30.

40. Hurley, "History and Commentary," 173.

41. Lamberigts, "Optatam Totius," 31.

42 Ibid., 31–32.

43. Hurley, "History and Commentary," 173.

44. See Hurley, "History and Commentary," 173.

45. Hurley, "History and Commentary," 174. The connection between the two documents, *Presbyterorum Ordinis* and *Optatam Totius*, is evident in the renewed emphasis on the threefold ministry.

46. Hurley, "History and Commentary," 175.

47. Ibid., 176.

48. Neuner, "Decree on Priestly Formation," in Vorgrimler, *Commentary*, 2:374.

49. While Hurley did not make much of these differences and in fact speaks highly of the leadership and communication skills of Mayer, a polyglot and a diplomat, Alberigo gives a more detailed report on the tensions and polarization. See Alberigo and Komonchak, *History of Vatican II*, 1:380.

50. Hurley, "History and Commentary," 176.

51. Neuner, "Decree on Priestly Formation," in Vorgrimler, *Commentary*, 2:372.

52. See Norris, *Decree on Priestly Training and Decree on the Ministry and Life of Priests*, 16, and Neuner, "Decree on Priestly Formation," in Vorgrimler, *Commentary*, 2:374.

53. Neuner, "Decree on Priestly Formation," in Vorgrimler, *Commentary*, 2:374.

54. Hurley, "History and Commentary," 177.

55. Neuner, "Decree on Priestly Formation," in Vorgrimler, *Commentary*, 2:375.

56. See Alberigo and Komonchak, *History of Vatican II*, 4:356.

57. Hurley, "History and Commentary," 178.

58. Lamberigts, "Optatam Totius," 37.

59. Henri Fesquet, *The Drama of Vatican II: The Ecumenical Council, June 1962–December 1965*, trans. Bernard Murchland (New York: Random House, 1967), 308.

60. Hurley, "History and Commentary," 179.

61. Neuner, "Decree on Priestly Formation," in Vorgrimler, *Commentary*, 2:375.

62. See Ralph Wiltgen, *The Rhine Flows into the Tiber: The Unknown Council* (New York: Hawthorn Books, 1967), 146. Also Fesquet, *The Drama of Vatican II*, 536–37.

63. There was no debate on this schema on November 13 or 15.

64. Alberigo and Komonchak, *History of Vatican II*, 4:357.

65. Fesquet, *The Drama of Vatican II*, 513.

66. Alberigo and Komonchak, *History of Vatican II*, 4:357. Schemas on liturgy, bishops, and priesthood were also important background texts for the discussion.

67. Lamberigts, "Optatam Totius," 38.

68. Alberigo and Komonchak, *History of Vatican II*, 4:357.

69. Ibid., 4:359. There was relatively little debate on chapter 2, the promotion of vocations, perhaps because the divergent ideas about vocation were surfacing and time was already a pressure in the debate.

70. Fesquet, *The Drama of Vatican II*, 513.

71. Alberigo and Komonchak, *History of Vatican II*, 4:357–58.

72. Neuner, "Decree on Priestly Formation," in Vorgrimler, *Commentary*, 2:375.

73. Alberigo and Komonchak, *History of Vatican II*, 4:358.

74. The subsequent appointment of Garonne to the commission was all the more significant because he had been one of the commission's most determined critics, especially at this third session.

75. Alberigo and Komonchak, *History of Vatican II*, 4:359.

76. Lamberigts, "Optatam Totius," 42.

77. Neuner, "Decree on Priestly Formation," in Vorgrimler, *Commentary*, 2:375.

78. Alberigo and Komonchak, *History of Vatican II*, 4:359.

79. Fesquet, *The Drama of Vatican II*, 526.

80. Alberigo and Komonchak, *History of Vatican II*, 4:360.

81. Fesquet, *The Drama of Vatican II*, 521.

82. Ibid., 522.

83. Ibid., 521.

84. Xavier Rynne, *The Third Session* (London: Faber & Faber, 1965), 223.

85. Ibid. Rynne asks a wry question as to who might be among the number of those bishops of the East that Staffa claimed to represent.

86. Fesquet, *The Drama of Vatican II*, 523. The encyclical *Humani Generis* of Pope Pius XII, "Concerning Some False Opinions Threatening to Undermine the Foundations of Catholic Doctrine," was promulgated on August 12, 1950.

87. Fesquet, *The Drama of Vatican II*, 525.

88. Ibid., 521–22.

89. Ibid., 520.

90. Ibid., 522.

91. Ibid., 520.

92. Hurley, "History and Commentary," 180. In an interview, Hurley commented on his surprise at his selection for the Central Preparatory Commission. "I went to Rome and right away realized that we were up against something: a big division between conservatives and progressives. Those resident in Rome, mainly cardinals, were strongly conservative in regard to theological attitudes, the training of priests, and the preservation of the Church in the established tradition. By contrast, I found myself wholly

in sympathy with the transalpine cardinals like Alfrink, Frings, König, and so on ... I had done a good deal of reading in the late forties and through the fifties; it was an exciting decade for me. It opened up my mind and heart to a different view of theology from the Scholastic "mathematics" I had learned as a student. This new view was much more scriptural and historical." An Interview with Denis E. Hurley, OMI, "The Struggle of Vatican II," January 6, 2002. Federation of Asian Bishops' Conferences (FABC) Papers, No. 115. <http://www.ucanews.com/html/fabc-papers/fabc-117.htm>; accessed 01/12/2007.

93. See Alberigo and Komonchak, *History of Vatican II*, 4:361.

94. Fesquet, *The Drama of Vatican II*, 514.

95. Ibid.

96. Alberigo and Komonchak, *History of Vatican II*, 4:361.

97. Ibid., 4:362.

98. Ibid.

99. Fesquet, *The Drama of Vatican II*, 523.

100. Ibid., 526.

101. Alberigo and Komonchak, *History of Vatican II*, 4:362.

102. Fesquet, *The Drama of Vatican II*, 526.

103. Alberigo and Komonchak, *History of Vatican II*, 4:358.

104. Ibid., 4:364.

105. Rynne, *The Third Session*, 225.

106. Alberigo and Komonchak, *History of Vatican II*, 4:364.

107. Hurley, "History and Commentary," 180.

108. Neuner, "Decree on Priestly Formation," in Vorgrimler, *Commentary*, 2:377; not all members were present at all voting sessions; thus the different total numbers.

109. Alberigo and Komonchak, *History of Vatican II*, 4:362, n.117.

110. Ibid.

111. Lamberigts, "Optatam Totius," 42, n.70.

112. Alberigo and Komonchak, *History of Vatican II*, 5:550.

113. Quoted in Alberigo and Komonchak, *History of Vatican II*, 5:229.

114. See George Vaillant, *Adaptation to Life: How the Best and Brightest Came of Age* (Boston: Little Brown & Co, 1977).

115. Archbishop Hurley was not only a significant contributor to the construction of this decree, he was a bishop with a deep commitment to priestly training. In his commentary on the document he also offers his own proposals for a major seminary curriculum, showing in concrete terms the three basic concerns of finality, unity, and humanity in an integrated studies program. Hurley, "History and Commentary," 207–11.

116. Hurley, "History and Commentary," 181.

117. Robert Harvanek, "Decree on the Training of Priests," in *Vatican II and Its Documents: An American Reappraisal*, ed. Timothy O'Connell (Wilmington, DE: Michael Glazier, 1986), 96.

118. Lamberigts, "Optatam Totius," 44–45.

119. George P. Schner, ed., *The Church Renewed: The Documents of Vatican II Reconsidered* (Lanham, MD: University Press of America, 1986), 55.

120. Hurley, "History and Commentary," 182.

121. See Norris, *Decree on Priestly Training and Decree on the Ministry and Life of Priests*, 18.

122. Harvanek, "Decree on the Training of Priests," 95.

123. See Norris, *Decree on Priestly Training and Decree on the Ministry and Life of Priests*, 18.

124. Unlike other decrees, *Optatam Totius* contains no endnotes to remind the reader that this section needs to be juxtaposed with *Lumen Gentium* 5.

125. Norris, *Decree on Priestly Training and Decree on the Ministry and Life of Priests*, 18.

126. Minor seminaries were omitted in first draft but requested by the bishops.

127. Neuner comments that this Christocentrism is an approach supported by Paul VI. "Decree on Priestly Formation," in Vorgrimler, *Commentary*, 2:383.

128. Drawing on his experience with other bishops and regions, Hurley comments that the tendency to keep a distance between students and staff is not helpful. Hurley, "History and Commentary," 188.

129. See Neuner, "Decree on Priestly Formation," in Vorgrimler, *Commentary*, 2:385–86.

130. Hurley, "History and Commentary," 190.

131. This chapter is the fruit of the request of Cardinals Suenens and Meyer and Archbishop Hurley for an integrated program of pastoral formation. See Neuner, "Decree on Priestly Formation," in Vorgrimler, *Commentary*, 2:386.

132. Hurley describes the importance of emotional education for the seminarian. See "History and Commentary," 192.

133. Neuner, "Decree on Priestly Formation," in Vorgrimler, *Commentary*, 2:387.

134. Ibid., 2:388.

135. See Hurley, "History and Commentary," 194, for an expanded list of these options.

136. See Hurley, "History and Commentary," 193–94.

137. Lamberigts points out that Latin lost its privileged place in the political and teaching world after the Peace of Münster in 1648 although its importance was maintained in teaching Catholic theology. Lamberigts, "Optatam Totius," 27.

138. Hurley comments that the price paid for the victory of the scholastic method in the thirteenth century "was the shadow it cast over the centuries that followed—a triple shadow: theological, philosophical and pedagogical." Hurley, "History and Commentary," 195.

139. Hurley, "History and Commentary," 195.

140. Neuner, "Decree on Priestly Formation," in Vorgrimler, *Commentary*, 2:397.

141. Harvanek, "Decree on the Training of Priests," 97.

142. Hurley, "History and Commentary," 198.

143. Both Neuner and Hurley support this view in their commentaries on this section.

144. Harvanek points out that even though teachers are to point out errors in other systems and religions, the tone in *Optatam Totius* 16 is much more positive and affirmative than it had been before. Harvanek, "Decree on the Training of Priests," 98.

145. The first version of the propositions did not have this article on the method of theological studies, but it was included as an essential supplement to the preceding articles on theology and philosophy studies.

146. Hurley "History and Commentary," 205.

147. Ibid.

148. Ibid., 206.

149. This is more fully dealt with in *Presbyterorum Ordinis* 19.

150. Cullmann was well-known in Rome because he had been teaching exegesis at the Swiss theological faculty in Rome for over fifteen years and was in contact with the Pontifical Biblical Institute. (See Fesquet, *The Drama of Vatican II*.)

151. Neuner, "Decree on Priestly Formation," in Vorgrimler, *Commentary*, 2:372–73.

152. Lamberigts, "Optatam Totius," 43.

153. Edward Schillebeeckx, *Vatican II: The Real Achievement* (London: Sheed & Ward, 1967), 37.

154. Ibid.

155. Ibid.

156. The appointment of Archbishop Garonne as permanent head of the curial office of the Congregation of Seminaries and Universities in that same period was all the more significant because he had been one of the congregation's most determined critics and, during the third session of the council, had called for the congregation's thorough overhauling. In commenting on this early reaction against the council's directions, Rynne adds that it is doubtful whether the decree would have been drawn up in the same language if Garonne had been the congregation's head at the time. See Xavier Rynne, *The Fourth Session* (London: Faber & Faber, 1966), 263.

157. Quoted in Rynne, *The Fourth Session*, 256–57.

158. Hurley, "History and Commentary," 183.

159. George P. Schner describes these complementary documents in *The Church Renewed*, 56–58.

160. John O'Malley, "Historical Background," in *Reason for the Hope: The Futures of Roman Catholic Theologates*, by Katarina Schuth (Wilmington, DE: Michael Glazier, 1989), 43. He also points out that the distinction has also disappeared from the 1983 Code of Canon Law.

161. Metz describes the basic difference between diocesan and religious clerics as one of the structural vocation of the diocesan priest and the charismatic vocation of the religious priest. See Johannes Baptist Metz, *Followers of Christ: Perspectives on the Religious Life*, trans. Thomas Linton (New York/Mahwah, NJ: Paulist Press, 1978), chapter 1.

162. Schner, *The Church Renewed*, 57. Schner discusses and develops the key ideas related to these documents.

163. This was termed the "propaedeutic year," a year of introductory studies to lay the formational foundations for theological studies and priestly spirituality.

164. *Ratio Fundamentalis Institutionis Sacerdotalis*, III Conclusion <http://www.ewtn.com/library/CURIA/CCESEMSF.HTM>; accessed 12/10/2006.

165. *Origins* 4/5 (June 27, 1974): 655.

166. Lamberigts, "Optatam Totius," 26.

167. Ibid.

168. *Origins* 4/5 (June 27, 1974): 67.

169. Schner, *The Church Renewed*, 60.

170. Ibid.

171. Schner comments that no mention is made of such helpful psychological theories as the stages of development described by Erikson, Kohlberg, or Fowler and especially of the crucial stages of adolescence and young adulthood, identification, and intimacy. Nor do there appear guidelines for the formation of that community which the documents take for granted. *The Church Renewed*, 60.

172. *Origins* 6/11 (September 2, 1976) and *Origins* 6/12 (September 9, 1976).

173. Schner, *The Church Renewed*, 57.

174. <http://www.ewtn.com/library/CURIA/CCESEMS.HTM>; accessed 11/14/2005. See also Schner, *The Church Renewed*, 56.

175. *Origins* 19/34 (January 25, 1990): 550–61.

176. *Origins* 23/32 (January 27, 1994): 558–71.

177. That during the 1960s there was a breakdown of meaning in so many areas of life in the the world and in seminaries did not help priestly vocations or ministry. As the church was entering the modern era, Western so-

ciety was moving steadily away from past securities and along the postmodernist continuum of questioning. The human capacity for lifelong commitment was also under scrutiny.

178. "On the Ministerial Priesthood" <http://www.christusrex.org/www1/CDHN/ministpr.html>; accessed 06/20/2004.

179. Daniel Donovan, *What Are They Saying About the Ministerial Priesthood?* (New York/Mahwah, NJ: Paulist Press, 1992), 22–23.

180. For an analysis of some key implications of this synod see Donovan, *What Are They Saying About the Ministerial Priesthood?* 21–25. See also Kenan B. Osborne, *Priesthood: A History of Ordained Ministry in the Roman Catholic Church* (New York/Mahwah, NJ: Paulist Press, 1989), 318–24, and Papesh, *Clerical Culture*, 65–71.

181. James Walsh, "Reaping Harvests, Sowing Seeds: Vatican Influences and National Developments in United States Seminaries from the Mid-Nineteen Eighties to the Present," in *Seminaries, Theologates, and the Future of Church Ministry: An Analysis of Trends and Transitions*, by Katarina Schuth (Collegeville, MN: Liturgical Press, 1999), 24.

182. A comparable flow of documents from religious congregations such as the Society of Jesus have followed the *Ratio Fundamentalis*. In 1968, the interim *General Norms for Studies* was promulgated by Pedro Arrupe; this was followed in 1980 with the definitive *General Norms*. Assistancies or provinces implemented these at the local level through Orders of Studies.

183. The large number of church documents, journal articles, and books relating to the common and ordained priesthood that were published in the decades following the council place them beyond the scope of this book to address in any depth. Representative texts have been selected to raise key issues related to *Optatam Totius*.

184. For a critique of this change and subsequent loss, see O'Malley, "Historical Background," in Schuth, *Reason for the Hope*, 43.

185. O'Malley, "Historical Background," in Schuth, *Reason for the Hope*, 43.

186. *Program of Priestly Formation*, 5th ed. (Washington, DC: USCCB, 2006).

187. Although there was much emphasis in the council on the issue of exemption in regard to religious clerics, it seems that this has disappeared in the formation process. There is no mention in the document or in the index itself. For some insight on this issue of religious exemption, see K. Rahner, *Bishops: Their Status and Function* (Montreal: Palm Publishers, 1964), section 7, 57–62.

188. O'Malley points out also that in those *PPF*s that did deal with novitiates there was some understanding of a training period for religious before formal theological studies were undertaken, but the rest of the PPF did not

address this difference or take account of it in any way. See O'Malley, "Historical Background," in Schuth, *Reason for the Hope*, 43–44.

189. O'Malley, "Historical Background," in Schuth, *Reason for the Hope*, 44.

190. See R. Scott Appleby, "Surviving the Shaking of the Foundations: United States Catholicism in the Twenty-First Century," in *Seminaries, Theologates, and the Future of Church Ministry: An Analysis of Trends and Transitions*, by Katarina Schuth (Collegeville, MN: Liturgical Press, 1999), 29.

191. Pfnausch points out that this apostolic exhortation provides a valuable commentary on canon 276 of the 1983 Code. See Edward G. Pfnausch, "The Conciliar Documents and the 1983 Code," in *The Spirituality of the Diocesan Priest*, ed. Donald B. Cozzens (Collegeville, MN: Liturgical Press, 1997), 156–72.

192. One of the problems that affect the shaping of spirituality is the problem of misunderstanding and of communication breakdown caused by various factors. This breakdown is not an uncommon factor in the relations between priests and bishops. See Pfnausch, "The Conciliar Documents and the 1983 Code," in Cozzens, *The Spirituality of the Diocesan Priest*, 169. Cozzens, however, points out that relationships between bishops and priests seem to be improving. See Cozzens, *The Spirituality of the Diocesan Priest*, 187.

193. Pfnausch, "The Conciliar Documents and the 1983 Code," in Cozzens, *The Spirituality of the Diocesan Priest*, 169.

194. Ibid., 170. For a contemporary "confession" of the spirituality of a diocesan priest, see William D. Hammer, "Confessions of a Pilgrim Pastor," in Cozzens, *The Spirituality of the Diocesan Priest*, 173–83.

195. This is analyzed in Timothy Costelloe, "A Critical Evaluation of the Theology of Ordained Ministry of Pope John Paul II" (Ph.D. diss., Melbourne College of Divinity, 1998), especially 273–81.

196. Costelloe, "A Critical Evaluation," 274.

197. Ibid., 277.

198. Secretariat on Priestly Life and Ministry. *The Basic Plan for the Ongoing Formation of Priests* (Washington, DC: USCCB, 2001).

199. Among the many benefits that have arisen from the encouragement of *Optatam Totius* to integrate minor and major seminaries with university training is that of the association of seminaries with Catholic colleges and universities. Seminary training has, through connections with theological consortia, divinity schools, and university theology departments, developed more universally recognized academic standards along with an expanded professional and pastoral expertise. Association with field education and Clinical Pastoral Education (CPE) programs has enabled not simply greater competence, but the advantage of opening up communities of ministry in new ways.

200. Hurley himself admitted that his own earlier attempts to move beyond the idea of theological training that involved separate blocks of material and to replace it with a harmonious integration of the theological, pastoral, and spiritual aspects of a priest's formation were not completely successful. See his proposals for a major seminary curriculum in Hurley, "History and Commentary," 207–11.

201. The Lilly Foundation has been funding a number of such studies since the 1980s. See Fred L. Hofheinz, preface to *Reason for the Hope: The Futures of Roman Catholic Theologates*, by Katarina Schuth (Wilmington, DE: Michael Glazier, 1989), xiii-xiv. See also Katarina Schuth, *Seminaries, Theologates, and the Future of Church Ministry: An Analysis of Trends and Transitions* (Collegeville, MN: Liturgical Press, 1999), 27, for a list of Lilly-funded studies on seminaries and formation of priests.

202. Mary L. Gauthier, ed., *Catholic Ministry Formation Enrollments: Statistical Overview for 2005–2006* (Washington, DC: The Center for Applied Research in the Apostolate, Georgetown University, April 2006), 1–16. For an analysis and critique of contemporary seminary formation, see also Papesh, *Clerical Culture*, especially 61–76.

203. Schuth, *Seminaries, Theologates, and the Future of Church Ministry*, 25.

204. Donald W. Wuerl, "Seminary Visitation," *America* 187/9 (September 30, 2002). <http://www.americamagazine.org/>; accessed 11/15/2005.

205. Schuth, *Seminaries, Theologates, and the Future of Church Ministry*, 25.

206. See Schuth, *Seminaries, Theologates, and the Future of Church Ministry*, 25–26. The text of the letter is in "The State of U.S. Free-standing Seminaries," *Origins* 16/18 (October 16, 1986): 315.

207. See Schuth, *Seminaries, Theologates, and the Future of Church Ministry*, 27.

208. The report of the 1980s visitation became the subject of a scholarly dialogue initiated by the Bishops' Commission on Priestly Formation. The papers delivered were published in *Priests: Identity and Ministry*, ed. Robert Wister (Wilmington, DE: Michael Glazier, 1990) and these were the basis of a position paper, "The Doctrinal Understanding of the Ministerial Priesthood," which became chapter 1 of the 1993 *Program of Priestly Formation*. See Schuth, *Seminaries, Theologates, and the Future of Church Ministry*, 29.

209. The tensions experienced within Roman Catholic seminaries between faculty members and between faculty and students were not unique. Justo Gonzalez wrote about the different types of students (and their characteristic approaches to learning) whom he taught in his theology courses during his years of teaching at the Protestant Candler School of Theology in Atlanta. For the discussion of three types of theology students see Justo L. Gonzalez, *Christian Thought Revisited: Three Types of Theology*, rev. ed. (Maryknoll, NY: Orbis Books, 1999).

210. For the *Instrumentum Laboris* (for The Apostolic Visitation of The Seminaries and Houses of Priestly Formation in The United States of America) 2002, see <http://www.bishop-accountability.org/resources/resource-files/churchdocs/InstrumentumLaboris_Seminaries.htm>; accessed 11/15/2005.

211. For a contemporary analysis of the impact of the sexual abuse scandal and the response of laity, see David Gibson, *The Coming Catholic Church: How the Faithful are Shaping a New American Catholicism* (New York: HarperSanFrancisco, 2003), 163–96.

212. See Roger Mahony, "My Hopes for Dallas," *America*, 186/18 (May 27, 2002). <http://www.americamagazine.org/gettext.cfm?articletypeid=1&textID=1973&issueID=374&search=1>; accessed 11/15/2005.

213. See Donald W. Wuerl, "Seminary Visitation," *America* 187/9 (September 30, 2002). <http://www.americamagazine.org/>; accessed 11/15/2005.

214. See Letter from Robert A. Fambrini, SJ, *America* 187/14 (November 4, 2002). <http://www.americamagazine.org/letters.cfm?article TypeID=47a&textID=2500&issueID=403>; accessed 02/01/2007.

215. James Gill, "Seminaries Await Vatican Visitation," *America* 187/2 (July 15, 2002). <http://www.americamagazine.org/gettext.cfm?articletypeid=1&textID=2254&issueID=395&search=1>; accessed 11/15/2005.

216. Ibid.

217. Gauthier, *Catholic Ministry Formation Enrollments*, 1–16. See also Papesh, *Clerical Culture*, 62.

218. Dean Hoge, *The First Five Years of the Priesthood: A Study of Newly Ordained Priests* (Collegeville, MN: Liturgical Press, 2002), 6–7.

219. Ellis, "The Priest and the Intellectual Life," 186.

220. Katarina Schuth, *Priestly Ministry in Multiple Parishes* (Collegeville, MN: Liturgical Press, 2006), 153.

221. Center for Applied Research in the Apostolate (CARA) Washington DC. <http://cara.georgetown.edu/bulletin/index.htm>; accessed 12/05/2006.

222. Ibid.

223. See also Schuth, *Priestly Ministry in Multiple Parishes*, 4.

224. <http://www.usccb.org/laity/laymin/factoids.shtml>; accessed 12/05/2006.

225. Reference is from Msgr. Philip J. Murnion and David DeLambo, *Parishes and Parish Ministers: A Study of Parish Lay Ministers* (New York: National Pastoral Life Center, 1999). <http://www.usccb.org/laity/laymin/factoids.shtml>; accessed 12/05/2006.

226. Reference is from David DeLambo, *Lay Parish Ministers: A Study of Emerging Leadership* (New York: National Pastoral Life Center, 2005), 88. <http://www.usccb.org/laity/laymin/factoids.shtml>; accessed 12/05/2006.

227. Lennan, *Risking the Church: The Challenges of Catholic Faith* (Oxford: Oxford University Press, 2004), 227–28.

228. For the document and the three recommendations from the dialogue, see: <http://www.usccb.org/seia/refrc_women_1971.shtml>; accessed 12/05/2006.

229. USCC, "Office for Women's Concerns Proposed," *Origins* 5 (November 1975): 398. Deborah Halter discusses this and other initiatives in her book, *The Papal "No": A Comprehensive Guide to the Vatican's Rejection of Women's Ordination* (New York: Crossroad, 2004), chapter 5.

230. The 1983 Code, the last document to emerge from Vatican II, neglected the egalitarian spirit of the council and maintained the male-only priesthood (canon 1024). For comments developing the implications of this, see Halter, *The Papal "No,"* chapter 9.

231. Sara Butler, ed., *Research Report: Women in Church and Society* (Mahwah, NJ: Catholic Theological Society of America, 1978), 10–11. This is also reported and the ideas on women and ministry are developed further in William J. Rademacher, *Lay Ministry: A Theological, Spiritual and Pastoral Handbook* (Eugene, OR: Wipf and Stock, 1996), 146.

232. Pontifical Biblical Commission, "Can Women Be Priests?" *Origins* 6/6 (July 1, 1976): 92–96.

233. <http://www.ewtn.com/library/CURIA/CDFINSIG.HTM>; accessed 12/05/2006.

234. *Ordinatio Sacerdotalis* (On Reserving Priestly Ordination to Men Alone), 4.

235. Prusak, *The Church Unfinished* (New York/Mahwah, NJ: Paulist Press, 2004), 340–41.

236. Sullivan, *Creative Fidelity: Weighing and Interpreting Documents of the Magisterium* (New York/Mahwah, NJ: Paulist Press, 1996), 182–83. An article in relation to this issue is R. Gaillardetz, "Infallibility and the Ordination of Women," *Louvain Studies* 21 (1996): 3–24.

237. See Donald B. Cozzens, *Freeing Celibacy* (Collegeville, MN: Liturgical Press, 2006); *Sacred Silence: Denial and the Crisis in the Church* (Collegeville, MN: Liturgical Press, 2002); *The Changing Face of the Priesthood: A Reflection on the Priest's Crisis of Soul* (Collegeville, MN: Liturgical Press, 2000).

238. Gill, "Seminaries Await Vatican Visitation."

239. Cozzens, *Sacred Silence*, 126.

240. Ibid.

241. Cozzens, *The Changing Face of the Priesthood*, 31.

242. Ibid., 43. For more on the development of priestly celibacy, see chapter 3, "Loving as a Celibate."

243. USCCB, "The Nature and Scope of the Problem of the Sexual Abuse of Minors by Catholic Priests and Deacons in the United States." See <http://www.nccbuscc.org/nrb/johnjaystudy/>; accessed 12/28/2006. The report is 145 pages in length and indicates that 4.3 percent of priests had been

accused of abuse. Between 1950 and 2002, there were 4,392 allegations against priests that were not withdrawn or known to be false.

244. The extent to which this is being addressed in the Vatican visitation process will be important to follow up. Interviews with bishops, rectors, and seminarians after the visitation indicated that there was no suggestion that there is a crisis today in moral theology in American seminaries. Yet it is in the area of moral theology that the visitation has made itself felt, especially in ensuring that papal texts such as John Paul II's encyclicals *Veritatis Splendor* and *Evangelium Vitae*, which deal with moral issues, are adequately covered, and that the way in which such material is presented to students is monitored. The issue of faculty who are trained in contemporary psychological and pedagogical disciplines, and who have the competence to enable effective collaborative and communicative techniques for ministry does not as yet seem to have received priority in the visitation reports. See <http://www.usatoday.com/news/world/2005-04-30-Vatican-US-review_x.htm>; issue date: January 6, 2006. Also see Anne Colby, Thomas Ehrlich, Elizabeth Beaumont, and Jason Stephens, *Educating Citizens: Preparing America's Undergraduates for Lives of Civil and Moral Responsibility* (San Francisco: Jossey-Bass, 2003), chapter 7, "Faculty the Cornerstone."

245. "Perspectives: John Jay Sex Abuse Report," *Religion and Ethics Newsweekly*, no. 276 (December 22, 2006). <http://www.pbs.org/wnet/religionandethics/index_noflash.html>; accessed 12/28/2006.

246. Gill, "Seminaries Await Vatican Visitation."

247. Jack Dominian, *Living Love: Restoring Hope in the Church* (London: Darton Longman & Todd, 2004), 47.

248. Ibid.

249. Ibid.

250. Ibid., 47–48.

251. Pilarczyk, "Priestly Ministry in the United States," *Origins*, 20/24 (November 22, 1990): 382.

252. Ibid., 384.

253. Bishop Wilton D. Gregory, Presidential Address (Washington, DC: November 11, 2002). <http://www.nccbuscc.org/bishops/gregory.shtml>.

254. In part 3 of her study of seminaries and theologates, Schuth offers a wide range of constructive comments about seminary programs that would surely be a help to those engaged in constructing such programs for contemporary seminarians. Schuth, *Seminaries, Theologates, and the Future of Church Ministry*, 124–206.

255. Hoge, *The First Five Years of the Priesthood*, 3–4.

256. Ibid., 4–5.

257. Ibid., 102.

258. James Gill, "The Study's Implications Related to Health," in Hoge, *The First Five Years of the Priesthood*, 119.

259. Hoge, *The First Five Years of the Priesthood*, 23.

260. Ibid., 103.

261. Gill, "The Study's Implications Related to Health," in Hoge, *The First Five Years of the Priesthood*, 117.

262. Ibid., 122.

263. Dean R. Hoge and J. Wenger, *Evolving Visions of the Priesthood* (Collegeville, MN: Liturgical Press, 2003), 22–23. Criticism of seminary education is found especially in 20–24.

264. Donald B. Cozzens, *The Faith that Dares to Speak* (Collegeville, MN: Liturgical Press, 2004), 88.

265. See Cozzens, *Sacred Silence*, chapter 7, and Papesh, *Clerical Culture*, especially part 2.

266. Hoge and Wenger, *Evolving Visions of the Priesthood*, 81.

267. Cozzens, *Sacred Silence*, 118.

268. William Baumgartner, preface to *Seminaries, Theologates, and the Future of Church Ministry*, by Katarina Schuth, xiii.

269. Ibid.

270. For greater development of these ideas and the research that has informed them, see Schuth, *Seminaries, Theologates, and the Future of Church Ministry*, 207–23.

271. Francisco F. Claver, SJ, "The Church in Asia: Twenty and Forty Years After Vatican II (Personal Reflections: 1985 and 2005)," in James H. Kroeger, MM, *The Second Vatican Council and the Church in Asia: Readings and Reflections*, FABC Papers, No. 117. <http://www.ucanews.com/html/fabc-papers/fabc-0.htm>; accessed 12/05/2005.

272. Ibid.

273. Ibid.

274. For a contemporary description of the changing relationship between laity and clergy, and also on some difficulties raised by the theological presuppositions of the 1997 Vatican Instruction entitled "Certain Questions Regarding Collaboration of the Lay Faithful in the Ministry of Priests," see Richard Gaillardetz, "Shifting Meanings in the Lay-Clergy Distinction, *Irish Theological Quarterly* 64 (1999): 115–39.

275. Federation of Asian Bishops' Conferences, Fourth Plenary Assembly, September 16–25, 1986, Tokyo, Japan, *Final Statement*. <http://www.ucanews.com/html/fabc_plenary/fabc-86.htm>; accessed 12/05/2006.

276. Schuth, *Seminaries, Theologates, and the Future of Church Ministry*, xix, 31.

277. Katarina Schuth, whose research on seminaries and theologates had its origins in 1984, lists such factors as the changing ethnic and racial makeup

of the Catholic population, the decline in the number of priests, the rising number of lay ministers, and the ideological configuration of Catholics. Ecumenism, interfaith relations, and dealings with non-believers are also areas that seminarians need to be able to engage in dialogically, as these are part of the ordinary Western parish communal context. See Schuth, *Seminaries, Theologates, and the Future of Church Ministry*, xix.

278. Katarina Schuth, *Reason for the Hope: The Futures of Roman Catholic Theologates* (Wilmington, DE: Michael Glazier, 1989), 210.

279. For this document, see <http://www.vatican.va/jubilee_2000/magazine/documents/ju_mag_01021998_p-54_en.html>.

280. The Official Response of the Japanese Church to the *Lineamenta*. Special Assembly for Asia of the Synod of Bishops, July 23, 1997. <http://www.cbcj.catholic.jp/eng/edoc/linea.htm>; accessed 12/05/2006.

281. "Continuing Formation for Priesthood in Asia," FABC Papers, No. 92e.

282. Appleby, "Surviving the Shaking of the Foundations," 1.

283. Ibid., 3. It is projected that although at the beginning of the twentieth century 80 percent of all Christians throughout the world were white and lived in the Northern hemisphere, it is projected that, by 2020, 80 percent of all Christians will be people of color who live in the Southern hemisphere. See Tom Tracy, "Priestless Parishes, Communion Services Worry Liturgical Expert," *National Catholic Reporter* (February 27, 2004).

284. See Appleby, "Surviving the Shaking of the Foundations," 3–8.

285. Appleby, "Surviving the Shaking of the Foundations," 6.

286. Thomas Beaudoin, *Virtual Faith: The Irreverent Spiritual Quest of Generation X Catholics*, quoted in Appleby, "Surviving the Shaking of the Foundations," 12. It is interesting to note that in exploring the faith dimension of his generation, Beaudoin's next book exploring faith was titled: *Consuming Faith: Integrating Who We Are With What We Buy* (Chicago, IL: Sheed and Ward, 2004).

287. A description of Generation Y from a business website: "At 60 million strong, more than three times the size of Generation X, they're the biggest thing to hit the American scene since the 72 million baby boomers." <http://www.businessweek.com/1999/99_07/b3616001.htm>; accessed 01/20/2007.

288. Such fundamentalist approaches are identified as "loyalist" approaches. Church teachings are reduced to facts. See, for example, "Faith Facts provide concise, complete, and easy-to-read answers to specific questions about the Catholic faith." <http://www.cuf.org/FaithFacts/view_all.asp>; accessed 02/05/2007.

289. Appleby, "Surviving the Shaking of the Foundations," 9.

290. Schuth, *Priestly Ministry in Multiple Parishes*, 153.

291. Ibid.,155.

292. See Donald B. Cozzens, ed., *The Spirituality of the Diocesan Priest*

(Collegeville, MN: Liturgical Press, 1997), 188. Cozzens points out that the present crisis of priesthood, and that of sexual abuse, has done much to dismantle this style of ministry.

293. Schuth, *Priestly Ministry in Multiple Parishes*, 167.

294. Derek Worlock, "Formation and Evangelization" *Origins* 20/23 (November 15, 1990): 328.

295. Ibid.

296. Ibid.

297. Ibid.

298. Fesquet, *The Drama of Vatican II*, 513.

299. These comments were made by Walter Lippmann—journalist, media critic, and philosopher—in 1914! Quoted in Robert D. Putnam, *Bowling Alone: The Collapse and Revival of American Community* (New York: Simon & Schuster, 2000), 379, 402.

300. For research that addresses the pedogogical and methodological approaches helpful in the seminary context, see: Charles R. Foster, Lisa Dahill, Larry Golemon, Barbara Wang Tolentino, and Lee S. Shulman, *Educating Clergy: Teaching Practices and Pastoral Imagination* (San Francisco: Jossey-Bass, 2005), and Anne Colby, Thomas Ehrlich, Elizabeth Beaumont, and Jason Stephens, *Educating Citizens: Preparing America's Undergraduates for Lives of Civil and Moral Responsibility* (San Francisco: Jossey-Bass, 2003).

301. The concerns of bishops from Latin American, African, and Asian countries during the debates on priesthood, and in consequent communications, are related to the lack of ordained priests. It is of interest to note the increased number of communities where lay leaders are forming Catholic communities without access to the sacramental life of the church.

III: ON THE ADAPTATION AND RENEWAL OF RELIGIOUS LIFE
PREFECTAE CARITATIS

1. *The Flying Nun* was a TV sitcom produced by the American Broadcasting Company from 1967 until 1970. The *Awful Disclosures of Maria Monk of the Hotel Dieu Convent of Montreal: The Secrets of the Black Nunnery Revealed* (Maria Monk, 1854) was a horror story of convent life as was, to a much lesser extent, Monica Baldwin's, *I Leap Over the Wall* (Rinehart, 1949).

2. While this section addresses both religious men and women, the primary focus will be on religious women because they serve the church in greater numbers than male religious; this was so particularly in the period under discussion.

3. For such an understanding see Jo Ann Kay McNamara, *Sisters in Arms: Catholic Nuns Through Two Millennia* (Cambridge, MA: Harvard University Press, 1996).

4. See John W. Padberg, "Understanding a Tradition of Religious Life," in *Religious Life: Rebirth Through Conversion*, ed. Gerald Arbuckle and David Fleming (New York: Alba House, 1990), 4. A comprehensive description of major historical forms of communities of commitment of men and women to Jesus Christ is presented in pp. 3–20.

5. Patricia Wittberg, *From Piety to Professionalism—and Back?* (Lanham, MD: Lexington Books, 2006), 8.

6. Wittberg gives the numbers and nations of the exponential growth of active orders for women in various European nations along with the decline of the contemplative orders. *From Piety to Professionalism—and Back?* 6.

7. Leon Joseph Suenens, *The Nun in the World: New Dimensions in the Modern Apostolate* (London: Burns & Oates, 1962), vi.

8. Ibid., 26.

9. Ibid., 27.

10. Angela Merici, founder of the Ursulines, and Ignatius of Loyola were both founders of apostolic orders in sixteenth-century Europe. Each established their companies of women and men respectively who shared their mission and ministry, but although their vision of apostolic service was similar, the ecclesiastical requirements for community life were very different. Suenens addressed the discrepancies between the church's treatment of men and women founders of religious orders at the time and subsequently. See also R. Kevin Seasoltz, "Institutes of Consecrated Life: Identity, Integrity and Ministry," in *Ordering the Baptismal Priesthood: Theologies of Lay and Ordained Ministry*, ed. Susan Wood (Collegeville, MN: Liturgical Press, 2003), 242–51.

11. Mary Ward was the foundress of the Institute of the Blessed Virgin Mary in the seventeenth century. For further information, see: <http://www.loretonh.nsw.edu.au/mary_ward/Mary_Ward.htm>; accessed 03/01/2007. Frances Xavier Cabrini was the foundress of the Missionary Sisters of the Sacred Heart of Jesus in the nineteenth century. For further information, see: <http://www.mothercabrini.org/legacy/life1.asp>; accessed 03/01/2007.

12. Suenens, *The Nun in the World*, 42.

13. Ibid., 48. Father van Biervliet is the canonist, and the reference is *Regina Mundi*, no. 5 (1956).

14. Secular institutes were created formally in 1947. See Giuseppe Alberigo and Joseph Komonchak, eds., *History of Vatican II* (Maryknoll, NY: Orbis Books, 1995–2006), 1:81.

15. Gerard Huyghe, *Tensions and Change: The Problems of Religious Orders Today* (London: Geoffrey Chapman, 1965), 6.

16. Padberg, "Understanding a Tradition of Religious Life," in Arbuckle and Fleming, *Religious Life: Rebirth Through Conversion*, 15.

17. Ibid., 15.

18. Ibid., 16.

19. It is of interest to note that this is also a characteristic of a number of religious ministries at the present time.

20. Huyghe, *Tensions and Change*, 7. Huyghe points out that while this is more true of French religious, it is not totally different for other nationalities.

21. Ibid.

22. Friedrich Wulf, "Decree on Appropriate Renewal of the Religious Life," in *Commentary on the Documents of Vatican II*, ed. Herbert Vorgrimler (New York: Herder & Herder, 1969), 2:301.

23. September 23, 1950, *AAS* 42, 657.

24. Joan Chittister et al., eds., *Climb Along the Cutting Edge: An Analysis of Change in Religious Life* (New York/Mahwah, NJ: Paulist Press, 1977), 75–76.

25. Ibid., 76. The struggles of Benedictine women at the time, both within their own communities and with the European ambivalence toward America, is told in Sr. Regina Baska's *The Benedictine Congregation of St. Scholastica—Its Foundations and Development: 1880–1930*. See Chittister et al., *Climb Along the Cutting Edge*, 78.

26. For a description of the role the Sister Formation Institutes played, see Lora Ann Quinonez and Mary Daniel Turner, *The Transformation of American Catholic Sisters* (Philadelphia: Temple University Press, 1992), chapter 1, "Changing Times," 3–30.

27. See, for example, Sister Ritamary, ed., *The Mind of the Church in the Formation of Sisters*, Proceedings for 1954–55 (New York: Fordham University Press, 1956), and Sister Mary Hester Valentine, ed., *Prayer and Renewal: Proceedings of the Sister-Formation Conferences 1969* (New York: Fordham University Press, 1970).

28. There are many volumes of the Canadian Religious Conference publications, along with undated consultation booklets on issues pertinent to adaptation and renewal of religious life. Volume 16, for example, is a compilation of papers given at the 1970 workshop on a comprehensive study of the vow of celibacy. *Consecrated Celibacy*, Donum Dei, no. 16 (Ottawa: Canadian Religious Conference, 1971).

29. Jo Ann Kay McNamara, *Sisters in Arms: Catholic Nuns through Two Millennia* (Cambridge, MA: Harvard University Press, 1996), 616. In 1889 Rome refused recognition to sisters who did not live in common and did not wear a religious habit. See McNamara, *Sisters in Arms*, 609.

30. Sandra Schneiders, "Religious Life: The Dialectic Between Marginality and Transformation," *Spirituality Today* 40 (Winter 1988

Supplement): 60. Each of these descriptions expresses what has been a characteristic approach to religious life in the past, and, sadly, they all still prevail in differing degrees in present church life, and in expectations of religious within their own ranks and in the ranks of clergy and laity.

31. Rousseau was described as one of the experts who was "often in the service of the Roman Curia." See Alberigo and Komonchak, *History of Vatican II*, 2:476.

32. See Alberigo and Komonchak, *History of Vatican II*, 1:185. For the background and approach to the documents under discussion I am indebted to Alberigo, Wulf, Rynne, and Fesquet in particular.

33. Alberigo and Komonchak, *History of Vatican II*, 1:105.

34. Ibid., 1:186.

35. Wulf, "Decree on Appropriate Renewal of the Religious Life," 301. Wulf's carefully documented history of the decree and his analysis of the document can be attributed to his presence in the process. See also Alberigo and Komonchak, *History of Vatican II*, 4:587.

36. See Wulf, "Decree on Appropriate Renewal of the Religious Life," 301.

37. Wulf, "Decree on Appropriate Renewal of the Religious Life," 301.

38. Alberigo and Komonchak, *History of Vatican II*, 1:187. The experience of the American Benedictines is an example of the consequence of efforts of adaptation.

39. The "zealots" were against dialogue with socialist countries and were supportive of authoritarian regimes. This group of zealots was against the reconciliating initiatives of Pope John XXIII. See Alberigo and Komonchak, *History of Vatican II*, 2:211–12.

40. See Alberigo and Komonchak, *History of Vatican II*, 2:473 particularly; Wulf, "Decree on Appropriate Renewal of the Religious Life," 301–32; and Xavier Rynne, *The Second Session* (London: Faber & Faber, 1964), 127–55, and *The Third Session* (London: Faber & Faber, 1965), 208–15.

41. See Alberigo and Komonchak, *History of Vatican II*, 3:349, 423.

42. See Alberigo and Komonchak, *History of Vatican II*, 2:473.

43. "Schutte counted 1050 Council fathers, Reetz spoke of 800 bishops who were religious. Reetz counted only bishops in the strict sense whereas Schutte included in his total the superiors general and also the prefects apostolic most of whom were religious." Alberigo and Komonchak, *History of Vatican II*, 2:473.

44. Even when women religious were admitted as observers in 1964, they were not permitted to speak during the discussions on the schema on religious life or to attend commission meetings.

45. Bishop Huyghe describes some of the issues that were important in the conciliar commissions on doctrine and religious life at a symposium held

in 1965. He gives the biblical and juridical basis for the term "state of perfection" and provides a brief overview of the development of religious life, addressing some of the salient points in relation to the two key documents, *Lumen Gentium* chapter 6, and *Perfectae Caritatis*. Huyghe, "What Do We Mean by Religious?" in *Religious Orders in the Modern World*, ed. Gerard Huyghe et al. (London: Geoffrey Chapman, 1965), 3–16.

46. Baum, as one of the council experts involved in the Commission on Religious Life, describes the stable and communal life that was being endorsed by the council in Gregory Baum, "Commentary," *The Decree on the Renewal of Religious Life of Vatican Council II* (New York/Mahwah, NJ: Paulist Press, 1966), 11. Because he was a religious himself at the time as well as a theological expert, his commentary on the document at the close of the council provides an understanding of the theological foundations of *Perfectae Caritatis* as promulgated.

47. Baum, "Commentary," 11.

48. The 1983 Code of Canon Law speaks of the "consecrated life" as the profession of the evangelical counsels in a stable form of life, in which the faithful, under the action of the Holy Spirit, follow Christ more closely. The counsels must be understood in the context of *Lumen Gentium*, chapter 5. See Joseph Komonchak, Mary Collins, and Dermot Lane, eds., *New Dictionary of Theology*, (Dublin: Gill and Macmillan, 1987), 355–56.

49. Baum, "Commentary," 12.

50. Rahner develops in some depth the issues related to the doctrinal commission's deliberations over whether to devote a whole chapter in *Lumen Gentium* to religious life alone or whether the passage concerning religious should form one section of the chapter on the holiness of the church, where it would appear in the context of "the vocation of *all* the faithful." Rahner, "The Theology of the Religious Life," in Huyghe et al., *Religious Orders in the Modern World*, 42. Alberigo and Komonchak, *History of Vatican II*, 3:365–67, also give a more protracted discussion of these debates.

51. Baum, "Commentary," 16.

52. Ibid., 16–17.

53. Ibid., 17–18.

54. Ibid., 18. For a more systematic analysis of the overall ecclesiology that informed these documents, see Richard Gaillardetz, *The Church in the Making* (New York/Mahwah, NJ: Paulist Press, 2006). For an analysis of the way in which these chapters in relation to religious life and the Commission on Religious Life were developed in conciliar commissions and debates, see Alberigo and Komonchak, *History of Vatican II*, 2:473–79.

55. Baum, "Commentary," 19.

56. Alberigo and Komonchak, *History of Vatican II*, 2:477.

57. Alberigo and Komonchak, *History of Vatican II*, 2:478.

58. Wulf, "Decree on Appropriate Renewal of the Religious Life," 303.

59. See Wulf, "Decree on Appropriate Renewal of the Religious Life," 304.

60. Wulf, "Decree on Appropriate Renewal of the Religious Life," 307. The analysis of this argument and of the role of Aquinas, the contradictory and unsatisfactory aspects of his approach to the counsels and the commandments, and the implications of this in the renewed understanding of religious life is presented in pp. 308–9.

61. Alberigo and Komonchak, *History of Vatican II*, 2:478.

62. Wulf, "Decree on Appropriate Renewal of the Religious Life," 305.

63. Ibid., 320.

64. Ibid., 322.

65. Ibid., 323.

66. The Congregation of the Immaculate Heart of Mary, popularly known as the Scheut Fathers; from the name of the suburb of Brussels, Belgium, where it was founded in 1862.

67. Wulf, "Decree on Appropriate Renewal of the Religious Life," 324.

68. See Alberigo and Komonchak, *History of Vatican II*, 4:46.

69. Alberigo and Komonchak, *History of Vatican II*, 4:22.

70. Ibid., 4:23, n.71.

71. See Rynne, *The Third Session*, 209; Alberigo and Komonchak, *History of Vatican II*, 4:365–67; Wulf, "Decree on Appropriate Renewal of the Religious Life," 329–32; and Henri Fesquet, *The Drama of Vatican II: The Ecumenical Council, June 1962–December 1965*, trans. Bernard Murchland (New York: Random House, 1967), 514–15 for more detailed descriptions of the debates and voting details from November 12 to 14.

72. Suenens, *The Nun in the World*.

73. Rynne, *The Third Session*, 209.

74. Ibid., 210.

75. Alberigo and Komonchak, *History of Vatican II*, 4:367.

76. Fesquet, *The Drama of Vatican II*, 515.

77. Rynne points out that in an interview Sr. Mary Luke was cautious in her remarks about the schema and the conservative nature of the Commission for Religious, but she expressed her hope that a new text would (a) modernize theological teaching with regard to the religious life in accordance with the aims and goals of *aggiornamento*; and (b) provide for the representation of women religious in ecclesiastical bodies which governed them. It is known that Sr. Mary Luke took an active, but not visible, part in the work connected with the revision of schema 8. Rynne, *The Third Session*, 215.

78. Rynne, *The Third Session*, 213.

79. Ibid.

80. Ibid.

81. See Alberigo and Komonchak, *History of Vatican II*, 3:93 for a description of the "brilliant Chilean solution" whereby exemption could be seen as a "concrete realization of collegiality" in act. The conservative groups wanted to keep exemption while others openly attacked it.

82. Wulf, "Decree on Appropriate Renewal of the Religious Life," 325–26.

83. See Rynne, *The Third Session*, 215.

84. Rynne, *The Third Session*, 215.

85. Wulf suggests that the number is deceptive, because between 350 and 500 bishops had subscribed to the same amendments, but it was still a very high number of amendments. Wulf, "Decree on Appropriate Renewal of the Religious Life," 328.

86. Alberigo and Komonchak, *History of Vatican II*, 4:585. Alberigo also commented on the frequent absences from and the indecisive role played by Antoniutti in the commission meetings (589).

87. Alberigo and Komonchak, *History of Vatican II*, 5:225.

88. Ibid.

89. For the details of the voting and the particular responses to articles under question in this session, see Wulf, "Decree on Appropriate Renewal of the Religious Life," 328–29, and Alberigo and Komonchak, *History of Vatican II*, 4:597–90, and 5:224–28.

90. Alberigo and Komonchak, *History of Vatican II*, 5:550.

91. Wulf, "Decree on Appropriate Renewal of the Religious Life," 329.

92. Wulf, "Introductory Remarks on Chapters V and VI," in Vorgrimler, *Commentary*, 1:253 states that chapters 5 and 6 "must be considered together because they form an essential whole. They also have a history which must be known if we would fully understand them." See pp. 253–79 for his commentary on these two chapters and the history.

93. Again, for some of the key insights to the development and importance of this decree I am indebted to Wulf, "Decree on Appropriate Renewal of the Religious Life," 333–404 and Baum "Commentary," 9-55.

94. Wulf reminds his readers that the phrase, "the practice of the evangelical counsels" should not be overemphasized because it appears relatively late in the development of religious asceticism. See Wulf, "Decree on Appropriate Renewal of the Religious Life," 335.

95. Wulf, "Decree on Appropriate Renewal of the Religious Life," 335.

96. Paul VI, *Ecclesiae Sanctae*: Apostolic Letter, Motu Proprio, On the Implementation of the Decrees *Christus Dominus, Presbyterorum Ordinis*, and *Perfectae Caritatis*, August 6, 1966.

97. Baum, "Commentary" 25.

98. Ibid., 26.

99. Ibid., 27.

100. Wulf comments that the cooperation of "all members" was problematic for some bishops who worried about "an unrestrained individualism at the expense of obedience." Wulf, "Decree on Appropriate Renewal of the Religious Life," 342.

101. Rahner offers a theological critique of this approach in "The Theology of Religious Life," in Huyghe et al., *Religious Orders in the Modern World*, 41–75.

102. See Wulf, "Decree on Appropriate Renewal of the Religious Life," 344, and "Introductory Remarks on Chapters V and VI," in Vorgrimler, *Commentary*, 1:253–61.

103. Wulf, "Decree on Appropriate Renewal of the Religious Life," 344.

104. See Wulf, "Decree on Appropriate Renewal of the Religious Life," 344–45.

105. Wulf, "Decree on Appropriate Renewal of the Religious Life," 348.

106. Ibid., 352.

107. Baum, "Commentary," 38.

108. Wulf, "Decree on Appropriate Renewal of the Religious Life," 354.

109. Ibid.

110. Ibid.

111. *Provida Mater* (February 2, 1947) is an apostolic constitution of Pope Pius XII concerning secular institutes. *Primo Feliciter* (March 12, 1948) is an apostolic letter of Pius XII written to celebrate the anniversary of *Provida Mater* and to expand on the nature of secular institutes.

112. Baum, "Commentary," 41.

113. Ibid.

114. Wulf, "Decree on Appropriate Renewal of the Religious Life," 355.

115. Baum, "Commentary," 45.

116. Briggs, *Double Crossed: Uncovering the Catholic Church's Betrayal of American Nuns* (New York: Doubleday, 2006). See especially, chapter 8, "Seeking Justice," 133–51.

117. Wulf, "Decree on Appropriate Renewal of the Religious Life," 361.

118. Ibid., 362.

119. See Baum, "Commentary," 49.

120. Wulf, "Decree on Appropriate Renewal of the Religious Life," 363.

121. Ibid., 365.

122. The apostolic constitution, *Sponsa Christi* (Spouse of Christ), on religious life is a document of high authority issued by Pope Pius XII on November 21, 1950. Apostolic constitutions become the basis for canon law.

123. See Wulf, "Decree on Appropriate Renewal of the Religious Life," 368.

124. Ibid., 369.

125. Ibid., 370.

126. Responses were taking place in all parts of the world, but for comparison it is helpful to be able to use publications that record these initiatives.

127. Joseph E. Haley, *The Sister in America Today* (Notre Dame, IN: Fides Press, 1965), 137.

128. Alberigo and Komonchak, *History of Vatican II*, 5:628.

129. There were numbers of these in Europe. Huyghe and Suenens were key contributors through their lectures and writings. See Huyghe, *Tensions and Change: The Problems of Religious Orders Today*.

130. Edward Schillebeeckx, *Vatican II: The Real Achievement* (London: Sheed & Ward, 1967), 46.

131. Ibid., 47.

132. Ibid.

133. See Huyghe, *Tensions and Change*, and Huyghe et al., *Religious Orders in the Modern World*.

134. Achille Liénart, preface to *Religious Orders in the Modern World*, ed. Gerard Huyghe et al., vii.

135. Huyghe, *Tensions and Change*, 4.

136. Huyghe et al., *Religious Orders in the Modern World*, 124.

137. Huyghe, *Tensions and Change*, 6.

138. Sister Gertrude Joseph Donnelly, *The Sister Apostle* (Notre Dame, IN: Fides Publishers, 1964), 163–64.

139. Chittister et al., *Climb Along the Cutting Edge*, 52.

140. Sister Mary Hester Valentine, *The Post-Conciliar Nun* (New York: Hawthorn Books, 1968), 20.

141. Canadian Religious Conference, Leadership Conference of Women Religious, *Widening the Dialogue: Reflections on* Evangelica Testificatio (Ottawa: Canadian Religious Conference, 1974).

142. *Religious and the Evangelization of the World*, Donum Dei, no. 21 (Ottawa: Canadian Religious Conference, 1974), 9–10.

143. Ibid., 152.

144. See for example, J. M. R.Tillard, *A Gospel Path: The Religious Life* and *There Are Charisms and Charisms*; Francis J. Moloney, *Disciples and Prophets: A Biblical Model for Religious Life*; and Jerome Murphy O'Connor, *What Is Religious Life? A Critical Appraisal*.

145. Sister Mary Charles Borromeo, ed., *The New Nuns* (London: Sheed & Ward), 1968.

146. See Sister Mary Charles Borromeo, ed., *The New Nuns*.

147. For a sociological analysis of what happened to the Glenmary Sisters in Cincinnati and to the IHM sisters in Los Angeles, see Helen Rose Fuchs Ebaugh, *Women in the Vanishing Cloister: Organizational Decline in Catholic*

Religious Orders in the United States (New Brunswick, NJ: Rutgers University Press, 1993), 138–42.

148. Ebaugh, *Women in the Vanishing Cloister*, 139–40.

149. A contemporary perspective on this from outside religious orders is found in Kenneth Briggs's *Double Crossed: Uncovering the Catholic Church's Betrayal of American Nuns*, 154–55.

150. Quinonez and Turner, *The Transformation of American Catholic Sisters*, 42. The "unflinching posture" of support of members of the Leadership Conference of Women Religious (LCWR) for the IHM sisters at the time is recorded on p. 121.

151. Quinonez and Turner, *The Transformation of American Catholic Sisters*, 83–84.

152. See, for example, E. F. O'Doherty, *Vocation and Formation: Psychological Aspects* (Dublin: Gill and Macmillan Ltd., 1971); William Meissner, *Group Dynamics in the Religious Life* (Notre Dame, IN: University of Notre Dame Press, 1965).

153. Sandra Schneiders gave the paper and this subsequently formed chapter 1 of her book, *New Wineskins: Reimagining Religious Life Today* (New York/Mahwah, NJ: Paulist Press, 1986), 11–17.

154. Schneiders, *New Wineskins*, 14.

155. Ibid.

156. Ibid., 15.

157. Ibid., 15–16.

158. Ibid., 16–17.

159. See, for example, the story of Agnes Mansour, RSM, in Quinonez and Turner, *The Transformation of American Catholic Sisters*, esp. 107–9, and in John Quinn, "Address to LCWR: Extending Our Dialogue About Religious Life," *Origins* 13/13 (September 8, 1983).

160. As the council came to its close, Wulf lamented that there was no theology of religious life at that period; rather, he saw that it was on the threshold of being generated. See Wulf, "Decree on Appropriate Renewal of the Religious Life," 278.

161. The first of these occurred in 1971 when the conferences of bishops and of religious of Latin America convened a group of heads of North American communities. "Its purpose was to make the North Americans aware of the problems caused by missionaries from Canada and the US and to protest the imposition on Latin American situations of practices that they felt reflected North American cultural biases more than religious values." Quinonez and Turner, *The Transformation of American Catholic Sisters*, 79–80.

162. Ricardo Antoncich, "Synthesis," in *Religious Life Tomorrow*, Donum Dei, no. 24 (Ottawa: Canadian Religious Conference, 1978), 220.

163. Maria Augusta Neal, *Catholic Sisters in Transition: From the 1960s to the 1980s* (Wilmington, DE: Michael Glazier, 1984), 16.

164. Ibid., 78.

165. Maria Augusta Neal, *From Nuns to Sisters: An Expanding Vocation* (Mystic, CT: Twenty-Third Publications, 1990), 114.

166. Ibid., 119.

167. Quinonez and Turner, *The Transformation of American Catholic Sisters*, 77.

168. Ibid., 85.

169. See Briggs, *Double Crossed*, 193.

170. Patricia Wittberg, *The Rise and Fall of Catholic Religious Orders: A Social Movement Perspective* (Albany: State University of New York Press, 1994), 265.

171. Ibid., 226.

172. Wittberg wrote of the "boundary maintenance, common living, and other commitment mechanisms" which held religious life together. If these were to break down, religious life itself would be subject to collapse. Wittberg, *The Rise and Fall of Catholic Religious Orders*, 253.

173. Quinn, "Addresses of the Pontifical Delegate, John R. Quinn, D.D., Archbishop of San Francisco," in *Religious Life in the U.S. Church: The New Dialogue*, ed. Robert J. Daly et al. (New York/Mahwah, NJ: Paulist Press, 1984), 11.

174. Ibid., 13–14.

175. Michael Buckley offers an analysis of both the letter of John Paul II to the American bishops and "Essential Elements" and points out ways in which the connection with the conciliar teachings on religious life and those contained in the Sacred Congregation's document may be seen to diverge. Michael J. Buckley, "Reflections on the Essential Elements..." In Daly et al., *Religious Life in the U.S. Church*, 256–82.

176. The interdisciplinary papers written in response to the data gathered for this pontifical commission have been summarized in *Origins* 16/25 (December 4, 1986); *The Crisis in Religious Vocations: An Inside View*, ed. Laurie Felknor (New York/Mahwah, NJ: Paulist Press, 1989) contains sixteen of these. See also Mary Ewens in *The Future of Religious Life: The Carondelet Conference*, ed. Dolores Steinberg (Collegeville, MN: Liturgical Press, 1990), 57–71.

177. John Quinn, "Address to the Leadership Conference of Women Religious Assembly," *Origins* 13/13 (September 8, 1983). See also Quinonez and Turner, *The Transformation of American Catholic Sisters*, 61–63.

178. John Lozano, "The Theology of the Essential Elements in the Teaching of the Church," in Daly et al., *Religious Life in the U.S. Church*, 106. Lozano was a Vatican consultant and professor of spirituality at Chicago Theological Union.

179. Pope John Paul II, *Consecrated Life*, Apostolic Letter to the Bishops of the United States of America, April 3, 1983.

180. Lozano, "The Theology of the Essential Elements in the Teaching of the Church," in Daly et al., *Religious Life in the U.S. Church*, 106.

181. Various forms of veils and of habit style marked one congregation from another. This was not an issue for male congregations, in which the opportunity to wear ordinary clothes was an option for times of relaxation or other occasions. Religious women did not have this option. They possessed only the congregational habit; in some cases there was also a summer habit, but this was not an option taken up by all congregations.

182. Diane Bergant, "The Rebirth of an Apostolic Woman," in *Ministerial Spirituality and Religious Life*, by John Lozano (Chicago, IL: Claretian Press, 1986), 86.

183. The Pontifical Commission on Religious Life, "Report to U.S. Bishops on Religious Life and the Decline of Vocations," *Origins* 16/25, (December 4, 1986).

184. Ibid.

185. *CLAR*, No.1, Mexico City, December 1966; 3rd edition Bogotá, 1969, pp. 32–39. Quoted in *Religious Life and the Poor: Liberation Theology Perspectives*, by Alejandro Cussianovich (Dublin: Gill and Macmillan, 1979), 45.

186. In 1968 the Second General Conference of Latin American Bishops was held in Medellín, Colombia.

187. Cussianovich, *Religious Life and the Poor*, 48.

188. Ibid., 48-49.

189. Ibid., 49.

190. Ibid., 63.

191. Marcello Azevedo, *Vocation for Mission: The Challenge of Religious Life Today* (New York/Mahwah, NJ: Paulist Press, 1988), 4.

192. Ibid., 5.

193. Ibid.

194. Ibid., 151 (italics in text).

195. Ibid., 8 (italics in text).

196. Ibid., 9.

197. Ibid., 166.

198. Ibid.

199. *The Role of Apostolic Religious Life in the Context of the Contemporary Church and World*, Donum Dei, no. 31 (Ottawa: Canadian Religious Conference, 1986), 86.

200. Margaret Brennan, "Decree on the Appropriate Renewal of Religious Life: *Perfectae Caritatis*," in *The Church Renewed: The Documents of Vatican II Reconsidered*, ed. George P. Schner (Lanham, MD: University Press of America, 1986), 71.

201. It is important to remember that theological education was not generally open to laity (including women religious). Theological schools opened their courses to laity only in the post-conciliar years. Prior to Vatican II women who wanted to study theology had to go to universities in Europe where gender discrimination was forbidden by law. Controversial and influential scholar Mary Daly took her doctorates in sacred theology and philosophy from the University of Fribourg, Switzerland.

202. These communities have maintained their Catholic identity through lay and/or religious leadership of varied styles, exercised in the absence of ordained priests.

203. The synod on "The Consecrated Life and Its Mission in the Church and the World." The papal homily at the synod reminds those present that "through the course of the centuries the tradition of the church gave these words doctrinal and practical expression. The state of perfection is not just a theory. It is life . . . the horizon of the kingdom of God is revealed in a unique way through the vocation to the consecrated life. And, one could also say, in the marvellous flowering in recent years of the secular institutes and societies of apostolic life, which are doing so much good in the church. We are also witnessing the birth of new forms of consecration, particularly inside the ecclesial movements and associations, which seek to express in ways adapted to the present culture religious life's traditional tension between contemplation of the mystery of God and the mission to our brothers and sisters." John Paul II, "The Consecrated Life and Its Mission in the Church and the World," *Origins* 24/18 (October 13, 1994).

204. Doris Gottemoeller, "The Priesthood: Implications in Consecrated Life for Women," in *A Concert of Charisms: Ordained Ministry in Religious Life*, ed. Paul Hennessy (New York/Mahwah, NJ: Paulist Press, 1997), 137. However, if the church were to allow religious sisters to be ordained then this would create some quite serious issues for congregational and personal discernment.

205. For example, there are numbers of religious represented in The Committee of Religious NGOs at the United Nations. This is a coalition of representatives of religious, spiritual, and ethical nongovernmental organizations who exchange varying points of view and are dedicated to the pursuit of peace, understanding, and mutual respect. See <http://www.rngo.org/1601.html>; accessed 03/01/2007.

206. Moses Anderson, "The Black Religious in the USA," in *Religious Life Tomorrow*, 191.

207. Jamie Phelps, "Religious Life and Cultural Inclusiveness," in *Journey in Faith and Fidelity: Women Shaping Religious Life for a Renewed Church*, ed. Nadine Foley (New York: Continuum, 1999), 261.

208. David Nygren and Miriam Ukeritis, "Executive Summary of Study on the Future of Religious Orders," *Origins* 22/15 (September 24, 1992): 258.

209. Ibid., 270.

210. An obverse benefit here may well be that the experience of seeing communion and other services conducted by lay men and women, celibate, married, and unmarried may enable parishioners to break through the stereotypes of liturgical leadership that characterized the pre–Vatican II church.

211. Sandra Schneiders, *Finding The Treasure: Locating Catholic Religious Life in a New Ecclesial and Cultural Context*, Religious Life in a New Millennium, 1 (New York/Mahwah, NJ: Paulist Press, 2000), 245–46. See also Paul Hennessy, "The Parochialization of the Church," in Hennessy, *A Concert of Charisms*, 1–8.

212. The more religious and lay people continue to exercise ancillary liturgical leadership in a variety of roles, and the more theological and ministerial education they engage in, the more they will be confronted with the issue of ordination. This brings to mind once again the importance of educating seminarians to an awareness of gender issues and of other related leadership issues that they will surely be faced with after ordination. For useful approaches to this, see especially: Victor Klimoski, Kevin J. O'Neill, and Katarina M. Schuth, *Educating Leaders for Ministry* (Collegeville, MN: Liturgical Press, 2005) and Charles R. Foster, Lisa Dahill, Larry Golemon, Barbara Wang Tolentino, and Lee S. Shulman, *Educating Clergy: Teaching Practices and Pastoral Imagination* (San Francisco: Jossey-Bass, 2005).

213. Schneiders, *Finding the Treasure*, 246.

214. Ibid.

215. Ibid.

216. Nygren and Ukeritis, "Executive Summary of Study on the Future of Religious Orders," 272.

217. David Power, "Theologies of Religious Life and the Priesthood," in Hennessy, *A Concert of Charisms*, 67. Power also addresses key elements of the synod and the exhortation in relation to religious priests.

218. The concern of Archbishop Quinn to work collaboratively with the episcopal conference and with the two conferences of major superiors, along with his proactive commitment to dialogue, enabled the growth in mutual respect and understanding that permeates the report.

219. For a more expansive description of the radical change confronting post–Vatican II religious, see Suzanne Campbell-Jones, *In Habit: An Anthropological Study of Working Nuns* (London: Faber & Faber, 1979).

220. Thomas O'Meara, *Holiness and Radicalism in Religious Life* (New York: Herder & Herder, 1970), 18.

221. For statistics on religious in Latin America, Asia, and Africa, see Bryan T. Froehle and Mary Gautier, *Global Catholicism: Portrait of a World Church* (Maryknoll, NY: Orbis Books, 2003), and also *Statistical Yearbook of the Church 2003* and *Catholic Almanac 1975*.

222. "Special Assembly for Asia," *Origins* 27/38 (March 12, 1998). The number of religious brothers has increased in Asia but decreased in Africa and Oceania.

223. "The Church in Contemporary Asia," *Origins* 24/06 (June 23, 1994).

224. Office of Consecrated Life, Federation of Asian Bishops' Conferences (FABC), "The Role of Religious in the Building Up of the Local Church in Asia." <http://www. fabc.net/offices/ocl/ocl.html>; accessed 01/16/2007.

225. Ibid.

226. See Evelyn Monteiro and Antoinette Gutzler, *Ecclesia of Women in Asia: Gathering the Voices of the Silenced* (Delhi, India: ISPCK, 2005). The six areas addressed in the conference were women and violence, women and the Bible, women and church structures, women and spirituality, eco-feminism and theological method, and women and world religions.

227. Jeong Ja Leo Kim, (Little Servants of the Holy Family of Seoul), "God our Ma/Father's Korean Women's Church," in *Ecclesia of Women in Asia: Gathering the Voices of the Silenced*, ed. Evelyn Monteiro and Antoinette Gutzler (Delhi, India: ISPCK, 2005), 170–71.

228. See Kim, "God our Ma/Father's Korean Women's Church," 172.

229. Kim, "God our Ma/Father's Korean Women's Church," 172.

230. See: <http://cara.georgetown.edu/bulletin/RelStatistics.html>; accessed 02/20/2007.

231. Pontifical Commission on Religious Life, "The Report to U.S. Bishops on Religious Life and the Decline of Vocations," *Origins* 16/25 (December 4, 1986) indicates the "multiple factors" for departure and for the decline in vocations. These include the absence of screening procedures and the cultural identity crisis of the time that affected religious and corporate identity.

232. Pontifical Commission on Religious Life, "The Report to U.S. Bishops." See also: <http://cara.georgetown.edu/bulletin/RelStatistics.html>; accessed 02/20/2007.

233. Among other cultural changes that affected Catholic identity were the impact of the Vietnam War, the Watergate scandal, and the psychosexual revolution.

234. Pontifical Commission on Religious Life, "The Report to U.S. Bishops."

235. See Pontifical Commission on Religious Life, "The Report to U.S. Bishops."

236. See, for example: the seminal trilogy of Sandra Schneiders, Religious Life in a New Millennium: vol. 1, *Finding The Treasure*; vol. 2, *Selling All: Commitment, Consecrated Celibacy and Community in Catholic Life* (New York/Mahwah, NJ: Paulist Press, 2001); and vol. 3, *Buying the Field* (forthcoming). See also Patricia Wittberg's sociological research, *The Rise and Fall of*

Catholic Religious Orders and *From Piety to Professionalism—and Back?* Mary Jo Leddy, in *Reweaving Religious Life: Beyond the Liberal Model* (Mystic, CT: Twenty-Third Publications, 1991) wrote her critique of U.S. society and religious life with their "liberalism and consumer capitalism." She argues for a "reweaving of religious life" that is able to discern the signs of the Spirit visible in renewed commitment to the poor, a more radical pluralism, and a more focused network of ministry. See especially pp.144–65. Judith Merkle also offers a critique of the "liberal model" in her examination of issues of autonomy and transformation in religious life thirty years after Vatican II, in Judith A. Merkle, *Committed by Choice: Religious Life Today* (Collegeville, MN: Liturgical Press, 1998).

237. See Lawrence Cada, Raymond Fitz, et al., *Shaping the Coming Age of Religious Life* (New York: Seabury Press, 1979), 2.

238. Cada, Fitz, et al. *Shaping the Coming Age of Religious Life*, 180.

239. See Nygren and Ukeritis, "Executive Summary of Study on the Future of Religious Orders."

240. Nygren and Ukeritis, "Executive Summary of Study on the Future of Religious Orders." In the summary the example was given of a small religious congregation, the Alexian Brothers, who were founded to help in the plagues of the Middle Ages and have moved to a ministry to AIDS sufferers. This community increased its numbers. The research engaged in through the Centre for the Study of Religious Life addresses some of the issues related to these criteria. See: <http://www.religious-life.org/research/index.html>; accessed 03/01/2007.

241. Wittberg points out that while redefinitions such as religious life described as "prophetic witness" had been promoted in writings on religious life, "structural changes in the daily life of sisters, and (to a lesser extent) religious priests and brothers had prevented the new frame from being enacted on a corporate basis... Religious communities had deprived themselves of some of the very communal commitment mechanisms that might have reinforced their new beliefs." Wittberg, *The Rise and Fall of Catholic Religious Orders*, 251.

242. Wittberg, *From Piety to Professionalism—and Back?* 259.

243. Ebaugh, *Women in the Vanishing Cloister: Organizational Decline in Catholic Religious Orders in the United States.*

244. Whether Ebaugh got the reasons for decline right or not, and that is debatable, the fact of the decline was real and not less so over a decade later.

245. Ebaugh, *Women in the Vanishing Cloister*, 141.

246. Ibid., 142.

247. In their 1997 General Chapter, the Congregation of the Brothers of St. Xavier, founded 150 years earlier, decided to eliminate all provincial and regional administrative structures from their international congregation. For fur-

ther details see: <http://www.religious-life.org/pdfs/KINDLING_SU04.pdf>; accessed 03/01/2007.

248. For an expansive bibliography on reconfiguration and for information on present research into religious life, see the publication from the Center for the Study of Religious Life: <http://www.religious-life.org/pdfs/KINDLING_SU04.pdf>; accessed 03/01/2007. Also see William Bridges, *Managing Transitions: Making the Most of Change* 2nd ed. (Cambridge, MA: Perseus Books, 2003).

249. Jeanne Schweickert *Standing at the Crossroads: Religious Orders and Reconfiguration* (Chicago, IL: Convergence Inc., 2002), x–xi). The instance is given of a community of Benedictine sisters who are changing from their original Roman Catholic identity to form an ecumenical Benedictine monastery, known as the Benedictine Women of Madison, Wisconsin.

250. The problematic issue of women's identity can be seen in the discussion on the ordination of women to the diaconate. On June 2, 1994, shortly after John Paul II's letter on the ordination of women to the priesthood, Cardinal Carlo Maria Martini, archbishop of Milan, is reported to have stated at the eucharistic congress in Siena that "the pope has said nothing about the ordination of women to the diaconate." The Canon Law Society of America took up this issue and an excerpt of its report, "Canonical Implications of Ordaining Women to the Permanent Diaconate" is in *Origins* 25/20 (November 2, 1995). The first two conclusions give an indication of the present impasse in the church regarding the place of women in relation to ministerial orders.

> 1. Historically, women have been ordained as deaconesses. While it would be anachronistic to call "deaconesses" the women whose ministry is recorded in the New Testament, by the third century there clearly were women deacons. What their ministry involved has varied from place to place and from century to century. Although some debate whether they were indeed "ordained," the evidence points to an ordination parallel to that conferred on men to be deacons. Although this past experience does not require that women be ordained to the permanent diaconate today, it does indicate that this possibility is not foreclosed to the church.

> 2. Cultural factors play a significant role in decisions to introduce the permanent diaconate today. Cultural factors were also significant factors in the decision to ordain deaconesses in local churches in the past. It is appropriate, therefore, that contemporary cultural factors recognized by church officials involving women be taken into consideration in determining whether to ordain women to the permanent diaconate today.

This issue may provide an opportunity for all women and men in the church to take note of the appeal of Pope John Paul II in 1995 during an audience with the Vatican's delegation to the Fourth World Conference on Women in Beijing: "I appeal to all men in the church to undergo, where necessary, a change of heart and to implement as a demand of their faith, a positive vision of women. I ask them to become more and more aware of the disadvantages to which women, and especially girls, have been exposed and to see where the attitude of men, their lack of sensitivity or lack of responsibility, may be at the root."

251. Congregations of brothers, often initially established for the school apostolate, are moving into new and diverse apostolic ministries. See, for example, the movement of the Christian Brothers, initially established in Ireland with an international educational outreach, from education in schools to its recently established collaborative Edmund Rice International, a non-governmental organization committed to advocacy on behalf of children and young people who are marginalized because of poverty, legal status, environmental degradation, or adult wars. It is sponsored by the Congregation of Christian Brothers and the Congregation of Presentation Brothers. It is a partner organization with Franciscans International in Geneva. <http://www.edmundrice international.org/>; accessed 03/01/2007. The brothers have opened up their education apostolate to lay leadership, see <http://www.edmundrice.org.au/Education/>; accessed 03/01/2007.

252. In suggesting these names I am aware of a number of other significant writers such as Judith Merkle, Michael Crosby, and Gerard Arbuckle, to name only three, but I have selected these three as representative and widely read researchers on the religious life itself.

253. Schneiders, *Selling All*, 406.

254. Ibid.

255. See, for example, *Consecrated Religious Life: The Changing Paradigms* (Maryknoll, NY: Orbis Books, 2005); *Poverty, Celibacy and Obedience: A Radical Option for Life* (New York: Crossroad, 1999); and *Reframing Religious Life: An Expanded Vision for the Future* (Slough, UK: St Pauls, 1995).

256. O'Murchu, *Consecrated Religious Life*, 209. The connectedness of these renamed vows to the evangelical counsels is a creative and provocative initiative. His research on quantum theory and evolutionary science has been foundational to the approach to the vowed religious life taken in this book. Another approach to religious life and to the vows that takes the cosmos into account and involves a transformation of consciousness informed by "Indian genius and modern psychology" is Vadakethala Vineeth's *Call to Integration: A New Theology of Religious Life* (New York: Crossroad, 1981). Vineeth also renames the vows against an alternative horizon of meaning. See chapter 2, "The Vows," 33–70.

257. O'Murchu, *Consecrated Religious Life*, 165.

258. Ibid., 237.

259. See Chittister et al., *Climb Along the Cutting Edge: An Analysis of Change in Religious Life*. Joan Chittister, *The Fire in These Ashes: A Spirituality of Contemporary Religious Life* (Kansas City, MO: Sheed & Ward, 1996) and *The Way We Were: A Story of Conversion and Renewal* (Maryknoll, NY: Orbis Books, 2005).

260. See also Quinonez and Turner's descriptions of the LCWR leadership efforts in renewal and adaptation and the Vatican response to American religious. "Not Without Struggle" in Quinonez and Turner, *The Transformation of American Catholic Sisters*, chapter 6.

261. Chittister, *The Way We Were*, 170–71.

262. Ibid., 188.

263. Ibid., 231.

264. Ibid., 252–53.

265. Johannes Baptist Metz, *Followers of Christ: Perspectives on the Religious Life*, trans. Thomas Linton (New York/Mahwah, NJ: Paulist Press, 1978), 26.

266. This quote is attributed to Cardinal John Henry Newman, but I have been unable to find the source.

FINAL REMARKS

1. Bernard Cooke, *Power and the Spirit of God: Toward an Experience-based Pneumatology* (Oxford: Oxford University Press, 2004), 189.

PART V

FURTHER READING

VATICAN AND SYNODAL DOCUMENTS

Committee on Priestly Life and Ministry. "Reflections on the Morale of Priests." *Origins* 18/31 (January 12, 1989): 497–505.

Congregation for Institutes of Consecrated Life and Societies of Apostolic Life. *Consecrated Life within the Church, a Testimony to Christ Yesterday, Today and Forever*. Rome: February 2, 2000.

———. *Directives on Formation in Religious Institutes*. Rome: February 2, 1990.

———. *Starting Afresh from Christ: A Renewed Commitment to Consecrated Life in the Third Millennium*. Rome: May 19, 2002.

Extraordinary Meeting between the Cardinals of the United States (Sala Bologna del Palazzo Apostolico Vaticano, April 23–24, 2002. *Message to the Priests of the United States of America*. Washington, DC: USCCB, 2002.

International Theological Commission. *Report of the International Theological Commission: The Priestly Ministry (5–7 October, 1970)*. Translated by Jacques Dupuis. Bangalore: St. Peter's Seminary, 1971.

———. *Doctrinal Propositions on the Ministerial Priesthood*. Rome: September 25, 1971.

John Paul II. *Consecrated Life*. Apostolic Letter to the Bishops of the United States of America. Rome: April 3, 1983.

———. *Mane Nobiscum Domine*. Apostolic Letter to the Bishops, Clergy and Faithful for the Year of the Eucharist. Rome: October 7, 2004.

———. *Pastores Dabo Vobis* (I Will Give You Shepherds). Post-Synodal Apostolic Exhortation. Rome: March 25, 1992.

———. *Pastores Gregis* (On the Bishop, Servant of the Gospel of Jesus Christ for the Hope of the World). Post-Synodal Apostolic Exhortation. Rome: October 16, 2003.

————. *Vita Consecrata.* Post-Synodal Apostolic Exhortation. Rome: March 25, 1996.

National Conference of Catholic Bishops. *The Ministerial Priesthood.* Washington, DC: NCCB, November 30, 1971.

Paul VI. *Ecclesiae Sanctae* (Apostolic Letter, Motu Proprio, On the Implementation of the Decrees *Christus Dominus, Presbyterorum Ordinis,* and *Perfectae Caritatis*). Rome: August 6, 1966.

————. *Evangelica Testificatio* (Apostolic Exhortation on the Renewal of Religious Life According to the Teachings of Vatican II). Rome: 1967.

Sacred Congregation for the Doctrine of the Faith. *Inter Insigniores:* Declaration on the Admission of Women to the Ministerial Priesthood. Rome: October 15, 1976.

————. "Certain Questions Regarding Collaboration of the Lay Faithful in the Ministry of Priests." Rome: August 15, 1997.

Sacred Congregation for Religious and Secular Institutes. *Venite Seorsum* (Instruction on the Contemplative Life and on the Enclosure of Nuns). Rome: 1969.

————. "Essential Elements in the Church's Teaching on Religious Life as Applied to Institutes Dedicated to Works of the Apostolate." Rome: May 31, 1983.

Synod of Bishops. *The Ministerial Priesthood: Justice in the World,* Washington, DC: USCC, 1972.

Union of International Superiors General. *With A Passion for Christ and Passion for Humanity.* Congress on Consecrated Life. Rome: November 23–27, 2004.

————. *Women Disciples of Jesus Christ: Bearers of Reconciliation in Our World.* Report of UISG Plenary and Assembly Meetings. Rome: May 9–16, 2004.

WORKS CONSULTED

Alberigo, Giuseppe and Joseph Komonchak, eds. *History of Vatican II.* 5 vols. Maryknoll, NY: Orbis Books, 1995–2006.

Alberigo, Giuseppe, Jean-Pierre Jossua, and Joseph Komonchak, eds. *The Reception of Vatican II.* Translated by Matthew J. O'Connell. Washington, DC: Catholic University of America Press, 1987.

Anderson, Floyd, ed. *Council Daybook: Vatican II.* 3 vols. Washington: National Catholic Welfare Conference, 1966.

Beaudoin, Tom. *Virtual Faith: The Irreverent Spiritual Quest of Generation X Catholics*. San Francisco: Jossey-Bass, 1998.

Bernier, Paul. *Ministry in the Church: A Historical and Pastoral Approach*. Mystic, CT: Twenty-Third Publications, 1996.

Beyer, Jean. "Life Consecrated by the Evangelical Counsels: Conciliar Teaching and Later Developments." In *Vatican II Assessment and Perspectives: Twenty-five Years After (1962–87)*, edited by René Latourelle 2:64–89. New York/Mahwah, NJ: Paulist Press, 1988.

Bridges, William. *Managing Transitions: Making the Most of Change*. 2nd ed. Cambridge, MA: Perseus Books, 2003.

Burns, James MacGregor. *Running Alone: Presidential Leadership JFK to Bush II—Why It Has Failed and How We Can Fix It*. Cambridge, MA: Basic Books, 2006.

Coll, Niall, and Paschal Scallon, eds. *A Church With a Future: Challenges to Irish Catholicism Today*. Dublin: Columba Press, 2005.

Committee on Women in Society and in the Church. *Strengthening the Bonds of Peace: A Pastoral Reflection on Women in the Church and in Society*. Washington, DC: USCCB, 1995.

Congar, Yves. *Report from Rome: The First Session of the Vatican Council*. London: Geoffrey Chapman, 1963.

Costelloe, Timothy. "A Critical Evaluation of the Theology of Ordained Ministry of Pope John Paul II." Ph.D. diss., Melbourne College of Divinity, 1998.

Dominian, Jack. *Living Love: Restoring Hope in the Church*. London: Darton Longman & Todd, 2004.

Fesquet, Henri. *The Drama of Vatican II: The Ecumenical Council, June 1962–December 1965*. Translated by Bernard Murchland. New York: Random House, 1967.

Fulton, John, Anthony M. Abela, et al. *Young Catholics at the New Millennium*. Dublin: University College Dublin Press, 2000.

Gaillardetz, Richard. *The Church in the Making*. New York/Mahwah, NJ: Paulist Press, 2006.

Gibson, David. *The Coming Catholic Church: How the Faithful are Shaping a New American Catholicism*. New York: HarperSanFrancisco, 2003.

Groome, Thomas H. *What Makes Us Catholic: Eight Gifts for Life*. San Francisco: HarperSanFrancisco, 2003.

Halter, Deborah. *The Papal "No": A Comprehensive Guide to the Vatican's Rejection of Women's Ordination*. New York: Crossroad, 2004.

Horton, Douglas. *Vatican Diary 1962–1965*. 4 vols. Philadelphia: United Church Press, 1964–1966.

Jedin, Hubert, ed. *History of the Church*. Vol. 10, *The Church in the Modern Age*. New York: Crossroad, 1989.

Klimoski, Victor, Kevin J. O'Neill, and Katarina M. Schuth. *Educating Leaders for Ministry*. Collegeville, MN: Liturgical Press, 2005.

Kloppenburg, Bonaventure. *Ecclesiology of Vatican II*. Translated by Matthew O'Connell. Chicago, IL: Franciscan Herald Press, 1974.

Komonchak, Joseph, Mary Collins, and Dermot Lane, eds. *New Dictionary of Theology*. Dublin: Gill and Macmillan, 1987.

Ladaria, Luis. "Humanity in the Light of Christ." In *Vatican II Assessment and Perspectives: Twenty-five Years After (1962–87)*, edited by René Latourelle, 2:386–402. New York/Mahwah, NJ: Paulist Press, 1988.

Lafont, Ghislain. *Imagining the Catholic Church: Structured Communion in the Spirit*. Collegeville, MN: Liturgical Press, 2000.

Latourelle, René, ed. *Vatican II Assessment and Perspectives: Twenty-five Years After (1962–87)*. 3 vols. New York/Mahwah, NJ: Paulist Press, 1988.

Martin, John Hilary. "The Ordination of Women and the Theologians in the Middle Ages." In *A History of Women and Ordination*, edited by Bernard Cooke and Gary Macy, 1:31–160. Lanham, MD: Scarecrow Press, 2002.

O'Connell, Timothy. *Vatican II and Its Documents: An American Reappraisal*. Wilmington, DE: Michael Glazier, 1986.

O'Malley, John. *Tradition and Transition: Historical Perspectives on Vatican II*. Wilmington, DE: Michael Glazier, 1989.

———. "Vatican II: Did Anything Happen?" Roland Bainton Lecture, Yale Divinity School, New Haven, CT, September 26, 2005.

Osborne, Kenan B. *Ministry: Lay Ministry in the Roman Catholic Church*. New York/Mahwah, NJ: Paulist Press, 1993.

Putnam, Robert D. *Bowling Alone: The Collapse and Revival of American Community*. New York: Simon & Schuster, 2000.

Reese, Thomas J. *Inside the Vatican: The Politics and Organization of the Catholic Church*. Cambridge, MA: Harvard University Press, 1996.

Rock, Austin, OP, ed. *Impact of Renewal on Priests and Religious*. Chicago, IL: The Priory Press, 1968.

Rush, Ormond. *Still Interpreting Vatican II: Some Hermeneutical Principles*. New York/Mahwah, NJ: Paulist Press, 2004.

Rynne, Xavier. *Letters from Vatican City*. New York: Farrar, Straus & Co., 1963.

———. *The Second Session*. London: Faber & Faber, 1964.

———. *The Third Session*. London: Faber & Faber, 1965.

———. *The Fourth Session*. London: Faber & Faber, 1966.

———. *Vatican Council II*. Maryknoll, NY: Orbis Books, 1999.

Schillebeeckx, Edward. *Vatican II: The Real Achievement*. London: Sheed & Ward, 1967.

Schner, George P., ed. *The Church Renewed: The Documents of Vatican II Reconsidered*. Lanham, MD: University Press of America, 1986.

Stark, Rodney, and Robert Finke. *Acts of Faith: Explaining the Human Side of Religion*. Berkeley, CA: University of California Press, 2000.

Sullivan, Francis, A. *Creative Fidelity: Weighing and Interpreting Documents of the Magisterium*. New York/Mahwah, NJ: Paulist Press, 1996.

Tilley, Terrence W. *Inventing Catholic Tradition*. Maryknoll, NY: Orbis Books, 2000.

Vaillant, George. *Adaptation to Life: How the Best and Brightest Came of Age*. Boston, MA: Little Brown & Co, 1977.

———. *Aging Well: Surprising Guideposts to a Happier Life from the Landmark Harvard Study of Adult Development*. Boston, MA: Little Brown & Co, 2003.

Vorgrimler, Herbert, ed. *Commentary on the Documents of Vatican II*. 5 vols. New York: Herder & Herder, 1969.

Wickham, E. R. "Appraisal." In *Priests and Workers: An Anglo-French Discussion*, edited by David Edwards, 124–53. London: SCM Press, 1961.

Wiltgen, Ralph. *The Rhine Flows into the Tiber: The Unknown Council*. New York: Hawthorn Books, 1967.

Yzermans, Vincent A. *American Participation in the Second Vatican Council*. New York: Sheed & Ward, 1967.

PRIESTHOOD

Cozzens, Donald B. *The Changing Face of the Priesthood: A Reflection on the Priest's Crisis of Soul*. Collegeville, MN: Liturgical Press, 2000.

Donovan, Daniel. *What Are They Saying About the Ministerial Priesthood?* New York/Mahwah, NJ: Paulist Press, 1992.

Ellis, John Tracy. "The Priest and the Intellectual Life." In *Secular Priest in the New Church*, edited by Gerard Sloyan, 186–218. New York, NY: Herder & Herder, 1967.

Fenton, Joseph, C. "The Spirituality of the Diocesan Priesthood." *The American Ecclesiastical Review* 116 (1947): 126–40.

Fink, Peter. "The Priesthood of Jesus Christ in the Ministry and Life of the Ordained. In *Priests: Identity and Ministry*, edited by Robert Wister, 71–103. Wilmington, DE: Michael Glazier, 1990.

Fischer, James A. *Priests: Images, Ideals, and Changing Roles*, with a foreword by Andrew M. Greeley. New York: Dodd Mead, 1987.

Goergen, Donald J., and Ann Garrido, eds. *The Theology of the Priesthood*. Collegeville, MN: Liturgical Press, 2000.

Kloppenburg, Bonaventure. *The Priest: Living Instrument of Christ, the Eternal Priest*. Translated by Matthew O'Connell. Chicago, IL: Franciscan Herald Press, 1974.

Lécuyer, Joseph. *What Is a Priest?* Translated by Lancelot Sheppard. New York: Hawthorn Books, 1959.

———. "Decree On the Ministry and Life of Priests: History of the Decree." In *Commentary on the Documents of Vatican II*, edited by Herbert Vorgrimler, 4:183–209. New York: Herder & Herder, 1969.

Liebard, Odile M., ed. *Clergy & Laity*. Wilmington, NC: McGrath Publishing Co., 1978.

Osborne, Kenan B. "Envisioning a Theology of Ordained and Lay Ministry." In *Ordering the Baptismal Priesthood: Theologies of Lay and Ordained Ministry*, edited by Susan K.Wood, 195–227. Collegeville, MN: Liturgical Press, 2003.

———. *Priesthood: A History of Ordained Ministry in the Roman Catholic Church*. New York/Mahwah, NJ: Paulist Press, 1989.

Papesh. Michael. *Clerical Culture: Contradiction and Transformation*. Collegeville, MN: Liturgical Press, 2004.

Philibert, Paul J. "Issues for a Theology of Priesthood." In *The Theology of the Priesthood*, edited by Donald J. Goergen and Ann Garrido, 1–42. Collegeville, MN: Liturgical Press, 2000.

Power, David. *Ministers of Christ and His Church*. London: Geoffrey Chapman, 1969.

Ratzinger, Joseph. "The Ministry and Life of Priests." *Homiletic and Pastoral Review* (August–September 1997): 7–18.

———. "Priestly Ministry: A Search for Its Meaning." *Emmanuel* 76 (1970): 442–53, 490–505.

Ryan, Herbert J. *To Be a Priest: Perspectives on Vocation and Ordination*. New York: Seabury Press, 1975.

Sloyan, Gerard, ed. *Secular Priest in the New Church*. New York: Herder & Herder, 1967.

Tartre, Raymond. *The Postconciliar Priest: Comments on Some Aspects of the Decree On the Ministry and Life of Priests.* New York: P. J. Kenedy, 1966.

Terwilliger, Robert E., and Urban T. Holmes III, eds. *To Be a Priest: Perspectives on Vocation and Ordinatio.* New York: Seabury Press, 1975.

Vineeth, Vadakethala. *Call to Integration: A New Theology of Religious Life.* New York: Crossroad, 1981.

Wister, Robert, ed. *Priests: Identity and Ministry.* Wilmington, DE: Michael Glazier, 1990.

Wood, Susan K., ed. *Ordering the Baptismal Priesthood: Theologies of Lay and Ordained Ministry.* Collegeville, MN: Liturgical Press, 2003.

Wulf, Friedrich. "Decree on the Ministry and Life of Priests." In *Commentary on the Documents of Vatican II*, edited by Herbert Vorgrimler, 4:210–38. New York: Herder & Herder, 1969.

THE TRAINING OF PRIESTS

Appleby, R. Scott. "Surviving the Shaking of the Foundations: United States Catholicism in the Twenty-First Century." In *Seminaries, Theologates, and the Future of Church Ministry: An Analysis of Trends and Transitions*, by Katarina Schuth, 1–23. Collegeville, MN: Liturgical Press, 1999.

Bellitto, Christopher M. "Revisiting Ancient Practices: Priestly Training Before Trent." In *Medieval Education*, edited by Ronald B. Begley and Joseph W. Koterski, 35–49. New York: Fordham University Press, 2005.

Colby, Anne, Thomas Ehrlich, Elizabeth Beaumont, and Jason Stephens. *Educating Citizens: Preparing America's Undergraduates for Lives of Civil and Moral Responsibility.* San Francisco: Jossey-Bass, 2003.

Coleman, Gerald. *Catholic Priesthood: Formation and Human Development.* Liguori, MO: Liguori Publications, 2006.

Cozzens, Donald B. *The Faith that Dares to Speak.* Collegeville, MN: Liturgical Press, 2004.

———. *Freeing Celibacy.* Collegeville, MN: Liturgical Press, 2006.

———. *Sacred Silence: Denial and the Crisis in the Church.* Collegeville, MN: Liturgical Press, 2002.

———, ed. *The Spirituality of the Diocesan Priest.* Collegeville, MN: Liturgical Press, 1997.

Ellis, John Tracy. *American Catholics and the Intellectual Life.* Chicago: Heritage Foundation, 1956.

————. "American Catholics and the Intellectual Life." *Thought* 30 (Autumn, 1955): 351–88.

————. "The Priest and the Intellectual Life." In *Secular Priest in the New Church*, edited by Gerard Sloyan, 182–218. New York: Herder & Herder, 1967.

Fesquet, Henri. *The Drama of Vatican II: The Ecumenical Council, June 1962–December 1965.* Translated by Bernard Murchland. New York: Random House, 1967.

Foster, Charles R., Lisa Dahill, Larry Golemon, Barbara Wang Tolentino, and Lee S. Shulman. *Educating Clergy: Teaching Practices and Pastoral Imagination.* San Francisco: Jossey-Bass, 2005.

Gauthier, Mary L., ed. *Catholic Ministry Formation Enrollments: Statistical Overview for 2005–2006.* Washington, DC: The Center for Applied Research in the Apostolate, Georgetown University, April 2006.

Gonzalez, Justo L. *Christian Thought Revisited: Three Types of Theology.* Rev. ed. Maryknoll, NY: Orbis Books, 1999.

Harvanek, Robert. "Decree on the Training of Priests." In *Vatican II and Its Documents: An American Reappraisal*, edited by Timothy O'Connell, 91–107. Wilmington, DE: Michael Glazier, 1986.

Hurley, Denis. "Pastoral Emphasis in Seminary Studies." *The Furrow* 13 (1962): 16–30.

Hurley, Denis, and Joseph Cunnane. *Vatican II on Priests and Seminaries.* Dublin: Scepter Books, 1967.

Lamberigts, Mathijs. "*Optatam Totius*: The Decree on Priestly Formation, A Short Survey of Its History at the Second Vatican Council." *Louvain Studies* 30 (2005): 25–48.

Norris, Frank B. *Decree on Priestly Training and Decree on the Ministry and Life of Priests.* New York/Mahwah, NJ: Paulist Press, 1966.

O'Donohoe, James A. *Tridentine Seminary Legislation: Its Sources and Its Formation.* Louvain: Publications Universitaires de Louvain, 1957.

O'Malley, John. "Diocesan and Religious Models of Priestly Formation: Historical Perspectives." In *Priests: Identity and Ministry*, edited by Robert Wister, 54–70. Wilmington, DE: Michael Glazier, 1990.

Schuth, Katarina. *Priestly Ministry in Multiple Parishes.* Collegeville, MN: Liturgical Press, 2006.

————. *Reason for the Hope: The Futures of Roman Catholic Theologates.* Wilmington, DE: Michael Glazier, 1989.

————. *Seminaries, Theologates, and the Future of Church Ministry: An Analysis of Trends and Transitions.* Collegeville, MN: Liturgical Press, 1999.

THE RENEWAL AND ADAPTATION OF RELIGIOUS LIFE

Arbuckle, Gerald, and David Fleming, eds. *Religious Life: Rebirth Through Conversion*. New York: Alba House, 1990.

Azevedo, Marcello. *Vocation for Mission: The Challenge of Religious Life Today*. New York/Mahwah, NJ: Paulist Press, 1988.

Baum, Gregory. "Commentary." In *The Decree on the Renewal of Religious Life of Vatican Council II*, 6–55. New York/Mahwah, NJ: Paulist Press, 1966.

Borromeo, Sister Mary Charles, ed. *The New Nuns*. London: Sheed & Ward, 1968.

Breen, Michael J., ed. *A Fire in the Forest: Religious Life in Ireland*. Dublin: Veritas, 2001.

Brennan, Margaret, "Decree on the Appropriate Renewal of Religious Life: *Perfectae Caritatis*." In *The Church Renewed: The Documents of Vatican II Reconsidered*, edited by George P. Schner, 63–72. Lanham, MD: University Press of America, 1986.

Briggs, Kenneth. *Double Crossed: Uncovering the Catholic Church's Betrayal of American Nuns*. New York: Doubleday, 2006.

Cada, Lawrence, Raymond Fitz, et al. *Shaping the Coming Age of Religious Life*. New York: Seabury Press, 1979.

Campbell-Jones, Suzanne. *In Habit: An Anthropological Study of Working Nuns*. London: Faber & Faber, 1979.

Chittister, Joan. *The Fire in These Ashes: A Spirituality of Contemporary Religious Life*. Kansas City, MO: Sheed & Ward, 1996.

———. *The Way We Were: A Story of Conversion and Renewal*. Maryknoll, NY: Orbis Books, 2005.

Chittister, Joan, et al., eds. *Climb Along the Cutting Edge: An Analysis of Change in Religious Life*. New York/Mahwah, NJ: Paulist Press, 1977.

Consecrated Celibacy. Donum Dei, no. 16. Ottawa: Canadian Religious Conference, 1971.

Cussianovich, Alejandro. *Religious Life and the Poor: Liberation Theology Perspectives*. Dublin: Gill and Macmillan, 1979.

Daly, Robert J., et al., eds. *Religious Life in the U.S. Church: The New Dialogue*. New York/Mahwah, NJ: Paulist Press, 1984.

Donnelly, Sister Gertrude Joseph. *The Sister Apostle*. Notre Dame, IN: Fides Publishers, 1964.

Ebaugh, Helen Rose Fuchs. "The Growth and Decline of Catholic Religious Orders of Women Worldwide: The Impact of Women's Opportunity Structures." *Journal for the Scientific Study of Religion* 32/1 (March 1993): 68–75.

————. *Women in the Vanishing Cloister: Organizational Decline in Catholic Religious Orders in the United States.* New Brunswick, NJ: Rutgers University Press, 1993.

Farnham, Janice, and Mary Milligan. "Women Religious and the Synod of Bishops." *America* (October 15, 1994): 22–23.

Fleming, David, ed. *Religious Life at the Crossroads.* New York/Mahwah, NJ: Paulist Press, 1985.

Foley, Nadine, ed. *Journey in Faith and Fidelity: Women Shaping Religious Life for a Renewed Church.* New York: Continuum, 1999.

Haley, Joseph E. *The Sister in America Today.* Notre Dame, IN: Fides Press, 1965.

Hennessy, Paul K. *A Concert of Charisms: Ordained Ministry in Religious Life.* New York/Mahwah, NJ: Paulist Press, 1997.

Huyghe, Gerard. *Tensions and Change: The Problems of Religious Orders Today.* Translated by Sr. Marie Florette. London: Geoffrey Chapman, 1965.

Huyghe, Gerard, et al. *Religious Orders in the Modern World.* London: Geoffrey Chapman, 1965.

Lawson, Veronica. "Tabitha of Joppa: Disciple, Prophet, and Biblical Prototype for Contemporary Religious Life." In *Transcending Boundaries: Contemporary Readings of the New Testament: Essays in Honor of Francis J. Moloney,* edited by Rekha Chennattu and Mary Coloe, 281–92. Rome: Libreria Ateneo Salesiano, 2005.

Lozano, John. *Ministerial Spirituality and Religious Life.* Chicago, IL: Claretian Press, 1986.

McEnroy, Carmel. *Guests in Their Own House: The Women of Vatican II.* New York: Crossroad, 1996.

McNamara, Jo Ann Kay. *Sisters in Arms: Catholic Nuns Through Two Millennia.* Cambridge, MA: Harvard University Press, 1996.

Meissner, William. *Group Dynamics in the Religious Life.* Notre Dame, IN: University of Notre Dame Press, 1965.

Merkle, Judith A. *Committed by Choice: Religious Life Today.* Collegeville, MN: Liturgical Press, 1998.

————. *A Different Touch: A Study of Vows in Religious Life.* Collegeville, MN: Liturgical Press, 1992.

Metz, Johannes Baptist. *Followers of Christ: Perspectives on the Religious Life.* Translated by Thomas Linton. New York/Mahwah, NJ: Paulist Press, 1978.

Moloney, Francis, J. *Disciples and Prophets: A Biblical Model for Religious Life.* London: Darton Longman & Todd, 1980.

Monteiro, Evelyn, and Antoinette Gutzler. *Ecclesia of Women in Asia: Gathering the Voices of the Silenced*. Delhi, India: ISPCK, 2005.

Murphy O'Connor, Jerome. *What Is Religious Life? A Critical Appraisal*. Wilmington, DE: Michael Glazier, 1977.

Neal, Maria Augusta. *Catholic Sisters in Transition: From the 1960s to the 1980s*. Wilmington, DE: Michael Glazier, 1984.

———. *From Nuns to Sisters: An Expanding Vocation*. Mystic, CT: Twenty-Third Publications, 1990.

Nygren, David, and Miriam Ukeritis. "Executive Summary of Study on the Future of Religious Orders." *Origins* 22/15 (September 24, 1992): 258–72.

O'Malley, John. "Priesthood, Ministry, and Religious Life: Some Historical and Historiographical Consideration." *Theological Studies* 49 (1988): 223–57.

O'Meara, Thomas. *Holiness and Radicalism in Religious Life*. New York: Herder & Herder, 1970.

O'Murchu, Diarmuid. *Consecrated Religious Life: The Changing Paradigms*. Maryknoll, NY: Orbis Books, 2005.

———. *Poverty, Celibacy and Obedience: A Radical Option for Life*. New York: Crossroad, 1999.

———. *Reframing Religious Life: An Expanded Vision for the Future*. Slough, UK: St Pauls, 1995.

Quinonez, Lora Ann, and Mary Daniel Turner. *The Transformation of American Catholic Sisters*. Philadelphia: Temple University Press, 1992.

Religious and the Evangelization of the World. Donum Dei, no. 21. Ottawa: Canadian Religious Conference, 1974.

Religious Life Tomorrow. Donum Dei, no. 24. Ottawa: Canadian Religious Conference, 1978.

The Role of Apostolic Religious Life in the Context of the Contemporary Church and World. Donum Dei, no. 31. Ottawa: Canadian Religious Conference, 1986.

Schneiders, Sandra. *Finding the Treasure: Locating Catholic Religious Life in a New Ecclesial and Cultural Context*. Religious Life in a New Millennium, 1. New York/Mahwah, NJ: Paulist Press, 2000.

———. *New Wineskins: Reimagining Religious Life Today*. New York/Mahwah, NJ: Paulist Press, 1986.

———. "Religious Life: The Dialectic Between Marginality and Transformation." *Spirituality Today* 40 (Winter 1988 Supplement): 59–79.

————. *Selling All: Commitment, Consecrated Celibacy and Community in Catholic Life*. Religious Life in a New Millennium, 2. New York/Mahwah, NJ: Paulist Press, 2001.

Schweickert, Jeanne. *Standing at the Crossroads: Religious Orders and Reconfiguration*. Chicago, IL: Convergence Inc., 2002.

Steinberg, Dolores, ed. *The Future of Religious Life: The Carondelet Conference*. Collegeville, MN: Liturgical Press, 1990.

Suenens, Leon Joseph. *The Nun in the World: New Dimensions in the Modern Apostolate*. London: Burns & Oates, 1962.

Tillard, J. M. R. *A Gospel Path: The Religious Life*. Belgium: Lumen Vitae Press, 1975.

————. *There Are Charisms and Charisms*. Belgium: Lumen Vitae Press, 1977.

Valentine, Sister Mary Hester. *The Post-Conciliar Nun*. New York: Hawthorn Books, 1968.

Wittberg, Patricia. *Creating a Future for Religious Life: A Sociological Perspective*. New York/Mahwah, NJ: Paulist Press, 1991.

————. *From Piety to Professionalism—and Back?* Lanham, MD: Lexington Books, 2006.

————. *The Rise and Fall of Catholic Religious Orders: A Social Movement Perspective*. Albany: State University of New York Press, 1994.

Wulf, Friedrich. "Decree on Appropriate Renewal of the Religious Life." In *Commentary on the Documents of Vatican II*, edited by Herbert Vorgrimler, 2:301–32. New York: Herder & Herder, 1969.

RECOMMENDED WORKS

Coleman, Gerald D., *Catholic Priesthood: Formation and Human Development*. Liguori, MO: Liguori Publications, 2006.

Cozzens, Donald B. *Freeing Celibacy*. Collegeville, MN: Liturgical Press, 2006.

————. *The Changing Face of the Priesthood: A Reflection on the Priest's Crisis of Soul*. Collegeville, MN: Liturgical Press, 2000.

Dominian, Jack. *Living Love: Restoring Hope in the Church*. London: Darton Longman & Todd, 2004.

Donovan, Daniel. *What Are They Saying About the Ministerial Priesthood?* New York/Mahwah, NJ: Paulist Press, 1992.

Goergen, Donald J., and Ann Garrido, eds. *The Theology of the Priesthood*. Collegeville, MN: Liturgical Press, 2000.

Hennessy, Paul K. *A Concert of Charisms: Ordained Ministry in Religious Life.* New York/Mahwah, NJ: Paulist Press, 1997.

Hoge, Dean R. *The First Five Years of the Priesthood: A Study of Newly Ordained Priests*, Collegeville, MN: Liturgical Press, 2002.

Hoge, Dean R., and Aniedi Okure. *International Priests in America.* Collegeville, MN: Liturgical Press, 2006.

Hoge, Dean R., and Jacqueline Wenger. *Evolving Visions of the Priesthood.* Collegeville, MN: Liturgical Press, 2003.

Lennan, Richard. *Risking the Church: The Challenges of Catholic Faith.* Oxford: Oxford University Press, 2004.

O'Murchu, Diarmuid. *Reframing Religious Life: An Expanded Vision for the Future.* Maryknoll, NY: Orbis Books, 2006.

Papesh, Michael, *Clerical Culture: Contradiction and Transformation.* Collegeville, MN: Liturgical Press, 2004.

Philibert, Paul J. *The Priesthood of the Faithful: Key to a Living Church.* Collegeville, MN: Liturgical Press, 2005.

Prusak, Bernard P. *The Church Unfinished: Ecclesiology Through the Centuries.* New York/Mahwah, NJ: Paulist Press, 2004.

Schuth, Katarina. *Priestly Ministry in Multiple Parishes.* Collegeville, MN: Liturgical Press, 2006.

Schuth, Katarina, Victor J. Klimoski, and Kevin J. O'Neil. *Educating Leaders for Ministry: Issues and Responses.* Collegeville, MN: Liturgical Press, 2005.

Smith, Karen Sue, ed. *Priesthood in the Modern World: A Reader.* Franklin, WI: Sheed & Ward, 1999.

Suenens, Leon Joseph. *The Nun in the World: New Dimensions in the Modern Apostolate.* London: Burns & Oates, 1962.

Wittberg, Patricia. *Creating a Future for Religious Life: A Sociological Perspective.* New York/Mahwah, NJ: Paulist Press, 1991.

———. *From Piety to Professionalism—and Back?* Lanham, MD: Lexington Books, 2006.

———. *The Rise and Fall of Catholic Religious Orders.* Albany: State University of New York Press, 1994.

Wood, Susan K., ed. *Ordering the Baptismal Priesthood: Theologies of Lay and Ordained Ministry.* Collegeville, MN: Liturgical Press, 2003.

INDEX